SUFISM REVISITED

FATIMA HUSSAIN

SANG-E-MEEL PUBLICATIONS
25, SHAHRAH-E-PAKISTAN (LOWER MALL) LAHORE.

297	Fatima Hussain
	Sufism Revisited / Fatima Hussain.- Lahore: Sang-e-Meel Publications, 2010.
	408pp.
	1. Sufism - Islam.
	I. Title.

2010
Published by:
Niaz Ahmad
Sang-e-Meel Publications,
Lahore.

ISBN-10: 969-35-2363-6
ISBN-13: 978-969-35-2363-8

Sang-e-Meel Publications
25 Shahrah-e-Pakistan (Lower Mall), Lahore-54000 PAKISTAN
Phones: 37220100-37228143 Fax: 37245101
http://www.sang-e-meel.com e-mail: smp@sang-e-meel.com
PRINTED AT: HAJI HANIF & SONS PRINTERS, LAHORE.

To,

FAKHAR

CONTENTS

Fatima Hussain
Introduction — 9

Abdul Haque Chang
Sufi, Mirasi and OrthopraxySpirituality,
Music and Religion in Eighteenth-Century Sindh — 21

Agha Saleem
Melody of Peace *(Sur Kalyan)* — 35

Agha Saleem
Life of Shah Latif Bhattai — 79

Ahmad Salim
Women Sufi Poets: Living Dangerously — 93

Chander Shekhar
Relevance of Sufism in Modern Times:
A Survey of Texts and its Impact on Human Mind — 127

Fahmida Hussain
Relevance of Sufism and Bhakti in Modern Times — 131

Fatima Hussain
The Social Role of Baba Farid & His Shrine:
A Multidimensional Approach — 142

Fatima Hussain
Role of Sufism in Spreading the Message of
Peace in South Asia
                                                                146

Fatima Hussain
Constructing Paradigms of Religious Conflict
Resolution Through the Heer Waris Shah   150

Hameedullah Hashmi
The Great Sufi Saint Baba Shaikh Farid, A Study
in the Life, Teachings and Achievements   161

Harbans Mukhia
Bhakti and Sufi Movements—
Significance of the Day   209

Iftikhar Arif
Sufism and the World in Crisis   219

Jigar Mohammed
Relevance of Sufi Thought and Practices to the of
Peace Promotion and Concept of Living Together   230

Karan Singh, M.P.
Sufism and Bhakti Movements as Part of Great
Indian Culture—with Special
Reference to Kashmir   239

Kazi Javed
Sufism, and the Tradition of Tolerance and
Enlightenment in South Asia   247

CONTENTS

Khawaja Masud
Role of Sufism in Pakistan — 255

M.D. Thomas
Kabir: A Pioneer of Social Harmony
and Upliftment — 261

Madhu Trivedi
The Contribution of Sufi and Bhakti
Saints in the Evolution of Hindustani Music — 275

Maqsood Ahmed Rahi
Mysticism in Kashmir — 290

Mohd. Zaman Azurdah
Elements of Sufism in Nundo Reshi's Poetry — 303

Muhammad Ali Siddiqui
Mysticism and Humanism — 307

N.A. Baloch
Shah Abdul Latif, the Great Saint Patron of Music — 313

Paul Jackson, S.J.
Maneri's Inward Journey and its Impact — 323

S.A. Hasan
Jalaluddin Rumi's Mystic Thought-
A Message of Love and Human Resurrection — 337

Saleem Raz
Sufism in Pashto Poetry — 348

Saral Jhingran
Sufi Experience of 'Fana' as Basis for
Religio-Ethical Life Today — 356

Shah Muhammad Mari
Must Taukli-A Great Baluchi Mystic Poet　　　　　　　369

Shehzad Qaiser
Khawaja Ghulam Farid's Doctrine of Oneness of
Being (*wahdat al wujud*) and its
Universal Realization　　　　　　　　　　　　　　384

W.H. Siddiqui
Baba Farid, Great Humanist of All Times　　　　　　401

SUFISM REVISITED
Introduction

The present collection of essays serves as a unique guide to the study of Islamic mysticism, Sufism (Tasawwuf). It is intended to draw the attention of students of history, culture, peace studies and conflict resolution, probing ways to establish sustainable peace in the world. Needless to say, it will be of some significance to the lay reader as well as to the powers that be, offering a glimpse into the contemporary urgency to study and follow the Sufi message. Though the importance of Sufism has long been underlined by the UNESCO, for resolving conflict and ushering in peace, certain individuals have debunked this on the ground that *Tassawwuf* should not be pressed into service for advancing the "imperialist agenda" through UN agency. For many in the west, as well as in South Asia, Sufism is largely understood as some kind of a "song and dance sequence" implicitly associated with sensuous love.[1]

Many Sufis are highly skeptical of such practices, charging them as lacking any essential links with Islam. Sometimes, individuals describe themselves as Sufis but not as Muslims, responding to the universality of ecstatic mystical experience and the particularity of Sufi routes to that experience.[2] This makes non-ecstatic Sufis suspicious of the wildness of many of the claims made by ecstatic Sufis, from Islamic point of view.[3] Certain aspects[4] of Sufism have been criticized by *Ulama-i-din* (scholars of *shariat* & *fiqh*) like Ibn al Taymiyah (d.728/1328), Ibn Khaldun (d.809/1400) and Ibn-al-Jauzi.

The present work offers a incisive insight into the various shades of Sufism and how they are interpreted through the lens of practitioners of various disciplines who are experts in their respective fields. What follows then, is a degree of inevitable overlapping in some of the chapters. The inter-disciplinary approach expressed in these chapters is indicative of a new direction in the study of social science, especially themes related to history, culture peace and conflict resolution. I hope this work heralds a new trend in Sufi studies.

In todays strife-torn society, oblivious to rising or plunging GDPs, happiness is at a premium. The overwhelming desire to possess, is an indicator of a consumerist culture propelled by the unbridled growth of capitalist enterprise. Neo-imperialism has fanned conflict everywhere, forcing people to take up violent means to seek redressal from injustice. People of different religious, racial and national affiliations view each other with suspicion.

In the present global context, when formal religions are often, not only the butt of ridicule, but also viewed as a deterrent to social cohesion, the role of popular religion in the form of mysticism, assumes a new dimension hitherto unknown. The current intellectual propensity is to debunk religion on the pretext that it has been the cause of bloodshed throughout history and serves to divide, rather than unite people. My personal opinion, as a student of comparative religion, is quite different since all religion of the world, be it Judaism, Christianity, Islam, Hinduism or Sikhism, took birth with a noble intent. It is only when they became pedantic and were increasingly institutionalized to sanctify political and economic designs, that they were considered repressive and hence abominable.

According to Elise Boulding, there are two contrasting cultures in every religion, the holy war and peaceable garden cultures.[5] Churches, instead of helping their societies develop the middle ground skills of negotiation and mediation, have insisted on a choice between two extreme behaviors; unitive love or destruction of the enemy. In international affairs, this has led to the identification of the church with the state in wartime and kept it from claiming the important middle ground of peace making. Institutionalized religion can pick up its missed opportunities by adopting the mystic message of accommodation for the "other".

Although one may believe that the religious texts like *the Quran* (*the Bible* and *Torah* as well), is the direct word of God, it still has to go through human interpretation. Historical, political, social, economic and cultural contexts of the interpreting agent, affect the way religious texts are understood.[6] However texts, and in particular religious texts are filled with ambiguities, contradicting statements and are written down in a distant time, usually in language that is different from the ones used by the current communities.[7] In this context, Sufism assumes an important role as the Sufi masters used language and symbolism which was accessible to the human collectives.

In the literary and linguistic landscape of South Asia, throughout history, regional vernaculars flourished in a complex interplay with the language of the ruling elite. In this context too, Sufis played a very important role since they preached in the language of the common collectives. While the religious and political elite talked down to people, the Sufis talked to the people, while imposing the conceptual structures of Islam through the use of popular ideas which were already in existence.[8] The Sufi teachings of human brotherhood, peaceful coexistence, egalitarianism and service towards humanity, provided fertile ground for bridging the gap between various religious and linguistic communities of South Asia.

While the communication of Sufi teachings enriched the language, the language augmented the reachability of teachings. In this context, as in various others, Sufism transcends the parochial and moves into the realm of the universal. The *tazkirat*, *malfuzat* and *maktubat* of the Chishti, Suharwardi and Naqshbandi *silsilahs* constitute an important genre of Sufi writing in Persian, written during the period of the Delhi Sultans and the Mughals. Other genres of Sufi writing include the *premakhyan* (written in Hindi), *qissa, dhohrey, athware, baramah, kafi* (written in Punjabi) etc. of the former, some have been considered 'spurious' or historically unauthentic; the latter genre, whether prose or poetry, is considered pure fiction. However, though the tales woven around the personality of the Sufi, might not be factually correct, the Sufi message was transtemporal with a resonance larger than life, that went beyond any single historical context. The recurring themes in *tasawwuf* literature consist of *karamat* (miracles), sundry life experiences and narratives of reconciliation, probably a device to resolve conflict or to at least, confine it to a latent form; in this sense there was a covert contribution of the Sufis towards state formation and consolidation.[9]

II

Defining Sufism or Tasawwuf is an almost impossible task, however for the sake of pedagogic convenience Sufism may be described as devotion to God and love for humanity, in order to achieve the ultimate objective of closeness with God (irfaan) the ecstatic, rapturous and blissful state, and finally wisal (union), then annihilation (fana) in God. It is believed that there are three ways to experience nearness with God, the Quran (Shariat), Hadith (Prophetic traditions and Marifat (Spirituality). J.S. Trimingham has delineated three phases in the evolutionary history of Sufism, the Taifa, Tariqa and Khanqah phase marked by ascetic life, theoretical development and organized orders.

The term *Tasawwuf*, like many other religious terms, might have come into use at a later stage, nevertheless it is an intrinsic feature of the *Shariat*. Broadly speaking, matters of *shariat* concerned with external practices like prayers, *Zakat* etc., fall under the category of *Fiqh* (Islamic jurisprudence) while those concerned with the esoteric and states of the heart (*qalb*) belong to the domain of *Tasawwuf*. Both encompass gratitude and devotion to the Almighty, expressed through service to humanity. Instead of dwelling on *mazhab* (rituals) Sufism emphasizes *deen* (essence) of Islam, which is, why it is sometimes wrongly criticized for *bidat* (innovation).

Though Sufism as a distinct organized form, came into being after the advent of Islam, its idea can be traced to the life time of Prophet Mohammad (PBUH) when some of his companions (and the Prophet (PBUH) himself) practiced meditation to realize Divine Love stressing the need for *Jihad-i-Akbar* (the greater Jihad or struggle) in order to conquer one's *nafs* (self). The Sufi practice of community living in the *Khanqah* (the Sufi hospice), *langar* (community dining, irrespective of race, religious, social status etc.) are ideal examples of means which can be adopted to resolve conflict arising over sharing of resources and to establish social justice. In the past Sufis have even rebuked kings for the plight of the deprived in their reigns. The Sufi message of *fana* (annihilation) of the ego, before the final annihilation of the self) and forgiveness can make peace sustainable. The non-acquisitive character of Sufism is akin to that of Marxist though, also in sync with the

Gandhian idea that nature has enough for everybody's need, but not greed. The Sufi message of condemning greed if vehemently disseminated, can go a long way in successfully combating the vitriolic menace of neo-imperialism.[10] This is possible since Sufism deploys popular means like *sama, rags*, love-tales to bring home its message in an easy way to the young and old, alike.

Often, Sufism is viewed as being a challenge to the flaws in the established order. Women saints were double transgressors, first, by their nature as saints and second by their nature as women. Their real transgression was not to develop an unconditional personal spiritual practice or experience the spiritual states. Their real transgression was to go public and enter the public arena of preaching, teaching, exhorting and being visible. Only by going public did saintly women break all cords of the safety net of being a good women "in patriarchal society".[11]

Sufi thought firmly repudiates Samuel Huntington's "Clash of Civilization" theses and proffers "Dialogue among civilizations"[12] A lot has been written on Sufism, already. William Chittick, Rushbrook Williams, Louis Massignon, Arnold J. Arberry, Ronald Nicholson, Paul Jackson, Bruce B. Lawrence, Khaliq Ahmad Nizami, Muhammad Habib, I.H. Siddiqui, Muzaffar Alam, Sunil Kumar, Christian W. Troll, S.Z. H Jaffri, Simon Digby and Richard M. Eaton are among the prominent scholars writing on the subject. The present work is the first of its kind since it is a humble attempt to relate Sufism to conflict resolution and peace building strategies.[13]

Dialogue and interaction between social groups, coupled with respect and accommodation for the other, are the prequisites for conflict resolution and peace. While the use of coercive tactics are proving to be futile in as much as it may establish 'cold peace' that may or may not last. Sufism promises to bring in warm peace since its philosophy advocates avoidance of confrontation, through dialogue and respect for the other, and annihilation of the ego.

III

A senior friend, once, asked me a very pertinent question and lambasted me for not writing anything about it in my previous book. I have, hence, decided to deal with it here, however cursorily and in as dispassionate a manner as possible. *Why is it that the lands of the origin and development of Sufism, became associated with violence and terror resulting in tendentious nomenclature for abominable activities (Islamic terrorism)?*

To begin with, all countries in the land of Sufism's birth, allowed themselves to be used as instruments of foreign policy of others, who worked with the twin objective of forwarding an imperialist agenda and discouraging the notion of a powerful power bloc in the developing parts of Asia. With the explicit purpose of vilifying, Islam as a religious tradition and *Muslim* as a socio-political subject became synonymous. Well before 9/11, terrorism in its modern form, did exist in the world – in Algeria, Ireland, Sri Lanka, Nepal, India (in the form of Khalistan, Naxalite and Kashmir struggle)[14], Chechnya and other parts of Russia. However, it became worth dealing with, only when it started hurting the privileged few of the world who are more equal than equal. (The earliest references to the Reign of Terror can be traced to the period of the French Revolution when passionate attempts were made to enforce the ideas of liberty, equality and fraternity).

Security and stability in the lands of Sufism's birth, have been disturbed by a variety of factors – internally, by the conflict of the people with authoritarian, autocratic regimes that were supported by the neo-imperialists for strategic and commercial reasons. The Arab-Israeli conflict has been a major unitive source of discontent due to the sense of injustice it has generated among many. The U.N. has proved to be totally ineffective in the sphere of peace and security since international law does not have an *international* enforcing agency.

From the late 18th century onwards, several European powers had shown keen interest in West Asia, as part of their imperialist agenda. The British, the French, the Dutch and the Russians, all started carving out colonies, on the pretext of establishing protectorates for religious minorities in the tottering Ottoman Empire. Coupled with it, was the missionary zeal to enforce 'their' idea of modernization and 'civilized' on others, to bring about political and social change.

As Britain started taking a lead in the race for colonies (due to its industrial superiority and control over Indian resources), it started elbowing out the French, Dutch, etc starting with Oman. Britain prohibited free movement of ships in West Asia in the name of preventing piracy, slave trade and smuggling of weapons, thus destroying the economy of the region along with ports, cities, etc. It also restricted the movement of tribes, therefore we have the Al Zaids in the UAE, Al Thanis in Qatar, Al Saud in Saudi Arabia, all part of the same tribe.

The British, as a final blow to the Ottoman Empire, promised complete liberation to the Arabs (Sharif-McMohan Agreement), but made contradictory plans with the French over sharing the spoils of the fragmentation (Sykes- Picot Agreement) and with the Zionists (Balfour Declaration), resulting in the creation of Israel on Palestinian land. Thus, the Ottoman Empire was disintegrated and yet, the promised freedom was not given. The discovery of oil was a major turning point and even before the World War I, the focus of economy shifted from coal to oil. The strategic importance of oil was realized since it enhanced the naval power.

Geopolitically and strategically, West Asia has been of crucial importance for the Western powers. The control over West Asia was important for British control of India and also, since it was close to the Soviet Union. The presence of oil resources which had fast started replacing steam power in industry and shipping, was a very important economic factor. West Asia was also of tremendous significance by virtue of its geo-strategic location, almost at the center of the world. It boasts of many nodal choke points, controlling world trade routes – the Strait of Hormuz (75% of world's energy passes through it), Barivel Bander, Dardanelles, to name a few.

The importance of West Asia for all the industrial nations is evident from the fact that the West took serious offence when the Suez Canal was nationalized; when it was closed in 1956 (for about a year and a half) and in 1967 (for 7-8 years), rationing of oil resources had to be introduced and Europe was brought to its knees. West Asia is a promising market for those trying to engage in exports, since it is a capital surplus region.

It is evident that a desire to control petro-energy resources has been a determining factor in the political economy of West Asia. At the time when oil was discovered, West Asia was a tribal dominated area. Oil was found in the hinterland, which was controlled by tribes where there was circulation of tribal leadership that exercised political and military power. The merchants lived in the coastal region and controlled the economy. With this kind of socio-political formation, it was imperative for the world powers to identify and consolidate the position of the tribal leader, in order to successfully pursue their oil interest and to be able to sign the deal. The simple tribes were not aware of the magnitude of oil wealth and had been supported by the merchants. However, with the discovery of oil, the entire political equation changed. The volume of royalty was a phenomenal sum for the tribal leadership, and they, no longer depended on the coastal magnates.

Without a system of taxation (which is linked to democracy) there was legitimacy to develop an authoritarian structure linked to oil. The state became very rich and there was state led development and welfare, in the name of sharing the wealth; the state drew legitimacy from Islam.

A rentier state created a rentier society, with oil gradually becoming the prime mover of the economy, resulting in a monoculture economy. As the desert area was landscaped and the construction boom led to the need for manpower, large migrations from South Asian countries took place. In many countries, the expatriate population exceeded the local population in numbers, with the exception of Iran and Iraq. Iran and Iraq had a fairly developed agricultural and industrial sector, with fully developed skilled labour, since they were old civilizations (not tribal like GCC countries). However, they were the worst to be affected by oil. At the time when the Nationalist Movement was going on in India, this region was influenced by socialist ideals.

In time, the Bath Socialist Party came up in Egypt, Libya and Iraq. The nationalist movement in West Asia leaned towards the Left. This threatened the capitalists who were afraid that this tilt might go in Soviet favour. Oil interest, coupled with the fear of the Red, started promoting right wing politics in West Asia, and as such, was a determining factor in controlling the ideology of the region.

The surmounting insecurity felt by autocratic regimes (internally and externally), boosted defence expenditure, while the capitalists who sold arms to them, laughed their way to the bank. To further their profits, the capitalists encouraged tension among the countries of that region and sharpened contradictions between the Shia and Sunni, which were caused by political factors.

In a situation of turmoil, each ruler wanted to be the ruler of the entire region and each one's hopes were whetted by a conscious policy of playing one against the other. It is another matter, of course, that the rulers were not foresighted enough to see through the trap and did not refrain from recurrent bickering over issues which could have been resolved amicably, had the Sufi ideals of austerity, forgiveness, equitable distribution of resources, and accommodation been adhered to. Mussadiq, earlier supported by the US, was removed in a CIA engineered coup — a fine example of the symbiotic relationship between autocratic regimes and the US (Saudi Arabia is a classic example, as well) with the exchange of oil for ensuring continuity and security of the regime. After the 1979, Islamic Revolution in Iran, the US could no longer endorse Iran and hence tried to raise Iraq against it.

The oil boom reached its peak between 1974-86. From the mid 80s onwards, the oil prices started declining. As a number of players started joining the international oil market, serious challenges rose for the Gulf countries. The leverage exercised by a few oil countries began to be questioned. The local people began raising questions as the state started cutting expenditure subsidies. With the advent of the ICT revolution, information from the outside world became freely accessible, despite filters. The state control over information ceased to exist as al-Jazeera changed society; disillusionment with the twin monsters of internal autocratic rule and external enemy, grew relentlessly.

As the 'state led economic development' model failed (the market also failed), liberalization was initiated with everyone clamouring to enter the bandwagon of WTO. This also meant that the legal system of WTO would be applicable; because of obligations to the WTO, the national legal system debated with it (judicial system, human rights and so on). This, coupled with the fact that the oil led economy had a limited capacity to create substantial number of jobs for its own manpower, was frustrating for the emerging youth bulge. The inequitable distribution of wealth, along with the social mores, made it difficult for young men, even to get married.

Subsequently, there was the rise of the private sector and knowledge economy. The knowledge revolution provided skilled manpower to meet the demands of the ITC (Information and communication technology) sector. Many educated, whose skills did not match the requirements of the industry, could not be absorbed. In the absence of industrial capital, cronie capital (finance capital) had held sway in West Asia, resulting in a dependent economy with limited employability (No attempts were made at industrialization for attaining self-sufficiency. This dependence suited the capitalists or Neo-liberals, as they were now called).

Clearly, there was growing unrest and demand for educational reforms. The abdication of responsibility by the state, swelled the manpower with no employability, but which was nevertheless, a part of the information outfit. The lapping up of foreign education brought an unprecedented change in the value and cultural ethics.

With recession looming large, efforts are required to build economies beyond oil, to make development sustainable and ensure that its fruit is equitably distributed. Early realization of the urgency of regional integration and encouraging women's participation, based on Sufi ideals of accommodation and justice, is imperative. At the international level, taking recourse to a diversified energy mix (comprising of hydrocarbons as well as, other forms of renewable and non-renewable energy) is recommended since a blown up profile based on oil is not going to be sustainable. In fact, there is an urgent need to revisit the entire relationship between human consumption and resources. For this, Sufi teachings assume great importance.

Similarly, in the case of South Asia the uneven impact of neo-liberal reforms has been the cause of unrest in the region. The denial of basic human rights and the absence of equitable distribution of resources, has been responsible for seething discontent that brews over, every now and then. Coupled with this is the fact that *hasad* and *hirs* (envy and desire, the twin evils which the Sufis and Bhakti saints guarded against) have been fuelled by the Neo-liberal (or Neo-imperialist) quest for more profits. A lifestyle of austerity (a hallmark of Sufis) is looked down upon. Self proclaimed custodians of religion (Islamists as well as Hindutva protagonists), encourage extremism and communal disharmony. Vested interests work hard to ensure that the rift between India and Pakistan (who have the potential to be natural allies) continues, if not widens. However, its worth remembering that *do billion ki ladai men Bandar roti kha jata hai.*

Extremists seem to suffer from selective amnesia when upholding the Shariat. The Quran categorically states not lament the birth of a daughter, to give rightful inheritance to daughters, to acquire *ilm* (education) even if you have to travel to a place as far away as China, along with clearly defined rules regarding the virtuosity of men. However, all this, and more, is conveniently forgotten.

Not very long ago, Al Qaida, under Osama, was deployed to fight Russian presence in Afghanistan. When the US entered Lebanon, Al Qaida, strengthened by its experience in Afghanistan, decided to oppose the US. It had a wider canvas compared to the Taliban, since it had recruits from all over. Ironically, the neo-imperialists extolled the virtues of 'jihad' in their fight against Socialism, until the tables were turned on them. As a matter of fact, the 'use and throw' policy of neo-imperialists has been counterproductive and has generated a strong sense of injustice among many people.

Pakistan has been used as an instrument of foreign policy, of the U.S. President Carter offered funds to the dictatorial regime of Zia-ul-Haq, to wage a proxy war. In this sense, it is ironic that the first 'jihad' in modern times was fought by the U.S., using Pakistani army. This gave strategic depth to Pakistan and contributed to the creation of the Taliban (Strangely, Talib means seeker, i.e., seeker of knowledge. The plural is Taliban, students).

All acts of violence and terrorism need to be dealt with, in a tough manner. At the same time, we need to be tough on the causes of terrorism. Sufism has the potential to lend a soft touch to this tough stance.

Fatima Hussain

Notes:

1. Philip Gowins says that there are three kinds of love. The first is love in the marketplace where we bargain with our partner and say "love me, and I might reciprocate", or "I love you, and I demand you reciprocate". The second is the love that sees others as beings to be tolerated with quirks that perhaps we accept. This is better than the first kind of love. The third is love that sees all others as part and parcel of the Almighty, which cannot be faked and is the Sufi kind of love. See Philip Gowins, *Sufism, A Path for Today,* Readworthy, New Delhi, 2008, p.158.
2. Oliver Leaman, *A brief Introduction to Islamic Philosophy, Polity,* Blackwell, UK, 2001, p.79
3. Ibid
4. The concepts of *sama, raqs and wahdat ul wujud* (unity of being) have been themes of hot debate.
5. Elise Boulding, *Two Cultures of Religion As Obstacles to Peace, Journal of Religion and Science,* Zygon ®, Vol.21, Issue 4, December 1986, pp.501-508.
6. S. Ayse Kadayifii- Ornella, "Religion, Violence and the Islamic Tradition of Non-Violence *"Turkish Yearbook of International Relations,* No.34, 2003, p.3; the *Surah-i-Kafirun* of the *Quran* explicitly states *Lakum Denokum Wale Ya Din,* to him his religion and to me mine. However, this is not highlighted by those who use Islam to sanctify their political, social and economic causes.
7. Ibid.
8. The Chistis adopted Buddhist and yogic practices of *zambil,* shaving of the head of new entrants to the *silsilah,* offering water to visitors and the *chillah i ma'kus*
9. Richard M. Eaton, *Essays on Islam and Indian History,* OUP, New Delhi 2004, p100-101, Fatima Hussain, *The War that Wasn't: The Sufi and the Sultan,* Munshiram Manoharlal, New Delhi, 2009.
10. Fatima Hussain, *Sufism and Bhakti Movement, Contemporary Relevance,* Classic Lahore 2008, p.18. Ali see Nicolae Leuin Imper, *Imperialism, The Last Stage of Capitalism,* 1916.
11. Scott Kugle, *Sufi And Saints Bodies Mysticism, Corporeality And Sacred Power in Islam,* University of North Carolina Press 2007, p.103.
12. Seyed Mohammad Khatami, *Islam Dialogue and Civil Society,* JNU, New Delhi 2003, p2-3.
13. British Orientalist Edward Palmer (1840-1882) considers Sufism "an Arian reaction of the Persians to the "homocentric" Semetic genius of the Arabs in Oriental Mysticism.
14. From Assam to Maharashtra, in India, there has been a corridor of Naxal violence triggered by discontentment with feudal and with transgression harming tribals; Since the Indo-Pak war of 1971,till 1988-89, Kashmir did not face any significant political problem, regarding independence and questioning the accession to India. However, in 1987, there occurred a major faux pas in the electoral process. Four people backed by the Jamat-i-Islami, were not allowed to contest elections; they turned into rebels demanding their democratic rights.

Abdul Haque Chang

Sufi, Mirasi and Orthopraxy

Spirituality, Music and Religion
In Eighteenth-Century Sindh

Introduction

The social phenomena embodied in the institutions of Sufi, Mirasi and Orthopraxy in the eighteenth-century Sindh is the focus of this study. In this context an attempt will be made to understand the manifestations of Spirituality (Heteropraxy), Music (non-conformity), and Orthopraxy (political practices of religious representatives). In studying religion, spirituality and music we find at certain places that relations of these are sometimes close to each other[1], while at other times boundaries are drawn or established among them. The social space divided between them is under constant flux. Each element through social actors is making inclusions and exclusions in their social space.[2]

Religion, spirituality and music are structured systems having principle governed by an apex of power holders at each place.[3] Institutional backing for each provides them space to produce professionals of their field, having legitimacy to use vocabulary of their field and draw canons from their learning to formulate conventional laws in society for continuity and existence of social institutions, which provide them subsistence, social hierarchy, social recognition and identity.[4]

This study is based on scientific inquiry of three major institutions of traditional society in the eighteenth-century Sindh. This study will focus on the role-based institutional relations of social bureaucracy in traditional society, with their wider social mechanism and how traditional leaders played their social roles. Sufi, Mirasi, and Orthopraxy, these three roles are treated as intermediary between God and man, Wali and man, (saint) man to man and Rasul (Prophet). These three elements have power, authority and legitimate social role for their particular and specific duties and responsibilities. But connotation of intermediary does not justify total scenario and strength of these roles and their relations with their wider social institutions.

Traditional structures have been made part of inquiry as per the understanding of western perspective, as they are mostly concerned to know about these social institutions for better understanding. All these understandings were based on conventional findings, which were treated as scholarly work by western social scientists in the early eighteenth-century.[5] Administrators, travelers, spies, missionaries, traders and adventurers wrote such accounts.[6]

Similarly accounts on religion, spirituality and music were written in Sindh and outside Sindh in the same time frame,[7] in various forms, such as manuscripts containing text on the development of religion through Madrassahs, religious treatises on various themes of life like government and state relations with people and social construct of eighteenth-century Islam in Sindh. Likewise the Sufis left poetry and other verbatim provide other perspective of same images. Poetry provided raw material to musical structure for its continuity, recognition and penetration in other social spaces.

3. Defining Terms

The suffixes prax, praxis and praxy are used for the practices instead of the doctrine, where as xommonly -doxa, or –doxy are used but this does not correspond with the actual practices carried out by the people, therefore throughout this paper-praxis is used instead of –doxy.

The term Sufi here is denoted to as a collective noun. Spirituality being the social phenomenon. Heteropraxy is used as synonymous for Sufi and Spirituality.

The term Orthopraxy is used to represent the practices of Religious leaders, as not being the part of doctrine but practices of specific group in the course of history.

Mirasis are traditional musicians, who play Music. Mirasi is an occupational caste, who sing for society, and they don't have fixed ideological identity in comparison to the Sufi or the Mulla; instead they can sing for both, even for non Muslims as it is the case, therefore the term to non-conformist is used for Mirasi with reference to Sindh's context in 18th century.

4. Relationship of Spirituality, Music and Religion

Social space is market for individuals and institutions where they come to interplay for bargaining. Sometimes these negotiations are based on equality but at other times bargaining is profit for the one, who is dominant in any way to impose his own decisions by any will, not being on equal level. Such relations are always changing, actors are moving in amorphous social order. These actions are sui generis in their essence. Nothing is played through a prescribed or organized way as offices run. Social actions are based on their own rules which some times move in one direction while at other times move in another direction. These relations exist because either sides or any one side closes door for equal dialogue. The level of dialogue depends on balance of power in economic, religious, diplomatic, military or any other spheres where both parties are at equal level in treatment with each other.[8]

Treatment of religion, spirituality and music, by scholars regarding Sindh in general and the eighteenth-century in particular, is scanty and based on generalizations or carrying on already prevailing notions about the subject matter, which in most cases is derived from colonial accounts, whereas, anthropological accounts are silent about these relations due to their so-called commitment for methodological limitations of micro level studies. Historians produced descriptive accounts neglecting unresolved questions and abstraction of past history.[9] Therefore it is aimed to define these abstractions in concrete way and pose questions in this study about unresolved questions and abstractions of history in objective and subjective manner.

5. Social Structures of Spirituality, Music and Religion

Religion, spirituality and music are social institutions having particular and specific role (s) in human life. These institutions are not operating in society in their individualities. Society is larger than these institutions. Therefore these institutions (individualistically) do not determine human relations. Social facts are wider than institutional relations. Institutional relations operate as Ideal type for having institutional identity. Man is not engaged in individual institutional relations all the time, because wider social needs and dependencies compel him (them) to opt for many social institutions at the same time. A single institution is not capable of fulfilling all human needs, like economic, religious, spiritual, psychological, emotions, leisure, and aesthetic, and so on. People in a society are similarly engaged in religious, spiritual and musical spheres because of interaction-based human relations, and most importantly because of undefined & unrecognizable needs.[10] Therefore social institutions fulfill the multiform needs of man collectively. Traditional societies are operating at multi-polar level in the societal affairs and social relations are not drawn out in defined way. Empirical grounds indicate that social spheres are open to be occupied, unoccupied and reoccupied but at the ideal level defined parameters are built for "self" and "other". As man is alienated in society in case of deviant behaviour, in similar manner institutions are conceptualized as deviant when self and other becomes at extreme level of discomfort.[11] We have to bear in mind that this exists at the ideal level: conceptualizing in particular way by the intermediaries. While this conceptualizing may not necessarily prevail empirically, it provides cognitive images about the self and other.

The eighteenth-century brought change in world images, and perception; it altered consciousness individually and collectively. The West invented new concepts for the East: "Primitive", "Barbaric", "uncivilized", "non-developed", "aborigines",[12] which needed to be replaced by modernity. At the same time there were different perceptions of modernity within the East. The Mughals and Persian had their own concepts of modernity. Similarly at different parts of South Asia, local models of development emerged in the eighteenth century. The wider disintegration converted into smaller integration(s). We observe that two major paradigms are emerging in the beginning of the eighteenth-century. One is the western perception, which made roots in India and began. Euro-centrism in the western academics and it reflected through the policies enforced by East Indian companies.[13] Other is the stagnant image of South Asia, while within the pre-colonial South Asia there were multiple conceptions of modernity.[14]

In the eighteenth century, Sindh was going through the processes of change of power from Mughals to local Sufi dynastic rule. Orthopraxy, Heteroprax and Non-conformists were in interplay to occupy and negotiate their space.

6. Religion

By religion here we mean Islam and Mulla as an operator of religious activities.[15] Mulla is represented in this study as having predominant role in orthodox religious operations and in day to day matters, being in direct contact with people, his role being representatives of Orthoprax elements of the religion. The Arabs brought Islam to Sindh and it spread here by Persian mystical influence; later, local mystical generations carried similar trends. Therefore Sindh had never been under the influence of orthodox Islamic elements. Two major trends are found in Sindh in the era under stuffy: Fiqahi approach of Islam, and the direct influence of the mystical approach of Islam, due to being mostly an agricultural area. Thatta was the center of Orthoprax school of thought, having four hundred Madras. Most of the population was *Sunni*, under the Hanafi school of thought. *Sheites* were also in small majority; they were from earlier generation of the Isna Ashari and Ismaili sects. In theory justice was dealt according to the *Quran* and *Sunnah*. But in practice *Ijamaa* and *Qiyass* were more preferred when dealing with law and order, civil, and criminal jurisdiction.[16] The *Kardars, Muftis, Munsifs* and *Qazis* practiced *qanoon-e-shariat* and *Qanoon-e-Urf* in court, thus performing both functions of magistrate and Judge.[17] Faqihi Islam was part of state matters in the legalistic issues and matters but it was functioning along with the traditional and customary justice system and under the influence of the mystical lines of saint cult. The *Kalhoro* ruler came to the throne because they had religious Sufi roots.

Orthopraxy was concentrated in legalistic Islamic perspective. This group consisted of *Mulla, Ulama, fuqaha*, religious hard liners, religious scholars and large number of theologians of Hanafi school of thought (Abu Hanifah, 699-767); madrasah and masjid were centers of their activities. Makhdum Muhammad Hashim Thattvi, born in a religious family of Mirpur Bathoro in 1104 H, studied under the tutelage of Allama Moeen Thattivi and at Makka and Madina under the studentship of scholars of Hanafi seminaries: Shaikh Abdul Qadir Makki, Shaikh Abdul Bun Ali Masri and Shaikh Abu Tahir Muhammad Madni. He was veteran spokesman to Tahrik-i-Tajdeedi-Shariat. His religious ideas confronted with Allama Moeeen on the matter of interpretations of Hadith and fiqah. He was an adherent to traditional tents of Islam. He laid weight on ritualistic theses of Islam according to Hanfia theology; under these confinements he launched a movement against the apostasies in Sindh, *Aeena-e-Jahan Nama*. The protection of *Sharia* for him was in restoration of Hanfia theology. Makhdum Muhammad Hashim Thattavi regarded prevailing sindh,[18] he encouraged efforts of mulla Nizam-ud-Din and implemented *dares-e-nizami* in Sindh.[19]

He served on the seat of *Qadi-ul-Quddat* (chief Justice) of Thatta; he was author of one hundred fifty religious treaties on various branches of Islamic theology. His religious ideas will be presented in detail in theses.

Mukhdum Abdul Wahid Sawistani, Muhammad Qaim Bin Salih Al-Sindhi Hanafi, Mukhdum Ziauddin, Mir Najmuddin, Mukhdum Rohullah, Mukhdum Inayatullah, Mukhdum Mohammad Ibrahim, Mukhdum Usman Tharo, Qazi Mukhdum Abdul Rehman, Shaikh Muhammad Hiyat Sindhi, and Shah Faqir Ullah Alvi were major components representing the orthoprax thoughts in there works. [20]

Radical changes were introduced in orthopraxy circles of Thatta, executed under increasing power of Kalhoras in the upper parts after 1700 AD (Kalhoro Ruled Sindh until 1783). They proposed to reduce lower parts grip under the mianwal movements's theocratic and political influence, on the bound principles of Hanafi theology. This movement transmogrified to mianwal Tariqa in upper Sindh. Agrarian social communes developed around the cantonments of the power: mianwal Tariqa nourished in power corridors. Kalhoras rose as spiritual pathfinders, saints and liberators of peasants, they traced their origin from Hazarat Abbas, paternal uncle of the holy prophet (pbuh) of

Islam. Through the saint cult they began to rise as a political force, affiliation with saint-cult provided them influence on the landowners and peasants. Its social design was radical mystical agrarian order or controlled peasantry movement. They had strong relations with the hard liner theologians of Thatta, which desired for Islamic caliphate. Hanfia theology, Mahdi Janpuri's theological philosophy, and the codex of mianwal were its ingredients. Thus, mianwal transformed from Sufi brotherhood to radical-cum political Orthopraxy. Thatta began to relinquish its importance as the capital of Sindh; Kalhoras initiated to draw the power center towards Chandka, mountains being the border, Saraiki Balochs were their *mureeds* and part of hard core military cadre of mianwalism. Under these circumstances, upper Sindh had risen as a semi-autonomous territory, at the beginning of 18th century. Under the administration of autocratic kalhoro rule Riyasat, state and siyasat, politics were imbuing principles of Hukoomat, government: embodied in the compendium, manual for princes and kings: constitution of state and principles of inheritance, *Manshoor-ul-Waseeat-wa-Dustoor-ul-Hukoomat.*

7. Spirituality

Understanding the length and breadth of spirituality is beyond the scope of this study. As far as this study is concerned certain parameters are drawn to describe the subject matter under inquiry. The term spirituality contains vast spectrum to explanation, but I am here dealing with spirituality as social phenomenon, having institutional roots and actors, which are parts of fraternities. Under the shadow of social organization, spiritual leader, residential complex, teaching places and peculiar and distinct ways of social super structure about philosophy of life about this world and life after this world, Sufism is identified with the spiritual practices and philosophy generally. Sufism in this study will be treated as phenomenon under which spirituality is being practiced in various forms and ways for achieving certain ends and means through certain method and approaches. Organization and structure of Sufism is mostly formal having structural and fixed laws, thus it is one of the most complex system of unseen visions and the world which have hierarchies and bureaucratic distributions of spiritual levels. Unseen world occupies major place in its social organization, which runs parallel to this world. Sufism operates in the visible and invisible world simultaneously. Nonetheless social perspective of Sufism derives its roots from Orthodox Islam but it operates in society at one eighty-degree parallel to its origin.[21]

Religious scholars, students and leading Sufis nurtured in the seminaries of Thatta and played active role in sustaining and voicing reforms under the teaching of social reformer Allama Moeen Thattvi. Hospices and shrines were new centers along with madrasahs for heteropraxy. Allama produced unorthodox treaties of his own, like his eminent teacher, besides this, he managed to secure attention of other leading mystics and ulemas, who afterwards presumed important role in reforms. He produced fifteen volumes on various branches of Islam. Qadiri Uwaisi mystic Shah Abdul Latif Bhitai, and other Naqshbandi mystics and religious scholars such as Sufi Shah Inayat Shaheed, Mukhdom Muhammad of Khuhra, Sahib Dino Faqir of Daraza, Mukhdom Mohammad Zaman of Lovari, and Makhdum Abdul Rahim Grohri were prominent personalities who emphasized need of change and flexible rational approach towards Islam.

Shah Abdul Latif of Bhittai was a prominent mystic, he wrote in philosophical and technically in passive manner about events occurring in the Eighteenth century in his poetic compendium. Shah institutionalized *Shah Jo Raag*. A Sufi musical tradition, which prevails even now in Sindh and India. Sachal Sarmast, Sufi Shah Inayat, and Makhdum Muhammad Zaman Linwari are few prominent figures of the eighteenth century, having negative image of Mulla in their poetic discourse, criticizing them for not having true approach towards Islam. Eighteenth century social scenario compassed in poetical expression of mystics, clearly demonstrates rejecting the past, based on irrational ground. Selection of the vernacular with new diction was prime need of time. Persian poetical metaphors roamed around *Gul-o-Bulbul* and *Saghar-o-Mina*. New stake of metaphors assimilated in poetical expressions, rooted in local landscape were introduced which were understood by every one easily. Local folk characters were intermediary between the poet and the audience. Metaphysical and subtle mystical thoughts were presented in local symbols, giving privilege to common and illiterate people to comprehend Islamic thoughts in simple language. It provided new vistas between the people and religion. Religion was no more in alien sacred Lingua Franca; therefore, people were inclined towards hospices where every one had equal chance to be a recipient. Shah Latif and Sachal Sarmast are two major poets who brought people to this fold. Below a brief review of these poets is given, who were catalysts for social change and development.

Shah Abdul Latif (1690-1752 A.D) did not write or compile his poetic verses, his verses complied by his disciples and local scholars. The first published compendium of Shah's poetry was compiled by Ernest Trumpp, printed in Leipzing, Germany, in 1866. Shah made religious philosophy accessible to common person: linguistic barriers removed distance between God and man via the saint. He broke hegemonic authority of religious interpretation of religious schools, hospices entrance criteria were not restricted, providing space to those people who otherwise stood no where.

Mian Abdul Wahab Alias Faqir Sacahl Sarmast, poet of revolt[22] was born in Daraza in 1738 (d. 1826 A.D). He was disciple of Mian Abdul Haque, his paternal uncle, and father in law. He was continuation of Shah's philosophy but his poetical expression was evocative and directly expressing heretical ideas. He was inspired by Hallaj's philosophy. Throughout his poetry he repeatedly uttered: 'say ana'l haqq, every one is Mansur in my tribe'. He criticized orthopraxy openly in his poetry, such criticism is rarely found in mystical discourse of any other South Asian Muslim mystic. Local as well as international scholars of mystical scholarship have not explored Sachal's innovative mystical ideas.

His mystical discourse's imaginative boundaries are expressed in uncomplicated metaphors but it is extremely complicated in premises of subtlety. Some scholars unveiled his splendid approach but wider community of Islamic scholars is not appreciative about his personification in restructuring 18th-century's social formation. He persuaded many generations of mystics who later played active role in upper Sindh. The network of mystical chain was organized during his life time and it is even apparent today in district Kahairpur, and Sukkur.

8. Music

Music like religion and spirituality is distinct in its total social phenomena. But having interaction based relationship; music is part of religion and spirituality, and religion and spirituality are intermingled with music. A complex relation exists between music, religion and spirituality in South Asia. Music in its basic structure has different rules and regulations but all these structures are meant to regulate function of melody, rhythm and providing a space, which is abstract image as well as social image. Social in the sense that nothing exists in music, that is not social.

We find serious debates of two major schools of thought regarding the texonomological classification of musicology in Sindh. One school of thought says, "originally Sindhi Music is found on folk tunes, it can be categorized under the category of Neem Classical Raag, not under the category of Pure Classical Music. Classical music prevailed in Sindh first as a derivation of North Indian classical musical Surs and Dhuns and secondly as an amalgamation of Folk Sindhi Surs and Indian Classical Raags. According to them whatever is sung in the name of Sindhi Classical Music is actually North Indian Classical music. As far as Balochi music is concerned it cannot be categorized in any way as Balochi Classical music; whereas Balochi music still has its roots in folk musical tradition". Others believe that "music of Sindh and North Indian Classical music is the same, as they trace the origin of North Indian Classical music in the Indus Valley Civilization. They believe that the North Indian Classical music evolved in Sindh and it has been sustained here through the centuries. They think that the Sindhi scholars tried to Islamitise it and deliberately denied the role of Mirasi[23] in continuity of the classical music in Sindh. In the beginning of the eighteen-century we don't have such debates about the classification or categorizations of music in Sindh, these development took places later on.

Music originates its own roots in society through a specific group that earns as a professional musician. Other than the scholarly debates we have historical evidence of the large caste based community having occupational relationships with music since the centuries.[24] The system and organizational structure in itself have wider social contexts as having roots in the past. It provides ample past record preserved through oral traditions by this occupational caste.[25] Although many studies have been conducted on the Mirasi from occupational perspective but no study has yet provided all connections in its totality regarding worth of social strength of this community of musicians. Mirasi and other heredity musical traditions exist as a large group in

South Asia, they earn their subsistence as a traditional musician. This group is part of mainstream and is distinct because of its occupation, musicality, tradition and stigma. Through a time and space connotation, the role of Mirasi has become some thing more than what musicians are expected to play. Their roles have been enlarged as genealogists, barbers, chefs, messengers, informers, news exchangers, traditional craftsmen, *fakirs* and providers of music to society on ceremonies of happiness and in rituals of pain. Mirasis are professional musicians, having hereditary occupationsl, informal and formal methods of learning this art, through oral traditions and in structural methods as well. Music for mirasi is means of earning as well as his identity. Mirasis were patronized at different levels of the society to provide music for layman, Sufi, and for the patron who provided economic benefits to them in exchange of music playing.

This social group grew around periodic gatherings at Muslim shrines (dargah) and hospices (Khanaqah). With and without accompaniment renditions of specific poetical forms (maulud, madah) by chanters and singers. (*Zakir, qawwal*) were the focus of this tradition. The content of the poetry was intensely mystical[26], and the poetic forms were chosen for their rhythmic nature. This order was major component of heteropraxy: thus, redefining meanings of religion in vernacular language. Under the shadows of heteropraxy the secular-hereditary tradition nurtured. This involved remunerated professional musicians (mirasi), who sang war stories (jang Nama), ballads, epic, love stories, tribal traditions with instruments accompaniment, and imbuing social events with a poetical and musical shape. In this tradition, both the text and context for musical rendition varied differently by the Mirasi according to demands of the patron. The terms also used by Shah for professional musicians are *jajak, atar, path, ragai,* and *kertia*, with reference to their specific specialization-instrumentalists, singers, and chanter acclimatized vernacular language in its all articulations.

Literature produced in *khanaqah* and seminaries advocated re-modeling of the role of the prophets as a human beings and more emphasis on *haqoqal-abad*, 'human rights'. "The mere reciting of kalma did not make a Muslim, it was something else.[27] Religion and society co-related for change and reforms, change meant reconciliation of man and God, which was again in the hands of man. Man to man relation urged to redefine *haqoqal-abad*, as for God these relations were more important then *haqoqal-Allah*, "rights of God".

9. Conclusion

In 18th century Sindh, religion was translated in Sindhi language by the mystical personalities, and the traditional Sufi singing became vehicle to transfer these ideas to people, that transmission was carried out by the Mirasi. Hence religion was redefined by the Sufi and it was made public by the Mirasi. Such tradition is even continuing till today.

Religion, Spirituality and Music are social phenomena. They posses space and have social organization. The social space where they are performing their activities is the same. Same space is divided among each, according to the cultural rules. Mulla, Sufi and Mirasi operate in the same social environment. Mosque and Shrine are religious and spiritual spaces. These spaces operate parallel to each other. Mirasi is occupational caste, which exists in Sindh as well as in South Asia since many centuries. This caste is part of social, cultural scenario of society and Mirasi is also service providing caste as has been argued previously in this article. The spaces of religion, spirituality and music are located in the same territorial unit, physically each one is interrelated with the other, while mentally or normative perspective is given more weight by the scholars, whereas the practices of one each in their original setting are given less importance, while that provides very different story. This is initial work, and the present author is working on this theme by historical anthropological research methods, and it is hoped that by having critical comments the thesis of the article can be improved.

Notes:

1. Shah Abdul Latif has used verses of Quran in his poetry. His massage is meant as containing spiritual thoughts, while this message is sung by Faqirs in *Shah Jo Raag*. Religion, Spirituality and Music here are together to create meanings of social images. For further reference see Lilaram Watanmal Lalwani. *The Life, Religion, and Poetry of Shah Latif, A Greatest Poet of Sindh*. Sang-e-Meel publications, Lahore, 1978. Vol 2-p.8-41.
2. Without going in detailed technical debate it is a fact that it is Mullah, Sufi, and Mirasi who define their subject matter to people.
3. *Masjid, Mudrasah, Durghah, Khanqah,* and *Muhfal*

4. *Mulla, Sufi* and *Mirasi* are role-based occupational identities. Religion, Spirituality and Music are also way to provide them economic means for subsistence.
5. "Research during the past decade has broken new ground and signaled fresh departures in the late Mughal and early colonial historiography". Sugata Bose and Ayesha Jalal. *Modern South Asia History*, Culture, Political Economy. Sang-e-Meel Publications Lahore 1998, p.48.
6. Willemem Floor, *the Dutch East India Company (VOC) and Diewel-Sindh (Pakistan) in the 17th and 18th centuries*. Institute of Central & West Asia Studies, University of Karachi in collaborations with Lok Versa, Islamabad 1993-4.
7. Other than secondary resource material we have the rich primary texts on the eighteenth century from religious scholars of the Thutta, Bhakkar and poets such as Shah Latif, Sachal Sarmast, Sufi Shah Inayat are examples of this.
8. "In every society, there are scattered beliefs and practices, be they individual or local, which are not integrated into a definite system" W.S.S. Pickering. *Durkheim on Religion a Selection of Readings* with bibliographies. Routledge & Kegan Paul, London 1975, p.74.
9. "It is now quite difficult to reconstruct the eighteenth century discourse of this world, not least because of the supposed illegibility of the sources of that time, but also because of a lack of specific historical and material contexualisation and heuristics" Jamal, Malik, p.230.
10. Society does not operate in mechanical way, in sense that each and every human relation is not defined in society in holistic perspective and in its totality. Human relations are always redefined.
11. Concept of deviant behaviour is relative concept in traditional and complex societies, changing in degree.
12. Ibid.
13. Karl Marx in his book *Notes on Indian History* (664-1858) provides detail chronological history of India and detailed accounts of European penetration. Second impression Foreign Language Publishing House, Moscow.
14. Jamal, Malik p.242 and similar concerns have been given in the detail by the Sugata Bose and Ayesha Jalal in Chapter 5 *India between Empires: Decline or Decentralization?* P.48-56 and chapter 6 *The Transition to Colonialism Resistance and Collaboration*. P. 57-66.
15. Mulla will not be treated as critically in this study as most of Eurocentric accounts suggest.
16. Ibid., p.59.
17. Ibid.
18. Muhammad Juman Talpur (1982). pp.8-207.
19. Muhammad Juman Talpur (1982) pp.208 and footnotes of page 208.
20. Ghulam, Rasool Mahar gives the Names of religious scholars. (1964). P.872-904.
21. Annemarie, Sachimmel. *Mystical Dimensions of Islam*. The University of North Carolina Press Chapel Hill, 1975.
22. Ajwani (1991) pp.117-129.
23. Dewsh Vijya, a storyteller of Rajistan describes in his epical poetry *Khaman Raso* history of war between Muhammad Bin Yahya and Raja of Chator Khaman Rai, who was killed in war around the 813-833 A.D. This story was composed around the 870-90. this is one of the earlier evidence of story telling by Charn, which is sub-caste of Mirasi. For further and detailed reference see *Dodo Chaneser* Published by National Institute of Folk and Traditional Heritage, Islamabad, Pakistan. 1975 p.12-33.

24. Dr. Baloch provides detailed descriptive story of music in Sindh from the remote past to present. He traces origin of the Sindhi music from ancient period of Moen-jo-Daro by relating present day musical instrument Keener with past. Dr. Baloch made excellent job by relating music of past with present but there are many factors, which lack sequence of evidences and continuity of music of the Moen-jo-Daro. He goes on to explain the relationships of Sindhian music with Iranian and Turkish traditions. According to him Sindhi music was rich in past having such a mature stage that Sindhi musicians went outside Sindh and they made the great name and fame in this regard. He tells us that Zaryab was most important musician in the court of the Baghdad, where he made great repute regarding his musical skills and due to this he was victimized by his teacher who told him to leave Baghdad because in his presence he was not able to make his name in city. He left Baghdad and went to Muslim Spain where he made unending fame and name which is part of history and that is also reflected in musical tradition of Cante Jondo of southern Spain. Ibid.
25. The name of Bhagho Bhan is famous for being storyteller and singing war songs for Soomro tribe. He was Bhat of royal family. Music, and story telling was tradition of his family, along with this his family was famous for having information about genealogies. *Dodo Chaneser*, Published by National Institute of Folk and Traditional Heritage, Islamabad, Pakistan. 1975. p.12-33.
26. See Ghulam Nabi Sadhaio (1992) pp.211-413: A. Schimmel (1982) pp.33 and pp.140: A. Schimmel (1976) pp.152-262 and S. Qudratullah Fatimi (1991) pp.125-135.
27. *The Risalo of Sachal Sarmast* (1739-1826 A.D), Usman Ali Ansari (1997).

Agha Saleem

Melody of Peace
(Sur Kalyan)

Introduction

The poetic collection of Shah Abdul Latif Bhittai is called Risalo meaning the message. It is a 30-part *magnum opus*. Each part is named after a Sur (Melody) of some classical raga, some fold tune, or a tune associated with some popular folktale. The opening Sur is Kalyan. It is Sunskrit word meaning well-being, inner peace, tranquility, calmness, or harmony. The sur by with poet's description of the monistic concept of God by enunciating begins His various attributes particularly his Oneness and Unity.

> *Allah, the very first the Omniscient, the Supreme,*
> *The Lord of universe,*
> *The Omnipotent is there since infinity by his omnipotence,*
> *The Uncreated,*
> *The Lord, the One, the Unique, the Provider, the Master, the Merciful,*
> *Praise the true Master, and sing hymn of the Wise,*
> *The Generous One Himself sustains the universe,*

Having praised God Shah affirms the prophethood of Muhammad (pbuh). as the cause, the source, and the medium of creation. Sufis, particularly Mansoor and Ibn Arabi, believed that Muhammad (pbuh) was the Reality of the Reality, the Logos which is defined and a creative, animating and rational Principle through whom God emerges from His Absoluteness and His Unknowableness into manifestation. But the Logo is Prophet Muhammad (pbuh) the man, who, like every human being, was born and died but spirit of Muhammad (pbuh) of which Muhammad (pbuh) and all other prophets, including Moses, Abraham and Jesus were individual manifestations. Hence prophet Muhammad (pbuh) combined in himself spirit of Muhammad (pbuh) the Prophet and Muhammad (pbuh) the man. Hence our poet calls him Karari, meaning the cause and medium of creation:

> *Who so believed that God is one,*
> *And heartily affirmed that Muhammad (pbuh)*
> *Is the cause and source of creation,*
> *None of such believer's baat*
> *Ever made and unfavourable landing.*

After that Shah expound his Sufi concept of God who according to Ibn-i-Arbi, is pure, without attributes and essence of all existence. He is endowed with attributes when He manifests himself either in the universe or in man (who is part of universe) and all created things and God's attributes are, therefore, identical with God. The relationship between Him and His creations is that of an object reflected in countless mirrors, which obviously cannot exist without Him. No doubt, there is multiplicity of Khalq (creation) but they do not have the reality in terms of their substance as opposed to essence. There is only one Reality that is *Al-Haque* (The Truth). *Al-Kalque* is not the cause but essence of self and centre of the universe. There is only one self. Each one of us is that self, only it radiates like a sun or a star. So as the sun has innumerable rays, or just as you can focus the whole sun through a magnifying glass and concentrate it on one point. Likewise Brahma wears all faces that exist, and they are his masks. They are not only human faces but also the supreme self (*Allan Watts*). To Hegel, it is the Absolute in which all opposites matter and mind, subject and object, good and evil-are resolved in unity and are one. To Shah, the *Al-Haqu* and the *Brahma* is Pireen meaning the Beloved. Having expounded his monistic idea of god, Shah elucidates the mystic idea of God, the *Pireen*:

> *Your manifestations are in billions,*
> *Your essence is in every being,*
> *But appearances are variant with each other,*
> *O my beloved, how can I enumerate*

All of your innumerable attributes?

*

He is this, He is that, He is death, He is Allah,
He is beloved, He is the Breath
He is the enemy, He is the guide.

*

He perceives Himself and Himself is the beloved
He creates beauty and he himself long for it.
He Himself is the majesty, Himself the essence of beauty,
Himself the visage of beloved,
Himself paragon of beauty,
Himself the guide Himself the disciple, Himself the idea of Himself,
All this I learnt from within myself.

Then we meet lovers whose agony of separation from the beloved like that of man on gibbet. The malaise of beloved's separation is incurable and cannot be diagnosed by the worldly physician, even and old hand is a blunderer:

O stupid physician, why are you burring my skin with hot spikes?
While my body aches, you make me drink concoction,
Death is perceiving the beloved for those
Who consider gallows a bridal-bed.

Sufis concept of love is pleasure, and with God there is no pleasure: for the stations of reality are astonishment, surrender and bewilderment. The love of God for man is that He afflicts him, and so renders him improper for the love for any but him (Arberry). To Shah it is the beloved who causes malaise and pain. This pain is of different sort, which cannot be cured by any physician, but by the beloved alone. And because He inflicts pain He is called merciless, but fact He is the real guide and bliss of the soul:

Having inflicted me, the beloved left,
My pains and pangs are all from him,
I now hate to hear of relief by physicians.

*

The beloved became my physician, the guide to relief,

He uprooted my malaise completely and turned illness into health.

*

Different is the infliction of which beloved is th reliever,
No physician can relieve it a mite
Beloved is my guide, protector, and medication.

*

Beloved is medication not affliction,
Though known as subduer, he is sweet in company,
Whome he makes friend with, he repeatedly stabs,
Lord, the Coverer, probes innermost of being.

Now we meet lovers who climb gallows and bridegroom climbs the bridal bed. After the crucification of Christ and hanging of Hussain Bin Mansoor Hallaj, the cross and the gallows came to symbolize, in religious as well as secular literature, the persecution of the proclaimers of truth and the seekers of change by the beneficiaries of falsehood and the custodians of status quo. The Muslim mystic philosophy, however, the gallows stands for pain, suffering and torture unto death, which a true lover of god must endure in his journey towards union with the Divine. The gallows, or the beheading, is frequently recurring expression in Sufi literature. It is also a venerated religious icon of Christianity. Later it elbowed in secular literature. It is too obvious allusion to the last moments of two great mystics of the Muslim world, one and Arab and the other a Sindhi. It is said of Mansoor Hallaj that before he was hanged his hand were chopped off. Before the resultant loss of blood could turn him pale, he lifted his handless arms and painted his face red in blood. Asked about the significance of his action, he replied that the did not want any one think that fear of death had turned him pale but that he was aglow with crimson ecstasy at his imminent meeting with the Beloved. To shah this is the real manner of lovers. A true lover is the one, who climbs gallows as onlookers marvel at the happiness that glows on his face while on gallows.

Why are they happy on gallows?
They take gallows as bridal bed since their eyes met with those
Of the beloved,
Mounting the bridal bed of gallows is the way of lovers,

The go forward and never look back.

*

Gallows is the adornment of lovers
Since before the advent of time,
To waver and step back is anathema to lovers,
They are, have always been, determined to die on gallows.

In sufi through, love is also annihilation. Abu Abdullah al-Nabaji, the prominent Sufi, has said: Love is a pleasure if it be for a creature and annihilation if it be for the creator. By 'annihilation' he means that no personal interest remains, that such love has no cause, and that the lover does not persist through any cause." (*The Doctrine of the Sufis*: A J Arabery). Shah's perception of love is the same. The lover has to annihilate his ego and his self, and it is only then that he can be aware of the real Self. And in fact this awareness is the true union with the Beloved and can be achieved through pain and suffering because to Shah pain and suffering cause cathartic effect on human soul and one can see through his so crystallized self the real Self. To bring home this perception of love, Shah draws images like dagger, daft, gallows, chopping of limbs by the butcher, etc.. from the concrete world and applies them to human being's inner would of pain, suffering and agony.

First stab yourself, then talk of love,
Let agony of separation vibrate in your being
Like wid in trumpet,
Grill your flash if you seed love.

*

Having learnt the way of lovers
Do not moan when knife is plunged in you,
The agony of love is not to be shared with other,
Keep it unto you with ecstasy.

*

I am in love with those who weild knife,
I enter the arena of love cherfully,
And place my head on the chopping block,
So that the beloved my behead me.

The beloved calls the lover to kill him and after killing him again calls him. This is also symbolic. By killing the poet means the annihilation of ego and thus the lover is transformed and reincarnated:

> *The beloved beckons then slaughters,*
> *He slaughters then beckons,*
> *Don't step aside when under the spear of love.*
> *O lover, cast aside your knowledge and wisdom,*
> *Go straight to face death.*
>
> *
>
> *One who kills takes care also*
> *And beckons with love to be near him,*
> *This is the way of the beloved for all times,*
> *He is the healer, who opens the wounds,*
> *And is delight of the soul.*

Another eminent Sufi Sahl, has said, "Whosoever loves God, is life: but whosoever loves other than God has no life". By the words "is life" he means his life is agreeable because the lover delights in whatever comes to him form the beloved, be it loathsome or desirable: and by "he has no life," he means that as he is ever seeking to attain what he loves and ever fearing that he might be prevented from attaining it, his whole life is lost (Arberry). And shah says:

> *Every thing whatsoever comes form the beloved is sweet,*
> *If you taste thoughtfully there isn't any bitterness.*

He moves on replacing gallows and daggers with killer-wine as symbolic mean for God, lovers to merge with the Divine:

> *Those in front are nearing the chopping block,*
> *While those in the rear are ready to be beheaded,*
> *Sever your head so that you may be accepted,*
> *No lesser offering would be acceptable,*
> *Don't you see heads of those slain in love scattered all ever?*
> *The gruesome game of beheading goes on in the tavern of the barmaid.*
>
> *
>
> *Levers, fond as they are of drinking venom,*

> *Its very sight delights them,*
> *They are addicts, ever cravers of the bitter and the deadly,*
> *Lateef says, being love-smitten separation from the beloved*
> *Is killing them,*
> *Even when their wounds smart, they never let on to others.*

Since ancient times wine is the favourite metaphor of physical as well as spiritual pleasure. Greek gods used to drink nectar on Olympus mountain, and Hindu gods and saints took Som Rus. God Shiva, in his attribute of *Mahesar (Maha-Eshwar* meaning great god) is the god of wine also. Dionysus is the Greek god of wine and vegetation. He is not only the god of pleasure of wine but is also said to be the god human nature. 'Every one of us carries inside him the "Dionysus cord," which make the gifts of Prometheus useless.' 'He reminds men to forget the insignificance of their existence. He is voluptuous, ecstatic power that produces pleasure and forgetfulness, and forgetfulness is considered bliss. Men forget for a while that life is short, youth is fleeting and death is the eventual end of life. Awareness of the brevity of life has given birth to two types of poetic attitudes: one of composing didactic poetry instructing the reader thereby to do good deeds as life is very short; and the other is of enjoying life voluptuously. Past is dead and has vanished forever, future is continuation of the present. Only the new and the is-ness is eternal and everlasting. Hence we should live in the present, the current moment; the now. One is call Appolonion and the other Dionysion poetry. The best example of Dionysion poetry is that of a renowned Persian poet, Umer Kyayam. In his poetry we feel an ever-looming presence of death and resultant intense feeling of forgetting brevity of youth and life. Wine, the gift of Dionysus to mankind for forgetfulness, makes us forget and enjoy every fleeting moment:

> *Today is the time of my youth*
> *I drink because it is my solace,*
> *Do not blame me, although bitter, it is pleasant,*
> *It is bitter because it is my life.*

In the sixteenth century English literature there was popular literary tradition known as Carpe diem, which means 'seize the day'. One poem, written in this tradition by a sixteenth century poet Robert Herrick, is still very popular:

> *Gather ye rosebuds while ye may,*
> *Old time is still a flying,*
> *And this same flower that smiles today*
> *Tomorrow will be dying.*
>
> *
>
> *Then be not coy, but use your time;*
> *And while you may, go marry,*
> *For, having lost but once your prime,*
> *You may forever tarry.*

In mystic poetry wine is symbol of joy, ecstasy, and rapturous love of God. To communicate this spiritual ecstasy and joy, sufi have used similes and metaphors from daily life of common men so that they could visualize and feel the abstract spiritual pleasure the Sufi experiences by compering it with mundane joys of every day life. In many ancient religions wine was considered synonymous with truth because one who drinks cannot hide truth. It was also regarded as a divine beverage. It has the effect of submerging the normal personality of the person who drinks it. The flowers of Dionysus, when drunk, lost their individual personality, went mad, became crazed and were taken over by their god. The actors in the play performed for Dionysus rite were masked; the mask symbolized that submersion of their identity into that of another. It is because of this quality of wine that Sufis have used it as a symbol of obtaining spiritual ecstasy and losing individual personality. We all know that Omer Khayam was a poet of pleasure and wine. In Western world was considered as an erotic pagan poet, but later be was adjudged as Sufi poet. J. B. Nicolas, who translated Omer Khayam's *Rubaiyat* in French in the year 1867, presented him as mystic poet like Hafiz Sheerazi: 'shadowing the Deity under the figure of wine wine-bearer; etc.

Shah has also used wine as mystic metaphor for merging one's individual identity with the ultimate Reality. If we go by the explicit meaning of Shah's verses pertaining to wine, it will appear that the poet is motivating people to drink wine, to go to wine-maid and offer their head for a tumbler of wine. But its implicit meaning is that the wine-maid and the wine both obliterate ego and the drinkers become one with the whole. Hence, we see drinkers crowding the tavern, their individuality under liquidation. The poet advises drinkers to go to the tavern and lay their heads beside the pitcher of wine and get sip from it. The wine-maid will torment them first, tear them to pieces and then give them wine. The drinkers are clamouring for wine of the god Shiva, which is not an ordinary wine but there is some mystery in it which squeezes life from the sinews:

If you yearn for sip of wine go the winery,
Lateef says, lay down your head beside the wineful picture,
Then gulp mouthfuls of the thick wine, o bridegroom,
That overpowers even the powerful,
A sip of such wine even for the price of head would be a bargain.

*

If you for a sip wine, go to the winery,
Lateef says: lay down your head near the wine picture
Trade your head and drink cupful.

*

If your yearn for a sip of wine, go to winer's lane,
Where there is always a clamor for the wine of god Shiva,
I have puzzled it out, a sip of that wine is worth one's head.

*

If you have no taste for the bitter, do not wish for wine,
For it squeezes life out of the sinews,
Lateef says, you can taste it only after you have chopped your head.

Beheading, killing and chopping symbolize annihilation of the wine-seeker's ego and individual identity. The imagery of drinkers and the beautiful wine-maid is taken from the folk tale *Mokhhi ain Mataara*. Mokhhi is a Sindhi variation of the Persian word *Mogi* derived from *Moghan*, a Zoroastrain priest who used to serve ceremonial wine on feasts and festivals hence *Peer-e-Mughan* in Persian poetry.

The Tale:

A maiden, Mokhhi by name, had a winery in a village called Kaunkar some where near Karachi. Famous for its high quality and strong wine, the winery was frequented by connoisseurs from all around. Among them were eight friends, young are strong, known as Mataaraas, who, though infrequent visitor, were the hardest to please. Mokhhi had to provide them strong and still stronger stuff every time. One day they came and demanded wine of same vintage. They were served all the varieties available in the winery, but none took them high. They demanded stronger wine, which could take them out of themselves. Mokhhi, remembering a pitcher of wine buried in a corner of the winery since long, had it unearthed and served its brimful contents to the Mataraas. The Mataraas emptied the picture and went away staggering. They returned after a year and were served all and the varieties available in the winery but non was equal to one they had drunk the year before. They clamoured for the same stuff so that the high level of blissful tranquility they had attained on their earlier visit could be recaptured. Mokhhi was baffled for the wine she had offered them they year before was from pitcher in which a cobra had fallen, its flash had dissolved in the wine and only bones had remained. The venom had fermented with the wine and had given it a new taste and effect. Mataaraas had drunk the wine and now no wine was having any effect on them. Mokhhi did not want them to know that they had drunk venom mixed wine, but she, finding them desperate for that wine, had to tell them the truth. Mataaraas were strong and brave but they were fragile like a picture made of unbaked clay. They had not trodden the path of fondness and longing, which leads to gallows, nor were they lovers who embrace death with smile. They had drunk only wine but had not known the taste of venom. They had not reached the state where venom is the real wine for lovers. When they learnt that the year before they had drunk cobra venom, they were so shocked that they died instantly.

What killed them was not wine,
But the words of reproach of the wine-maid,
Which touched their hearts and they died.

*

Thine wine-maid had nothing against them, nor did the wine kill them,
Sayyed says, they crowded the tavern for a sip of wine,
Behold the graves near the brewery of those
Who were chilled to death by words.

Musical Interpretation

Kalyaan is a Sanskrit word meaning peace of mind and tranquillity. Traditionally it is devotional raga and mostly hymns are sung in it. As regards its origin, it is associated with Kalyani, a city which was one under the domain of Nazam of Hyderabad and is now a part of Andhra Pardesh. It is said that Kalyan raga was invented during the reign of Somaswara, the son of Vikremaditya, who was an authority on the art of music. He wrote a book on music in Sanskrit language with the title *Manasolasa*. Kalyaan is name of that (Frame) also. We know that raga are related to human passions and emotions. The very word raga means colouring of passion. The ancient musicologists of the sub-continent analyzed the impression that each of its notes and micro notes moves on the listener and thus determined their emotive value and equated each note and micro note with a particular human emotion. The point which needs collaboration is that every raga contains at least five notes and many micro notes and every note and micro note has different emotive value. Thus every raga, at one time, would evoke many emotions. Mr. Gosvame, the renowned Indian musicologist, has elaborated the point. According to him each raga always gives prominence to one or two notes. This emphasis on a particular note or notes is thus continued throughout the raga, maintaining its swing and over powering effect by the subordination of other notes, hence, the emotional appeal of *vadi* and *somvadi* notes of individual raga help to determine the emotional value inherent in raga.

The ascending and descending notes of raga Kalyan are:

SA-RE-GA-MA-PA-DHA-NI-SA
SA-NI-DAH-PA-MA-GA-RE-SA
With Vadi not GA and Samvadi note DHA

Shah Lateef probably knew the emotive value of each raga and thus the mood and feel of the verses given under Sur Kalyaan synchronise with the emotive value of raga.

The Melody

Chapter I

داستان ٻهريون

اول الله عليم، اعلیٰ عالم جو ڌڻي
قادر پنهنجي قدرت سين قائم آه قديم
والي واحد، وحده، رزاق رب رحيم
سو ساراه سچو ڌڻي رچئي حمد حکيم
ڪري پاڻ ڪريم، جوڙون جوڙ جهان جي

Allah, the very first, the Omniscient, the Supreme,
The Lord of Universe,
The Omnipotent is there since infinity by his omnipotence,
The Uncreated,
The Lord, the One, the Unique, the Provider, the Master,
The Merciful,
Praise the true Master and sing hymn of the Wise,
The generous One Himself sustains the universe.

اول الله علیم، اعلیٰ عالم کا دھنی،
قادر اپنی قدرت سے، قائم اور قدیم،
والی، واحد، وحدہ، رازق رب رحیم،
مدحت کر اس سچے رب کی، کہہ تو حمد حکیم،
وہ والی وہ کریم، وہ جگ کے کام سنوارے،

✥

MELODY OF PEACE

وحدہ لاشریک لہ، رجان تو چئین ایئن
تان مج محمدؐ کارئی نر تون منجھان نینھن
تان تون وِجیو کیئن، رنائین سرین کیں؟

"He is the one and no one shares his Oneness",
When you say this,
And accept with love Muhammad (phuh) as the cause of creation,
How then you bow before others?

وحد لا شریک لہ، کہہ دے جب اکبار،
احمدﷺ ہی تخلیق کا باعث، پیارے کر اقرار،
پھر کیوں غیر کے دوار، جا کر سر کو جھکائے۔

❖

وحدہ لاشریک لہ، جڈھن چیو جن
تن مجیو محمدؐ کارئی ھیجان سانئہ ھنین
تڈھن منجھان تن رأوٹڑ کو نہ اولیو

"He is One and no one shares his Oneness"
Those who said this with firm faith
And earnestly accepted Muhammad (pbuh)
As the cause of creation,
None of them ever strayed to an unfavorable landing.

وحد لا شریک لہ، کہا جنہوں نے یار
محمدﷺ ہی تخلیق کا باعث، دل سے تھا اقرار،
پہنچے وہ سب یار، کبھی بھی مشکل گھاٹ نہ آیا،

❖

وحدہ لاشریک لہ، جن اتو سین ایمان
تن مجیو محمدؐ کارئی قلب سانئہ نسان
اوہ فائق م فرمان، أ وٹڑ کنھن نہ اولیا

"He is the One and no one shares His oneness"
Those who said this with firm faith,
And accept in heart and with tongue that Muhammad (pbuh)

Is the cause of creation,
It is decreed in Quran that they shall never stray to an unfavorable landing.

وحد لا شريك له، كہيں اور ہو ايمان،

احمدﷺ ہی تخلیق کا باعث مانے قلب و زبان،

یہ فائق کا فرمان، کبھی نہ مشکل گھاٹ گئے وہ

❖

They did not stray to and unfavorable landing, and reached the Shore unharmed,
And all sarvants became one with the One,
They were graced with love by God since the advent of time

راہ مشکل گھاٹ نہ آیا، ناؤ رہی سالم،

ایک سے مل کر ایک ہوئے ہیں، ایسے سارے عالم،

بن گئے وہ سب بالم، رب کے روز ازل سے

❖

Since the advent of time God made them all light,
The truthful ones have 'No fear, neither remorse, nor worry,'
Eternal immersion in love is their Divine destiny.

رب نے انکو روز ازل سے، کیا سراپا نور،
لاخوف علیھم ولا ھم یحزنون، کبھی نہیں رنجو،
ہو گئے وہ معمور، بدل دی رب نے قسمت۔

❖

Slain by the Oneness they chant that there is none but God,
Hearts absorbed in *Haqeeqat*, they measure *Tareeqat*
With silence of *Ma'arfat* they search far places,
They never sleep, nor settle down, nor give up their search,
Lateef says, lovers chop off their heads night from their shoulders.

وہ جو قتیلِ وحدت ہیں اور، لب پر الا اللہ،
جن کو ہے عرفانِ حقیقت، جن کی طریقت راہ،
معرفت کی مہر ہے لب پر، ڈھونڈے دور نگاہ،
سکھ سے پل بھی آنکھ نہ جھپکیں، من میں درد اٹھاہ،
ان کی عجب ہے چاہ، وہ کاٹیں سر کندھوں سے۔

❖

وحدہ جی ودیار الا اللہ اذ کیا
محمد رسول چئی مسلمان ٹیا
عاشق ,عبداللطیف چئی انہین ہے ہیا
تیلان ڈٹی ڈنا ,جیلانی ویا وحدت گڈ جی

Slain by Oneness, they are cut into two halves,
By their belief that there is no God but Him,
Having accepted the Prophet hood of Muhammad they became Muslims,
Leteef says, God washed the lovers,
Who took this path and became one with oneness

وہ جو قتیل وحدت ہیں اور، الا اللہ کے بسمل،
کہا کہ "برحق محمدﷺ ہیں" اور، ہو گئے دل سے قائل،
کہے لطیف کہ جس عاشق نے، پائی ہے یہ منزل،
وحدت سے گئے مل، تب رب نے اس کو دھو دیا،

❖

وحدہ جی ودیا ,کیا الا اللہ اذ
سی ڈڑ پسی سڈ کنھن آیاگی ء نہ ٹھی

Slain by Oneness and cut into two halves,
By the belief that there is no God but Him,
Seeing them in this state only an unfortunate would not Yearn to be like them.

وہ جو قتیل وحدت ہیں اور، الا اللہ کے بسمل،
کون ابھاگا ایسا ہو جو، چاہے نہ یہ منزل،

❖

وحدہ لا شریک لہ رہتے نہ ہوڑا
کہ تو کنین نہ سٹا رجی کھٹ اندر گھوڑا
گاڑیندین گھوڑھا رجت شاہد تیندو سامھان

MELODY OF PEACE

"He is the One and no one shares His Oneness,"
Didn't you hear?
Nor did you hear you inner exhortations,
Your eyes will shed tears when witness to you deeds
Will confront you.

وحدہ لا شریک لہ، سنا نہیں اے غافل،
باطن کی آواز سے بھی تو، ہو سکا نہ قائل،
ہوں گے گواہ مقابل، روئے گا تو دن محشر کے،

❖

وحدہ لا شریک لہ،اہو وھائج وی
کٹین جی ھارائین ،ھنڈ تنھنجو ھی
پاٹان چوندء پی رپری جام جنت جو

"He is One and no one shares His Oneness," Should be your trade,
Loss or gain you carry on this barter,
He Himself will offer you cupful of heavenly wine to drink.

وحدہ لاشریک لہ، یہ ہی کر بیوپار،
یہی تیری منزل ہے اب، جیت ہو چاہے ہار،
کہیں گے سرکار، پی لے جام تو جنت کا۔

❖

وحدہ لا شریک لہ،ای ھیکڑائی حق
پیائی کمی ھک جن وڈو رسی ورسیا

"He is the One and no one shares His oneness" Is the only truth,
Whosoever adopted duality went stray and lost the path.

وحدہ لاشریک لہ، یہ ہے حق یکتائی،
منزل کبھی نہ پائی، دوئی میں جو الجھ گئے۔

❖

سر ڏونڍيان, رڌ نہ لھان, رڌ ڏونڍيان, رسرنا ہ
ھٿ ڪراہون آ گريون, ويا ڪجي ڪاند
وحدت جي وھان ۔ رجي ويارسي وڍبا

I search for my head and lose my body,
I search for my body and lose my head,
My hands, arms and fingers are out like reeds,
Those who experience ecstasy of Oneness, are chopped into pieces.

سر ڈھونڈوں تو دھڑ نہ پاؤں، دھڑ پاؤں تو سر کہاں،
جیسے سرکنڈے کٹتے ہیں، کٹے ہیں ہاتھ اور انگلیاں،
تن من خون افشاں، وصل جنہیں وحدت کا۔

❖

عاشق چو م ان کي رم کي چو معشوق
خالق چو م خام تون رم کي چو مخلوق
سلج ننھن سلوک جو ناقصا نگيو

Don't call Him lover, nor the beloved,
Neither the creator, not the creation,
Tell this secret only to him,
Who has risen above all imperfections.

عاشق مت کہہ اس کو تو، اور نہ ہی کہہ معشوق،
نہ ہی خالق کہہ اے ناداں، نہ ہی کہ مخلوق،
بتا نہ رمز سلوک، ناقص اور ناداں کو،

❖

وحدتان کثرت ٿي رکثرت وحدت کل
حق حقيقي ھيکڙو ہولي ہي م پل
ھو ھلا چو ھَل, ربا الله سندو سچئين

Plurality is unity, unity is plurality,
Truth is one; don't be misled by any gossip,
All this turmoil is because of Beloved.

وحدت سے ہی کثرت ہے اور، سب کثرت ہے وحدت
حق تو حقیقی ایک ہے سائیں، چھوڑ تو سب غفلت،
ہر سو پی کی نوبت، واللہ باج رہی ہے،

❖

پاڻهين جل جلاله , پاڻهين جان جمال
پاڻهين صورت يار ، جي, پاڻهين حسن ڪمال
پاڻهين پير مريد ٿئي ،پاڻهين هاڻ خيال
سڀ سهوئي حال , منجھان ئي معلوم ٿئي

He is the gloriously supreme; he is the essence of all beauty,
He is the countenance of beloved, He is the ultimate beauty,
He is the guide, He is the guided, and He is the idea,
All this is revealed unto one from one's own inner self.

خود ہی جل جلالہ، خود ہی جان جمال،
خود ہی صورت یار کی، خود ہی حسن جمال،
خود ہی پیر مرید بنے اور، خود ہی یار خیال،
سارا یہ احوال، اپنے آپ میں ڈوب کے پایا۔

❖

پاڻهين پسي پاڻ ڪي پاڻهين محبوب
پاڻهين خلقي خوب ,پاڻهين طالب تن جو

He perceives Himself and Himself is the beloved,
He creates beauty and then yearns for it.

خود ہی دیکھے خود کو، خود ہی ہے محبوب،
خود ہی خالق خوب، خود ہی اس کا طالب،

❖

سو ھی،سو ھو، سو اجل،سو اللہ
سوہرین، سو ہساھ ر، سو ویری ،سوواھرو

He is this, He is that, he is death, He is Allah,
He is beloved, He is breath,
He is enemy, He is the guide.

یہ بھی وہ اور وہ بھی وہ، اجل بھی وہ اللہ بھی وہ،
پریتم وہ اور جان بھی وہ، دشمن اور پناہ بھی وہ۔

ہڑاڈو سو سڈ ور وائي ء جو جي لہین
ہٹا اکھین کڈر بڈن م ھ تیا

You ponder and will discern that
Echo is in fact the sound,
They were one but in listening became two.

ایک صدا ایک گونج، سننے میں ہیں دو
غور سے گر سن لو، مخرج ان کا ایک ہے

❖

ایک قیصر ،در لک ،کوڑین کٹس گڑکیون
جیڈانھن کریان ہرک ،تیڈانھن صاحب سامھون

The palace is one, its doors and widows are numerous,
Wherever I look, the Lord is there.

ایک قصر در لاکھ، اور کروڑوں کھڑکیاں،
جدھر اٹھے یہ آنکھ، ادھر ہے سندر روپ سجن کا۔

❖

MELODY OF PEACE

کروڑین کایائون تنھنجیون ، لکن لک ہزار
جی ۔ ۔ سبہ کنھن جی ۔ سین ، درسن ڈارون ڈار
ہرہم ! تنھنجا ہار ، کھڑا چٹی کیئن چوان

You manifestations are in billions,
Your essence is in every being
But appearances are variant with each other,
O my beloved, how can I enumerate all your innumerable attributes?

ساجن! کیا کیا روپ ہیں تیرے! درشن لاکھ ہزار،

جی جڑے ہیں جی سے سائیں! الگ الگ دیدار،

تیرے روپ ہزار، کیا کیا روپ میں دیکھوں۔

❖

وائی

سیکا برہان کون بوجھی
نینھن نیہن و کٹی کالھہ وو
جا چتایم چت مرو سجن ساٹو بجھی
لاتُ جا لطیف جی سڈ تنھنجو سجی

Vaaee

Every one worships the beloved,
His eyes shine with love, his talk is virtue,
Whatever is my mind, he knows it all,
Whatever Lateef sings is at your behest, o beloved.

وائی

اکھین پریت، ریلی بتیاں، ایسے پی کو سب ہی پوچھیں،

جو بھی میرے من میں ہے وہ، تو ہی جانے جاناں!

دوہے، بیت لطیف کوی کے، تیری صدا ہیں سبحاں!

Capter II

داستان پہو

اکھی اکھائی رنج بریان کی رسیو
چکیم چکائی رسورانگھی سوری ۔ تان

His commiseration for my affliction
Shows I am in beloved's grace,
I am in the pink after crossing the gallows.

دیکھی جب بیماری میری، پیا ہوئے رنجور،
سولی کو اور انگا میں نے، روگ ہوا سب دور۔

❖

انڈا اونڈا ویج! کل کچاڑیا کا نمہین؟
اسان ڈکی ڈیل م, تون بیارئین ایچ!
سوری جنین سیج رمرٹ تن مشاہدو

O stupid physician, why are you burning my skin with hot spikes?
While my body aches, you make me drink concoction,
Death is perceiving the beloved for those,
Who consider gallows a bridal-bed.

اندھے نیم حکیم بھلا کیوں، اور تو روگ بڑھائے،
روگ ہے میرے من میں پر تو، دارو اور پلائے،
سولی سیج سہائے، موت تو پیا ملن ہے،

❖

سوری ۔ سڈ ٹیو کا ہلندی جیڈہون
ویں تن بیورنالو نینہن کھن جی

Gallows beckons, would any of you accompany me mates?
Those who love will be to go.

MELODY OF PEACE

سولی نے ہے بلایا سب کو، کون چلے گی ساتھ،
ان سے رہا نا جائے کریں جو پیا ملن کی بات۔

❖

سوري : سڈ کري اچی عاشقن کي
جی اٿيٿي سڌ سکن م رت کو م ھر ھري
سسی ڊار ڏري رچچ ھوء پريتو

The gallows beckons lovers to come,
If you for love do not step away,
First keep your head aside, then talk of love.

جن کے من میں پریت ہے ان کو، سولی نے ہے بلایا،
پیچھے قدم ہٹا نہ عاشق! گر ہے عشق کا دعویٰ،
کاٹ کے سر تو لے آ، پھر کر باتیں پیار کی،

❖

سوري آھ سينگار آڳھين عاشقن جو
موڙ موٽڻ مهڻو ٿيا نظاري نروار
کسن جو قرار، اصل عاشقن کي

Lovers have deemed gallows adornment since eternity,
To waver and step back is a reproach for them,
For they came to perceive the beloved,
To be slain in love is the lovers original covenant.

سولی روز ازل سے سائیں! عاشق کا سنگھار،
لوٹ کے آنا طعنہ جائیں، سولی پر دیدار،
مرنے کا اقرار، ان کا روز ازل سے ہے۔

❖

سوري سينگاري، اصل عاشقن کي
لڏيا کين لطيف ٿي ٿيا نيزي نظاري
کونيو کناري، آئيو چاڙهمي اُن کي

Gallows is the real adornment of lovers,
Lateef says, they never wavered when they sighted spikes
Of the scaffold;
They were speared as the reached there.

سولی روز ازل سے سائیں ! عاشق کا سنگھار،
پاؤں کبھی نہ ان کے لرزے، دیکھ کے بھالے، دار،
آن چڑھائے یارا پریت انہیں سولی پر۔

❖

سوري مٿي سيڻ، کهڙي ليکي سزا؟
جيله لڳا نيڻ تي سورياڻي سيج ٿي

Why are they happy on gallows?
They take gallows as bridal bed since their eyes met with
Those of the beloved,
Mounting the bridal bed of gallows is the way of lovers,
On and on they go, never looking back.

سولی پر یوں سجنا، کیوں کر ہیں مسرور،
جب سے لاگے نیناں، تب سے سولی سیج ہے،

❖

سوري چڙھڻ سيج پسڻ اي کم عاشقن
پاھون کین پسن رسائو ھلن سامھان

Mounting gallows and considering it a bridal bed
Is the way of lovers
They look not behind, they go forward.

سیج سمجھ کر سولی چڑھنا، یہ ہے ان کا کام،
رکیں نہ وہ ایک گام، آئیں مقابل سولی کے۔

❖

MELODY OF PEACE

سوري تي سوار ,ڏھاڙيو چنگ چڙھين
جم ورچي چڏنين ,رسڪن جي ڀار
پرت نہ پسين ھار نينھن جنان نئي نگيو

Lovers mount gallows hundred times every day,
This should not discourage you from yearning,
Love knows no bounds, it spring from the infinite.

عاشق سولی پر چڑھتے ہیں، دن میں سو سو بار،
پریت کی ریت کو بھول نہ جانا، دیکھ کر نیزے دار،
جا تو اب اس پار، پنپ رہی ہے پریت جہاں پہ۔

❖

پھرین ڪاتي پاء بيج ھوء پريتو
ڏک ھريان جو ڏيل ۾ ,واجت جئن وڃاء
سيکن ماہ پڇاء رچي نالو گيڙوء نينھن جو

First stab yourself, then talk of love,
Let agony of separation vibrate in your being like wind in a trumpet,
Grill your flesh if you seek love.

دل میں چھو کے خنجر، پھر کر باتیں پریت کی،
درد سجن کا صورت نغمہ، گونجے دل کے اندر،
انگاروں میں پک کر، پھر لے عشق کا نام،

❖

ڪاتي ڪونھي ڏوہ , جن وڍيندڙ ھٿ ۾
پسيو پر عجيب جي ,لڃيو وڃي لوہ
عاشقن اندوہ , سدا معشوقن جو

Knife can't be blamed, as its handle is the cutter's hand,
Finding itself poised to kill, the steel blade trembles,
Lovers forever pine for the beloved.

تیغ پر کیا الزام، تیغ سجن کے ہاتھ میں ہے،
دیکھ ادائیں محبوبوں کی، لرزے تیغ تمام،
دکھ ہی دکھ ہر کام، عاشق کو ہے پریتم کا

❖

کاتي تکي م ٹٹي سر منياني هوء
مان ورسن توءِ سون هريان جا هٹڙا

I want the knife to be blunt, not sharp,
So that my beloved's hands touch my body a little longer

دستِ یار میں خنجر ہے وہ، تیز نہ ہونے پائے،
ہاتھ ذرا رک جائے، یار کا میرے تن پر پل بھر۔

❖

کاتي جا قريب جي , سا هڏ حيري چم
عاشقن پنهنجو انگ , اللـــه کارڻ وڍيو

Beloved's knife cuts flesh and bone,
Lover lets himself to be dismembered for the sake of Allah.

دستِ یار کے خنجر سے، کٹ کٹ جائے چام،
لے کر یار کا نام، عاشق انگ کٹائیں،

❖

جي تون سگڻ سکيو ته کاتي رھڻي م کنجهہ
سپريان جي سور جو , ماٿھن ڍڄي نہ منجهہ
اندر اي اهنج سانڊيج سڪائون ڪري

MELODY OF PEACE 61

If you wish to learn the way of love,
Don't cry out when knife is stabbed,
The agony of love should not be shared with others,
But to be kept deep inside with joy.

پریت کی ریت جب سیکھی تو پھر، خنجر سے کیا ڈرنا،
پریتم نے جو زخم دیے ہیں، عام کبھی مت کرنا،
ہنس ہنس راز میں رکھنا، درد کی اس دولت کو،

❖

جان ودین ,تان ویہ , نہ تہ ونیو واٹ ون ءُ تون
ھي ءُ تنین جو ڈیہ , کاتی جنین ھٹ م

Stay if you wish to be slain, else go away
This land is of those who wield knife.

کاٹیں گر وہ انگ تو آجا، ورنہ راہ لے اپنی،
یہ ہے ان کا دیس کہ جن کے، ہاتھوں میں ہے کٹاری۔

❖

کاتی جن کری ,مان لنو لگي تن سین
محبت جي میدان م ,روجان پیر ہري
اڈي ء سر ڈري ,مان کھنٹوں سہرین

I am in love with those who wield knife,
I enter the arena of love cheerfully,
And place my head on the chopping block,
Wishing the beloved to behead me.

ایسے پی سے پریت لگی کہ، ہاتھ میں ہے خنجر،
الفت کے میدان میں آؤں، کیسا خوف و خطر،
آگے رکھ دوں سر، شاید کاٹ لے پریم۔

❖

اڳيان اڌڻ وٽ رھين سر سنباھيا
ڪٽ تہ ھوين قبول ھر مٿڻ پائين گھٽ
مٿا مھائين جاڙيا نہ ڏسين ھت؟
ڪلالڪي ھٽ ڪسڻ جوڪوپ وھي

Those in front are near the chopping lock,
While those in the rear are ready for being beheaded,
Severe your head so that you may be accepted,
No lesser offering would be acceptable,
Don't you see heads of those slain in love scattered all over?
The gruesome game of beheading goes on in the tavern of
The barmaid.

کچھ تو مقتل میں جا پہنچے، باقیوں کی ہے قطار،
تجھ کو مان ملے گا ہو جا، مرنے کو تیار،
کیا تو دیکھ نہ پایا ان کے، سروں کے ہیں انبار،
سروں کا کاروبار، دیکھ کلال کے ہاٹ پہ ہے،

❖

جي اٿيئي سڌ سرڪ جي ,تہ ون ۽ ڪلاڻ ڪاڻي
لاھي رک لطيف چٽي ,مٺو وٽ ماڻي
تڪ ڏيئي پک ھي ۽ توڻ ,منجھاڻ گھوٽ ا گھاڻي
جو ورڻہ وھاڻي ,رسو سِر وٽ سرو سھا نگو

If you yearn for a sip of wine, go to the the winery,
Lateef says, lay down beside the wineful picture,
They gulp mouthfuls of the thick sine a bridegroom,
That overpowers even the powerful,
A sip of such wine even for the price of head would be a bargain.

MELODY OF PEACE

ے پینا گر چاہے تو پھر، پاس کلال کے جا،

ے کے خم کے پاس تو جا کر، کاسئہ سر کو جھکا،

ایک ہی گھونٹ میں پی لے اور، جام پہ جام چڑھا،

شہ زوروں کے ہوش گنوائے، یہ ہے وہ مدار،

بھاؤ بڑا سستا، سر دے کر ے مل جائے،

❖

جي اٽيئي سڌ سرڪ جي رتہ ون ءُ ڪلالڪي هٽ

لاهي رک ,لطيف چئي مٽو ماني وت

سر ڏني م ست پيچ کي پاليون

If you long for a sip of wine, go the winery,
Lateef says, lay down your head near the wine pitcher,
Trade your head and drink cupfuls of wine.

جا کلال کے ہاٹ پہ ہے، ے کی خواہش کر،

کہے لطیف کہ سر کو کاٹ کے، مٹکے پاس تو دھر،

سر کا سودا کر، جام پہ جام تو پی لے

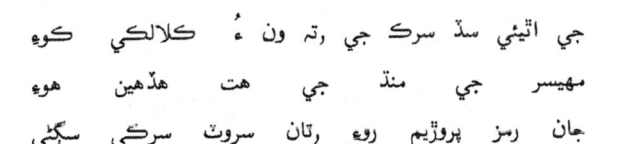

❖

جي اٽيئي سڌ سرڪ جي رتہ ون ءُ ڪلالڪي کوء

مهيسر جي منڌ جي هت هڍهين هوء

جان رمز پروڙيم روء ,تان سروٽ سرڪي سڄڻي

If you yearn for a sip of wine go to winer's lane,
Where there is already a clamour for the wine of god shiva,
I have puzzled it out, a sip of that wine is worth one's head.

گر ہے مے کی خواہش تو پھر، کوچہ کلال میں جا،
مھیسر، کی مے کا ہر دم، وہاں ہے شور بپا،
رمز میں یہ سمجھا، کہ سر کے بدلے مے سستی ہے۔

❖

جي اٽيئي سڌ سرڪ جي ، تہ ون ۽ ڪلالڪي گھر
وڍن، چيرڻ، رچچرڻ ، ڀت انين جي ڀر
جي وٽي پوئي ور ، تہ سھنگي آھ رسيد چٽي

If you yearn for a sip of wine, go to the winer's house,
He cuts up, mangles, lacerates the seeker of his wine,
Sayyed syas, getting even a cupful this way is a bargain.

گر ہے مے کی خواہش تو پھر، گھر کلال کے جا،
کاٹیں تیرا انگ انگ، تو مے کی ریت نبھا
سودا ہے ستا، گر جام ملے جاں دے کر

❖

ناھي ناھ ڪڪو ۰ ،ڪي سلھہ مھانگو مند
سنباھج سيد چٽي ،ڪائي ڪارڻ ڪند
ھي تنين جو ھند رمتن ھاس مرن جي

This wine is very precious, it cannot be purchased with money
Syed Says, prepare to lay your head beside a wine-jars
This is a place where seekers lay their lives.

مے کا کوئی مول نہیں ہے، مول ملے کب مدرا،
کہے لطیف کہ سجا کے سرکو، پاس کلال کے لے آ،
پیتے ہیں جو مدرا، واریں سر مدھ شالے میں۔

❖

MELODY OF PEACE

عاشق زهر پياك ، وه ڈسي وهسن گهٽو
كڙي ء قاتل جا ،هميشہ ميراك
لڳين لنو لطيف چئي فنا كيا فراق
توئي چڪن چاك تہ به آه نہ سلن عام كي

Lovers fond as they are of drinking venom,
Its very sight delights them,
They are addicts, ever cravers of the bitter and the deadly,
Lateef says, being love-smitten separation from the
Beloved is killing them,
Even as their wounds smart, they never let on to others

عاشق عادی زہر کے ہیں اور زہر سے ہیں مسرور،
کڑوا قاتل زہر جو دیکھیں، مستی میں ہوں چُور،
کہے لطیف کہ عشق یار میں، مٹ کر ہیں مسرور،
زخموں سے ہیں چُور، کبھی نہ زخم کھائیں،

❖

م ڪر سڌ سري جي تون ٿارئين نوه
پتي جنهن ھاسي ٽٺي ، منجهان رڳن روح
ڪاٺي چڪ ڪڪوہ ، لاهي سرلطيف چئي

If you have no taste for the bitter, ask not for wine,
For it squeezes life out of sinews,
Lateef says, you can taste it only after you have chopped
You head.

کڑوی مے گر پی نہ پائے،مت لے مے کا نام،
جان رگوں سے کھینچے یہ مے، لرزاں جسم تمام،
چکھ لے کڑوا جام، سر دے کر تو پی لے گھونٹ۔

❖

سدریاں شراب جون , کہ پچارون کن؟
جہ کاٹ کلان کیدیا , تہ مونیو ہوء وین
پکون سی پین رس جن جا ست ہ

Why those, who only yearn, talk of wine?
They went away, when venders drew their daggers,
Only those will get sips, who offer their heads in barter.

جو بس خواہش کرنا جانیں، لیں کیوں ہے کا نام،
جونہی کلال نے تیغ نکالی، لرزاں جسم تمام،
وہی چڑھائیں جام، جو سر کا سودا کر پائیں۔

❖

سر جدا ,دڑ ڈار ,دوک جنین جا دیک ہ
سی سر کن پچار رحاضر جن جی ہٹ ہ

Their heads are severed from their trunks,
And their limbs are boiling in cauldron,
They may wish for wine, who have their heads ready.

سر جدا ہیں جسم سے اور، دیگ میں جسم تمام،
حق ہے ان کا جام، سر جو سجا کر لائیں۔

❖

دیکین دوک کڑہن رجت کڑئین کڑکو نہ لہی
تتی طبیبن رچاک چکندا چڈیا

Where the limbs were boiling in a cauldron,
And the sound of boiling never ceased,
There the physicians left wounds festering

انگ ابلتی دیگ میں ہیں اور، گر گر کرے کڑھائی،
زخموں کی رعنائی، دیکھ کے بھاگے دید۔

❖

MELODY OF PEACE

سسي سي کھرن , جي واتيندڙ وچ م
اوء کي پيو پڇن , سرو جن سنباهيو؟

Those who serve wine, demand head,
But those who are in the brew it demand something else.

مدرا پینے آئیں ان سے، سر مانگے ہے ساقی،
جن کی مدرا بھٹی، وہ کچھ اور ہی مانگیں۔

❖

اصل عاشق پنهنجي , سسي نه سانڊين
لاهيو سر لطيف چئي , ساه سلهاڙيو ڏين
کلهڻون کورين پڇن هوء پر يتو

True lovers never save their heads,
They sever their heads, says Lateef, and give up life,
They chop off right from their shoulders and then talk of love.

جو ہیں پریت کے مارے ان کو، کب ہے پیاری جان،
سجا کے سر وہ لے آتے ہیں، جان کریں قربان،
سر کا دے کر دان، بات کریں پھر عشق کی۔

❖

اصل عاشق جو سر نه سانڊين کم
سو سسنئان اڳرو ,سندو دوسان دم
هي هڊو ء چم پک پريان جي نه پڙي

It is not the way of true lovers to save their heads,
A moment with beloved is more precious than hundred heads,
These bones and flesh are not worth a sip.

جو ہیں پریت کے مارے ان کو، کب ہے پیاری جان،
یار کی ایک جھلک کی خاطر، لاکھوں سر قربان،
میرا جسم یہ جان، یار کی خاک پا پہ صدقے۔

❖

جی مٹی وٹ مڑن, تہ سیکھن سنڈ ٹھی
سر ڈنی ست جڑی ،رنہ عاشق انّ اچن
لڈا تی لین ،ملھہ مہانگا سپرین

If union with the beloved were possible by giving up one's head,
Every one would aspire for it,
Were head a barter all the lovers would come chopping it,
Thinking it a bargain,
Only with good fortune the union with the precious and priceless
Beloved is possible.

سر کا صدقہ دے کر سائیں، پریتم گر مل جائے،
ستا سودا جان کے عاشق، سر اپنا کٹوائے،
قسمت جب بر آئے، تب ملتا ہے ساجن،

❖

ملھہ مہانگو قطرو سکئ شہادت
اسان عبادت نظر ناز پرین جو

A drop of wine is so precious that even longing for
It is worth giving up life,
The amorous playful glance of the beloved is like prayer for us.

مئے انمول کے اک قطرے کی، آس شہادت ہے،
یہ بھی عبادت ہے، گر ہو پی کا روشن،

❖

MELODY OF PEACE

وائي

مند پٺندي مون, ساجن سھي سڄاتو
پي پيالو عشق جو سيپڪي سمجھيو سون
پريان سندي ٻار ,اندر اڳ جي اٿون
جٽ ناھي جڳ م , ڏينھن مڙيئي ڏون
الا! عبداللطيف چئي ,آھين تون ئي تون

Vaaee

While drinking wine, I recognized my beloved.
As I drink the cup of love-wine, all the mysteries were unraveled,
Fire of love burns inside me,
It is only for two days that we live in this world,
Abdul Lateef says, it is only you who pervades all phenomena.

وائی

پی کر ے کے جام، ساجن کو پہچان لیا،
عشق کے پیالے پی کر ہم نے، جانا بھید تمام،
انگ انگ میں پیار کی اگنی، سلگیں سب اندام،
جھوٹے جگ میں رات بتائی، صبح کیا آرام،
کہے لطیف کہ تو ہی تو ہے، باقی تیرا نام،

❖

Chapter III   داستان ٽيون

اٺياري اُ ٿي ويا , منجھان مون آزار
حبيب لڏي ھٽي ويا پيڙا جي پچار
طبيبن تنوار ,رھڏ نہ وٽي ھاڻ مون

Heaving inflicted me, the beloved left,
My pains and pangs all are from him,
I now hate to hear of relief by physicians.

مجھ کو چھوڑ گیا ہے ساجن، پریت کا روگ لگا کر،
ایسا درد وہ دے گیا، دل کو میرا یار وہ دلبر،
کوئی نہ چارہ گر، میرے من کو بھائے۔

❖

هڏ نہ وٹی هان مون ,ویجن جی وصال
هن منهنجي حال , حبيب ٿي هادي ٿيو

I thoroughly dislike physician's company now,
For beloved has became my guide and healer.

من کو اب نہ بھائے کوئی، پی بن اور طبیب،
وہ ہی یار حبیب، میرے حال کا ہادی ہے۔

❖

حبيب ٿي هادي ٿيو , رهنما راحت
پيڙا نيائين پاڻ سين لائي ڏيئي لت
سپريان صحت ,رڌنيم منجهان ڏکندي

The beloved became guide and comforter,
He cured my affliction completely and turned my illness to health.

ہادی ہوا حبیب وہ میرا، راہ نمائے راحت،
پی نے روگ مٹایا سارا، قائم ہو گئی نسبت،
ہم نے پانی صحت، روگ سے تیرے ہاتھوں۔

❖

اور ڏکندو او ٿئي هادي جنهن حبيب
تر تفاوت نہ کري تنهنکي کو طبيب
رهنما رقيب ,ساڻر صحت سپرين

MELODY OF PEACE

Different is the infliction of which beloved is the reliever,
No physician can relieve it,
Beloved is my guide, protector, and medication.

اور طرح کا روگ لگے ہے، ہادی ہو جب حبیب،

ایسا روگ مٹا نہ پائے، کوئی اور طبیب،

راہ نما ہے رقیب، دہی درد کا درماں ہے۔

❖

ساٹر صحت سپرین آھي نہ آزار
مجلس وير منو تئي , کوئيندي قھار
خنجر تنھن خوب ھٿي , جنھن سین تئي یار
صاحب رب ستار , سوجھي رڳون ساھ جون

Beloved is medication not affliction,
Though known as Subduer, he is sweet in company,
Whom he makes friend with, he repeatedly stabs,
Lord, the coverer, probes innermost of being.

جب وہ چارہ ساز ہوا تو، دور ہوا آزار،

گاہے بول سے رس گھولے اور، گاہے قہر کا وار،

اس کو ہی وہ گھائل کر دے، جس کا ہو وہ یار،

صاحب رب تار، وہ ہی من کی پتا جانے۔

❖

رڳون ٿيون رباب , وجن ویل سپکنھین
لچن , کڇن نہ ٿیو , جانب ري جباب
سوئي سنڈيندم سپرين کیس جنھن کباب
سوئي عین عذاب , سوئي راحت روح جي

All my veins vibrate like the strings of rebeck,
The beloved is indifferent and irresponsive,
I can neither moan nor groan,
Who has grilled shall mitigate the suffering,
He is the tormentor, as also comfort of soul.

پل پل جھن جھن باج رہے ہیں، رگ رگ تار رباب،
میرے لب پر مہر لگی ہے، ساجن دے نہ جواب،
وہ جو میرے زخم کا مرہم، دل کو کرے کباب،
وہ ہی عین عذاب، وہی راحت روح کی ہے۔

سوئی راہ رد کری سوئی رہنماءُ
وتعز من تشاءُ وتذل من تشاءُ

He is the one who leads astray and a perfect guide too,
"You elevate whom so you with and you abase whom so you wish."

وہ بھٹکائے راہ دکھائے، عجب ہے اس کی عادت،
جس کو چاہے عزت دے اور، جس کو چاہے ذلت۔

✣

بر م پچھانیون عشق جي اسباب ڪي
دارون هن درد جو, ڏايو ڏسيائون
آخر والعصر جو انين اتائون
تھان پوءِ آئون سڪان ٿي سلام ڪي

He secretly inquired about the causes of my love-ailment,
He then prescribed an appropriated medicine,
He advised me to have patience,
Since then I am yearning to meet and pay homage to him.

کیا ہے درد کا کارن؟ پی نے چھپ کر پوچھا،
درد کا درماں بخشا یار نے، مجھ کو پاس بلایا،
"آخرو العصر" پریتم نے فرمایا،
تب سے یہ من میرا، ترسے پی درشن کو۔

✣

MELODY OF PEACE

سکین کے سلام کی ، کرین کے نہ سلام
پیا در تن حرام ، ای در جنین دیکیو

Why do you yearn only, why don't you go and pay him homage?
Those, who see his door once, never turn to any other.

دور سے بیٹھا کیوں ترسے ہے، جا اس یار کے دوار،
ٹھکرایا سنسار، جس نے دیکھا دوار پیا کا۔

❖

منایان منو گھٹو کڑو ناہ کلام
سکوت نی سلام ، پریان سندی پار جو

His words are sweetest of all the sweets and are never bitter,
Even his very silence is a response,

شیرینی سے شیریں تر ہے، میٹھا ہر ایک بول
ساجن ہے انمول، چپ بھی پیار کی باتیں ہیں۔

❖

پریان سندی پار جی ، مڑیٹھی مٹھائی
کانھی کڑائی چکین جی چیت کری

Whatsoever comes from the beloved is sweet,
If you taste thoughtfully, there isn't any bitterness.

شیرینی ہی شیرینی ہے، جو کچھ پریتم دے،
دل سے گر چکھ لے، ذرا نہیں کڑواہٹ۔

❖

جائی بجھی جن ،تو سین سو سج کئی
تون کین سندیون تن ، پر سین پچارون کرین

He who willed the prize of pain for you,
How is it that you reveal his secrets to others?

جان بوجھ کر پی نے تجھ سے باندھا درد کا رشتہ،
پریت کے درد کی باتیں پیارے!، غیر کو مت بتلا۔

❖

تو جنین جي ٻاتر، تن پڻ آهي تنھنجي
فاذ كروني اذ كر كم ،راي پروڙج ٻات
ھٽ كاتي ڪڙ وات ، ٻچڻ ٻر ٻرين جي

Those whom you remember all the time, remember you too,
"Remember me and I will remember you." Ponder over these words,
The beloved has a knife in his hand and sweet words on his lips.

جس کی چاہ میں تڑپ رہے ہو، وہ بھی تجھ کو چاہ ہے،
فاز کرولی از کر کم، پی کی بات سمجھ لے،
ایسا وہ پریتم ہے، شیریں لب اور ہاتھ میں خنجر۔

❖

جيئن ھيڪار ،منجھان مھر سڏ ڪيو
سو مون سپ جمار ، اورڻ اُھونئي ٿيو

It was only once that the beloved called me with kindness,
I am fated to recount it all my life.

پریتم نے اک بار پکارا، مہر سے مجھ برہن کو،
بس اس ایک سخن کو، سکھیو! دل دہراتا ہے۔

❖

ھاٻوھي ھيڪار ،مون ڪان ٻڌيو سڄين
الست بركم ، چيائون جنھن وار
سندي سور ڪنار ،تن تڎاھڪون نہ لھي

The beloved had once asked lovingly, "Am I not your Lord"?
Since then the pain of separation never leaves me.

MELODY OF PEACE

پیارے سے پریتم نے پوچھا تھا، مجھ سے یہ اک بار،
"کیا میں تیرا رب نہیں ہوں"، میرا تھا اقرار،
درد کی تیز کٹار، تب سے دل میں اتری ہے۔

❖

جو؟	حبیب	ہٹ	رکئی	پچن	ہابوہیو
کن	نہ	ہاٹ	ہاسی	جی	نینہن	ہینان	نیزی
اچن	کٹات	اوچی	سامہان	اجل	عاشق
مشاہدو	تن	مرݨ	جن	قُرب	کُسن

The beloved beckons, then slaughters, then beckons,
Don't step aside when under the spear of love,
O lover, cast aside your knowledge and wisdom,
Go straight to face death.

پوچھ رہے ہیں یار، پی نے باندھا کدھر نشانہ،
عشق کے بھالے برس رہے ہیں، خود کو کریں نثار،
دیکھ کہ کیسی سج دھج سے وہ، آئیں سوئے دار،
سر دیتے ہیں وار، مر مٹنا تو پیا ملن ہے۔

❖

سا	کُھݨ	رکوئی	سہرین	کُھی	کوئی
ہاٹ	کرم	ہاسی	جی	نینہن	ہینان	نیزی
سامہون	اجل	عاشق!	جاݨ،	وِجائی	ر	جُل

One who kills takes care also and beckons with
Love to be near him,
This is the way of the beloved for all time,
He is the healer, who opens the wounds,
And is delight of the soul.

پاس بلا کر قتل کرے اور، پھر وہ پاس بلائے،
لاکھ گڑھے ہوں عشق کے بھالے، قدم لرزنہ پائے،
موت سے آنکھ ملائے، بھول کے اپنی خودداری کو۔

❖

The beloved's summon is verily a banishment,
This paradox inspires more love,
Never despair, though he severs relationship but in fact he ties it.

پی کا پاس بلانا بھی تو، گویا ہے دھتکار،
جس کو کوئی سمجھ نہ پائے، ایسا اس کا پیار،
آس اسی کی یار!، جو توڑ کے ناطہ جوڑے۔

❖

When he kills, he takes care, when he takes care, he kills,
O mother, he is the killer as well as delight of the heart.

قتل کرے تو مہر کرے اور، مہر سے قتل کرے وہ،
میرے روح کی راحت ہے اور میرا قاتل ہے وہ۔

❖

One who kills takes care also
And beckons besides him,
This is the way of the beloved for all times,
He is the healer, who opens the wounds,
And he is delight of the soul.

MELODY OF PEACE

قتل کرے اور مہر سے پھر وہ، پاس بلائے یار،

یہ بھی اس کے ناز و ادا ہیں، عجب ہے اس کا پیار،

زخم وہ دے ہر بار، وہ ہی روح کی راحت ہے۔

❀

وائي

ٽيندو تن طبيب، دارون منهنجي درد جو

بُڪي ڏيندم باجھ جي راڄي شال عجيب

پرين اچي هاڻ ڪيو، رسندو غور غريب

ڏڪندو سيوئي ڏور ڪيو، رنجهون تن طبيب

اديون! عبداللطيف چئي، هاتڪ آہ حبیب

Vaaee

Beloved will cure me, he will be medicine of my affliction
The wondrous one will come and give me potion of mercy,
Beloved himself came and diagnosed my disease,
My physician cured me of it,
Abdul Lateef says, O mates my beloved is indeed an expert physician.

وائي

ہوگا درد کا درماں، میرا یار حبیب سکھی ری!

درد کا آ کر کرے مداوا، مہر سے میرا سجناں،

میرے انگنا آ کر دیکھا، میرا حال پریشاں،

مجھ روگی کا روگ مٹایا، آن کے میرے انگنا،

کہے لطیف کہ تجھ سا جگ میں، اور طبیب نہ جاناں!

❀

کُهن ۽ ڪونين راءِ پُر سندي سڄين

سوري چاڙهيو سپرين، ڏنپ ڏهائي ڏين

ويڻا وره وٽين، آءُ واڍوڙيا! وهاءِ تون

He kills and calls beside him,
He makes lovers mount gallows,
And burn their skins daily,
He deals in the commodity of the agony of love,
O wounded one, come and buy some of it.

پاس بلا کر گھائل کر دے، ایسے ناز و ادا،
وہ ہی دار پر لٹکائے اور، دے وہ زخم نیا،
سر کا کریں سودا، آجا تو بھی سودا کرلے،

❖

Agha Saleem

Life of Shah Latif Bhattai

Shah Abdul Latif Bhattai, the mystic poet of Sindh, was born at Hala Haveli, a village in Hala Taluka of Hyderabad District. It is at a distance of about 80 miles from Bhitt, the last resting place of Shah Latif. As it often happens in the case of great men, the dates of birth and death of Shah are also controversial. Nevertheless a majority of notable scholars, after intensive research, agreed that he was born in the year 1689 and died in 1752 at the age of 63.

Shah's ancestors came from Hirat (Afghanistan) with Tamerlance and settled in Sindh. His great grand father, Shah Abdul Karim of Burri was a renowned poet and a saint. His father, Sayyed Habib Shah, was also a pious man. Habib Shah was in Hala Haveli, when Shah Latif was born, and after his birth, Shah Habib shifted to Kotri, a place at a distance of about four miles from Bhitt and now in a ruins. This is where Shah Latif, in his prime youth, fell in love with the daughter of a powerful landlord, Mirza Mughal Beg. Shah Latif wanted to marry her but Mughal Beg opposed the match and turned hostile to the family. Habib Shah had to leave Kotri and settle in a small village near Kotri.

Shah had found beauty of his dreams in a human form and he was all the time so absorbed in its contemplations that he was oblivious of what was happening around him. His condition alarmed his father and one day finding him covered head to foot in dust he talked to him and recited an extemporaneous line of the verse:

"The wind blew and covered all her limbs"
To which Shah replied impromptu:
"She breaths just for seeing the beloved".

His father hoped that his son would come out of the infatuation but the rejection of his suit had shattered Shah completely and in a fit of despair and desperation he left home for destinations unknown. Coming across a group of wandering Hindu ascetic Jogis, he joined them in their foot journeys to Hinglaj, Junnagarh Lahoot, lassernere and Thar, the desert area of Sindh. He journeyed on the mountainous route, which the heroin of the popular folk tale *Sassi Punhoon*, had traveled in search of her beloved husband Punhoon who had left her after marriage. During this journey Shah experienced all the hardships and sufferings Sassi had endured and the intensity of love that had driven her. At a later stage he composed five melodies of Sassi's love, her determination and her sufferings of separation and search. These wanderings broadened his vision and widened canvas of his poetry. Hence we see the landscape of his teeming with people from different walks of life; ironsmiths striking anvil with their hammers and blowing up fire. Lovers climbing gallows as a bridegroom climbs the bridal bed. Moths hovering on flames and burning themselves to ashes. The drinkers gulping venom mixed wine and hiccupping wine. Archers, wounding lovers with darts of love Groaning patients of love and physicians. Sufis who do not believe in sectarianism and who guided even those who were their enemies. Lover riding a camel in full moon night yearning for union with the beloved whose face is brighter than the full moon. The seafarers navigating sea of their being to find our new spiritual horizons. Sea merchants preparing for new voyage and their youthful wive imploring them not to leave them alone in the season of lovers union. Killers of the beast in man. Restless ascetic jogis wandering in search of peace. Many folk historical and saint historical characters. Rivers, sea, mountains, lakes, desert, oasis, trees, jungle, cobras, swans, crows. Love afflicted damsels sending messages to their lovers through messenger crows and weaver girls. Over these animate and inanimate images are painted human feelings of pain and pleasure.

After wandering for three years, he felt an inner urge to go to Thatta, where he met Makhdoom Mohammad Moen the great *Wahdatal Wajudi* scholar and Sufi of the day. Under his influence Shah became a Sufi, and on his advice he gave up aimless wanderings and retuned to his parents. Meanwhile situation at home had changed. Some robbers had ransacked Mughal Beg's house and killed all the male members of the family. The ladies, took this incident as a curse fallen on them because they had annoyed their Murshid. Habib Shah, came to him, sought his forgiveness and offered Mughal Beg's daughter Bibi Sayyada in marriage to Shah, whom he had fallen in love with. Thus Shah was united to the beauty of his dreams that he had seen in human form. But physical union was no longer a compelling urge. The company of Hindu ascetics and his sojourn at Thatta with the Sufi scholar had purged him and sublimated his love sickness into channels of Sufism and thus he had embarked upon a spiritual voyage. According to Sufi creed, the mundane beauty kindles flame of love and the pangs of separation intensify it. Lover reaches stage where he yearns for Eternal Beauty. The human beauty, Shah fell in love with, was a veil of the Eternal Beauty and the pangs he had suffered had purged him and he had perceived the Eternal Beauty through his crystallized self. This philosophy he expounded in all his poetry particularly in the melodies he wrote about Sassi.

The brutal murder of Shah Inayat the great Sufi of his time, and the overall socio-political scenario of the country despaired Shah Latif so much that he decided to retire in seclusion on a Bhitt (sand dune) and it is because of the Bhitt that he is called Shah Bhitai meaning Shah of the Sand Dune. It was on that dune that he composed great poetry.

In the year 1752, he intuited his death. He asked his disciples to play music and sing the verses he had composed in raga Sohni. Wrapping himself in white sheet of cloth, he retired to *Hujra* (antechamber) and listened to music for three days, and when his disciples went in, they found him dead. He was buried on the Bhitt.

Historical Background

Sindh, except for its short-lived annexation first to Iran and then to Delhi, had always been an independent country. Even during these periods of annexation Sindheans struggled against foreign occupation and as such the history of Sindh is the history of its battling for independence and its songs giving their lives for their motherland. Porus the great unflinching hero of Indus Valley fought with Alexander so valiantly that even Greek historians acknowledged his valour and valiance and acclaimed that no king, whosoever, fought Alexander with that valour throughout his conquests. But after his dignified surrender he accepted to act as satra and commander of Alexander fought with his won countrymen on his behalf whereas in Sindh Sambos and Oxycanos, the rulers of Sehwan and Alore, and the Brahman intellectual youths, not caring for their lives, fought him and were massacred mercilessly.

Arabs conquered Sindh in 712 A.D. and ruled for about 300 years Soomras, a local Rajput tribe, liberated Sindh and regained its freedom in 1011 A.D. In 1333-34 A.D. Sammas, another local tribe, started gaining power and eventually defeated Soomras and ascended the throne. By the year 522 A.D. Samma rule degenerated and Arghoons and Tarkhans, the militant tribes from Central Asia, usurped Sindh's independence. Sindheans started guerilla war against them. Meanwhile Akber, the Mughal imperor, conquered Sindh and annexed it to Delhi. Sindh was divided into three administrative provinces of Bakhar, Sehwan, and Thatta and governors were appointed to rule on emperor's behalf. Aurangzeb died in 1707 and with his death the Mughal Empire started crumbling. It was difficult for the emperor to keep peace in Sindh. He therefore appointed Mis Yar Muhammad Kalhoro, head of the local tribe of Kalhoras, as governor of upper Sindh. The Kalhoras had acquired considerable following in upper Sindh in the garb of religion and were striving for political power and after getting governorship they eventually succeeded in ascending the throne of Sindh. It was during Kalhora rule that Shah Latif composed the poetry, great for all times to come. Kalhora period was a period of prosperity in Sindh. Though they were embroliled in many battles throughout their reign and the armies of Nadir Shah and Ahmed Shah trampled Sindh, but, despite that Kalhoras brought affluence and well-being to the people and Sindh flourished economically, culturally and intellectually.

But appraising the period by modern norms it was a period of intellectual dormancy, barrenness and a long cultural winter sleep. No new ideology was bred. The only progressive ideology was *Tassawuf* that too, with the passage of time, had lost its vigor and vitality. It was in this icy well that Shah Inayat put in appearance. He jolted the society with his declaration that all land belonged to God and its produce to the tiller. The custodians of status quo killed him. Shah Latif was 30 years of age and the murder of Shah Inayat left permanent-mark on his mind. Shah Inayat emerged in his poetry as a lover, who smilingly climbs the gallows as bridegroom climbs the nuptial bed. Probably one of the reasons of our Shah's denouncing the society and settling on a dune even after achieving his love object. It was from there that he assailed the social order of the time, criticized the static social order and revitalized *Tassawuf* with the vigor of his poetry. He exalted the common man and restored his human dignity the society had deprived him of. In my opinion no other poet, whosoever, has ever depicted the miseries of downtrodden people as poignantly as Shah has done.

Shah Inayat

Sufis were against private property and accumulation of wealth and considered it to be the root cause of all social evils and human miseries. They quote many verses of Quran and traditions in support of it. For instance, they quote Prophet Muhammad (pbuh) to have said: "All creatures of God are the family of God, and he is the best loved of God who loves His creatures best". According to another tradition the prophet said that on the Day of Judgment God will admonish man "O son of Adam! I was ailing and you never inquired after me, I was hungry and you did not offer me any food, I was thirsty and you failed to provide water to me". The man will submit puzzled. "O Lord! You are the Cherisher and the Sustainer of the worlds, how could all this be possible with you?" God will then say: "Was it not that such and such persons in your neighborhood were sick and suffered from hunger and thirst? Had you attended to them you would have felt my presence at no distance, from them." Sufis set example and declassed themselves. They lived poor and desired to be raised poor on the Day of Judgment. Their *khanqahs* were the social asylums for the poor. There are many real and allegorical episodes in Sufi literature that reflect their concept of private property and amassing wealth. One of the allegorical episodes is that once a king brought two small bags of golden nuggets to famous saint, Hazrat Abdul Qadir Jeelani. He held one bag in his left and the other in his right hand and squeezed both the bags and, to the utter awe of the king, blood started oozing from the bags. Hazzat Jeelani said to the king: "Don't you feel ashamed of bringing to me the blood of the people you have sucked".

In modern times it is theorized that possession of property is not a biological instinct but an acquired instinct in human being. Kropatkin, a well-known anarchist, hypothesized pre-historic society as without class and authority based on egalitarian social and economic relationship. Lewis H. Morgan, a nineteenth century social scientist supported the idea of primitive communism in Ancient Society. There were ancient societies which existed without class and state and where collective right to basic resources was guaranteed. Angles worked on Morgon's paper and analyzed its relationship to historical materialism in "Origin of Family, property and the State. This hypothesis may not be true but it is certainly true that man has been whishing and dreaming of such a society ever since. For instance it was in the fourth century B.C that Arisisppus, pupil of Socrates, held that pleasure is the highest goal in human life. This goal could only be achieved when man neither governs nor is governed, which means a society without government and state. Zeno, another philosopher of the period, dreamt of a community without government. Man should not be subject to the law of the state but to moral law. If man is allowed to be guided by his instincts he would have no need for police, prisons, temples and army. During the Middle Ages there were the Hussiles, the Anabaptists, the Brothers and sisters of the Free Spirit all of whom repudiated the state and church institutions and private property. In 17th century we meet Gerard Winstancly a clergyman who founded communal sect called 'Diggers'. He identified Jesus as a universal liberty and regarded private property an evil. Then the 'Levelers', who believed that of all the institutions that stood in the way of human equality the monarchy was the highest and most in need of leveling. Their agitation was in past responsible for the execution of King Charles I. Thomas More dreamt of a utopia of agrarian society, where there was no private property. All goods were deposited in a central warehouse from which each man could withdraw sufficient material for his needs. In 1755 Rousseau declared that all inequalities except constitutional differences in men are unnatural. He condemned land owning by individuals and said, "The fruits of the earth belong to us all and earth to nobody". The western society was fermenting for change, but here in Sindh the pathfinders of human progress were illuminating people's soul and asking people to do good deeds to get place in paradise. As people were not aware of their potentials to change their life style and the unjust and sinister system, they accepted all the miseries and sufferings with complacency. This was the social scenario when Shah Inayat Shaheed proclaimed, "Land belongs to God and its yield to the tiller." Hazrat Shah Inayat was Sufi of Sahurwardy order. It is said that his elders migrated from Baghdad and settled in Uch. This does not sound convincing because Langah to which Shah Inayat belonged is a local Rajput clan. However, his family was follower of Sahurwardia Makhdooms of Uch and his father came to Sindh as their representative. Shah Inayat was born in the year 1655-56. He received education in *Tasawwuf* from a renowned Sufi of Multan Shams Shah who sent him to Hyderabad Deccan to acquire further knowledge from Mubarak Shah Abdul Malik. From there he came to Meeran Pur also known as Jhok Sharif. Within a short time of his stay in Jhok Sharif, he became popular as an ascetic Sufi among the masses. His popularity touched the zenith when he distributed his family's land and the land granted by the rulers to Dargah, amongst the landless peasants without any compensation and share in the yield. Thus he became a threat to the neighboring landlord Sayads and with the consent of the Mughal governor of Thatta, Mir Lutuf, they attacked Jhok Sharif and killed many of Shah Inayat's followers. Shah Inayat complained to the Mughal King Forkh Sere at Delhi. The king forfeited all the land of the Sayyads and gave it to Shah Inayat as compensation. The king also granted more land for the expenses and maintenance of the Dargah. This land was also distributed among the peasants. Shah Inayat had set an example of transforming feudal society into an agrarian egalitarian society in which collective well being for all had become a reality. But it was not easy to change the settled static social order. The result was that the system retaliated with full force and pounced upon Shah Inayat. All custodians of the status quo united. The Mughal governor and the neighboring landlords complained to the king that Shah Inayat was organizing revolt against the King in the guise of spiritual movement. King ordered his governor, the zameendars and the Kalhora rulers of upper Sindh to crush the insurgency of Shah Inayat ruthlessly. Hence the governor of Thatta, Kalhora ruler, Pirs, Sayyads and landlords sent their forces to besiege the fort of Jhok. It might have been easy for government forces to topple the mud walls of the fort but it was very difficult to topple the wall of determination and conviction of the Faqirs of Shah Inayat. They started a guerilla was against the government forces and inflicted heavy losses on them. The siege continued for six months. Seeing the losses of government forces and the resistance the Faqirs had put up, the governor decided to capture Shah Inayat by deceit. He sent a copy of the Holy Quran to Shah Inayat and invited him for dialogues according to the teachings of the Quran. Shah Inayat knew that it was a trap of treachery and deceit but to honor the Holy Quran he decided to surrender. He instructed all his Faqirs not to take up arms whatsoever may happen because the matter was with Allah. And then he went to meet the governor. The governor, as he had planned, immediately ordered the executioner to behead him. When he was being beheaded he gave blessings to the executioner by reciting a verse:

"You liberate me from the evil of existence
May God reward you for that in this and the next world."

Shah Inayat was like a lone star which shined for a while, illuminated the path to progress, and then faded away. Darkness triumphed and spread over centuries.

Sufi Music & Dance

In Sufi terminology mystic music is called *Sama*, which means listening. But in Sufi orders Sama denotes listening to devotional music. Before the advent of Islam, Arabs used to organize musical concerts where erotic, obscene and profane love poetry was sung and beautiful slave girls served wine. This eventuated in over sexual indulgence. Male singers sang heroic epic poetry, which instigated listeners to revenge and resulted into orgies. Male singers sang heroic epic poetry, which aroused listeners to revenge leading to the sanguineous feuds among tribes. It was because of this reason that Islam disallowed all such music and poetry and permitted only that poetry which was useful for the society. Imam Ghazali said that Prophet was against only those songs, which provoke sensuous desires and promote diabolic acts, but the music that intensifies the love of God in human hearts can by no means be equated with such songs".

In the days of Prophet (pbuh) *Sama* meant listening to Holy Quran. Prophet's companions, while listening to holy Quran, were moved to tears. Even prophet himself wept when some verses of Quran were recited to him. It is reported that during prayers "sound like that of the boiling of a small cauldron was heard from his breast." An eminent follower, Ibne Jarir said to have expired of ecstasy during the 'Sama' of the Quran.

Later in 9th century and onwards, *Sama* meant only to listening of that music and poetry, with or without musical instruments, which evoked spiritual ecstasy and purified emotions. Thus *sama* became a technical term used in a particular context and was distinguished from common musical concerts for its esoteric value. It is said that in *sama* the connotations of poetic works, rhythm, and the modulation of song move the Sufi to spiritual rapture and he dances in spiritual ecstasy. This state of Sufi is called Wajd, which can be evoked even by mundane music. It is reported in Sufi literature that once some thieves organized a music concert. A Sufi happened to pass by and listened to it. It moved him to such spiritual rapture that the thieves, seeing him spiritually exhilarated, were extremely impressed. They gave up thieving and became pious men. Sufi literature abounds, in such anecdotes. However, there is a lot of controversy about the permissibility of *sama* among the *Sufis*. Many of them declare it unlawful while some consider it permissible and some adjudge it even as an act of worship. Hajvery said "Any one who says that he has no pleasure in sounds and melodies and music, is either a liar and a hypocrite or not in his right senses and is outside the category of men of hearts."

Abul Qasim Muhammad Aljunayad, an eminent Sufi has said "Sama is an occupation which admits one to the Court Hall of the Divine Audience." Once Ibne al Khair Abu Saeed, the notable Sufi of early eleventh century, was engrossed in Sama. When there sounded a call for prayer, he did not get up to offer prayer. When some one drew his attention to it he said, "I am already in prayers".

Some Sufis consider sama a recollection of God's sound when He asked humans beings "Alastu Be Rabbekum" (Am I not your God?) and the humanity answered "Baja" (Yes). The memory of the covenant is preserved in the human heart as a close secret, which is recollected during sama. The voice of God was the first sama for the ears of human beings. Shah elucidates this point in his melody of Marui:

> *When the words of Allah-"Am I not your Lord?" fell on my ears,*
> *I at once said heartily "yes" at that time,*

It was then that I made covenant with the Beloved.
When there was no sound of "Kun Fayakun" (be and it become)
Neither there was any trace of moon (prior to creation),
Nor was there any awareness of virtue and vice,
And there was only Unity par excellence,
It was at that juncture, says Lateef, that
He unfolded the mystery (of creation),
O my Beloved! My eyes and soul have
The remembrance and awareness of that state.

Some Sufis, in the height of ecstasy, faint in Sama and it is believed that they faint on hearing the voice of *Alast*. Sama reminds them of Primordial Covenant. The sound of *Alast* was musical, as such some Sufis have identified even the musical mode in which it sounded. Hazrat Nizammudin Aulia has said that he heard the sound of *Alast* in Purbi raga, which he liked very much. Some of his disciples say that he heard it in Yeman raga because the Prophet had felt the breath of the Merciful coming from Yamen. Jalaludin Rumi (1273) has said that the sound emanating from the musical instrument reminds the lovers of the first covenant and works as a clue to have access to the knowledge of Reality. He further says, "Sound of human throat and that of tambourine both are in fact heavenly sounds."

Sufis have different views about the effects of sama on the listener. Sirri Saqti, the great Sufi of 9th century, said, "Sama makes lovers cheerful, fearful; and the desirous impassionate. It is like a shower of rain, which turns a very good soil into verdant." Ziauddin Suharwardi a prominent Sufi has said, "Sama brings into motion what is already filled in the heart be it, joy, grief, fear, hope or devotion. At times it stimulates pleasure and at times it leads to lamentation. The effect of sama, whatsoever, is called ecstasy and when it is exhibited in movements it is called Wajd." No one can define Wajd. It can only be experienced. Elaborating as to what Wajd is Ziauddin Suharwardi further says: The nature of ecstatic movements depends on the state (haal) of mind. If one is overwhelmed by the feelings of grief, fear, anxiety, he starts weeping, crying and shouting; becomes restless and even faints then and there. On the other hand, if the listener is already occupied with feelings of happiness and good cheers, he claps and dances out of mirth and merriment." When harmony in the music and the inner feelings of listener is actualized, Sufi feels a kind of exhilaration, which becomes the aesthetic state. He is distracted from the physical world and becomes unconscious of his surroundings and is led to the super-sensory plane where, if hurt, he does not feel pain. This is a state of mind, which Sufis call *Wajd*.

While listening to Sufi music one transcends all the barriers of creed and breed. Hence in the sama gatherings of Chishti Sufi's *Bishan Pad* (hymns of Vishnu) were sung and Muslim listeners were enraptured by them.

Again there is difference of opinion among the Sufis about *Wajd*. Some say that in the state of *Wajd* one can dance because dance is the spontaneous expression of *Wajd* and manifestation of the ecstasy acquired in sama. It is natural for a man to leap and dance when overwhelmed with joy. The point of difference is not the dance itself but the way of dance as to whether the dance should be organized and governed by set rules or it should be disorderly movements. The Sufis of Moulvia creed dance in an organized manner prescribed by their preceptor. While Hajveri differs and considers the dance based on prescribed rules as unlawful. He prefers to call it "movements" rather than dance. Some Sufis call it agitation (*Izterab*) and manifestation of agitation cannot be in an organized manner; it cannot necessarily be harmonious and rhythmic. Though Sufis do not approve of methodological dance, they also do not appreciate disorderly and ridiculous movements of body. There are three types of Sufi dance, namely:

1. Gashthani (encircling)
2. Dawidani (running)
3. Paidani (stepping to and fro)

Each denotes a particular spiritual activity. Gastani stands for journey round the world; Dawidani, leaping for upward ascension; and Paidani, stepping to and fro for trampling the sensuous desire. A renowned poet of Chistia order, Hazrat Usman Harooni, aptly describes this state of Sufi, in one of his famous ghazals:

In the love of a friend I dance in the middle of fire, for every moment,
Some times I flounce on dust,
And some times I dance on thorns.

*

come, O barmaid, play mystic music;
in an ecstasy of union with the friend
I dance like a frenzied man.

*

I am Usman Harooni, a friend of Mansoor,
I am not afraid of ignominy and I dance on gallows.

Wajd is always momentary and Sufi's soul sinks back to the ordinary level of consciousness. If the state of *Wajd* continues, it can cause death. Hazrat Bakhtiar Kaki, a well-known Sufi of Chistia order, died while listening to music because his soul did not sink back to normal consciousness.

Since ancient times scholars and musicologists have been endeavoring to find out as to how music effects human temperament. Hakim Zahir played three tunes on his violin in the audience of the Caliph. The effect of the first tune was that all present burst in uncontrollable laughter. The second tune made them lament and the third one set stupor over them. The Indian musicologists of yore analyzed impression, which each note moves on the listener and hypothesized that each musical note, in its own right, has emotive value. When it is sounded it evokes the particular human emotion. And then they tried to determine the emotive value of each note and of combination of notes. In the West also research has been made in this regard and their findings are in accord with the views of Sufis. According to their findings music stimulates the forgotten and vague vigue or imageless impressions clearer. This is a state when according to Sufi belief, the listener recollects his covenant and this remembrance evokes ecstasy in him and he dances in mystic rapture. The ancient Indian musicologists also tried to find out basic human emotions, which, according to them, are:

1. Erotic (sringra)
2. Anger (roudra)
3. Comic (hasya)
4. Ridiculous (bibhatsa)
5. Heroic (vira)
6. Pathos (karuna)
7. Disgust (jugupsa)

8. Wonder (vishmaya)
9. Peace (shanta)

Every note or combination of notes evokes these emotions. Hence when Hazrat Nizamuddin Aulia said that he heard the sound of Alast in raga Purbi, it was because the arrangement of Purbi raga's notes evoke feelings of love, pain, relationship, enthusiasm, humility, harmony, friendship, and pathos.

American psychologist Max Schoen, also conducted experimental study by using gramophone records and found that music produces change in the existing state of the listener. These changes he classified under nine leads as under:

1. Dreamy, tranquil, soothing, soft.
2. Sentimental, passionate, yearning, melting.
3. Sad, pathetic, tragic, mournful,
4. Solemn, spiritual, grave.
5. Cheerful, gay, joyful.
6. Graceful.
7. Spirited, exciting, exhilarating.
8. Martial, majestic.
9. Sensational and thrilling.

I have stated earlier that musicologists of yore attributed emotive value to each musical note and each note evokes some basic emotion of the listener and they determined the emotive value of each note and combination of notes. It appears that Shah was well aware of this attribution and he has compiled his poetic collection in the melodies, which harmonizes with the mood and feel of his poetry. For instance, the arrangement of notes of raga *khambat* is such that it evokes feelings of happiness and the poetry that Shah Lateef has complied under the melody of *khambat* that relates to the feelings of love and happiness.

Shah Lateef belonged to the class of Sufis who regard music as the source of spiritual exaltation and sublimity, and even at his deathbed he listened to his own poetry composed in raga Sohni. Shah was not only I lover of music but also a great musicologist. His virtuosity is evident from his poetic collection, which is compiled in various ragas. He appropriated and refined folk tunes that "come and go on the lips of the people," and included them in his system of ragas. His poetic collection consist of thirty ragas. Some of which are classical ragas like Shudh Kalyan. Aeman, Khanihat, Srirag, Abheri, Disi, Hussaini, Kaamode, Kedara, Sarfang, Aasa, Bero, Ramkali, Purbi, Pirbhati, Bilawal.

Some are indigenous ragas like *Samoondi* (melody of seatarers). Khahori (melody of seekers), *Ghatoo* (melody of killers), *Kapaaiti* (melody of spinning girls), *Rip* (melody of calamity love) *Karayal* (melody of black colour), *Dahar* (melody of a valley between two dunes).

Some ragas are named after folk tales of love and valour. These Moomal Raano, Marui, and Leela Chanaser, while some titles of the folk tales are names of ragas also like Sohni and Sourath.

Shah also invented some ragas based on occupational folk songs, seafarer's songs and songs of spinning girls. Unfortunately all songs of his invention are lost and we are left with their names only. Shah was an innovative artist. He was the first Sufi in Sindh who introduced the musical instrument Danboor (variation of the word Tanboor) in Sufi Sama. Not only that but he also altered that traditional instrument, which previously had four strings and was called Chou Tara. He added one more string to it and made it Punj 'law Tanhooro. It reminds us of Zaryab, the great musician of his times. Zaryab was a Sindhi but the torrent of time burled him to Arabia and from there to Spain. His influence on Spanish music was immense. He, about eight hundred years before Shah, added one additional string to the Arabian four stringed musical instrument *Aoud*, and made it five stringed.

Ahmad Salim

Women Sufi Poets: Living Dangerously

Abstract

This paper documents the place of women Sufi (mystic) poets in the Indian Subcontinent and India; their role in bringing about the emancipation of women in particular, and of the society in general, and the dangers faced by them in the medieval Indian social milieu. The paper seeks to explore to what extent women Sufi poets functioned within the traditional paradigm, and to what extent they managed to break out of it, what impact their lives and ideas produced on society, and how far the status of women in medieval Indian society reflected their economic position in terms of the production process and ties of dependence. The first part of the paper deals mainly with the biographies of women Sufi poets and the dangers faced by them in context of the social milieu. The second part is more analytical and tends to critically examine the emergence of women Sufi poets and their contributions in bringing about a change in the social order. The author also brings personal understandings and experiences of the culture that is portrayed. It has been attempted to convey effectively the intuitions and subtleties of an oral culture where information is passed through word of mouth, from person to person and from family to family. The research carries a strong element of linguistic anthropological study of discourse and poetry used in devotional settings. A range of theories, including ethnography of speaking, is applied to interpret the data in the paper. The transliteration of live speech and its context in the performances is based on a conversation analysis scheme with adaptations, especially in the turn- taking among the *qawwals*.

Introduction

Sufi poets like Rabiya Balkhi, Lal Ded, Mira, Qurat-al-ain Tahira and Peero Preman were part of a widespread emancipation movement in the Indian Subcontinent and the Middle Eastern countries that started almost 1200 years back and lasted till the nineteenth century. Interestingly, these women fought for women's rights and freedom of society at a time when even these concepts were unknown in the West. This movement saw the emergence of women saints on an unprecedented scale and was one of the most powerful characteristics of the medieval age in the region. It was, by and large, marked by the rejection of the existing male chauvinism, ritual hierarchy and Brahmanical superiority; the use of the vernacular in preference to Sanskrit; and the emergence of the low-caste "non-literate" persons as great spiritual leaders. The peasantry, artisans and other lower classes, as well as the ritually interior but economically powerful groups such as merchants and craftsmen participated in this movement on a large scale.

Women Sufi Poets: Life Stories

Rabiya al Basri

The central leitmotif of early Sufism dates back to the most famous eighth century woman Sufi, Rabiya al Adawiyya. Mention of Rabiya is most relevant here as she is seen as the model mystic. She ran down the streets of Basra of present day Iraq, carrying torch in one hand and a bucket of water in the other, saying that she wanted to set heaven on fire and extinguish the flames of hell so that the seekers of God could rip down the veils of distraction and focus on the true goal—the Divine Beloved!

Rabiya al Basri lived in Basra in Iraq in the second half of the eighth century A.D. She was born into poverty. Many spiritual stories are associated with her and what we can glean about her is reality merged with legend. These traditions come from Farid-ud-Din Attar, a later Sufi saint and poet who used earlier sources. Rabiya, herself, though, has not left any written works.

After her father's death, there was a famine in Basra, and it was during this period that she was parted from her family. It is not clear how she was traveling in a caravan that was set upon by robbers. She was taken by the robbers and sold into slavery.

Her master made her work very hard, but at night, after finishing her chores, Rabiya would turn to meditation and prayers, praising the Lord. Foregoing rest and sleep she spent her nights in prayer and she often fasted during the day.[2]

One day the master of the house espied her at her devotions. There was a divine light enveloping her as she prayed. Shocked that he kept such a pious soul as a slave, he set her free. Rabiya went into the desert to pray and became an ascetic. Unlike many Sufi saints she did not learn from a teacher or a master but turned to God himself.

More interesting than her absolute asceticism, however, is the actual concept of divine love that Rabiya introduced. She was the first to introduce the idea that God should be loved for His own sake, not out of fear, as earlier Sufis had done.

Rabiya was in her early mid-eighties when she died, having followed the mystic way to the end. By then, she was continually united with her Beloved. As she told her Sufi friends: 'My Beloved is always with me.'

Rabiya Balkhi/Khuzdari

Rabiya Khuzdari, an eminent poetess of the Persian language, was contemporary to Roadki, Daqiqi and Abu Shakoor.[3] The love story of Rabiya Khuzdari is one of the main cultural myths of Khuzdar, Balochistan. Amir Ka'ab, father of Rabiya, was a General of the Sassanied Dynasty. The Sassanieds were the rulers of Khurasan and Mawara-un-Nahar. Their rule starts from 272 AD. The ancestors of Amir Ka'ab came to Khurasan during the Abu-Muslim's period. Amir Ka'ab had two children, a son Harris and a daughter, Rabiya. Due to her extraordinary beauty and intelligence she was known as Zain-ul-Arab (the beauty of the Arabs). She has been considered as the first poetess of the Persian language. Her impassioned style of poetry was neat and clean.[4]

Besides all these qualities, Rabiya is known for her love affair with Baktash, a brave soldier and faithful slave of her brother Harris. Harris succeeded his father Amir Ka'ab after his death. Due to his charming personality and good character, Baktash gained an important place among the other staff of Harris. Stories about his beauty, charm and character spread all over the country. The house of Baktash was next to the palace of Harris. It is said that one day while Rabiya was on the roof of the palace, she saw Baktash. Rabiya fell in love with Baktash. Subsequently, exchange of love letters and messages through an old-aged nurse ensued. When the love affair of Rabiya and Baktash was at its peak, a neighboring king attacked Harris' country. At one stage during the battle, Baktash was surrounded by enemies and was about to fall down. Suddenly a veil-wearing horse rider speedily appeared in the battlefield and quickly picked up wounded Baktash and went away. After a long period it was disclosed that the horse rider was none else but Rabiya. The love story of Baktash and Rabiya soon became public. This news reached Harris as well. He got irritated and decided to punish both. He arrested Baktash and put him in a dry well. To punish Rabiya, his sister, he ordered the veins of her hands to be cut and then put her in a cell. That's how Rabiya died a slow death. Before her death, Rabiya wrote many verses of her poetry on the walls with her blood. Soon afterwards, Baktash escaped from confinement and killed Harris. Then he went to the grave of Rabiya and committed suicide.

The tragic story of Rabiya makes us praise her courage, sacrifice, rebellion, and true love. Maulana Jami and Maulana Abu Saeed-ul-Khair declare her a Sufi.[5] Rabiya sacrificed her life for truth and stood against the chains of orthodoxy and conviction.

Mira

Mirabai holds a prominent place among the women Bhakti poets in the Indian Subcontinent. She made a significant contribution towards social change, the emancipation of women and interfaith harmony.

The dates of Mira's lifespan are uncertain and much disputed. According to an account she was born in 1493, and died in 1546. She is believed to have been the daughter of Ratna Singh of the Medtiya Rathore clan. Mira's maternal great-grandfather, Jodhaji, was the founder of Jodhpur. Her paternal grandfather, Dudaji, had conquered Medta city and 360 villages around it. He gave Mira's father, Ratna Singh, 12 villages, of which the central village was Kudki. Mira was born in the small fort at Kudki.[6]

She was married into the royal family of the Sisodia Rajputs of Mewar. The identity of her husband has not been established beyond dispute. Traditionally, she was believed to have been the wife of Maharana Kumbli, but most scholars now agree that her husband was Bhojraj, the eldest son of the famed warrior, Rana Sanga. Some interpret the marriage as part of a political alliance between the Ranas of Mewar and the Rathors of Jodhpur against the royal family of Merwar. According to some accounts, Mira was accompanied from her natal to her marital home by her maidservant and companion in *Bhakti*, Lalita, who remained with her throughout her life, acted as her amanuensis, and died with her. Dhruvdas, in his versified account of Mira's life, says that Mira said, 'I will take Lalita with me, (wherever I go), I have great love for her.'[7]

Thus, Mira's, *Bhakti* first became conflict ridden in the context of her resistance to the attempt of her husband's family's attempt to mould her, as the new daughter-in-law, according to their requirements.

Many of Mira's verses refer to ill treatment by the Rana of Mewar, her mother-in-law and sister-in-law, Udhabai:

The mother-in-law fights
The sister-in-law teases
The Rana is angry
They guard me
They spy on me
Imprison me with heavy locks.[8]

Modern scholars have been at great pains to argue that Mira 'lived happily with her husband' until his death, and then turned to intense Krishna *Bhakti* as a sort of compensation: 'As soon as she was separated from her *patidev* (husband as God) she suddenly shattered all worldly ties, averted her attention from all else, and became even more immersed in her chosen diety.'[9] Vishwanath Tripathi indignantly repudiates the idea that her rebellion may have been directed against her husband, saying: 'She was not a light-minded or psychologically abnormal woman.'[10] Chaturvedi, too, condemns the traditional idea of Mira as a rebel against her husband: 'The blot of being a rebel against her husband has been wrongly placed on her pure character.'[11]

However, the accepted tradition is at variance with this view. Nagaridas, a *bhakta* of the Vallabh Sampradaya, who also happened to belong to the same Rathor clan, as did Mira, in his verses composed in 1743, says that Mira was offered poison because she preferred the company of other devotees to physical contact with her husband. Legend has it that Mira remained a virgin after her marriage. Considering herself wedded to Krishna, she refused to consummate the marriage. In two of her songs she describes herself as 'virgin through life after life.' This, however, could be meant as a metaphorical rather than a literal description.

Traditionally, the 'Rana' addressed in Mira's songs has been interpreted as her husband. Later *bhaktas* who narrated her life in their versified anthologies of *bhaktas'* lives established this interpretation and referred to her husband as 'Rana'. Recent scholarship, however, tends to identify the 'Rana' addressed in her songs with her husband's brother Vikramjit Singh who succeeded to the title of 'Maharana' after the death of Mira's father-in-law and husband. By this account, the conflict escalated only after Mira became a widow.

Vikramjit did not like Mira's attitude. He thought that Mira should not mix freely with the saints, as it was below the dignity of the royal family. The idea that a woman stepped out of the house was inconceivable; he therefore made every effort to stop her from joining the congregational meetings. Mira, in her spiritual endeavor, had taken a revolutionary step of coming out in the open and mixing freely with the saints without any qualms on account of her status and sex. Mira is seen as a saint and considered as a symbol of legendary devotion, but also as a historical figure who resisted the power of princely, feudal patriarchy and became a critic of certain forms of social oppression.[12]

Lal Ded or Lalla Arifa

Lal Ded, or Lalla Arifa, as she is known among Pakistani scholars, was a great saint and mystic from the Kashmir province of India. She lived in the fourteenth century, which was a period of great religious upheaval and change.

Lalla was married at an early age but was badly treated by her mother-in-law. It is said that her mother-in-law used to place a stone in her plate covered with a thin layer of food, thus virtually starving her. On the festive occasion of *grihashanti* (literally 'peace at home'), Lalla's friends teased her about the excellent food she would get to eat to which she replied with the now famous verse:

They may kill a big sheep or a tender lamb
Lalla will have her lump of stone all right.[13]

Despite the bad treatment and lack of food she acted with forbearance and equanimity. However, this cruel upbringing encouraged her to enter the life of a renunciant and she found a guru called Sidh Srikanth.

During her life, Lalla composed many hundreds of songs. Primarily, these spoke of her great longing and love for her beloved Shiva. Indeed, there are many similarities between her life and her near contemporary Miranbai. Her poems or *Vakyas* formed an important part of Kashmiri language and culture and are still very much revered.

The period in which Lalla lived was important. It was one in which the divisions between religions were broken down. A saint like Lalla was able to appeal to the heart of the people. Her spiritual realizations crossed caste and religious barriers and are still admired.

Zeb-un-nisa Makhfi

A poetess of distinction, a patron of scholars, herself a scholar of Arabic and Persian languages, a *hafiza* of the Quran, and an excellent calligraphist, Zeb-un-nisa distinguished herself in almost all major literary pursuits of her age.[14]

Zeb-un-nisa Begum was the gifted daughter of Aurangzeb. She was born on 15 February 1638. she was the eldest child of Aurangzeb and his chief queen, Dilras Bano Begum,[15] who hailed from Persia. She was the daughter of an Iranian noble Badiuz Zaman entitled Shah Nawaz Khan Safvi. Zeb-un-nisa had two sisters and two brothers. Of the two brothers, prince Azam Alijah was born in 1653, and the young prince

Akbar was born in 1657. since Dilras Bano died while giving birth to the child, the responsibility of taking care of the newborn fell upon the nineteen year old Zeb-un-nisa. Her love and affection for her brother remained unaffected by the vicissitudes of fortune suffered by the latter.[16]

Zeb-un-nisa was not only a highly educated lady but also an active patron of learning, who encouraged education and learning by various means. Her court was a sort of literary academy crowded with renowned scholars and poets of the time. She spent most of her annual allowance of four hundred thousand rupees in patronizing them.[17]

Zeb-un-nisa wielded a facile pen and was well aware of contentious theological issues. She was often asked to handle controversial religious matters. It is important to remember that unlike her father she was not of an orthodox disposition, instead she had the liberal, mystic bent of mind when any dispute came up in the court, she resolved it in a very satisfactory and agreeable manner. Consequently, copies of her decision were sent to Iran and Turan.[18]

Not much is known about the personal life of Zeb-un-nisa, since it was not considered pertinent to write on such aspects of the life of a royal princess. The absence of authentic information, naturally, has led to the circulation of numerous stories and anecdotes about Zeb-un-nisa, many of which do not stand the test of simple commonsense, let alone historical scrutiny. Some of the authentic information about her, however, can be gleaned from stray observations and comments. Zeb-un-nisa took an interest in music. She was one of the best singers among the women of her times. She had an exceptionally sweet voice. When she recited the Quran, she moved her listeners to tears. She was fond of gardens and herself laid out a garden near Lahore, which was known as Char Burji (now Chau Burji) or Four Towers.[19] The stories of her flourishing love affair with Aqil Khan in that garden were circulated among a few people. However, this is controversial as history books written in Persian don't endorse their love affair. Many people go as far as declaring that this love affair was the main reason for her conflict with Aurangzeb and also for her remaining unmarried all her life.[20]

Only three of the four tall minarets of Chau Burji now survive beside the gateway, which is covered with turquoise, amber, and azure tiles. She built one more garden at Lahore, known as Natvan Kot Bagh, which was not far from Chau Burji. Here she was buried and in compliance with her wishes the minarets of her mausoleum were built and carved to represent four slender marble palms.

Qurat-al-ain Tahira

Qurat-al-ain Tahira, born in the nineteenth century, was a famous Iranian Sufi poetess. She was a follower of Ali Muhammad Bab, the founder of Baha'i faith. When Bab was being persecuted for an assassination attempt on Nasiruddin Shah, the king of Iran, she was also persecuted for plotting the murder of her father-in-law and also for following the Baha'i faith.[21] The issue of her revolt and consequent death is dealt with in detail in the latter section of this paper.

Qurat-al-ain Tahira threw aside her veil despite the ancient custom of the women of Persia, and although it was considered impolite to speak with men, she carried on debates with learned men, and in every meeting she vanquished them. The Persian government took her prisoner; she was stoned in the streets, anathematized, exiled from town to town, threatened with death, but she never failed in her determination to work for the freedom of women. She bore persecution and suffering with the greatest heroism. To a minister of Persia, in whose house she was imprisoned, she said: 'You can kill me as soon as you like but you cannot stop the emancipation of women.' At last the end of her tragic life came—she was carried into a garden and was strangled. For her execution she put on her best attire, as if she were going to a bridal party. With such magnanimity and courage she gave her life.[22]

Peero Preman

Peero preman (Preman, the lover), a mystic poet of the nineteenth century, belonged to a very poor Muslim family. She is also know as Peeran Ditti, Peer Bano, and Peer-un-nisa.

Peero fell in love with a middle-aged *faqir* (saint) and left home for Lahore when she was only 12 or 13 years old. The *faqir* died after few years, leaving the young, beautiful Peero at the mercy of ravages of time. She finally reached Hira Mandi (the Red Light area in Lahore). She wanted to leave the place and shared her intentions with her customers. Someone told her about Saint Gulab Das, a bhagat and Punjabi poet, who lived in Liliani, Kasur.

Peero went to saint Gulab Das and thus occurred the union of two lovers and poets. However, she did not stay with him for long. The *kasbi* with his men followed her to Kasur to take her back to the Red Light area. They imprisoned her at Wazirabad. The main charge levied against her was that she had joined up with a Hindu, which was an insult to Islam. They asked her to come back to her faith.

When Gulab Das came to know about Peero's imprisonment, he sent his men, who brought her back to him.

Peero has narrated this whole account in her versified autobiography, the very first of its kind in the Punjabi language by a woman.

She died in 1872. Gulab Das ordered his disciples to bury him in Peero's grave after his death. Soon afterwards he also died.

Some Patriarchal Trends

In the South Asian and Middle Eastern patriarchal societies, the position of women has for long been regarded as inferior. This became progressively emphasized in the medieval period. The birth of a son continued to be looked upon as highly desirable, while that of a daughter was deplored. Two primary factors behind the social exploitation of women were the lack of education and economic independence.

In the Indian Subcontinent, foreign invasions led to a further deterioration in the position of women. These invasions invariably prompted the orthodox society to erect barriers to freedom of women. Fear of the invading hordes descending on their women was indeed taken seriously by orthodox Hindus. It was believed that any relationship between Hindu women and outsiders would result in the mixture of castes (*Vamasankara*) and the breakdown of the social order.

This led, on the one hand, to the imposition of greater restrictions on women and, on the other, to their increased exploitation.[23]

The birth of a daughter was unwelcome because she was a source of expense, trouble, and anxiety to her parents under whose custody she normally stayed till marriage. A daughter was considered a burden, as she constituted an economic drain because without any prospect of material returns one had to spend a fortune as dowry or groom price at the time of her marriage. A girl's sexuality was considered dangerous and a force that had to be contained within the bonds of marriage. Hence, pre-pubertal or child marriage was encouraged. In fact, custom and orthodox tradition stipulated that the girl should be modest and subdued so that she did not attract male attention:

Just as the tobacco leaf loses its freshness if it is kept open, a girl loses her modesty if she laughs.

A girl who laughs too often and walks too provocatively is a prostitute.[24]

The women Sufi poets had to often deal with disapproving opinions in the wider society. Mira frequently refers to what 'people' and 'people of the world' say about her, but does not more closely specify who these people are: 'The people of the world speak bitter words, and laugh at me.'[25]

Child marriage and *purdah* (segregation) was widely prevalent in society. Women entered the homes of their husbands as child-brides and were conditioned into a position of total dependence and helplessness. They were illiterate and knew little else besides domestic chores. Subordination and servitude were intrinsic to their being. *Purdah* was common among the Muslim women in general and upper class Hindu and Rajput women in the North India, while in the south, respectable women rarely stepped outside the bounds of their homes. Polygamy demeaned the position of women even further. A woman was not considered a man's equal instead she was regarded as an object of enjoyment. The practice of having many wives was widespread among the royalty and the nobility and not uncommon even among the ordinary people. Women as objects of male lust figure prominently in the erotic literature produced in South Indian regional languages during the period.

The life of a respectable woman ended on her husband's funeral pyre. The origin of the term and practice of *sati* is associated with Shiva's divine consort Sati, who threw herself into the sacrificial fire because her father Daksha had insulted her husband. This was, therefore, regarded as the ultimate act of devotion, which a chaste wife could perform. Lots of those women who opted to remain alive after their husband's death were miserable. They had to tonsure their head, divest themselves of all ornaments and avoid being seen by people who considered them inauspicious.

Not much is known about the property rights of women in the medieval period. Surely, they did not enjoy any equality with men in this respect. However, there seems to have been some improvement during the period under review in this study. Women mystic poets and the influence of the Bhakti movement favorably affected women's property rights.[26]

Women mystic poets, whether associated with the Bhakti movement or not, emerged in an atmosphere of discrimination and suppression, but blossomed forth into thinkers, scholars, and spiritually advanced and emancipated being. Their lives and works constitute the supreme forms of self-expression. Sharply breaking away from the traditional role assigned to a woman as wife, daughter or mother, these women saints consciously or unconsciously departed from the established norms of social behavior and spurned the limitations imposed on them by family and society. Not only did their compositions carry the overtones of protest, their emergence was in itself a revolt.

This revolt was on the social as well as intellectual grounds against male hegemony. Most women mystic poets under review in this study excelled in debate and discussions with their male counterparts. The initiator of the movement, Rabiya Basri, once came across Hassan Basri near a lake. Hassan Basri, her contemporary male mystic, laid his prayer mat on the surface of water and invited her to say the prayers on it. Instead of being impressed, she said showing off of this sacred ritual isn't apt in this bizarre world. Rabiya laid her prayer mat in the air and said, 'Let's say our prayers at a height so that everyone comes to know the significance of prayers.' At this Hassan Basri remained silent. Then, Rabiya said, 'You demonstrated in a way fish do and I in the way flies do, our real job is totally different from these demonstrations. We should focus on that.'

Here one is compelled to think what is the real job Rabiya refers to? Her implication becomes evident by the following incident. One night Hassan Basri and few other friends visited Rabiya. There was no arrangement for light at Rabiya's place. When the visitors asked for light, Rabiya lifted her principal finger and the light emanated from it. In that light they kept talking till morning. Rabiya Basri said, 'Live your life like a candle so that people draw light from you and you can enlighten the world.'[27]

Similarly, Rabiya Balkhi once met Roadki, the eminent Persian poet who was her contemporary. An exchange of verses started between them. Rabiya handled the situation very intelligently. Roadki was impressed by the wit of the young lady and narrated the incident in the court of the King in Bukahra.[28]

Poverty

Women like Rabiya Basri and Peero Preman were born in poor households, whereas women like Mira, Lalla, and princess Zeb-un-nisa were born rich. However, all these mystic poets had to live poverty-ridden lives.

Throughout her life, Rabiya Basri's poverty and self-denial were unwavering. She did not possess much other than a broken jug, a rush mat, and a brick, which she used as a pillow. She spent all night in prayer and contemplation chiding herself if she slept, for it took her away from her active love of God.

Mira, born in a royal family was reduced to a state of absolute poverty after she flouted the social convictions and left her home to mingle with saints. In some songs she refers to the symbols of poverty such as tasteless vegetables and ragged clothing, which she prefers to the luxuries of the life she has given up. The world she has found is posed as the polar opposite of the world where the Rana rules:[29]

I don't like your strange world, Rana,
A world where there are no holy men,
And all the people are trash.
I have given up ornaments, given up braiding my hair.

I have given up putting on *Kajal*, and putting my hair up.

Zeb-un-nisa Makhfi had to face solitary confinement and she also led a poverty-ridden life. As regards the reason for her sudden fall in the eyes of the emperor Aurangzeb, it was because she had secret correspondence with her brother Akbar when he openly rebelled against his father in 1681. when Prince Akbar's rebellion failed and his camp near Ajmer was seized by the Imperialists on 16 January 1681, Zeb-un-nisa's letters to Akbar were recovered because of which she had to bear her father's wrath.[30] However, her poetic effusion in the prison has also been recovered.[31]

So long these fetter cling to my feet
My friends have become enemies.
My relations strangers to me
What more have I to do with being anxious to keep my name, honored when friends seek to disgrace me
Seek not relief from the prison of grief, O Makhfi, the release is not poetic.
O Makhfi, no hope of release hast thou until the Day of Judgment come.
Even from the grave of Majnun the voice comes to my ears, 'O Laila there is no rest for the victim of love even in the grave.'
I have spent all my life, and I have won nothing but sorrow, repentance, and the tears of unfulfilling desire.

Long is thine exile, Makhfi, long thy yearning, long shalt thou wait, thy heart within thee burning. Looking thus forward to thy home returning. But now that home hast unfortunate? The years have passed and left it desolate; the dust of ages blows across its gate. If on the day of Reckoning God says: 'In due proportion I will pay and recompense thee for thy suffering.'[32]

Let all the joys of heaven
It would outweigh,
Were all God's blessing poured upon me yet
He would be in my debt.

Gendered Literature

Revolt against Patriarchy

Interestingly, we do not find a simple reversal of the 'male versus female' idea in the works of women sufi poets. Mortal man does not appear in their work as a charmer who must be shunned lest the mind be distracted from devotion. The husband or prospective husband, who often appears in their work as an impediment to the quest for truth, is perceived not as a temptation but as an obstruction, pure and simple. It is not his beauty or other allurements that must be resisted, but his interference, even tyranny.

What is represented as a temptation is the status marriage confers on a woman. There is a special emphasis on this temptation in the work of Mira. Many other women sufi poets use imagery drawn from kitchen and household drudgery in their poetry—the spinning wheel, the water-pot, the cooking fire. Mira's poetry is more replete with symbols of *suhag* (wedlock)—*sindoor*, bangles. For a woman of the Rajput nobility, marriage confers not only respectable ritual and social status but also makes many luxuries accessible. Dressing in finery is an important privilege of the married woman. These luxuries too recur as images in Mira's work—delicate food, silk saris, the high towers of the palace, and, most often, various kind of jewellery, which represent women's special form of wealth.

Spiritualism: A Means to Transcend Social Norms

The spiritual path helped these women to break out of stereotypes, the chains of tradition, orthodoxy and convention, which sought to control their sexuality. Numerous Sufi brotherhoods and *pirs* brought variations of Ibn-i-Arabi's thinking to the Indian Subcontinent, where their shrines continue to attract a great deal of interest. There are five major schools of Sufism, all of which played an important role in social, cultural or political life during the time of the Mughals. These are Qadria, the Chishtia, the Naqshbandia, the Suhrawardia and the Sattaria. The princess Zeb-un-nisa Makhfi was associated with all of them—except the Suhrawardias—at different times and for different reasons.[33]

When Sufism reflects radical forms of gender equality, this is because gender is considered irrelevant of the ultimate goal of the mystical path, which makes equal demands on men and women. As a saint, a woman could transcend the normally accepted limits and seek God even as a naked saint—Lalla and Rabiya Basri.

Rabiya Khuzdari, as mentioned earlier, became the first victim of *Karo Kari*. In the male driven society she lived, it was impossible for her to express her love openly. Poetry and mysticism helped her break the chains of tradition.

Her exquisite verses take us to a high plane of mystic thought and absorption. She has caught up the sum of love, and uttered it with an intense feeling of suppressed emotion. We soar to those heights of contemplation and ecstasy where the real is lost in the ideal and visions take the place of facts. Withal, there pervades in her poems an inextinguishable hope of everlasting union with the Spirit of Love.[34] At one point she says: [35]

Again has this love made me his prisoner
And all my efforts to free myself were vain.
Love is an ocean without shores. Oh! Intelligent men!
It is impossible to sail on it indeed
If thou wantest to be a perfect lover, thou must accept
All the difficulties which it will cause.

Another characteristic of Rabiya's poetry is the dominant note of Persian theosophy. The eager inquisitive spirit that flared up during the Renaissance in Persia could not exhaust itself entirely in the expansion of poetry or the creation of literary models. The wider outlook brought about by the kindling of new desires and aspirations deepened the sense of mystery, and sought an appropriate expression. The soul turned away with dissatisfaction from the seen, and yearned after the Divine. This was the dawn of mysticism in life and poetry.[36]

Recognition in Life and After

Our knowledge of most women mystic poets is inadequate. This is partly because unlike male saints, only a few of them established a steady following with disciples to preserve accounts of their lives and compositions. Very few women under review in this study gained any recognition of their spiritual greatness during their life. They were usually scorned by their contemporaries as 'mad' and 'shameless.' Lalla was called *matsar* or mad, and referred to herself as *diwani* or one who is not in her senses.[37] Qurat-ul-ain Tahira and Rabiya Balkhi were persecuted in different ways.

As mentioned earlier, several male mystic poets gained recognition in their life and are well known even today because they established a steady following of disciples. They also attained a symbolic significance. For instance, mystic poets from lower caste groups, who refer to the injustice they encountered, or who are constructed through legend as having encountered such injustice (Kabir, Ravidas), became symbols for self-respect movements amongst the lower castes. Although they may not have tried to set up sects, groups of people chose to name themselves after these mystics, explicitly identifying with the egalitarian implications of the message of their teachings. Even today, Kabirpanthis and Raidasis are organized bodies of opinion whose faith has a political and social dimension.

Similarly, in her poetry Mira refers to the injustices perpetrated on her. although Mira does not directly generalized about women's situation on the basis of her experience, yet her account of her struggle for personal freedom from societal restrictions imposed on her because she was a woman is perhaps the most sharply delineated account that survives in the work of women mystic poets. Mira, however, was not picked up as a symbol for any such movement for self-respect amongst women, even though her life and work would seem to lend themselves very well to such a role. This is true of all women mystic poets. None have any sect established in their name, and though many are integrated in mainstream traditions, none have been picked up by women collectively for any specific relevance they may have for women's lives.

Rabiya Khuzdari's revolt against stern social restrictions and her consequent death excited general sympathy, and invested her with a halo of romantic idealism. She is well known and remembered in Afghanistan, Iran and Balochistan, more specifically in Khuzdar, where various organizations and monuments exist in her remembrance. She was a daughter of the soil. The people of Balochistan feel great affiliation with her. There is a literary and cultural organization namely Rabiya Khuzdari Arts Academy which has been working in Khuzdar for almost 20 years. A main road in Khuzdar town, which links colony road with mosque road, is named Rabiya Khuzdari Road. There is another social and educational organization namely Rabiya Khuzdari Social and Educational Society. Besides these social organizations, there is a public library by the name of Rabiya Khuzdari Library in Khuzdar town. Rabiya Khuzdari is remembered as a symbol of grace, honor and distinction for Khuzdar.[38]

But the question is whether or not she is also remembered for her revolt against social injustices and being a martyr for the cause of emancipation of women?

Unfortunately, there is no mention of her in the local folk literature, particularly in Brahvi and Balochi. Prof. Nadir Qambrani has published only one complete booklet about Rabiya Khuzdari in Brahvi.[39] Only a few of Rabiya's own verses are available, the rest of her poetry has disappeared in the course of centuries. However, these verses are sufficient to prove how rare was her feeling of beauty and greatness of spirit. Great Persian poets such as Jami, Heravi, and Sheikh Atar, confirm her status as an artist.[40]

There are no monuments and relics to commemorate Lalla, neither has she a steady following of disciples or organizations by her name. The accounts of her life are also surrounded by myths and legends. Like her birth, her death is also legendary. In one version, her end came behind the wall of Juma Masjid at Vejibror, twenty-eight miles southeast of Srinagar, where she is said to have disappeared in a flash of light.[41] according to *Rishinama*, one day Lalla sat in a large earthenware vessel and placed another on top. As such gone without a trace. As one scholar says: 'It is a matter of surprise that there should not have been a *samadki* (temple) or *maqbara* (tomb) to mark the place where her body was cremated or laid to rest.'[42] Similarly, there is no monument, no relic in a region renowned for widespread sacred memorabilia; the only thing close to such commemoration is now a dry pond. Given the internecine strife in Kashmir, one does not know its state, and chances are it too has gone from sight. In other words, there is really nothing concrete to 'show' that Lalla ever existed.

Yet Lalla was such a person who is corroborated by some of the greatest saints of Kashmir, both Hindu and Muslim, and subsequently also by numerous hagiographers and historians. But the greatest witness is the *Lalla Vaakh*, a collection of profound spiritual poetry, which has been studied by numerous scholars. It is important to note that these verses live on in the oral tradition of Kashmir, which enjoy a stature similar to the poetry of Mira, Kabir, Bulleh Shah, Baba Farid, Guru Nanak and other great mystic poets/saints of the subcontinent.[43]

Why Rebellion?

Women mystic figures in South Asia and Middle East can be classified into a few broad categories on the basis of their choice of spiritual path and their interaction with the traditional society. If at one end of the spectrum were rebels like Zeb-un-nisa, Mira, Qurat-al-ain and Rabiya Khuzdari, at the other were pious and chaste housewives, the ideals of womanhood like Vasukiyar, the wife of Tiruvalluvar, Gangambika and Nagalochane, Basava's wives, Vishnupriya, wife of Chaitanya, and Bahinahai. The women mystics of the latter category are not covered by the scope of this study.

Zeb-un-nisa was severely punished for her rebellion against her father. Her rebellion was somewhat different from that of Mira and was mostly attributed to her love for her younger brother Akbar. In her poetry, she also revolts against her passionate love for God, and despairs when she can no longer endure her suffering. Then she dreads she has made a mistake and gets filled with doubt. She goes to the extent of questioning her faith, fearing she may have become a *kafir*, a non-believer. Similarly, in another poem, she is plunged in the deepest abyss of doubt but finally emerges to retrieve her faith in the Beloved:[44]

I am near to Thy heat as is Thy gown,
At Thy feet, haughty Beloved,
I lay down the pride of my brow.

The figure of Mira, constructed in popular imagination through legend and the supporting interpretation of her songs, has accumulated many meanings over time. She is seen as a saint, a mystic, as one who gave up the world for God, and also as a rebel. Many of the Sufi poets are perceived as rebels against injustice of various kinds perpetrated by the established order, but Mira is perhaps the only one in the subcontinent whose rebellion is against injustice within the family and kinship group, injustice done to her because she was a woman. This dimension is present in the life, legends and compositions of some other women Sufi poets, but is perhaps most clearly and forcefully articulated by Mirabai.

Mira's rebellion acquires its dramatic quality. She stands out as a lone and extraordinary figure, the exception that proves the rule. She does not seem to emerge from any known tradition of women's rebellion of this or of any other kind in her community, nor, after her, did any such tradition develop. Rajasthani Rajputs and Rajasthan in general did not, even in the nineteenth century, throw up a social reform movement around women's issues, even though at this time such movements emerged in many other communities and regions.

Flouting the Marriage Institution

Qurat-al-ain Tahira refused to live with her husband because he did not accept Bab's claims. She was married to Mullah Mohammad, son of her paternal uncle Haji Mullah Taqi.

Her paternal uncle, who was also her father-in-law cursed Bab and punched her in great anger. At this she said: 'Uncle, I see your mouth filled with blood.'[45]

Her father tried his best to restore relations between husband and wife but Qurat-al-ain would not yield, saying that her husband, not having accepted the truth, was *khabith* (impure) and that the pure and impure could not remain in conjunction. She further held that this amounted to divorce and therefore no formal divorce was needed. Haji Mullah Taqi, her father-in-law, was murdered by the Babis on account of his hostility, and it was suspected that Qurat-al-ain had incited the murder, after which she fled to Khurasan. After this she was divorced formally by her husband.[46]

Lalla and Mira were both reluctant brides. Lalla was married off to a Brahman at the age of twelve and Mira was married to Prince Bhoj Raj of Mewar. Both walked out of their homes mainly because of domestic ill-treatment, which was occasionally combined with an unnatural husband-wife relationship and the fear engendered in the husband by the wife's unconsciously manifested supernatural powers.[47]

Lalla believed that her husband was actually her son in a previous birth and claimed in one *vak*: 'I have not been confined nor have I borne a son.'[48]

Lalla's mother-in-law is said to have agitated her son with tales of Lalla's infidelity. In anger her husband allegedly stoned the pot which Lalla carried on her head. Though the pot broke, the water purportedly remained frozen on her head. This terrified her husband to such an extent that he could not think of retaining her as his wife.

Like many other women sufi poets, Zeb-un-nisa remained unmarried. Marriages of the Mughal princesses were always difficult. Much importance was given to the status of suitors which demanded that the suitor to be of the same rank, standing and qualities. She received many proposals but she insisted on meeting the princes before fixing of marriage and found none of them suitable. Mirza Farrukh, the son of Shah Abbas II of Iran, also wanted to marry her. The records show how Mirza Farrukh came with a splendid retinue, and was feasted by Zeb-un-nisa in a pleasure house in her garden while she waited on him with a veil upon her face. She told her father that in spite of the Prince's beauty and rank, his bearing did not please her and she refused the marriage. The disappointed prince returned to Persia.[49]

Why did Zeb-un-nisa not marry? Few circles believe that Zeb-un-nisa's literary activities and the subsequent praise accorded to her rendered her so high-headed that she denied living as a wife. A few believe that she lost interest in the world because of her father's cruel treatment of her brothers and cousins. Others are of the opinion that she did not marry because her father had engaged her to Dara Shakuh but later killed him. This political action of his father strongly disappointed her and she sternly refused to marry anybody.[50]

The 'Bride of the Lord' Concept

Several women saints looked upon God as their husband. To this category belong Mira. Significantly, while the 'Bride of the Lord' concept came naturally to women saints, it was not uncommon among the male saints of the Bhakti movement to see the Jivatman (individual soul) and paramatman (supreme soul) relationship as that of a husband and wife.[51]

Mira posits her God as a husband and also as a lover, even an adulterous lover. It would be a mistake to simplistically see this as the substitution of one male dominated structure by another.[52] For one thing, many *bhaktas*, including males, address God as husband and beloved. The mystic marriage, the *bhakta* as bride waiting for God as husband to lift the veil, and as woman pining for her distant lover, are by no means restricted to women *bhaktas*. They are all pervasive in *bhakti*. This is a prevalent idiom of mysticism—not an idiom specially chosen by women *bhaktas* because they happen to be females.

Mira, in her songs, adopts a demanding tone towards God, reproaches Him for staying away and neglecting her. Joy resides in presence, pain in absence. Nor in any song is God represented as telling her to do or refrain form doing anything. He is not a commandment-giving but a delight-giving presence. Among the attributes seen in Him by Mira, one that seems special to her work as compared to that of others, is the sweetness of His words and His voice, which recurs in more than one song, perhaps as a contrast to the bitterness of the words she mentions that people spoke against her.

While she experiences the pain of separation and longs for union with God, she also repeatedly says that God is within her. Finding the beloved is indistinguishable from finding that which is within. 'The doctor dwells within the sick one, the doctor alone knows the cure,' indicates the interiority of the entire experience.

Zeb-un-nisa Makhfi viewed God as a beloved. The opening poem in her *Diwan* (book of verses), is a passionate religious invocation of God.[53]

To Thee first,
From whence clouds of great mercy are born,
The rose that blooms in my garden, I look!
Let praise of Thy love the beginning adorn,
Of these few verses I mark here in my book.

However, at another place she most ardently expresses this passion: [54]

O love, I am in thy thrall.
As on the tulip's burning petal glows

A spot intense, of deeper dye, withal,
And see the dark stain which within it blows,
Of its intensity, more acute than all,
My heart is torn to pieces in its throes.
As for the shining diamond of the soul,
I pine in vain, Beloved one, my goal.

Subversion of Gendered Behavior

The women mystic poets subverted the conventional notions of gendered behavior. In the spiritual sphere of Sufism, physical distinction between male and female was often completely overlooked and the two became fused and identified. Many of the saints believed that all creation, being the product of the supreme creative power, was feminine.

Apart from being a symbolic representation of the idea that in Paradise truth will appear as it is, unveiled—the naked image of Lalla also speaks of certain psycho-spiritual dimensions of gender relationships, especially the key episode regarding her nakedness. This has to do with her claim that she wandered around unashamedly because 'there are no men in Kashmir' till she met one, as some would say, a Muslim saint. While discussing notions, such as the Divine feminine, it is important to remember that we are dealing with symbols which, because of human limitations, do indeed have a literal dimension. However, to the extent that they have to do with the life within, with ideas of the unseen and life after death, their psychological substance is primarily symbolic—or vice versa. Thus, in the context of religion or archetypal psychology, 'feminine' and 'masculine' are primarily symbolic terms, not man or woman.[55]

Life is male and female, and both are essential as represented by the totality of the Yin and Yang. As a psychological symbol, 'masculinity', among other qualities, may represent a certain type of intellectual attitude, one that is penetrative and analytic. Similarly, femininity may refer to a more receptive and inwardly focused attitude. The human experience of the Divine requires a feminization of consciousness, irrespective of gender.[56]

Whether we choose celibacy or commit to partnership; whether we are female or male, the same work remains of polishing the mirror of the heart, of being in remembrance moment by moment, breath by breath. Each moment we reaffirm the inner marriage until there is no longer lover or Beloved but only the Unity of Being. Little by little, we die to what we thought we were. We are dissolved in love, and we become love, God willing. As Rabiya says: [57]

In love, nothing exists between breast and Breast.
Speech is born out of longing,
True description from the real taste,
The one who tastes, know;
The one who explains, lies.
How can you describe the true form of something
In whose presence you are blotted out?
And in whose being you still exist?
And who lives as a sign for your journey?

Shunning Female Virtues of Modesty

Mysticism helped transcend normally regarded feminine virtues of beauty, modesty, and gentleness. Several women mystics showed complete freedom from inhibition and flagrantly defied all notions of women's sexuality. With no consciousness even of body, Akka Mahadvi went naked with her body covered only by her long luxurious hair. In one of her *vachanas* she thundered: [58]

To the shameless girl
Wearing Mallikarjuna's light, you fool,
Where is the need for cover and jewel?

Lalla too is said to have discarded her clothes and danced naked. In her *Vaakh*, Lalla sang:

Lalla, think not of things that are without
Fix upon thy inner self thy thought
So shall thou be freed from doubt.
Dance then, Lalla, clad but in the sky
Air and sky, what garment is more fair?
Cloth, says custom, (but) does that satisfy? [59]

When Lalla's father-in-law tried to point out her unbecoming conduct in front of many men, she is reported to have retorted: 'I see no men, I see only sheep.'[60]

By all accounts the 'most famous and most persistent legend' about Lalla occurred in the state of nakedness. It concerns her encounter with the Persian/Iraqi sufi Sayyid Ali Hamadani, popularly known in Kashmir as Shah Hamadan and who is considered one of the greatest patron saints of Kashmir. As the story goes, when Lalla was asked why she wandered around naked, the answer would be: 'Because there are no men in Kashmir.' One day, somewhere near Srinagar, she saw Shah Hamadan approaching and realized that here was a real man and ran to hide herself in a grocer's shop. However, she was turned away because of her scandalous state, whereupon she jumped into the nearby baker's oven. The poor baker was stunned, even more so when he saw Lalla emerge from the burning oven fully clothed in green colored garments of Paradise. One version has it that this transformation took place under the aegis of Shah Hamadan, another attributes it to Lalla alone. Others mention the story only to dismiss it as fabrication, while some consider it authentic but with respect to an unnamed man, not Shah Hamadan. Whatever the precise nature of the story is, it is generally accepted as true in spirit, and in any case is never refuted to deny her nakedness. True or false, it remains the most renowned tale associated with her, indelibly enshrined in the current kashmiri proverb *ayeyi wa'nis gay iandras* (she [Lal Ded] had gone to the grocer but [instead] arrived at the bakers).[61]

Flouting Social/Religious/Domestic Authority

Apart from the flouting of social and religious authority in which all the mystics had to some extent engage, the woman mystics had to also flout the absolute authority of their husbands and their families over their lives, since they now acknowledged a higher authority.

Lalla was critical of religious ceremonies and religious orthodoxy. Her teachings and poems are thus reminiscent of Kabir (although Kabir came later).[62]

Idol is of stone, temple is of stone;
Above (temple) and below (idol) are one;

Which of them wilt thou worship O foolish Pundit?
Cause thou the union of mind with Soul.

Qurat-al-ain Tahira flouted social and religious authority by embracing Baha'i faith—for which she had to give her life. When she was arrested and presented to Nasir-ud-din Shah, the king of Iran, he said, 'Let this beautiful woman go. Set her free.'

While she was imprisoned in the house of Klantar, Shah wrote a letter to her in which he said that if she left Baha'ism and became a true Muslim once again, he would raise her status considerably, i.e. he would make her the principle woman of the *haram sara* and marry her.

Tahira wrote few verses on the back of that letter and sent it back to the Shah. In those verses she told him that kingdom, respect, and government were for him, and wandering like a *faqir* was for Tahira. If he thought that his status was good, he should keep it for himself, and if Tahira's status was bad he should leave it for her—for she longed for this status.

The king praised her courage. He said, 'Never has history presented such a valorous woman to me.'

The king was not in favor of persecuting Tahira. However, without his knowledge she was murdered by the officials of the court.[63]

Mira flouted social conventions in her own way. Though a Rajput queen, who should have strictly observed the *purdah*, she publicly danced with anklets on her feet in the motley company of devotees and sang in abandon: [64]

Pag ghunghroo bandh Mira nachi re
(Mira dances with anklets on the feet).

Anklets and dancing being associated in contemporary society only with courtesans or *devadasis*, Mira's dancing in public like a nautch-girl showed the extent of her defiance.

Slander against a woman's moral character is a powerful weapon often used to intimidate women into accepting restrictions on their movements and associations. In Rajput culture, with its emphasis on women's sexual virtue, this weapon was especially potent. Mira renders it impotent in the only effective way she could, by declaring her refusal to be ruled by this norm: 'I have given up the norm of family honor, what can anyone do to me?'65 By stepping out of family and womanly *Maryada* (which means both 'limit' and 'honor'), Mira disarms her detractors—the poison of slander fails to work. The hostility she faces then takes sterner forms. The Rana's hostility appears to have taken the form of an attempt to kill Mira. The incident of his sending her a cup of poison, which according to legend is turned to nectar when she drank it, is repeatedly referred to in her songs. It acquires the potency of a major symbol of her faith in her God, her triumph over her detractors, and the transmutation of her pain into joy.

Many women saints left their homes to mingle freely with male saints. Mira acknowledged: 'By keeping company with saints, I have lost the respect of society.' In a strong gesture of deliberate defiance towards her persecutors, she asserted:

Rana, to me even this shame seems sweet
Let anyone insult or laugh
I walk with firm unfaltering steps.
When I talk with saints, wicked people rebuke me
But Mira's Lord is Giridhar Gopal
May the wicked feed the kitchen flames (*angithi*). 66

For a married woman to establish associations with people outside her family and mingle with them on her own is even today generally frowned upon in Indian society. This is so even when her associates are of her own caste and class status. Mira says:

Today I am in the company of
Good people, Rana, how fortunate I am.
Those who mingle with good people are dyed four times over
Do not associate with the *shaktas*—your devotion will be disturbed.
Sixty-eight holy places, crores of *Kashis* and *Gangas* are at the feet of saints.

Whoever slanders them will go to hell; will become blind and crippled.

Mira's God is the lifter of mountains;
I am clad in the dust of the saints' feet.

The above song suggests that the female mystics were criticized by many in contemporary society. Many of their practices were certainly unorthodox. Numerous legends relating to various male and female mystics revolve around their conflicts with established religious authority and practice. Many relate to the breaking down of caste taboos. For example, in one legend, Kabir got into trouble with Pundits because he chose it as an act of piety to feed poor *Shudras* instead of Brahmans.

Empowerment of Women and the Downtrodden

Despite the limitations and constraints of the social milieu, most women Sufi poets contributed significantly to the religious and social developments of the period. Mira was able to find a respected place among contemporary mystics because of her tendency to subvert many value systems. Women, like the lower castes and other despised groups, were able to find in mysticism more space than was available to them in ritualistic religion.

The parallel idealization of 'subalternity', and the new and easy modes of salvation opened to the subaltern are an inversion of fear of the empowerment of women and *Shudras* (lower castes). Thus, a new social order evolves which tries to cut across caste and gender barriers. Mira contributes as a catalyst when she breaks these conventions. In fact, Mira's role in the spiritual foray is to break the quantum of spirituality granted to women through *smritis* and *puranas* which consider women as low born and do away with the hierarchal structure of spiritual economy, and takes her to the metaphysical realm.[67]

Rigors of caste did not weigh heavily on most women saints. Even Bhinabai, a Brahman and scrupulous observer of social norms, accepted the low caste Tukaram as her guru. Mira, belonging to a princely Rajput family, found in untouchable Raidas her ideal guru. Neither of these, however, made any conscious effort to critically examine or overturn the existing social order, and in many cases the overtones of protest are to be found not so much in the role perceptions of women saints, as in the very fact of their emergence. Several women saints, however, provide more concrete examples of the rejection of the existing social structure and behavioral modes. Akka Mahadevi, for example, asserted:[68]

O brothers, why do you talk to me
Who has given up her caste and sex

Having united with Chenna Mallikarjuna.

As mentioned earlier, Mira chose Ravidas, also known as Rohidas or Raidas, the Chamar *bhakta*, as her guru. In a song attributed to her, she says: [69]

I have found a guru in Raidas, he has given me the pill of knowledge,
I lost the honor of the royal family, I went astray with the *sadhus*,
I constantly rise up, go to God's temple, and dance, snapping my fingers,
I don't follow the norms as an oldest daughter-in-law, I have thrown away the veil,
I have taken refuge with the great guru, and snapped my fingers at the consequences.

The first circle of opposition that Mira had to break through was that the immediate family. This opposition took the form of restricting her movements by locking her in. Paradoxically, Mira resists this opposition and goes her own way, with the aristocratic self-assertion and valor, even while she is flouting community norms.

Interfaith Harmony

The present seemingly endless 'celebration' of cultural difference and diversity is in danger of being rendered meaningless if it implies abandoning the significance of unity. With the worldwide rise of religious fundamentalism, it is imperative to search for frameworks, which unify rather than divide. In the lives and works of the women sufi poets both these dimensions of diversity and unity merged into a creative and powerful message. Peero Preman's attachment with a Hindu mystic and Lalla's association with Shah Hamadan, a Muslim mystic, celebrate the inter-communal harmony in the region.

Lalla, Mira, and many other women sufi poets occupy a peculiar position within the scholarship on Hinduism and Islam and the history of these religions in the subcontinent. Obviously, the literature on the history of the subcontinent and its saints is vast, but a brief review of some of the most well known general texts and some main ones on women sufi poets demonstrates the controversial nature of these remarkable women. The main controversy about some of these women sufi poets in a nutshell is: Were they Hindu or Muslim? Were they

Yogis, or as the Sufis/Muslims refer to women who attain gnosis: Arifa?

For example, we take the case of Lalla. In an extensive study of Lalla and her poetry by Jayalal Kaul, the author claims that Lalla was an adherent of the Trika School of Kashmiri *Shivism*, a branch of Hindu mysticism that arose in Kashmir during the thirteenth and fourteenth centuries. However, as Kaul himself points out, the earliest recorded mention of Lalla is in a chronicle by a Muslim, Dawud Mishkati, and his Asrar-ul-Abrar (Secrets of the Pious), written in 1654 A.D. Kaul also states that while there were Hindu chronicles in Sanskrit written earlier than 1654, none of these mentioned Lalla. As stated by Dawud Mishkati, Lalla 'was one of those who wander in the wilderness of love, wailing and lamenting for the Beloved,' and he refers to her as Lalla Arifa. Mishkati uses Islamic spiritual idioms to describe Lalla as, 'she was a knower of the path of the Valley of Truth (*huqq*).' The author cites the Muslim Sheikh (spiritual master), Nasir-ud-din, as having written about Lalla:[70]

Passion for God set fire to all she had
And from her heart rose clouds of smoke
Having a draught of *ahd-e-alast*
Intoxicated and drunk with joy was she
One cup of this God-intoxicating drink
Shatters reasons into bits...

The main point here is that the first extremely reverential acknowledgment of Lalla's spiritual status is not in the Sanskrit/Hindu chronicles but in Persian/Muslim hagiography: as *ahd-e-alast* implies. Lalla was described in purely Islamic terms. Similarly, other Muslim writers do not consider her Brahmin ancestry as something to fuss over, comparing her to the great Muslim woman saint, Rabiya of Basra.[71] For example the *Tarikh-i-Hasan*, a generally well-acknowledged history of Kashmir written by a Muslim in 1885 says:

The saintly lady Lalla Arifa, a mystic of the highest order, was a second Rabiya...this chaste lady was born in a Brahmin family in the village of Sempor. During the early days of her life she was under the influence of an extraordinary spell of ecstasy—she was married at Pampor.[72]

Another chronicle says: 'Bibi Lalla Arifa was one of the perfect saints and a second Rabiya of Basra.'[73] Similarly, there are numerous stories about her having become a Muslim through Shah Hamadan, or one Muslim saint or another. An undated pamphlet in Lahore, perhaps of the nineteenth century, claims she became a Muslim at the hands of the Persian Sufi saint Sayid Hussain Samnani.[74]

Lalla, a disciple of priest Srikanta and the companion of such Muslim dervishes as Sayyid Ali Hamadani and Sayyid Husain Samnani, boldly declared in her *Vaakh*.[75]

The idol is but stone, the temple is but stone.

It is interesting that like Kabir, Lalla is now equally revered by both the Hindus and Muslims. In fact, Muslim chroniclers like Pir Ghulam Hassan call her Lalla Arifa and a Rabiya (saint).[76]

The works of Zeb-un-nisa Makhfi also celebrate interfaith harmony among Islam, Hinduism, Zoroastrianism and Christianity. While imprisoned, she was filled with bitterness, but she kept her dignity, and her agitated muse sought higher realms than the facile, limited precepts of the royal court. Her brothers Azam and Akbar were both dissatisfied with her and neither wished to see her *Diwan* because it did not accord with accepted modes. In fact, it is a classic model of Sufi poetry, with some overtones of Hinduism and Zoroastrianism. In a few verses she refers to the fire, which consumes and purifies; in one of her poems she describes a Brahmin ascetic:

The knotted veins his wasted body bears,
Are like unto the sacred thread he wears.

In a poem she speaks of her own sacred thread, which is a purely Hindu concept. There is an element of Platonism in her writing as well; for example, in another poem she seeks 'truth', and platonic learning is apparent throughout her works. Furthermore, there are several references to Biblical themes. She compares herself with the suffering of Ayub (Job); she refers to Noah. She is moved by Yousuf's (Joseph) legendary beauty, which she lauds in poem in her *Diwan*. In the opening poem she hopes, above all, to see her prayers answered as Solomon's were, and further on she regrets that she will never be able to follow Abraham, Friend of God, to contemplate the Holy Kaaba. She writes:

'Alas, the torch of Moses has not guided her,' and in poem number VII in her *Diwan* she alludes to the revelation on Sinai.[77]

Epilogue

Throughout the centuries, women as well as men have continued to carry the light of Sufism. For many reasons, women have often been less visible and less outspoken than men, but they have nevertheless been active participants and stood against male social and intellectual hegemony. But their rebellion came with a price. Rabiya Khuzdari, Mira, Qurat-al-ain Tahira and many others had to endure rigors and social contempt and some were even persecuted by death.

Within some Sufi circles, women were integrated with men in ceremonies; in other orders, women gathered in their own circles of remembrance and worshiped apart from men. Some women devoted themselves to the spirit ascetically, away from society, as Rabiya did; others chose the role of benefactress and fostered circles of worship and study. Many of the great masters with whom people in the West are familiar had female teachers, students, and spiritual friends who greatly influenced their thought and being. And wives and mothers gave support to their family members while continuing their own journey towards the union with the Beloved.

As discussed earlier, the cultures in which Sufism existed tended to convey more material orally than in written form, and women in particular may have had less of a tendency to write, preferring instead to simply live their experience. Nevertheless there were women who did write of their mystical experience in songs, in journals, and in critical exposition. As scholarship translates more of these works, more of the story of mysticism is becoming accessible to the world. As this unfolds, we are discovering the lives and work of many women mystical poets.

Notes:
1. SHAIKH, Sa'diyya, *Islam and the Path of the Heart*, 6 May 2006 www.religiousconsultation.org
2. www.maryams.net
3. FATEHPURI, Dr. Farman, 'Farsi ki Pehli Shaira – Rabiya', *Balochistan ka Adab aur Khawateen*, Karachi, 2006, p.25.

4. SABIR, Dr. A. Razzak, 'Rabiya Khuzdari – A Cultural Tradition of Khuzdar', *Bi-Annual Research Journal Balochistan Review*, Bsc, Zob, Quetta, vol. IV-V, 2000.
5. FATEHPURI, Dr. Farman, op.cit., p.27.
6. KISHWAR, Madhu, and VANITA, Ruth, 'Poison to Nectar – The Life and Work of Mirabai', *Manushi*, nos.50-51-52, 1989, p.77.
7. CHUPRA, Sudershan, *Mira Parichay Tatha Rachnayen*, New Delhi: Hind Pocket Books. 1976.
8. CHATURVEDI, Parashuram, *Mirabai ki Padavali*, prayag: Hindi Sahitya Sammelan, 1955-56, p.113, as quoted in RAMASWAMY, Vijaya, 'Anklets on the Feet: Women saints in Medieval Indian Society', *The Indian Historical Review*, vol. XVII, nos 1-2, New Delhi, 1993, p.77.
9. CHATURVEDI, p.21, as quoted in Madhu Kishwar and Ruth Vanita, op.cit., p.78.
10. TRIPATHI, Vishwanath, *Mira ka Kavya*, New Delhi: Macmillan, 1979, p.43.
11. CHATURVEDI, p.220, as quoted in KISHWAR, Madhu, and VANTA, Ruth, op.cit., p.78.
12. SHARMA, Sunita, *Veil, Sceptre and Quill-Profiles of Eminent Women 16th-18th Centuries*, Patna, p.123.
13. KAUL, Jayalal, *Lad Ded (Lalla)*, New Delhi: Sahitya Academy, 1973, p.10.
14. SHARMA, Sunita, op.cit., p.106.
15. Ibid, p. 106.
16. SHARMA, Sunita, op.cit., p.106.
17. NAUMANI, Maulana Shibli, *Swaneh-i-Zebun Nisa Begum*, Aurangabad, 1934, p.7.
18. LAL, Magan, *Diwan of Zebun Nisa*, London, 1913, pp.12-13.
19. STUART, C.M. Villiers, *Gardens of the Great Mughals*, Allahabad, 1979, pp.134-35.
20. SINI, Dr Pritam, 'Zebun Nisa Makhfi ki Shairi', *Monthly Aaj Kal*, August 2000, p.26.
21. BUTT, Abbas Ali (tr), *Quratulain Tahira* by Martha Rote, Karachi, 1966, p.26.
22. ESSLEMONT, j.e, *Baha'u'llah and the New Era*, Karachi, 1990, p.155.
23. RAMASWAMY, Vijaya, 'Anklets on the Feet; Women Saints in Medieval Indian Society', *The Indian Historical Review*, vol. XVII, nos.1-2, New Delhi, 1993, p.61.
24. Proverbs quoted from S. Shanmugam, *Image of Women in Tamil Culture*, Institute of Traditional Cultures Bulletin, University of Madras, 1975, p.253ff.
25. KISHWAR, Madhu, and VANITA, Ruth, op.cit., p.82.
26. RMASWAMY, Vijaya, 'Anklets on the Feet; Women Saints in Medieval Indian Society', op.cit., p.21.
27. Ibid.
28. QAZALBASH, Dr. Ali Kameel, 'Rabiya Khuzdari', *Balochistan ka Adab aur Khawateen*, Karachi, 2006, p.29.
29. KISHWAR, Madhu, and VANITA, Ruth, op.cit., p.83.
30. ASKARI, S.H. 'Princess Zebun Nisa—Fact and Fiction', *Pranjna Bharti*, vol. V. Patna, 1988, p.106.
31. SHARMA, Sunita, op.cit., p.113.
32. SHARMA, Sunita, op.cit., p.113.
33. KRYNICKI, Annie Krieger, *Captive Princess – Zeb-un-nisa Daughter of Emperor Aurangzeb*, Oxford, 2005, p.56.
34. LAL, Rev. Joel Waiz, *An Introductory History of Persian Literature*, Lahore, p.76.
35. RAHMANI, Magdalene, *Rabea-i-Balkhi-Afghan Poetess*, Afghanistan, July, August, September 1947, p.18.
36. LAL, Rev. Joel Waiz, op.cit., p.76.
37. RMASWAMY, Vijaya, op.cit., pp.62-71.
38. SABIR, Dr. A. Razzak, op.cit.

39. Ibid.
40. RAHMANI, Magdalene, *Rabea-i-Balkhi-Afghan Poetess*, Afghanistan, July, August, September 1947, p.18.
41. KHUYIHOM, Pir Ghulam Hasan, *Tarikh-e-Hasan*, 1885, no.9048.
42. AHMED, Durre S., 'Real Men, Naked Women and the Politics of Paradise: The Archetype of Lal Ded', *Women and Religion*, vol. II, Heinrich Boll Foundation, Regional Office Asia, 2000, p.72.
43. Ibid., p.72.
44. KRYNICKI, Annie Krieger, op.cit., p.171.
45. BUTT, Abbas Ali, op.cit.,, p.61.
46. ALI, Maulana Muhammad, *History and Doctrines of the Babi Movement*, Lahore, 1933, p.10.
47. RMASWAMY, Vijaya, op.cit., pp.76-7.
48. KAUL, Jayalal, op.cit., p.11.
49. SHARMA, Sunita, op.cit., p.113.
50. AHMAD UDDIN, *Dur-e-Maktoom*, Lahore; Khadam-ul-Taleem, p.27.
51. RMASWAMY, Vijaya, op.cit., pp.78.
52. KISHWAR, Madhu, and VANITA, Ruth, op.cit., p.88.
53. KRYNICKI, Annie Krieger, op.cit., p.171.
54. Ibid., p.171.
55. AHMED, Durre S., 'Real Men, Naked Women and the Politics of Paradise', op.cit., p.94.
56. AHMED, Durre S., 'Women, Psychology and Religion', *Women and Religion*, vol. I, Heinrich Boll Foundation, 1997, p.7.
57. UPTON, Charles, *Doorkeeper of the Heart: Versions of Rabi'a*, Putney, VT: Threshold Books, 1988, p.36.
58. RAMANUJAM, A.K., *Speaking of Siva*, p. 129.
59. BAZAZ, Prem Nath, *Daughters of the Vitasta*, New Delhi: Pamposh Publications, 1959, p.133.
60. KAUL, Jayalal, op.cit., p.15.
61. AHMED, Durre S., 'Real Men, Naked Women and the Politics of Paradise', op.cit., p.71.
62. www.kashmirherald.com
63. BUTT, Abbas Ali (tr.), op.cit.,, p.92.
64. CHATURVEDI, Barsanelal, *Mira Padaali*, Sahitya Snagam, Mathura, 1965, p.66.
65. Chaturvedi lists this as part of a variation of No. 23, p. 106, as quoted in Madhu Kishwar and Ruth Vanita, op.cit., p.82.
66. CHATURVEDI, Barsanelal, op.cit., p.66.
67. SHARMA, Sunita, op.cit., p.125.
68. TIPPERUDRASWAMI, H.T. op.cit., p.163.
69. Ibid., p.80.
70. AHMED, Durre S., 'Real Men, Naked Women and the Politics of Paradise', op.cit., p.75.
71. SMITH, Margaret, *Rabiya: The Life and Work of Rabiya and Other Women Mystics in Islam*, Oxford: Oneworld, 1994.
72. KAUL, p.5, as cited in Durre S. Ahmad, 'Real Men, Naked Women and the Politics of Paradise', op.cit., p.75.
73. Ibid., p.75.
74. Ibid., p.75.
75. BAZAZ, Prem Nath, *Daughters of the Vitasta*, New Delhi: Pamposh Publications, 1959, p.132.
76. RMASWAMY, Vijaya, op.cit., p.88.
77. KRYNICKI, Annie Krieger, op.cit., p.172.

Chander Shekhar

Relevance of Sufism in Modern Times: A Survey of Texts and its Impact on Human Mind

Beginning of Sufism or emergence of Bhakti movement in Indian sub-continent may be termed a renaissance in Indian sub-continent. No fix date, era or period can be fixed for it. But it definitely began in the form of a confluence of two diverse schools of thoughls, related to mysticism or the subjects related the study of devotional and divine subject of practice and study. One misconception about Hinduism which is oftenly found is that it does not adhere to the oneness of God. While it is not true as Yusuf Husain writes," There are ample evidences to prove that this religion (Hinduism) addresses to the belief of One God." It is the very way a Muslim brethren has to recite the first pillar of Islam i.e. Kalima-e-Shahadat. Sufi thinkers interpreted the scriptures in the light of their spiritual experiences. A Sufi does affirm his faith in the God (One God) but indicates towards the oneness of God. The renowned Sufi of Iran, Abu said Abhilkhair who is considered revered Sufi in the chain of first Sufi thinkers says;

> Faith in oneness of God lies in seeing only one God
> rather than just repeating that God is one.

Even the word Bhakti existed at the commencement of the 2nd B.C. In fact the first ongoing Bhakti movement was in process from 2nd B.C. to 9th B.C. in central and south and from *12-13-16th* BC. in northern and western as well as eastern India. The second phase was the period of assimilation and amalgamation of various analogies. Islamic Sufism which had gone under various upheavals itself in central

Asia and Iran when arrived in India faced fresh inputs and exchanged elements of common interests with the people who took interest as the followers and those who only wanted to know about the essence of their thoughts on mysticism. The attitude of Sufis was just opposite to the new masters who were their faith followers. Sufis did not believe in hurting beliefs of people. For them the only way to win the pleasure of God was to win the hearts of people. Because for them human beings were equal and without any discrimination of any type. When Hafiz says:

> Do what you please only see that you do not harm
> others because that is the only sin in our creed.

Or in later period Naziri said:

> I don't intentionally hurt anybody's feelings,
> because I know you reside in heart

Political upheavals and innumerable massacres which caused psycho-phobia amongst human beings in the then Iran made the Sufis to think of how to give a healing touch to the victims. Hafiz and Maulana Rumi consistently scold the oppressors, both political and religious and ask human beings to love their fellow being, and to strengthen the faith in God.

This factor was the leading aspect towards Love in its various *forms* and stages. Besides laying emphasis on Love of man for man as a preliminary to spiritual love, Sufis have dealt with the purpose of creation, for this they refer to the holy tradition which say: 1 was a hidden treasure and I desired to be known so I created the universe. Why should God have this desire to manifest? Because God is beauty and beauty has an irresistible urge to reveal itself. When Nizarni Ganjwi says:

> A beautiful face cannot bear concealment. If you close the door it will peep out of the window"

Or as Khayyam says:

> The idol asked the idol worshipper, oh my devotees do you know why you are prostrating yourself before me? The reason is that He who is watching me through your eyes, has manifested His beauty through me"

Don't we find the commonality of thought in this quatrain of Khayyam when we think over the process of *Pranprithistha* of an idol.

However, apart from these imbibed characteristics the Sufis did carry with them the doctrine of *Wahadatul Wajood* which has been stated to be equal vent to *advaitwad*. Though this equality led to severe differences amongst the Sufis themselves and in 17th century Baqi Billah resisted this belief and insisted on *Whadatusshahud*. The task was taken up by *Mujaddid-e-alife Sani* and it resulted in the forceful establishment of Naqashbandi silsila. It may be stated, after suppression of more than a century Wahdat-ul-Wajood again emerged in 18th Century. *Nala-e-Andlib*, by Khawaja Andalib, father of Khawaja Mirdard, is an example of this doctrine. (I am not going deep in the said aspect)

Therefore, the process of amalgamation paved way for a new socio-cultural environment in an effort to provide space to every one to live with dignity in an integrated world of human beings. When Amir Khusro (d.1325 A.D.) says:

> Every community has got a path,
> a faith and a worshipping object,
> I straightened my direction towards a curly caped
> (beloved)

In fact it also hints to the holy tradition:

> Every community is happy with whatever they
> have got"
> Or as he says in the *mathnavi nuh sipihar*"

Their faith may not be like us but every group has their own track, belief and qibla and the last destination is same. Or many other verses where Amir Khusro without caring for the bigoted fellow followers goes on praising the way of worship of non-Muslims. One should keep in mind the period when Khusro recites these praiseworthy verses. That was the period when Hazrat Nizamuddin Aulia was summoned to the royal court for his participation in the mehfil of Sama. In the same period Amir Khusro who was his true disciple speaks of the mind of a Sufi. After all what is Sufism or who is a Sufi? There are innumerable explanation and interpretation of this beautiful word which on just listening thrills a man worldly desire. A very simple, straight and explicable explanation of this word can be found in the words of Abul Hasan Noori, a contemporary of Junaid-e-Baghdadi, He says:

"Sufi is one who is not under the control of anyone and as well does not want to control anyone. He does not want to be a prisoner of any want or materialistic desire as only the un-wanton state is the icon of annihilation." The way of life of a Sufi is like transparent glass not a mirror which allows one to see himself only. World for him is as clean and clear as the nature without any adulteration and artificiality," In a very simple interpretation, Sufism or mysticism is neither only sense-perception, nor intellectual thinking and reasoning. It is an inner illumination of the soul when, weaned of its physical and mental covers, it comes in direct contact with reality. Without actual experience this idea is had to grasp: The renowned Sufi Attar said:

In the ocean that I am, neither am I not the ocean of this secret one does not know. Save one who has been thus.

It may be mentioned that Sufi poets of Iran like Maulana Rum, Senai, and Attar, Hafiz, Sadi , Khayyam, Abusaid Abilkhair and many other are constantly-imitated by the non-Muslim saints in Indian subcontinent particularly the cults which spread more humanistic approach towards understanding religions and their teachings. Their sayings have been related with the verses from the above said poets. Even Sikhism followed the khanqahi system of langar and later on Radha swamis too followed the same. The centers of Radhaswami and Prannathis even translated the works of the poets into regional languages.

Fahmida Hussain

Relevance of Sufism and Bhakti in Modern Times

In the polarized world of today where mankind seems to be drifting towards violence and chaos; disaster and misfortune seem inevitable. Mankind is divided on the lines of race, color, faith, sects, language, caste, creed and many other differences, within or outside af human control. Hatred, fanaticism and intolerance are the order of the day, with the future looking bleak. Uncertainty grips the common man. Even intellectuals and men of learning are filled with disillusionment and doubt, rendering them inactive and indecisive. This state of affairs has created a sense of despair and cynicism among the masse. In such situations it is either religion that offers refuge or a drift towards various forms of escapism to forget and block out grim realities. However, objective realities demand a third option.

Religion, which is supposed to give man solace and a sense of security, has become a set of mere rituals, sans spirit. With the growing over-emphasis on religious rites and formalism by the orthodox clergy, many youth, intellectuals and the educated are showing signs of silent indifference towards religion. The formalities, rituals and rites are in reality just the exoteric or the outer side of every religion. The esoteric or the inner substance is the essence and the wisdom which elevates man and provides solace and comfort in times of despair. That essence has somewhere along the way been lost. Formalists may hold their faith in esteem but their souls lack the actual wisdom that blesses the hearts. They claim to be followers of great messengers of love and peace, yet fail to respect the basic faith of others. They lack the realization that a person can have trust and understanding with followers of other religions without giving up one's own. In such a situation who should be looked upon for guidance? Who will bring that much-needed revolution that returns peace and harmony to the world? What we need are people who believe in the singular spirit of all religions; people who believe that religions may differ in fundamental respect, formal procedures, terminologies and languages, but are not far from each other in their spirit; people, who believe that all human beings, irrespective of their beliefs, are equal in the eyes of their Creator. What we need are "Sufis" — people who believe in tolerance, love and the well being of all humanity.

The ideology of a Sufi is not opposed to any religion, faith or belief, it is rather the essence of all religions that it supports and defends. The turmoil and tribulation that surrounds us today, where enmity, hatred, prejudices and biases among individuals and nations persist, it is increasingly necessary to follow the doctrine of "Sufism", the main ideal of which is to accept diversity yet remove differences. Today we need Sufism more than ever before, because only by adopting this code can we rise above all the prejudices that divide mankind.

Sufism appreciates diversity in Man and teaches us to accept that all people of the world can not be same; all cannot follow the same customs or religions. That despite our diversity. God has made each in His image. "What is my belief should not be considered inferior by others, it should not be mocked at by others if they do not understand it" — this is the call of the Sufi. It is the Sufis who belief that "what you do not like for your own self, do not like it for others; and what you wish for yourself, also wish for others" [1]

Before embarking upon the actual thesis of my essay it is necessary to understand different related terms such as Mysticism, Sufism and Bhakti, and the difference and similarities between them.

According to the Encyclopedia Britannica, "Mysticism is intellectually outlined as the science of awareness of soul and discipline of body."[2]

In Sufi Inayat Khan's view, "Mysticism is the essence of all knowledge, science, art, philosophy and literature. Mysticism is neither a path, nor a belief, nor is it a principle or a dogma; being a mystic means having a certain temperament, a certain outlook on life".[3] The proponent of Darazi school of Sufi thought, Sakhi Qabool thinks that "Mysticism is universal, name it whatever you wish, practice under any faith or philosophy that is best suited to your own code of conduct, even then the reality would be the same. Go to search Truth in any corner of the world, you will find the same Truth"[4].

Regarding Sufism we find quite interesting comments. Considering Sufism a mystical movement, the online encyclopedia Wikipedia states, "Beliefs which go beyond purely exoteric practice of mainstream religions, while still related to one's own religion. 'Kabbalah' is mystical movement in Judaism, 'Sufism' is significant mystical movement of Islam, 'Gnosticism' is related to the mystic sects of Christianity and 'Vedanta', that of Hinduism. Mysticism is the pursuit of communion with or conscious awareness of ultimate reality, the divine spiritual truth or God, through direct experience, intuition and insight. This state of one-ness with reality is called *'Irfan'* in Islam, *'Nirvana'* in Buddhism, *'Moksha'* in Jainism, *'Samadhi'* in Hinduism and 'Salvation' in Christianity." (www.wikipedia.com, 9.11.2007). This statement demonstrates that conventionally the word 'Sufism' is considered synonymous with the word 'Mysticism' and that it is a single tradition — although within Islam, i.e., Islamic mysticism is Sufism.

Most of the interpretations of Sufism agree that it is the esoteric school of Islam founded on the pursuit of spiritual truth as a definite goal to attain. A Sufi takes up the inner journey to attain the knowledge of 'self', a knowledge that leads towards an understanding of the divine. "The Sufi in his tolerance allows everyone to have his own path and does not compare the principles of others with his own, allowing freedom of thought to all since he himself is a free thinker"[5]. Religion for a Sufi is the path that leads man towards the attainment of his ideal, worldly as well as heavenly. "Sufism is the spirit of Islam but in a broader perspective, it is the pure essence of all religions and philosophies and there have been Sufis in all nations of the world, following different faiths, speaking different languages, they have oneness in the understanding of the universal truth"[6].

Sufi Qubool has summed up the different definitions in these words "Sufism means the religion and philosophy of love, the acknowledgement of all faiths, the equality of human beings, revolt against falsehood, adoption of truth, relief from egotism."[7]

Sufism should be considered a historical phenomenon which emerges whenever the formalistic approach of any religion overshadows the actual reality and the eternal and absolute truth in it. "It has its own theories and practices, its ideals and realities, its achievements and failures and its points of strengths and weaknesses and its areas of light as well as of shades."[8] We will discuss these in detail in the latter part of this article.

When Sufism first came to the Indian Subcontinent, it changed significantly due to local influences, especially in its metaphysical aspect. The Indian version of Mysticism, the amalgamation of Sufism and the thought of 'Vedanta' (philosophy of the Vedas) is known as 'Bhakti'. "The term 'Bhakti', which literally means devotion, humility and seeking grace from God, also makes room for metaphysical quest or rational endeavour to know oneself besides the Supreme Self and to get merged ultimately in Him"[9].

Scholars have different views about the influence of the two philosophies on each other. Some scholars think that the Sufi thought underwent the change under the influence of Hindu Vedanta, while others not only refute this view of Indian impact, but assert that under the influence of Sufi thought there arose amongst Hindus of North Western India including Punjab a movement called 'Nirguna Bhakti'.[10]

There is striking similarity between the two systems. Many scholars support the idea that "simultaneously with the advent of Sufism in India there arose among Hindus a movement popularly known as Bhakti movement. The ideology of this movement, especially of Nirguna — also called Gurmat — school is so identical to that of Sufism that it has become a point of elaborate study to find out the extent of impact, if any, of Sufism on the ideology of Nirguna school of thought" and that of Bhakti movement on Sufism. Some even think that Sufism adopted Vedantic pantheism, which is quite akin to Ibn Arabi's *Wahdatul Wajudi* school of Sufism.

The most popular Hindi poet of Bhakti was Kabir who helped in bringing the Muslims and Hindus together through his poetry. Kabir was a Sufi who was later influenced by Ramanand, the Bhakt. "Though the doctrine of *Wahdatul Wajud* (Unity of Being), pronounced by Ibne Arabi is quite akin to Vedanta, but the former gained popularity among the Sufis of India only after the Indian Bhakts had gained ascendancy in spiritual field with their Vedantic monoism."[12]

Looking at the common, similar aspects of the three, i.e. Mysticism, Sufism and Bhakti, it is not difficult for an intelligent person to understand and infer that these are one and the same, albeit with different terminologies adopted according to the source of their origin. We can therefore infer from all this that Sufism is a form of mysticism which developed among Muslims, influenced by the ascetic movements of the areas and regions wherever they moved.

Sufism as a movement appears in all major religions, with different names. In every religion there is a tendency in its followers to prefer observance of rituals and rites without understanding the essence of the religion or the purpose of these practices. Sufism aims at reviving and reliving the true spirit of the faith, which in its view is love of God and all His creatures.

In Sindh and Punjab the Sufi movement, which had its origin in Muslim societies, was entirely changed due to the modifications under similar practices of the indigenous faiths of the Indus Valley. After the Muslim conquest of India and after the first phase of orthodox methods of preaching and conversions, there came a phase when various Sufis had migrated here who represented the peaceful, friendly and tolerant element of Islam. They were able to attract followers from all over the country. In Punjab, Fariduddin Ganj Shakar, Data Ganj Baksh and in Sindh Shahbaz Qalandar were among such Sufis. They preached the concept of love, equality and brotherhood of all human beings and respect for all religions. They did not denounce religious faith but accommodated everyone irrespective of caste, creed, culture, race and faith.

Then there comes the role of those Sufis who were also great poets. They were able to reach the hearts of the common folk by rendering their poetry in their own languages. Shah Hussain, Bulleh Shah in Punjab and Shah Latif and Sachal in Sindh were able to spread their message of universal brotherhood equality and love, eternal and everlasting valid for all times and all climes.

"The great Saint poet of Sindh, "Shah Latif was against the Mullah and Pandat, for they both had become blind towards their true path and had engaged themselves in the religious rituals of reciting holy maxims, observing fasts and praying to God for a fixed number of a day. He made it clear to them that though the prayers and sacred fasts were virtuous things; it was certainly another art which brought us before the Beloved face to face"[13]

> Fasting, Prayer are indeed rituals revered
> The Wisdom that gets you to the Beloved
> Is yet to be discovered

The result was that the people of this part of the subcontinent followed a different kind of faith which was not orthodox, nor fanatic, nor was it extremist in any way — and this is what we need today.

With such a track record we may recommend to follow the Sufi philosophy in this modern age, albeit with some modifications, such as the removal of medieval superstitions, practice of *Piri-Muridi* (in place of teacher-student relationship of the master and his disciples), which found their way in this system during the rule of autocracies and the colonialists. It is pertinent to also give some background of some of the wrongs done by some false Sufis or patrons. The great Sufi masters who had guided people to follow the spirit of religion were often men of learning and wisdom, and brought enlightenment to their order and improvement in the quality of life. But after their death, they and their shrines were transformed into idols of worship in which the *murids* (followers) were made to believe blindly.

"Every village or group of villages acquired its local saint, to be supported and revered who provides deliverance from suffering for all mankind, and when he dies they make him the object of pilgrimage and hasten to the shrine...some kiss his grave"[4] Ignorant and misguided people corrupted the environment at the shrines of real great Sufi Saints, where charity and *nazranas* (offerings) were used not for the betterment of life of the common man as intended but used by the persons of the hereditary *pir, sajjada nishins* and *muttawalis* (caretakers).

This in turn led to feuds for control of the shrines among the successors of the saints.

To attract more people to the shrines, fake *pirs* and their agents took advantage of ignorant masses by duping them into believing in their different *karamat* (miracles), magic powers, charms and amulets. Drugs, intoxication and gluttony were promoted to produce a false sense of ecstasy, which made these shrines a thriving business for the drug mafia. The autocratic foreign rulers from the East and our colonial masters from the West strengthened this system by patronizing these hereditary *pirs* as true custodians. They co-opted them into their political system and bribed them through granting *jagirs* (estates), vast areas of land and government positions to exert control over the large following of these *pirs*. Succession disputes among the heirs of saints were exploited in return for continued support. Today the descendants of these *pirs* are no Sufis or Saints, but continue to enjoy the patronage of the government and exercise the same influence and control over the ignorant masses. Visits of political figures and heads of state and provinces and politicians to the shrines and the laying of expensive *chadars*, are not meant to pay tribute to the Saints but to give an impression of religiosity, contributing to the continuation of this culture of exploitation.

"Although Islam is more unyielding in its monotheism than any other religion yet several Muslim societies practice 'folk religions', of which saints, tomb worship, veneration of shrines and other aspects of *Piri-Muridi* are the main ingredients'. This has confused the average Muslim; on one hand he sees his *Pir* beckoning him to a shrine for remedies for all his problems of this life, while on the other he finds the *Mullah* summoning him to the seminary for salvation in the life hereafter. Both the *pir* and the *Mullah* demand a price for their favours."[5] These are the role models and so called saviors of an ignorant and illiterate society.

Avoiding these shortcomings related to the practice of Sufism, we can still adopt it as a code of conduct for modem times. There is a common perception that the Sufis were impractical persons who had no knowledge of worldly affairs. However, "the true Sufis were openly hostile to orthodoxy and bold against authority of every kind, and they generally maintained a decent respect for study and constantly advised people to acquire *ilm* (knowledge)"⁶. They also advised and encouraged people to earn an honest livelihood through some *kasb* (work/labour).

Modern, scientific education has brought secular branches of knowledge, which should be adopted by all. Secular and liberal sections of society need a common ground for removing differences and hostilities among the different sects and communities that have been created by extremists. Biased political, social, economic philosophies have created unequal groups and classes and modem Sufism can play a role in reducing these differences, helping people to rise above narrow sectarian and communal boundaries to create a harmonious culture of love, tolerance and brotherhood.

The discovery and subsequent study of Sufism by the orientalists in Europe seems to have interested that part of the world. "Most importantly, creating Sufism as a new category of culture permitted it to be enjoyed and appropriated by Europeans (and Americans) precisely because it was separated from the newly emerging (and, to them, largely negative) category of Islam. This tendency has continued to the present day, especially in the realm of popular culture, where Sufism has been assimilated to generic New Age spirituality."⁷

Today there is a negative perception of Islam in the world, and especially in the West, where Muslims are all generally labeled as fundamentalists, and this can only be countered through the adoption of this softer image of Islam — Sufism. What is fundamentalism? We will have to understand the actual meaning of the term. "Fundamentalism can be used as a descriptive term with a specific meaning in a variety of religious contexts. Bruce Lawrence has defined it as 'selective interpretation of scripture'. This term can be applied to Muslims, Christians and Hindus or any other group because any group who portrays his interpretation as literal 'and true and believes in formalism and rituals more than the spirit, the essence, is a fundamentalist group. They ignore history and tradition and try to emphasize on the purity and primitive authenticity of the religion as believed to be practiced by the founder."⁸ This purified form of religion has nothing to do with the local culture, language, customs, arts and other finer things. The fundamentalists in all the religions have always tried in the past, and will continue to try to resist any such attempt which defies rigid religious bigotry and fanaticism. Sufism has faced resistance in the past and will have to do so in the future also.

According to Masood M. Khan, "In the history of Islam, hostility more than hospitality to Sufism has been a traditional feature of orthodox Islam. Since the beginning Sufism has had to face opposition from the Ulema and the rulers"[9], yet it can be tried in modern times. Sufism can render unique service to mankind by promoting inter-faith tolerance and sectional harmony.

The modern man is depressed when he looks around and finds unrest and turmoil everywhere and the condition of humanity in general and his nation in particular quite disturbing; he finds that in spite of all the material progress, there is lack of happiness and an increase in ill-feeling among people. Each is concerned with his own interests, ignoring the interests of his fellow human beings or even his friends, and this creates pessimism. The ideal of Sufism can help in such a situation. It can guide humanity to have a vision of a life devoted to the service of mankind.

"Although the different religions in teaching man how to act harmoniously and peacefully with his fellow-men, have given out different laws, they all meet in this one truth 'love God, love his creatures'.[20]

Realizing this one truth the Sufi frees himself from national, racial, and religious boundaries, uniting him in the human brotherhood, which is devoid of all types of differences and distinctions. At this juncture of history we all know that behind all wars, there is a suggestion of religion. "Whenever there has been a war, (even at present,) we can always see the element of religion. People think that the reason for war is mostly political, but religion is a greater war-mongerer than any political ideas. Those who give their lives for an idea always show some touch of religion". [21]

By practicing Sufism, war and catastrophe can be avoided because it preaches to shun all bias and spreads the message of unity, love and wisdom. The world should endeavour to have a better understanding of peoples, nations and their civilizations. We need to appreciate the moral and spiritual achievements of others and acquire new vision and a clear insight into the fundamentals of ethics. In Pakistan we can spread this message through the Sufi poets of Pakistani languages. Sufi poetry is the most appreciated legacy of Sufi tradition, together with the music and dance that have accompanied it for hundreds of years.

"Extreme radicalism that is fearless thinking and acting, is the chief characteristic of the Sindhi poet. Deadly opposition to the priest and brave resistance to the cruel, autocratic rulers were the marked features of their lives. They shocked the susceptibilities of .the orthodox priest to no small extent."[22]

Sindh's great Sufi poet Shah Abdul Latif Bhitai says:

> If you are not sincere to your infidelity
> Do not call yourself an infidel
> If you are not a true Hindu
> You do not deserve janya (beads)
> Nor a *tilk* on your forehead
> Because these suit only to those
> Who are true to their faith

Sufi Sachal Sarmast says,

> Religions confuse countries
> Pirs and Priests create mysteries
> Some bow in mosques, some temples grace
> But in all their wisdom. Love hath no place

Notes:

1. Dr. Riazul-Islam, *Sufism in South Asia*, Oxford University Press, 2003, pg. 307
2. *Encyclopedia Britannica*, (macropedia), 7th Vol., Chicago, page-786
3. Hazrat Inayat Khan, Sufi Message, Vol X, Motilal Banarasidas Publishers, Delhi, 1990, page 13
4. Dr. Sakhi Qabool Muhammad Faruqi, *Study of Mysticism in Darazi School Of Sufi Thought*, Darazi Publications, Khairpur Mir, Sindh, Pakistan, 2002, pg 54
5. Masood Au Khan, Sufism & Nakshbandi Order, Anmol Publications, New Delhi, 2003, pg VII
6. *Hazrat Inayat Khan, Sufi Message*, Vol V, Motilal Banarasidas Publishers, Delhi, 1990, pgs 16-17
7. Dr. Sakhi Qabool Muhammad Faruqi, Study of *Mysticism in Darazi School of Sufi Thought*, Darazi Publications, Khairpur Mir, Sindh, Pakistan, 2002. pg 39
8. Dr. Riazul-Islam, *Sufism in South Asia*, Oxford University Press, 2003, pg. 307
9. S.R. Shardha, Sufi Thought, Munshiram Manahoralal Publishers, 1974, pg 144
10. Ibid, pg 145
11. Ibid, pg 70
12. Ibid;
13. Ibid, pg 245
14. K.K. Aziz, *Religion, Land & Politics in Pakistan*, Vanguard, Lahore, pg. 121
15. Ibid, pg. 122
16. A.J. Arberry, *Sufism*, George Allen and Union Ltd., London, 1950, pg 119.
17. Carl W. Ernst, The *Shambala Guide to Sufism*, Shambala South Asia Edition, 2000, pg 199
18. Hazrat *Inayat Khan, Sufi Message*, Vol II, Motilal Banarasidas Publishers, Delhi.
19. Masood Au Khan, *Sufism-Nakshbandi Order*, Anmol Publications, New Delhi, 2003, pg 119
20. Hazrat Inayat Khan, *Sufi Message*, Vol II, Motilal Banarasidas Publishers, Delhi,
21. Ibid;
22. Jethmal Parsram, *Sindh and Its Sufis*, Indian Institute of Sindhology, Adipur, Gandhiham, 2000, pg 62

Fatima Hussain

The Social Role of Baba Farid & His Shrine: A Multdimensional Approach

Within the context of Islam, Sufism constructs a dichotomy- one between the head and the heart, between cold formalism and the warmth of personal experience. It implicates a hegemonic versus a universalist dichotomy, in which the head stands for conquest and subordination, the heart for universal love and compassion.

The *Chishti Silsilah* was the forerunner in this regard and this was the major reason for its immense popularity and success.

Baba Farid was the founder of the *Chishti* Order in Punjab and carried forward the pluralistic ideals of the *Chishti Silsilah*. His activities promoted the composite culture of South Asia, the proverbial *Ganga Jamni tehzib*.

Baba Farid, initially settled at Hansi in Hissar district. Later he shifted to Ajodhan, which came to be known as *Pakpattan* (meaning, the "Holy Ferry"). He was the disciple of Sheikh Qutubuddin Bakhtiyar Kaki of Delhi. He had a long list of eminent disciples and Khalifas, of which the most outstanding was Sheikh Nizamuddin Auliya under whom the *Chishti Silsilah* reached the highest watermark. Sheikh Jamaludin Hansvi and Sheikh Sabir, were his other important disciples. It is well known that his title *Ganj-i-Shakar* originated from his mother's inducement for prayer.

Baba Farid's interaction with the Hindu Yogis, not only motivated him to adopt several yogic practices such as the *Chillah-i-ma'akus*, but also resulted in the sublimation of misunderstandings between Hinduism and Islam. The practice of *Zambi* shaving of the heads of new entrants to the silsilah offering water to visitors were other *Chishti* practices which had Hindu or Buddhist origin.

Mir Khwurd reports that *Baba Farid's khanqah* was accessible to people from all walks of life, scholars merchants, artisans etc irrespective of caste, creed and religion. His renunciation endowed him with a spiritually, which enabled him to guide and help those who came to his khanqah by a kind of 'spiritual osmosis'.

It was believed that the distribution of *Tawiz* (amulets) at Baba Farid's shrine passed on the baraka of the saint, which ameliorated the suffering of the people, curing psychological as well as psychosomatic ailments. That this popular belief had a basis in reality is supported by recent research, which suggests that "faith healing" can have marked psychological and physiological effects. This is known as the placeco effect, whereby, the prescription of a chemically inert medicine results in a successful cure. There existed, a shared set of beliefs between the Sheikh and the patient. The ideology and the ritual supplied the patient with a conceptual framework for organizing his chaotic mysterious and vague distress, giving him a plan of action, helping to regain a sense of direction and mastery, to remove his inner conflicts.

Though Baba Farid used his prophylactics and curative powers to ameliorate the sufferings of the masses, he seldom used this ability to resolve his own travails. The ability to assimilate local customs, his renunciation, spirituality and compassion, coupled with devotion to God all these factors posited immense moral authority on Baba Farid's persona. This resulted in the immense popularity of Baba Farid and later his shrine among the rural masses which consisted primarily of Jat tribals.

To the non-literate non-Arabic speaking villages or pastoralists of Punjab, Islam was not what the Quran, the word of God conveyed; Islam was what the Sheikh practiced and preached. This resulted in the popularity of Islam and conversion by means of precedence (Richard M. Eaton).

The recognition of Baba Farid and his shrine, spread even beyond the frontiers of India. This was corroborated by Ibn-i-Batuta when he visited the shrine in 1334 and later recalled, "we reached the city of Ajudhan, a small city belonging to the pious Sheikh Farid-ud-Din of

Badaun about whom I had been foretold by Sheikh Burhanuddin Araj, at Alexandria".

This popularity of Baba Farid played a significant role in the conversions of the local tribal groups to Islam. However, this conversion was distinct on account of two factors.

Firstly this conversion did not belong to the oeuvre of conversions, which took place at the behest of Ulama and the Sultans, as the latter might have involved the use of coercive means. Secondly, this conversion did not involve the transformation from Hinduism to Islam since the dominant social groups, the Jats, lay outside the pale of formal Brahmanical Hinduism at that time.

The Chinese traveler Hsuan Tsang, and Al Biruni describe the Jats as pastolarist "low *sudras*" century period. However, by the 16th century, the Jats had moved upwards from the Sind-Multan area and spread prodigiously throughout Punjab and were listed as the dominant zamindar caste in the Ain-i-Akbari of Abu Fazi.

The northward migration of Jats from Sind to Punjab, their rise in social status from sudra to zamindars and their gradual transformation from pastoralists to fanners following Islam can be explained in the light of the accuturalizing influence of Baba Farid's teachings and his shrine.

The shrine allowed the Jat clan leaders and their followers into it's wide orbit of social and political influene, paving the way for the Jats' gradual integration into its ritual and religious structure.

Thus Baba Farid and at a later stage his *dargha*, became the local manifestation of the larger universal culture of Islam. His tomb became the first of the few Muslim holy places within larger India. This meant that South Asian Muslims were no longer compelled to look exclusively to the Middle East for spiritual inspiration. The shrine of Baba Farid, made universal culture system available to local groups, connecting them politically with Delhi and religiously with Islam.

Since the shrine was patronized by the rulers at Delhi, it received vast amounts as *futuh* which was distributed among the needy. In this context; the shrine of Baba Farid helped in the redistribution of the social surplus.

The shrine was endowed with tracts of lands from which it received revenue in kind. Therefor, it was in the interest of the shrine's *diwan* that agriculture be expanded at the expense of *pastorialism*. Though there is not collaborating evidence to this effect, yet it suggests that the *diwans* might have promoted agriculture.

Baba Farid's influence on *Guru Nanak*, the *Guru Granth Sahib* and several other Sikh practices like *langar, sangat* etc. is well known.

Another significant aspect of the shrine is the role it played in urbanizing Ajodhan. Mir Khurd describes Ajodhan as dasht-o-biyaban (waterless desert), which later metamorphosed into a bustling town.

Baba Farid's teaching and social significance was relevant not only during his life time, but continued to exercise moral authority even after his death.

Fatima Hussain

Role of Sufism in Spreading the Message of Peace in South Asia

The great Chishti saints like Sheikh Muin-ud-Din, Qutub ud-Din Bakhtiyar Kaki, Baba Farid and Nizam ud-Din Auliya left a deep impact on the life and times of medieval South Asia - specially in socio-religious reform movements, art, literature, culture and languages. The verses of Baba Farid called *Farid Bani* form the core verses of *Adi Granth*, the sacred book of Sikh Community. No wonder, he was called the father of Punjabi literature. Amir Khusro, a disciple of Nizam-ud-Din Auliya, similarly is considered the father of Urdu and Hindi literature. He is one of the greatest saint poets, who consistently attempted to bridge the gulf between Hindus and Muslims. One of his verses reads: "Condemn not the idol whispers; Learn from them the way of worship."

I am reminded of Prophet Muhammad's journey to Medina and his treaty with the Jews whom he guaranteed protection to life and to their place of worship and made it obligatory on each Muslim to abide by this, even at the cost of their lives. This action of the Prophet (pbuh) is a reaffirmation that Islam means peace, the basis of peace is respect towards each other and that peace has to be achieved at any cost.

The Sufis of South Asia were true inheritors of the Prophet (pbuh), in their message for a peaceful and harmonious relationship between the communities. They did so, by embracing disciples from all faiths, opening their *Khanqahs* to all and sundry and treated every one at par. Thus, Jaypal, the great magician became a disciple of Sheikh Muin-ud-Din and Raja Har Dayal became a disciple of Sheikh Nizam-ud-Din

Auliya and so on. There are evidences in the *Fawaid ul-Fua'ad*, a contemporary Persian work that Hindu *Yogis* visited Baba Farid and Sheikh Nizam ud-Din Auliya, which set the process of inter-faith dialogue and learning from each other.

When Islam came to South Asia, it came in two ways - one as warrior Muslims led by Muhammad Bin Qasim, Mahmud Ghazni and Mohammed Ghori respectively and followed by host of others including Turks and Mughals. The other way was the advent of the Sufis and their disciples to spread the message of Islam, which literally means peace. The inhabitants resisted the first category i.e. warrior Muslims and were reluctant to accept their religion, presence and ruling over them. And probably these classes projected to the inhabitants a distorted notion of Islam. However, it was the advent and spread of Sufism in South Asia, which was the greatest factor for social stability in South Asia, leading to political stability. People understood through them that Islam was a religion, which is not all about wars and orthodoxy, but a religion of piety, liberalism, virtue, sacrifice, simplicity, equality and devotion. Thus Islam got accepted in the communally divided and strife torn society and once Islam got accepted, Islamic rule of Sultans and the Mughals gained legitimacy. The moral pressure of Sufis was also writ-large on the Muslim rulers who were constrained to care for general welfare of the society and treat all the communities equally well. Bakhtiyar Kaki's impact on Sultan Shamsuddin Iltutmish, Baba Farid's impact on Balban and Nizam ud-Din Auliya's impact on Alauddin Khilji and Feroz Shah Tughlaq etc. are well known facts. The rulers conducted themselves in such a way that they kept getting the blessings of the respective Sufi Saints and thus it was incumbent on them to work towards the general welfare of the people - both Hindus and Muslims and usher in an era of peace and prosperity.

Another important impact of Sufism was the creation of Sikhism and development of Punjabi language. Sikhism took birth as a reactionary force against the evils of then caste-ridden and ritualistic society and as a reflection of Sufi piety and devotions. The Guru Granth Saheb contains verses relating to Baba Farid, Sheikh Rukn ud-Din and Sheikh Baha ud-Din Zakaria. Baba Farid's verse of reprimanding Dhola against the evil designs of villain Umru to intoxicate him and abduct his beautiful wife is well known. This verse is a reminder to the society against evil designs of others and also not to indulge in immorality that disturbs peace, prosperity and harmony.

Sufism set the process of social reformation in South Asia and was a major contributor to the emergence of Bhakti movement. Sikhism is a part of Bhakti movement and is a beautiful creation of Medieval South Asian History. It has tremendous impact on art, music, literature etc., besides its important contributions in philosophy and theology, especially mysticism and socio-religious movements. Sikhism owes a great deal to Sufism and certainly it bridged a great deal the gap between two civilizations—the Hindu civilization and Muslim civilization. Sufism thus brought about the ethos of religious pluralism in South Asia. It set the process of peaceful and harmonious inter-faith relations.

Its contribution in literature is also outstanding. *Kashf al-Mahjoob* to *Fawad al-Fua'd, Khairul Majalis* etc. and thousands of other Persian and Urdu and Punjabi works are great contributions of Sufism to the present day world, encompassing debates and thoughts, on man's relationship with God and fellow human beings. The essence of all these works is love and peace.

Sufi *Khanqahs* were places of service of humanity and peace. Sheikh Muin-ud-Din held that the highest form of devotion to God is possible through redressing miseries of the distress, helping the needy and feeding the hungry. Sheikh Nizam ud-Din Auliya similarly divided devotion into two categories - *Lazmi* and *mutaaddi*. The first one includes prayer, fasting, hajj etc. whereas *mutaaddi* devotion or transitive devotion includes service towards humanity, the reward for which is unlimited, it is this aspect of Sufism in South Asia, which makes the Sufis most revered by people from all walks of life irrespective of caste, creed and religious differences. Their message of service towards humanity and peaceful coexistence has no parallel in human history. Today their *dargahs* are places of pilgrimage for all people. They preached love and peace when they were alive and they preach the same today while lying buried. Thousands throng to their *mazars* in search of peace and solace. This is one of the greatest legacies of Sufi saints that we must cherish and adhere to. Through their deeds, actions, writings and uttering they always preached love. Love is the basis of peace. Without love all adjustments and compromises will be of temporary value. This is the essence of peace. Sufis' message of peace has global connotations which transgresses boundaries of nations and religions. Let peace be here, let peace be there and let peace be in between. Let peace be everywhere. Let peace not be torn into pieces.

Fatima Hussain

Constructing Paradigms of Religious Conflict Resolution Through the Heer Waris Shah

In the current global scenario, where formal religions are viewed with suspicion due to their real or perceived propensity to divide, rather than unite, popular religions like Sufism & Bhakti assume an ever increasing importance.

For long, UNESCO has been mulling over the idea of deploying Sufic ways to resolve conflict and usher in peace. Sufism is of significance because of its intrinsic ability not only to syncretize, but also to proffer relief from the hair splitting orthodoxy & exclusivist character of institutionalized religion.

For the ubiquitous hatred, avarice, strife and terror, Sufism provides ready answers.

I

The study aims to explore the relevance of the *Heer Ranjha* in today's turbulent times and how practicing the Sufic ideals of Waris Shah can be instrumental in resolving conflict & ushering in peace in South Asia.

The *Heer* of Waris Shah is a universal text which holds as much significance today, as it did at the time when it was written. Even now, singing *Heer* gives pleasure & mesmerizes one with the message of peace & love.

The Urs of Waris Shah is held on 9th of Sawan every year. Devotees attribute wonders to the author. In the past, the festival's bazaar was a major point of buying & selling. Besides the singing of Kalam, Dhamaal is also a hallmark of the festival.

The message of human brotherhood & love, as encapsulated in the *Heer* transcends the boundary of religion. History has proved that partition along religious lines has failed to produce stability and to deliver security & coherence in South Asia. Often, texts, and in particular, religious texts, are full of ambiguities, contradicting statements and are written down in distant time, often in a language, which is different from the one used by current communities. The Heer is stylistically succinct, written in a language which is and has been the language of the masses and its message appears to be humanly reachable. Its easy to understand, and preaches through live experiences which the people of the region can relate to. It holds out the possibility of coexistence and mutual prace in South Asia, promising the potential availability of a new and better life free of religious intolerance.

The study aims to highlight the continuing significance of *Heer* in the struggle for peace & freedom. The attractive simplicity of the text, if available to a wide readership, may successfully complete the unaccomplished task of the great sufi poet.

Cultural otherness is often cited as the reason for the partition of India, along religious lines. However, the tale of *Heer* contradicts the notion of cultural otherness. For millions of Punjabis, in Pakistan, as well as in India, *Heer* is the hallmark of a shared culture. The present study aims to highlight the *sanjhi virasat* (shared legacy) of Punjabis which transcends political boundaries. The *Heer* defies the notion of hard boundaries posited between Hindu & Muslim in the late medieval period. In a subtle manner, it underlines the presence of an amorphous identity/culture.

Though, a great deal of research has been done on the *Heer Ranjha* by specialists in the field of language, but hardly any historian has ventured to explore the field. The *Heer* of Waris Shah has critical bearing on the study of 18th Century (which has been the hotbed of debate among historians). The 18th Century witnessed the decline of the Mughal Empire and a process of reconfiguration of power. Several historians have debated on the happenings of the 18th Century through the lens of court chronicles or fiscal records. Few, if any, have ventured into the realm of literature to understand the social, economic or political reality of the time.

Historians like Muzaffar Alam, Chris Bayley etc opine that though the edifice of the Mughal empire was crumbling, the regional economies were thriving. However, the literature of this period offers a glimpse into a Punjab which was bleeding, despite all the revenue records indicating a thriving economy. This is how the Sufi, Bulleh Shah, who was the contemporary of Waris, describes the scene in Punjab:

Dar khulla hashar azab da, bura haal hoya Punjab da.

The portals of Hell are wide open, Punjab is in a state of calamity.

My own preliminary research highlights the need to further refine and qualify the hypothesis relating to 18th century Punjab. The narrative of Waris Shah is beautifully woven into the larger trajectory of political and social developments in Punjab. The romance may construct a fantasy world to liberate the imagination, but the fantasy has to be examined within the historical circumstances of its articulation, for fantasy does not mean the hesitation between the real and imaginary world. *Heer* is a mirror which effectively articulates resistance against the prevailing social, economic and political order. The characters of Chuchak, *Heer's* father and Kaido, her paternal uncle, represent the villainy and intolerance of a feudal set up. In a similar vein, Balnath Jogi is a symbol of social withdrawal & resignation which Ranjha adopts but another character Aiyali, the shepherd, challenges the sense of honour of Ranjha and spurs him on to aggressive action, in order to attain union (*wisal*) with his beloved.

Waris Shah has seamlessly blended the reflection model (i.e. literature is an inert reflection of existing social reality) and the substitution model (i.e., since reality is mundane, literature provides an escape/subliminating, from reality – an alternative reality) into one. The romance of Heer & Ranjha was narrated by Waris in a manner that had already attained a standard form. It was in the Bait metre, which too had been perfected by his predecessors, markedly Muqbal, the poet refers to the requests made by friends to him, to write afresh the love story of Heer. He, however, reconstructed it, to convey his own interpretation of society.

Waris Shah is a Muslim writer working with a Punjabi language, whose extant vocabulary was conditioned to a great extent, by Hindu ideational constructs. The use of Hindu idioms, by Waris in an unabashed manner, allows us to investigate how narratives frame cross-cultural interactions and make them serve higher ideological purposes. Unable to attain union (*Wisal*) with his beloved Heer, Ranjha makes his way to *Tila Bal Nath*, to seek refuge from a *Guru* who belongs to the order of *Kan-Phad* Jogis. Herein, we see a Muslim Ranjha converted into a Hindu Jogi without any hesitation, with his ears pierced and *Mundras* (ear-rings) inserted therein. Concomitant with this is Ranjha's visit to the *Panj Pirs* (5 divines), in order to seek their blessings. There are references to the Barah Mah, Athwara, Raja Bhoj, Kauravas, Pandavas, Ravana and so on.

The popularity of Heer suggests that the people of Punjab, resisted the domination of the higher languages of the Muslim ruling class. The present study aims to explore the possibilities in understanding language as historical evidence. The Heer opposes the hegemonic influence of the language of power and affirms that languages are socially constructed and socially negotiated. Languages are also agents of integration.

II

One of the major genres of pre-modern north Indian poetry is the Punjabi Qissa (which literally means an account or a story) composed by Sufi poets of Punjab, mainly in the 18th century. These narrative poems, called sufi romances by modern critics, are commonly assumed to put forward 'the equation of human love and love for a divine being'. They mark the inauguration of a new literary culture in a local language, and Indian Islamic tradition. These mystical romances describe the ascetic quest of the hero towards the revelatory beauty of a heroin (or God) by linking mortification, fasting, and prayer with a female object of desire. While eroticism and asceticism have often been linked, the hero's attainment of the heroine takes place only after an arduous ascetic quest in a hostile world.

The dominant theme of the Qissa – resistance to the existing order, is beautifully woven into the larger trajectory of rural Punjab. Qissa became not only an overpowering means of expression, it also attained immense popularity, as the poets deployed folk idioms and rural imagery of Punjab. As such, it was instrumental in bringing out its message in a subtle manner.

Waris Shah is a name to be reckoned with, in the tradition of Punjabi Qissa poetry, best known for his seminal work *Heer Ranjha*. Waris Shah's own life remains shrouded in mystery, except for a few facts gleaned from the text of the Qissa he wrote. He writes:

Waris Shah wasneek Jandyal daa, shaagird Makhdoom Qasoor daa ey.
i.e he was a resident of Jandyal & a pupil of Makhdum Gulam Murtaza of Qasoor.

Qasur was an important centre of learning in those days. It is said that Bulleh Shah, another important Punjabi poet, was also educated at Qasur. Nothing is known about Waris' career except that he was holding a middle ranking government post. Possibly, it was due to this that his form of resistance is somewhat oblique, as opposed to that of Bulleh Shah who was more forthright in his criticism. The exact date of his birth, family background and lineage remain obscure. According to one version, he was born in 1735, though 1722 is taken as the generally accepted date of his birth. After completing his education at Qasur, Waris Shah moved to the village of Malka Hans where he lived in a small room (*hujra*), where he wrote the immortal tragedy of Heer & Ranjha in 1766. Some 76 writers including well known names such as Damodar, Mukbal, Ahmad Gujjar, Charagh Awan, Peelo and Hafiz Barkhurdur have written their own versions of the Heer story. However Waris Shah's Heer is considered one of the quintessential works of classical Punjabi literature. Waris borrowed the story and plot of the legend Heer Ranjha and structured it to a nuanced narrative. The earlier version of Heer written by Damodar, around the time of emperor Akbar's reign, had a happy ending. Waris Shah's Heer, however, ends on a sad note. This could be attributed to several factors.

Waris Shah's own experience of unrequited love for Bhagbhari who was a Hindu girl, might have made him critical of the contemporary social norms and inspired him to rewrite the Qissa, as an ever fresh tragic dialogue of immutable love, highlighting a range of human emotions.

It is also likely that there existed a belief that if one wrote the Qissa Heer one self, one's desire (*mannat*) would be fulfilled, quite like the way there existed a belief in the efficacy of getting a copy of *Fawaid ul Fuad* written, in the Sultanate period.

Another reason could be the atmosphere of pessimism which prevailed in Punjab in those days. Waris Shah captures it thus in the completion note of his tale. He says:

The book was completed in the year 1180 Hijri.

The Bikram Calendar year was 1882.

These were the stormy ears when Jats (tillers) of the land turned rulers and new governments came to be formed from house to house.

The lament over the rise of Jats shows that he himself belonged to a superior class, most likely Syed.

The elite are in bad shape & the have-nots have turned into haves ones. The peasants and tenants rejoice, thieves have became masters and the corrupt and debased are then worshipped. The demonic & evil ones have gathered strength. They are at the top (Gurcharan Singh Pg.71).

Clearly, Waris Shah was finding it hard to come to terms with the reconfiguration of power, taking place in Punjab after the onslaught from the North West.

Waris Shah the *Jogi* was looted by the roving bands, Punjab and India, both tremble at the mention of Nadir Shah.

Though the Afghan marauders are often held responsible for the turmoil in Punjab, there is no derogatory reference to the Sikhs. Bulleh Shah says:

Khadda pitta lahe da,
Baki Ahmad Shahe da.

This highlights the fact, that Bulleh Shah too, held the Afghan invaders responsible for the misery in Punjab, remaining oblivious to their being Muslims.

Punjab was an area which, on account of its natural and human resources, as well as their strategic location, played a crucial role in the political fortune of the subcontinent. Economically, this area was one where money economy, trade and manufacture had developed and reached a fairly high level. Traders (*Khatris*) and administrators (*Hakims*) played an important role because Punjab was strategically placed at the juncture of important trade routes to Central Asia. As a result, the history of Punjab had been witness to many storms, along with several peaceful interludes.

In the eighteenth century, the period in which Waris Shah writes, Punjab lay exposed to several invasions from the northwest, as it had been earlier. The Mughal empire was disintegrating and historically, the eighteenth century was a century of turmoil and contradictions, as has been debated by historians like Muzaffar Alam, Satish Chandra, Irfan Habib, P.J. Marshall, etc. The people of Punjab had to undergo immense turmoil and this was, perhaps, the reason why the Punjabis are a determined, resilient lot, even today.

Coming back to the point, Punjab faced the brunt of Nadir Shah's and Ahmad Shah Abdali's invasions. This, along with his personal failure, perhaps, was the reason why Warish Shah gave a tragic ending to the tale. It was a continuation of the pessimism, which prevailed in the eighteenth century.

One wonders, if such was the turbulence in Punjab, then why there are the vivid descriptions of scenic beauty in the *Heer*. Images can motivate. They can inspire feelings of security, peace, warmth and hope. Waris Shah's imagery, was perhaps a conduit to support the healing process in Punjab.

While describing Heer's beauty, Waris Shah writes:

Her beauty slays rich *Khojas* and *Khatris* in the bazaar, like a murderous *kizilbash* trooper riding out of the royal camp armed with a sword. (Usborne, p.41).

Literally meaning *hot head*, Kizilbash was the name of a soldierly tribe in Iran, a number of whom came to India with the armies of Nadir Shah. The word "murderous" denotes aggression, therefore the invasions of Nadir Shah & Ahmad Shah Durrani Abdali were seen as causes for the ravaged state of Punjab.

Another reason why Waris Shah wrote the qissa afresh, could be his inclination towards *tasawwuf* and *bhakti*. Waris writes that when Ranjha is trying to cross the river Chenab, along whose banks the story is set, the boatman Ludden, for whom pecuniary benefits are of prime importance retorts:

Even the son of a Pir like Waris, we will not take into our boat for nothing.

So Waris Shah projects himself as a Pir. Also, the Qissa starts with a prayer to God and an Ode to Love – the foundation of creation; and an obeisance to the Prophet, his four friends; Chishti, the well known founder of the Chishti silsilah; his successors, including more specifically Baba Farid of Pakpattan (Gurcharan Singh, Heer Waris Shah, p.13). He also refers to himself as a *Jogi*, on several occasions.

The elusive Heer, like the formless absolute, i.e. God, awakens in Ranjha, the Sufi, a desire that overpowers his mind and heart, and does not allow him any peace. However, some scholars like Saeed Ahmad construe Heer as the Sufi and Ranjha as the formless absolute. So Heer says:

Ranjha, Ranjha kar di ni, main aape Ranjha hoi.

This is in the same note as *An al Haq* pronounced by Mansur al Hallaj. This alludes to the annihilation of the seeker with the Asbolute. The impulse towards union, i.e. wisal, is avoided through a series of narrative incidents that delay the satisfaction of desire, until the seeker is purified. This is likened to the several stations or *maqamat,* that a *mureed* has to pass through before he attains the final union with the beloved, i.e. Allah. To achieve this goal, he has to seek the assistance of his spiritual master, the *peer* who is the Kamphad yogi of Tila Balnath in Jhelum.

Ranjha is also blessed by the Panj Pirs. The union is entwined the widespread Sufi notion of annihilation or *fana,* which is a cause of celebration for the Sufi. The death of a Sufi heralds the ultimate union with the beloved God and is celebrated by Urs. In fact, this is the true birth of the Sufi. The divine form of Heer suggested both Allah's might and majesty (*jalal*) and his gentle grace (*jamal*).

Earning love can be a protracted and painful process, for which everything wordly, has to be abandoned, a process which involves much self-mortification. For this, the path of truth (*haqiqat*), has to be followed, apart from reposing an unending trust in God (*tawakkul*). Waris Shah describes, in vivid hues, the pain and sorrow inflicted by separation.

The vocabulary, the similies deployed by him, convey devotional emotions with skillfull restraint. Though the formulaic plot of Sufi romance contains a set of easily predictable conventions and motives. Waris Shah's Qissa Heer Ranjha shows a great deal of inventiveness in reinterpreting the formula and intensifies the experience.

Some scholars of Punjabi literature, like S.S. Nur are of the opinion that by the time, Waris Shah wrote his Heer, European works of Aristotle, Plato etc. had become known in South Asia which had a profound influence on his writing, though it was by no means, a case of mechanical appropriation of Western thought. In its own way, Heer Waris Shah is marked by a diversity of sources & a richness of literary imagination.

In was this period of turbulence spanning around a hundred years, which forms the richest period of Punjabi poetry. It was a bleeding Punjab, turbulent and chaotic, that produced the best poetry – mystic, romantic, lyrical & heroic in the form of *Qissa, Kafis, Masnavis, Dhorey* or *Dohe, Dholla, Mahiye* etc.

III

When we look at history, we have the propensity to depict women as being trapped within oppressive systems. Heer takes the lead – be it taking Ranjha to her father Chuchak, to be employed as cow herd (or rather buffalo herd), or be it assuring Ranjha of good times ahead, or rebuking her mother Malki for arranging her marriage, forcibly against her will and accuses her family of being unfair to her.

Only those without brains would fix a high dome brick into a drain.

This means fixing marriages without the consent of girls was not the norm. A very active, dynamic Heer, stands in stark contrast to the relatively passive Ranjha, who needs constant prodding from Almighty to move towards *wisal*.

S.S. Hans of Patiala University has interpreted the Heer Ranjha from the point of view of geography, talking of the notions of *watan*, *desh*, etc.

In a characteristic Sufi style, Waris Shah, was not discriminatory on the basis of religion and was against the bigotry of the clergy. He exposes the hypocricy of the priests (*ulema*) and is obliquely critical of the divisions in society, the dichotomy between precept and practice in Islam. He gives a strong pedagogic message of accommodation in society.

BIBLIOGRAPHY

A.L. Dallapiccola, ed., *Islam in Indian Regions*, 1000-1750 2 Vols. (Heidelberg : University of Heidelberg, 1992).
Afzal Khan ed., *Heer Waris Shah* (Lahore, 1969).
Aitzaz Ahsan, *The Indus Saga* (Karachi : Oxford University Press, 1996).
Ali Abbas Talal Puri, *Muqamat-e-Waris Shah* (Lahore : Kitab Nama, 1972).
D.J. Matthews & C. Shackle, *An Anthology of Classical Urdu Love Lyrics* (London : OUP, 1972).
Dr. Mohan Singh Diwana, *A History of Punjabi Literature (1100-1932)* (Lahore: Punjabi Adabi, 1982).
Fakhar Zaman, *Punjab, Punjabi aur Panjabiat* (Lahore: Al Hamd Publishers, 2003.
Francis Robinson, *Islam and Muslim History in South Asia* (OUP, 2003).
Ganda Singh ed., *The Punjab : Past & Present*, Vol.II & IV (Patiala : Punjab University, 1968).
Ghafran Syed and Bashir Nazim, *Punjabi Classical Adab* (Lahore : Aziz Book Depot, 1973).
Gurcharan Singh, *Heer Waris Shah* (Lahore : Suchet Kitab Ghar, 2001).
Hari Ram Gupta, *Later Mughal History of the Punjab* (Calcutta : Sungmeel Publication, 1924).
Harjot Oberoi, *The Construction of Religious Boundaries, Culture, Identity and Diversity in the Sikh Tradition* (OUP, 1997).
I.H. Qureshi, *Ulema in Politics : A Study Relating to the Political Activities of the Ulema in the South-Asian Subcontinent from 1556 to 1947* (Delhi : Renaissance Publishing House, 1985).
Jadunath Sarkar, *Fall of the Mughal Empire* (Calcutta, 1924).
Jadunath Sarkar, *Nadir Shah in India* (Patna, 1925).
Lajwanti Ramakrishna, dri, *Panjabi Sufi Poets* (London: Humphrey Milford, 1938).
Latif S.M., *History of the Punjab*, (Lahore, 1891).
Lock Hart, *Waris Shah*, (London: Lusacand Cor, 1938).
M. Afzal Khan ed., Monthly Journal *Panj Darya*, Waris Shah Number (Lahore, 1969).
M. Waseem Tr., Garcin De Tassy, *Muslim Festivals in India and Other Essays* (OUP, 1995).
Muzaffar Alam and Sanjay Subrahmanyam, *The Mughal State, 1526-1750* (Delhi : 1998).
Muzaffar Alam, *The Crisis of Empire in Mughal North India : Awadh and the Punjab, 1707-1748* (Delhi, 1986).
Penelope J. Corfield, ed., *Language, History and Class* (Oxford & Cambridge : Basil Blackwell, 1991).
Prof. Saeed Ahmed, *Great Sufi Wisdom* (Rawalpindi : Adnan Books, 2005).

Richard M. Eaton, *Essays on Islam and Indian History* (OUP, 2004).
S.A.A. Rizvi, *Shah Wali Allah and his Times : A Study of Eighteenth Century Islam, Politics and Society in India* (Canberra : Marifat Publications, 1980).
Sang-i-Meel, *Heer Waris Shah* (Lahore, 1991).
Seema Alavi ed., *The Eighteenth Century in India* (OUP, 2007).
Shafi Aqeel, *Punjabi Adab Key Panch Qadim Shair* (Karachi : Tarraqi-i-Urdu, 1994).
Talal Asad, *The Idea of an Anthropology of Islam*, Occasional Papers Series (Washington, DC : Centre for Contemporary Arab Studies, Georgetown University, 1986), pp.14-17.
Varis Shah, *The Adventures of Hir and Ranjha*. Tr. Charles F. Usborne (London : P. Owen, 1973).
Waris Shah *International Conference Report*, World Punjabi Congress (Lahore, 2005).

Hameedullah Hashmi

The Great Sufi Saint Baba Shaikh Farid
A Study in the Life, Teachings and Achievements

Baba Farid's grandfather Qazi Shu'aib, disappointed by the political conditions in Kabul migrated to Lahore[1] around 1157 A.D. with his three sons. He settled in Multan[2] as Chief Gazi at Kothewal One of his three sons was Jamaluddin Sulaiman, father of Shaikh Farid.

Jamaluddin Sulaiman married Qarsum Bibi, a daughter of Shaikh Wajih-ud-din Khojendi in Kothewal. Baba Farid's mother Qursum Bibi was a lady of fervent piety and patience. It was in the lap of his mother that his education began. She generated that spark of divine love in him which lasted throughout his life and later on which developed and dominated his entire personality. From the very beginning of his career in Kothewal he became well known for his intense devotion and piety.

Baba Farid (Farid-ud-Din Mas'ud *Ganj-i-Shakkar* was born in 571 A.H/1175 A.D. or according to others two years earlier in 569 A.H./1173 A.D. There is a dispute about the year of the Christian era as to Shaikh Farid's birth. The more commonly acceptable view puts it at 1173. Some traced his descent from Farrukhh Shah King, a noble of Kabul, but others from the Caliph Umar.

Early Education:

Baba Farid's first teacher whose influence was most lasting on him was his mother, Qarsum Bibi. Baba Farid had his early education at Kothewal and went to Multan[3] at the age of eighteen years to receive higher education from Maulana Minhaj-ud-din Tirmidhi who used to teach in his mosque/*Madrasah* near the *Sara-i-Halwai*. Farid committed to memorize the Holy Quran and recited it once in twenty-four hours. There he met and took *Bait* (initiation) at the hands of Qutb-ud-din Bakhtiyar Kaki whom he accompanied to Delhi. Under his inspired guidance, he completed his mystic training, living in the cell of a *Khanqah* of Khawaja Qutb-ud-din Bakhtiar Kaki at Delhi. There he met Khawaji Mu'in-ud-din Chishti and was blessed by both the masters and master's Master —Bakhtiyar Kaki and Mu'in-uddin Chishti. It was a unique honour in the history of the *Chishtiyah* order *(Silsilah)*. Khawaja Mu'in-ud-din Chishti Ajmeri happened to visit Delhi; he inquired about Baba Farid and seeing him remarked, "Baba Bakhtiyar! You have caught a noble falcon which will not build his nest except on the holy tree of paradise. Farid is a lamp that will illuminate the *Silsilah* of the *Derveshes*." Khawaja Ajmeri bestowed upon him his robe and Shaikh Qutb-ud-din conferred his *dastar* (turban) and other articles of *Khilafat*. Baba Farid enjoyed the unique privilege in the *Chishti* order of being initiated both by the director, Shaikh Qutb-ud-din and the director of the director (Shaikh Mo'in-ud-din Chishti).

Sufism:

While Sufism or Islamic mysticism is traceable to the contemplative aspect of the Prophet's life and while Hazrat Ali (R.A) is regarded for all the *Silsalas* as the first Sufi, the genesis of *Silsilas* is traceable to the post-*Umayyad* period, i.e. the second century Hijra, 7th century A.D. moved by compassion at the *Ummayad* atrocities, perpetrated for 90 years (41-132/661-750) on the innocent inhabitants of the sacred places. The Muslim conscience was fully exploited by the *Abbasid* agents in Iraq and Iran. They subverted the *Umayyad* throne and the scepter that passed into the hands of the *Umayyads* was the philosophy of Hazrat Abu Zar Ghafari (d-32/652), Hassan Basri (d-110/728), Ibrahim Bin Adham (d-161/777) and other who had held the material world in contempt and had emphasized for every sinner the importance of *Tauba* (repentance before being overtaken by death. Other feeders arose during the *Khilafat* of *Abbasid* in the third century Hijra/10th century A.D. such as Zulnun Misri (d-245/85) and Mansur Hallaj (d-309/920) who spun out mystic philosophy so elaborately that a curriculum of service of *Sufi Ibadat* evolved, comprising the technique of *Hal* and *Maqam* (literally state and stage) and also the doctrines of

Hulul and *Tanasukh* (transmigration). In this manner, the foundation was laid of the different *Sufi* schools each with a distinct philosophy. Ghazzali who lived in the 5th century Hijra/11th century A.D. treated *Tasawuf* (Such being the Arabic name for mysticism) as a substantive science. He defined the abstruse term of *Sufism* and pointed out the difference between *Ulema* and *Mashaikh*- the former being the *Ulema-i-Zahir*, and later *Ulema-i-Batin*. In this manner, he removed the conflict that had been raging between *Shari'at* and *Tariqat*.

In the seventh century Hijra/13th century A.D. appeared Ibne-Arabi (d-646/1248), Shaikh Shihab-ud-din Soharwardi (d-632/1234) and Jalalu'ddin Rumi (672/1273). They explained further Islamic mysticism or *Tariqat* and expounded the meaning of the discipline of the soul and the role of emotions. Ibn-e-Arabi stressed the *Wahdat-e-Wajud* principle or the pantheistic aspect of *Sufism* and emphasized the manifestation of the divine being everywhere and in everything. Shahab-ud-din Suharwardi expounded the principle of *Khanqah* life and Jalal-ud-din Rumi gave a fillip to *Sufi* pantheism. All this was approved by Shaikh Farid-ud-din Ganj-i-Shaker who associated himself with the above-mentioned *Sufi* thinkers of the Muslim world, and as a token of his regard for them used the standard work of Shaikh Shihab-ud-din Soharwardi entitled *Awariful Maarif* as a text book in his *Khanqah*/seminary at Ajodhan. Such were the years of *Tasawuf* prepared in the Muslim countries of western Asia, and the same, brought into India, by the *Mashaikh* gave rise to different *silsilahs*. But the real cause behind the rise of *silsilahs* was the wholesale destruction of Islamic culture at the hands of the Mongol hordes in 657/1258. Since the Mongols had destroyed the territorial foundations of Muslim society, the *Sufi* fathers rebuilt the same on a different plane. They gave their social system new names and spiritual values. Taking the universe as a unit they divided it into *Wilayats* and organized the *Silsilahs* in such a manner that each *Silsilah* should be able to promote the *Khanqah* life. There were six significant *Silsilahs*.i.e. *Chistiya, Suharwardiya, Qadiriya, Naqshbandiya, Firdausiya* and *Shattariya*.

The *Chishttiya* order was founded in the village Chisht near Herat in 940/1533 by Khwaja Abu Ishaq of Syria; the Suhrwardiya was founded by Abdul Qadir Suharwardi about 565/1169 in the town of *Jibal*, the ancient Media; Qadiriya was founded by Abdul Qadir Gilani in 562/1166 near Baghdad; the *Naqshbandiya* was founded by Khwaja

Bahau'din Naqshbandi of Turkistan about 792 A.H./1389 A.D. The Firdausiya was founded by Najumu'din Kubra of Bokhara about 633 A.H./1235 A.D. The *Shattariya* came into existence in Iran in the year 890/1485 and was introduced into India by Shah who died in Malwa (664/1265) His disciple Muhammad Ghaus of Gwalior made the *Shattariya* order better known by securing the professing of different religions and speaking different languages.

Farid as a Saint:

A teenager saint as he then was, Farid had so regulated his time that he was performing his *Namaz* (Prayers) *Qiyam* (Vigils) and *Saum* (Fasting) at the proper hour and without deviation, and he also performed the *Salat-i-Ma'kus* which looked like the Hindu *Sadhus* penance. They hang their heads downwards, suspended from a high tree and chant mantras. Shaikh Farid performed a similar penance as he was a true lover *(Aasihq)* of God and had a burning desire for a true UNION *(Wisal)* with him. In this way he believed he would remove all earthly hurdles that had been obviating his much desired union with the Master of the souls, the Almighty Creator. Another way that he adopted to precipitate the UNION was to observe the *Saum-i-tary*— a three-day fast during which he abstained from all food and drink. At the close of each day, he broke the fast with only a few drops of water. When at last the fast was over, Shaikh Farid felt extremely hungry. He ate a piece of bread that was offered him by a passer-by. He felt uneasy and vomitted it immediately. Later, he reported the matter to Shaikh Qutbu'din Bakhtiyar Kaki who reprimanded him, saying "Farid! You have broken your fast with the bread that was brought by a drunkard. By God's grace, that bread did not stay in your stomach. Go and observe the fast again. This time break your three-day-long fast with whatever appears from *Ghaib* (the unknown)." Shaikh Farid acted accordingly. At the end of this newly stipulated fast, some pebbles came into his hands. He put them into his mouth and they turned into sugar in his mouth. But considering this transformation as satanic, the Shaikh spaty that sugar out of his mouth and prayed earnestly to God for the remission of his sins. In the morning he related this incident to Shaikh Bakhtiyar Kaki who said, "You did the right thing by breaking your fast with the pebbles. Whatever appears from *Ghaib* is good. Go, you will be sweet like sugar. From this penance he earned the epithet of *Ganj-i-Shakar*.

Ganj-i-Shakar:

The Shaikh was popular not only for his teachings, but also for his miracles, which made people see in him the divine light. On the basis of a number of such incidents he became known as *Ganj-i-Shakar*- an epithet which means "treasure-house of sweets". Ferishta gives various versions of the derivation of this epithet. These versions are as follows:

Being weak from fasting, the Shaikh, once while on his way to his spiritual guide, saw his foot slipped and he fell in the mud, since those were the days of the rains. Some of the mud, consequently, entered his mouth. But to his utter surprise, it was converted into sugar. His guide had had intuition of the event. He told him that the Almighty had designed him to be a storehouse of sweet things and would preserve him in that condition. On return to his house, in that condition, he found that the epithet *Ganj-i-Shakar* had spread among the people so well that all those who met him, called him by that epithet.

Another incident substantiating this epithet is associated with the Shaikh's meeting with some female gypsies *(Banjaran)*, who, at that time, were on their way to Delhi with some bags of salt. They requested the saint to bless their bags so that they might sell the salt bags with profit. The saint touched the bags one by one and, on their arrival in Delhi, they found the bags full of sugar.

The third story also is connected with the Shaikh's childhood. While as a child, the Shaikh's mother, in order to teach him to offer his prayers regularly every morning, told him that the Almighty gave sweets to those who offered their morning prayers regularly. She would put some sugar wrapped in paper under his pillow without his knowing. The child thus rewarded formed the habit of offering his morning prayer regularly. When he was twelve years of age, she thought it was time to discontinue the practice, yet the Shaikh continued to get sugar supplied to him by the Almighty.

Gunj-i-Shakar or *Shakar Gunj* (Sugar-store) which became the regular epithet for Shaikh Farid was the term, first used by Shaikh Qutb-ud-din Bakhtiyar Kaki. Afterwards, it was used by all. Till today, the Shaikh is remembered as Gunj-i-Shakar.

Apart from the cause, behind it, which has been mentioned above, there are two stories- one given in the *Ajaibul Asfar* (P-8) and the other in Prince Dara Shikoh's *Safinatul Auliya*. According to the former, Baba Farid, being the title used by Shaikh Alau'ddin Ajodhani- saw a caravan of merchants once passing nearby and carrying bags full of sugar. Baba Farid enquired what the caravan was carrying. The merchants thought that Baba Farid was an ordinary beggar and would ask for only a little sugar, if he came to know about the contents of the bags. So they told him that they were carrying salt in the bags. Baba Farid replied, "Let it be salt". The caravan then proceeded to its destination where when the bags being opened, they were found to contain salt instead of sugar. The merchants then came to Baba Farid and supplicated for his blessings. He prayed; and the salt was then transformed into sugar. According to the *Safinatual Auliya* (P. 163) Baba Farid had become so thin and lean by continuous fasting and his body had thereby become so pure that whatever he put into his mouth to allay his hunger including subsequently. The Shaikh, as he grew old, had in him the miraculous power of turning into sugar whatever he put into his mouth. Even clay and stones, put into his mouth, were turned into sugar, it is reported. Owing to this miracle he was known as *Gunj-i-Shakar* or *Shakargunj*.

Stay at Hansi and Ajodhan;

After completing his course of mystic discipline at Delhi, Baba Farid settled at Hansi in the Punjab where once came Maulana Nur Turk, an excellent speaker and an eminent mystic on a visit here introduced Baba Farid to the public by addressing him as *Sarraf-i-Sukhan* (the appraiser of true speech). Shaikh Jamal-ud-din joined his discipline and lived at Hansi for 12 years. Baba Farid lived at Hansi for 19 or 20 years. The Shaikh took leave of his master and went to Hansi. Shaikh Kutb-ud-din Bakhtiyar Kaki allowed and said, "It has been pre-ordained that you will not be present at the time of my death. On the death of his mystic teacher Khawaja Qutb-ud-din Bakhtiyar Kaki, Shaikh Farid-ud-din went to Delhi, where he received the mystic regalia of Khawaja Qutb-ud-din from Qazi Hami-ud-din Nagauri. But a few months after Sultan Iltutmush also died (1236) and political intrigues began. To keep himself away from this, Baba Farid left Delhi for the lonely place of Hansi and further to avoid the stream of visitors, the

Shaikh shifted to Kothewal and then again to Ajodhan now known as Pakpattan meaning "Sacred Ferry in his honour where he lived till he died in 1265. He spent some 60 years of his life at Ajodhan.

Ajodhan was in those days the ferry of the Sutlej at the confluence of roads from Dera Ghazi Khan and Dera Ismail Khan. But the chief reason behind the Shaikh's desire to choose it as the site of his *Khanqah* was the fact that Ajodhan then comprised a majority of downtrodden and misguided Hindus, who needed a help and guidance. Also it abounded in unexplored forest where dangerous reptiles and animals had been attacking the innocent inhabitants. Once it is said that Shaikh Farid himself was attacked by a ferocious snake and subsequently, his revered mother, Qarsum Bibi, was killed and eaten by a tiger. The local Hindus welcomed the saint who used to sit amongst them under the trees (*Siyarul Auliya*).

Because of his fame, he earned the animosity of local officers, *jagirdars* and even of the *Qazi*, and the governor of Ajodhan. But as he cared little for worldly power and government patronage none could do him harm. For want of food and clothing, his family members had to live a very hard life and suffered from starvation. The Shaikh lived a life of hunger and starvation. Once Shaikh Nizam-ud-din Auliya purchased some salt on credit and prepared *delhas*. When the dish was served, Shaikh Farid asked him to remove the dish from the *Jama'at Khanah* and admonished him thus: "*Derveshes* prefer dying of starvation to incurring any debt for the satisfaction of their (baser) desires. Debt and resignation are poles apart and cannot subsist together."

Whatever came as *futuh* to the Shaikh's *Jama'at Khana* at Ajodhan was distributed and nothing was kept for the next day because that meant lack of trust in God. Just opposite to the *Chishtiya* principle of *tuwakkul* the *Suhrwardiya Khanqah* of Shaikh Baha-ud-din Zakariya at Multan was a sumptuous palace and well furnished.

Baba Farid's *Jammat Khana* was a small building of unbaked bricks where all inmates slept and prayed on the ground. No discrimination of any kind was permitted. All had to live under the same conditions. The inmates had different duties assigned to them. Some fetched water, others collected firewood. Some went to the forest to pluck *pelu* and *delha*. It was through the efforts of all inmates that a saltless dish could be prepared. "It was an *Eid* day for us if we had a square meal in the

Jamat Khana of Shaikh Farid", Shaikh Nizam-ud-din Auliya used to say. "And what type of people had collected together in *Jamaat Khana* of the Saint-government servants, *Ulema*, businessmen-all disgusted with their professions and longing for a life of spiritual solace and satisfaction. They rejected the hectic life of the world torn by dissensions and disputes and devoted their time and energy to building up their personalities in consonance with the highest tradition of the *Chishti Silsilah*. Let us not forget that it was at a time when ugly distinctions divided people. The Turkish aristocracy lived a life of luxury and affluence, while the common people toiled and struggled for a loaf of bread. The Turkish *sultans* dismissed the low-born people from public office. What a contrast to the ideas of Shaikh Farid! He declared as a corrective to this corroding atmosphere. "If you want greatness, associate with the downtrodden." To him all human beings were equal, made of the self-same clay regardless of race, creed, colour or status. Once a place of great importance as the meeting place of the great western roads from Dera Ghazi Khan to Dera Ismail Khan, Ajodhan was now an area with a deserted look. Its people were hard-hearted and stingy, and lacked in education and culture. Except *pelu* and *delah* no fruit was found in the surrounding forests. It was an ideal place for a Sufi anxious to work out the principles of his *Silsilah* and try their efficacy in a hostile and barren locality. It may be pointed out in this context that it was Shaikh Farid who consolidated and crystallized the teachings of the *Chishti Silsilah* in India. Shaikh Moin-ud-din Chishti of Ajmer had to spend most of his time in clearing the ground and sowing the seeds while, Shaikh Qutb-ud-din Bakhtiyar Kaki did not live long. Shaikh Farid, who unique as it was in the history of the *Chishti Silsilah*, was blessed by both the saints simultaneously, gave a form and content to the *Chishti* ideology and articulated it as a powerful factor in the life of the people. His eminence in the history of Indo-Muslim mysticism rests primarily on his ceaseless activity as a teacher of higher morality. He gave a pan-Indian status to his order and sent his disciples to distant parts of the country to propagate his ideal of salvation through service of mankind.

At Ajodhan Shaikh Farid married and had a family there. The Shaikh had five sons and three daughters, namely Khwajah Nasir-ud-din, Khawajah Shahab-ud-din, Shaikh Sulaiman, Shaikh Nizam-ud-din, Shaikh Ya'qub, Bibi Masturah, Bibi Sharifah and Bibi Fatimah. Among his Khalifahs were Shaikh Najib-ud-din Mutawakkil, Maulana Badr-ud-din Is-haq, Shaikh Jamal-ud-din Hanswi, Shaikh Nizam-ud-din Auliya, Shaikh Arif, Shaikh Ali Sabir, Maulana Fakhar-ud-din Safahani. Khawaja Muin-ud-din's disciple in the second generation was Baba Shaikh Farid, who in his turn had the great Shaikh Nizamuddin Auliya as his disciple. Thus these holy men began in this country a tradition of piety, which was grounded in the spiritual doctrines of the *Chishti Sufi* order.

Stories about his marriage with a daughter of Balban, fondly circulated by the author of *Jawahir-i-Faridi* during the time of Jahangir, are a fiction and the story attributing a prediction about the accession of Balban is an interpolation of a later date. His real attitude towards Balban is reflected in a brief Arabic letter reluctantly addressed to the Sultan. When a person who was in great distress insisted upon it. Without any regal titles, he addressed the Sultan thus: "I referred his matter first to God, and then to you. If you will grant anything to him, the real giver is God, but you will get the credit for it. If you do not give anything, the real authority is God and you are helpless in the matter." Every word of his brief letter is dignified and shows the extent to which the Shaikh maintained his self- respect and dignity before the rulers of the day.

When Balban, says Mir Khurd, author of the *Siyarul Auliya,* appeared before Shaikh Farid in his *Khanqah* at Ajodhan with the object of seeking his blessings before ascending the throne, the Shaikh wished him well, saying.

"*Faridun* was neither an angel, nor was he made of ambergris. He obtained the throne through his bounty and generosity. If you do justice and be generous you would become a *Faridun*." But the Shaikh did not accept the gold which, Balban had desired to present to him.

Shaikh Farid spent his life in voluntary poverty, guiding and serving the people. He was accessible to the humblest, whose sorrows he allayed with the sweet touch of his personality. He, made himself a bridge of understanding and harmony between Muslims and non-Muslims and is known to have had spiritual commerce with *yogis* and other spiritual teachers.

Guru Nanak, born three centuries after Shaikh Farid, sought to unite our people through adherence to great universal ideas. He made the spiritual compositions of Shaikh Farid a part of the tradition which he himself initiated. These compositions, in beautiful Multani Punjabi, from part of the Granth Sahib, the Sikh scriptures, and are venerated by all Sikhs. Shaikh Farid thus, whose name literally means 'unique', has the unique distinction of having been accepted as a teacher in a tradition other than his own. He is also the first recorded poet in the Punjabi language.

Shaikh Farid's Period:

On the political background of Shaikh Farid's period, Dr. Mohan Singh Diwana in his book *History of Punjabi Literature* writes. "The twelfth century saw not only the consolidation of Muslim rule in India with its capital transferred from Lahore to Delhi but also the spread of early Islamic mysticism which from the three centers, Multan, Lahore and Delhi, radiated its light with the greatest force and refulgence, never equaled since. Shaikh Farid belongs to the age when Muslim rule was dominating the Indian society. Islam was being preached by some *Sufi* saints. They were preaching their own ideology for the salvation of the people.

Philosophy of *Sufism*

The philosophy of *Sufism* is a product of the reaction against caste-fanaticism among followers of Islam. Shaikh Farid believed in this philosophy because this was based on human values. This philosophy is part of the struggle against Muslim rulers and their officials who preached the religion by force. The philosophy of Shaikh Farid followed the principles of those *Sufi* saints who raised voice against intolerance.

They openly declared that God was not to be found in mosques and *Masjids*. For achieving God-consciousness one should have a burning faith, all conquering love and purity. There should be no hypocrisy. When the rulers of the Islamic countries tried to suppress the teachings of the *Sufi* Saints, they failed. It could not be checked by all their efforts. The teachings crossed the frontiers and entered the neighbouring countries. Shaikh Farid was the first to start this *Sufism* in

India. He advocated the principles of Sufism through the medium of Panjabi language.

Principles of Sufism:

1. Love of God
2. Search for *Murshid* (Guru).
3. Sense of separation.
4. Renunciation (not from the world but from the worldly temptations.)
5. Condemnation of religious ceremonial fanaticism. 6. Transition of Life.

Philosophy of Shaikh Farid

"According to Sufi philosophy, Reality is the universal will, the true Knowledge, eternal light and supreme beauty, whose nature is self manifestation, reflected in the mirror of the universe." *(Outlines of Islamic Culture by Shushtery)*.

The philosophy of Shaikh Farid is entirely scientific spiritual philosophy. Shaikh Farid never avoided domestic life; he sought spiritual attainment while living in the family. Farid never followed the philosophy of escapism. Guru Arjan Dev selected the compositions of Shaikh Farid for the *Adi-Granth* only due to the philosophy of Shaikh Farid which was in line with *Gurmat* philosophy. One of the couplets of Shaikh Farid explains that there is no use of wandering in forests in search of God. God is always realized from within. It is an internal light which is attained through self-realisation.

The spiritual philosophy of Shaikh Farid revolves around the attainment of the highest bliss. It can only be achieved through pure thoughts, a controlled mind and by working without expectations of reward. Shaikh Farid believed that the reward was the output of one's work one had done. Shaikh Farid stresses that the man who sows a seed will surely get its fruit. It was not possible to plant a mango tree and hope to harvest grapes. If one spins the wool how one can get silk? After cutting down a mango tree, you cannot plant a *neem* tree in its place and expect to reap the tasty mangoes from it, even if you water the *neem* with milk. So, *Sufi* philosophy believes that reward is the result of the work you have put in.

Story tellers harm the personality of a great saint through their extravagant and irrational praises. Shaikh Farid was such a dominant personality that thousands of Hindus were fascinated by his teachings and many of them embraced Islam. What the sword of the Muslim rulers could not do that much what Shaikh Farid did that by his magnanimous conduct.

Love:

"The *Sufi* theory of spiritual development is based on complete self-abnegation and absolute absorption in contemplation of God. The *Sufi* believes that by this absorption and mental concentration he can attain a far closer communion with the Divinity and truer cognition of Truth.[4]" So, love is the vital force of spiritual life according to *Sufi* saints. Love is nature's glittering robe, smile of heaven and joy of the world. Love is the golden link, the only tie which unites man to the divine and man to man. Love is, therefore, not merely an uncontrolled or extreme emotion but it is something which can only be experienced and felt. What we can do for another is the test of the power. What we can suffer for others is the test of love. So, Shaikh Farid believes in love which stands like a rock when the problem, suffering and the challenges come. Describing true love Shaikh Farid writes:-

"The street is full of mud and it is raining heavily. The destination of the lover's shelter is far distant. The beloved has promised to meet him. Now the question comes should she stay at home or go to see her lover?"

Shaikh Farid himself replies, "If there is true love, problems and sufferings become very minor compared to the attraction. Let the rain pour more heavily, let the clothes be drenched, the true beloved must go to see her master."

In the words of A.M.A. Shushtery[5], "Man is the microcosm in whom divine attributes are manifested in most imperfect diminutive form. God is eternal beauty and the nature of beauty is self-manifestation and desire to be loved."

The essence of God's essence is love, revealed Himself to Himself. "If you cleave the heart of one drop of water there will issue from it a hundred pure Oceans. Love is not a confined term, love means to give away all that you have, to him whom you love. You should attribute everything to him so that nothing remains to you of your own. Conquer desire through the power of love; love God for His own sake and not for any reward. If love is based on reward it becomes 'selfish', Shaikh Farid asserts:

"That ego and love are not on speaking terms, the former takes one to hell and the latter to heavenly directions.

".....the all important factor in this work is Love, — a Love, which as we have already seen, rises from the seen and temporal to the Unseen and External."

The Sufi does not sink into "nothingness", but into 'Omnipresence', into the universal divinity. 'He becomes' an *Insan-e-Kamil*- the perfect man."

Self Realisation

Shaikh Farid believes that weeding out the wild growth from the field increases, the yield in increased. If the desires are curbed, the soul will step towards self-realisation. God is not to be found in the woods, he is to be realized from within. "Soul is like a mirror, with reason only part of it is polished and only part of the mirror is reflected in it; but when it is wholly polished, it reflects everything[6]. G.R. Bhai explaining realization writes, "There are pearls in the deep sea, but you must hazard all perils to get them. If you fail to get at them by a single dive, don't conclude that sea is without them. Dive again and again and you are sure to be rewarded in the end. So, also in the quest for the Lord, if your first attempt to see Him is fruitless, do not loose heart and you are sure to realize Him at last.

"Polished soul becomes like a mirror and it reflects inner self. Do not go to the woods in the search of God. God is always in the procession of life and not somewhere in isolation. There are some spiritual steps for self-realisation. According to Sufi Saints, "The spiritual life has often been described as a journey and the maps of the road are many. One "gives seven stages or stations." 1.Repentance. 2. Abstinence. 3. Renunciation. 4. Poverty. 5. Patience. 6. Trust in God. 7. Satisfaction[7].

The absolute bliss the enlightenment which ends all fears comes when you place your trust in your inner possibilities and understand that you are the transcendent flame that is burning to enlighten your inner-self.

Death-Consciousness

"Man's origin was from dust, lowly. But his rank was raised above that of other creatures. God breathed into him his Spirit[8].

Death is not the end of life, life persists even after death. All the *Sufi* saints were death conscious. They meant that physical existence in this world is temporary and after some time this body will go under the dust. Why not to make the most of the time, man has got in his hands.

Death lays her icy hands on everybody. Fear of death is not only an alarm to the man but it is a boon if man becomes death conscious. Those people are really blessed who accept the challenge of death. Shaikh Farid believed:

Worldly power, position and pelf are vague. These don't come to the rescue of man at the last hour. Consciousness of death is must, because it is inevitable. Too much worldly involvement carries the man away from his real goal. When the divine light goes out of this body it descends into dust.

Time does not favour anybody. It destroys everything later or sooner. Before the time comes to perish, why not to make the necessary spiritual awakening? Icy hands of the death won't spare anybody.

Shaikh Farid's poetry gives the reflection and image of the pain symbolized in inspiration for the higher purpose. Prof. Diwan Singh writes that the absolute impression of Farid's poetry is melancholism, pathos and sadness." There are two attitudes towards life, one is optimistic and the other is pessimistic. These are two different angles of life which are so integrated that it becomes difficult to separate them. Sadness is very near to life. Optimism is provisional, it is not permanent. Sadness is the real controller of life, happiness is only a fleeting shadow. It is an ideal expectation. Nobody gets the permanent relief in life; everybody is tolerating the grief for the sake of happiness.

Sadness is the sentiment which is very much near to the spiritual element. Shaikh Farid stresses sadness because it is the real remedy which gives reconciliation to face the problems of life. It opens the door for spiritual discovery also. All the mystics and *Sufi* Saints adopted sadness and renounced worldly desires. Prior says, "The artist never writes" It is spontaneous flow which gives words to the inner feelings:

"Verses come from Heav'n like inward light.
Mere human pains can never come by it;
The God, not we, the poem makes,
We only tell folk what he speaks."

Shaikh Farid and *Sufism*:

Prof. Sir Hamilton says: "Baba Farid is a seminal personality in the development of the Islamic mystical movement in India."

Actually Shaikh Farid is not a true Sufi-poet, because first factor on which the foundation of *Sufism* stands is the voice against fanaticism. Philosophy of *Sufism* is entirely based on self-realisation through love *(Ishk)* temples, mosques and other religious centers are not the dwelling place of God.

Baba Farid conventionally asserts upon man that *Namaz* in the mosque five times a day is essential. Baba Farid goes up to the extent that man who does not come in the mosques to pray five times is a dog. By calling the man as dog who does not go to the Shrine to pay homage, he also shows his conventionalism.

Baba Farid avoids confusion and contradiction to live an ideal life. God may not be in the churches, mosques and temples but the faith in these holy shrines certainly gives contentment, a peace of mind and calmness. Farid was a philosopher poet who gave call to the conscience. If a man acquires all the knowledge of world, but if he does not know himself, he is actually ignorant.

S.T. Coleridge says, "There was never a great poet who has not at the same time been a profound philosopher."

Baba Farid emphasizes the religious ceremonies only to develop the concentration. Concentration leads to the eliminations of impurities and cleans the mind of externalized sensual desires.

This purity, bliss, blessedness and peace make up the atmosphere of the state of meditation.

Meditation is an exercise to balance the mind,

It is best way to set the mind at rest,
Gives it the rest without doubt.

Baba Farid used to be in the meditate for hours together. So, Farid's philosophy is an essence of Absolute Reality.

Language of Shaikh Farid:

The language of Shaikh Farid bears the influence of many languages. We find much influence of Persian on the language of Shaikh Farid. His language is very sweet. *Lehndi* has given a polishing colour to the compositions of Shaikh Farid. Many words of *Sanskrit* are also found in the vocabulary of Farid.

Brij Bhasha has also influenced his verse. All these languages very much befit his writing. Farid selects his words like pearls to be fixed in the necklace of ancient Punjabi poetry, "Best words in their best order." This is the secret of the good poetry Farid has produced.

"The synthetic and magical power of Shaikh Farid's poetry lifts the wings of his imagination and reveals the secret of humanity in all its glory."

Linguistic survey of Shaikh Farid's composition reveals that he was the master of old Punjabi language. He was the source from which the fountain of modern Punjabi literature has flown. Symbolism in Farid's poetry is really marvelous.

"To set forth invisible or audible likeness what cannot be really or fully expressed to the physical eye or ear, or even clearly conceived by the limited faculties of the human mind. All language is in the last resort symbolic, and religious language to an especial degree, for it endeavours to present a mystery." [9]

In Farid's poetry the beloved stands for soul and the lover is a symbol of God. Meeting of the beloved and lover is a symbol of Union of the soul with the Sublime.

"Symbolism has become almost a style. Such writings carry a double meaning. One is the outward and apparent, the other is inner and real." [10]

Many reputed writers have paid rich tributes to Shaikh Farid.

Teachings:-

Baba Shaikh Farid lived his life at a time when vast revolutionary changes were occurring in the history of our land and those in our immediate neighborhood to the north-west. In that period Rajput hegemony over Northern India was breaking down, and the rule of certain Turkish dynasties was being established at Delhi and further east. But in the lands where Muslim culture had a glorious flowering such as Turkistan, Kabul, Khorasan, Iran and Iraq, the newly assertive Mongol tribes from Central Asia were bringing about vast devastation. These very tribes later, during the life-time of Shaikh Farid himself, under the conqueror Changez Khan and his grandson Halagu Khan overran the whole of west Asia and penetrated as far as Eastern Europe. In this period large numbers of Muslim scholars, divines and Sufis left their homes in Samarkand, Bokhara, Kabul, Herat and Ghazni and sought shelter in our country, which promised a peaceful atmosphere. In the high traditions of our country, these refugees were welcomed and they established their religious and missionary centers all over Punjab and other parts of northern India. The famous Khawaja Moin-ud-din Chishti, whose shrine at Ajmer is the principal pilgrim centre in India, came in the course of this wave of migrations during the reign of Prithviraj Chauhan, king of Delhi and Ajmer.

Scholars speak about the significance of Sufi mysticism. And mysticism has its own metaphors. But the simplest person can understand the relationship of life to death in lines such as described by Farid:

"Life is the bride; death the bridegroom will carry her way."

Shaikh Farid has been called the first great poet of the Punjabi language. Expressions from the common speech of the region coloured his poetry. He spoke of the songs of the flying cranes of autumn, the forest-fire of summer and lightning flashes of *Sawan*. With its music and imagery, poetry speaks to the heart. Kabir and Tulsidas have transformed great truths into thoughts which have given a philosophy of life to many in our country and abroad. What gives such lasting fame and permanence to the life and teachings of Shaikh Farid? In one of his very fascinating letters Maulana Azad observes that the value of an individual's life lies in the ideals that it sets before it, and in the sincerity of purpose with which it is pursued. Shaikh Farid's ideal of life flowed from his concept of religion which was revolutionary in its content and dynamic in its potentialities. His God was neither a theological myth nor a logical abstraction of unity, but an all-embracing personality present in his ethical, intellectual and aesthetic experience and furnishing the inspiration for creating an ideal realm of values in a distressed and struggling world. He strove to understand him in His dynamic relation to this finite world. It made him a citizen of that universal society in which God is the supreme intelligence and all human beings are his manifestations. He sought to reach the creator through his creation and identified religion with service of humanity. Again and again he emphasized the fact that faith in God means "Love of His creatures."

This revolutionary concept of religion has been thus explained by his disciple, Shaikh Nizam-ud-din Aulliya: Devotion of God is of two kinds; *Lazmi* devotion (intransitive) and *Muta'addi* (transitive), the benefit which accrues is confined to the devotee alone. This type of devotion includes praying, fasting, pilgrimage to Mecca, recitation of religious formulae, turning over the beads of rosary etc. the *Muta'addi* devotion, on the contrary, brings advantage and comforts to others, it is performed by spending money on others, showing affection to people and by others means through which a man strives to help his fellow human beings. The reward of *Muta'addi* devotion is endless and limitless."

This concept of salvation through service brought the Sufis into close touch with the masses that they strove to help, to educate and to reform. Shaikh Farid used to say that a mystic becomes dangerously egocentric if the overflow of divine love in him does not enrich the sources of his humanism.

Shaikh Farid articulated this concept of religion in the country's spiritual life, and with this ideal inspiring his life, he devoted all his energies to reducing human misery by inculcating a sense of moral values and by eliminating 'fear' from the human heart which is at the root of all human miseries. A careful psychological analysis of the people who brought their problems to him and the way he tackled them, will bear out this conclusion. Those who attribute asceticism or inertia to him do grave injustice to his thought and misunderstand the core of his activity. His was a life of faith, confidence, suffering and struggle. His advice to his disciples was:

"You will get honour in proportion to the pains that you undertake in you work."

He believed that a heart overflowing with emotion was instrumental in the progress of the soul. May God give you *dard* —with these words he blessed his favourite disciples. Secondly, Baba Farid strove ceaselessly to build up healthy and morally autonomous personalities in his disciples by removing their inner conflicts and tensions and by developing emotional integration' wherein lay the solution of the problems of a multi-religious, multi-lingual and multi-racial society. When a visitor presented a pair of scissors to him, he said: "I need a needle, not a pair of scissors. I sew and join, I do not cut and separate." The remark was symbolic of his efforts. He brought human hearts nearer and closer, believing that, "Having one heart is better than speaking one language." He was the first Muslim saint of the Punjab who prescribed for his disciples' religious litanies and formulae in the Punjabi language. He believed that what obstructed emotional integration was hypocrisy which drew a screen over one's personality and hindered its development on sound lines. Contradiction in one's feelings, thought and action was the root cause of all evils. He attempted through his own methods a harmony between these three. His own life was an example and an inspiration to his followers. After his death, his closest disciple and son-in-law, Shaikh Badr-ud-din Ishq was asked about the qualities of the Shaikh. He did not refer to his miracles or vigils. He said: "There was complete identity in his thought and action and action in his exterior and his interior." This was the highest achievement of a morally integrated personality.

Shaikh Farid reacted sharply if he found in any of his disciples any trace of arrogance or pride, intellectual or otherwise. Shaikh Nizam-ud-din Aulliya reached Ajodhan after having won his laurels in the highest academic circles of Delhi. One day when Baba Farid was giving lessons in *Awarif-ul-Ma'arif* to his disciples, Shaikh Nizam-ud-din Aulliya interrupted him. Shaikh Farid discerned in this a trace of intellectual arrogance and punished him by withdrawing his favours for a few days. The admonition had its effects and Shaikh Nizam-ud-din remembered the incident all through his life. One of his sayings recorded in the

Siyar-ul-Auliya is: If you want to make the entire world your enemy, develop pride." But at the same time he used to say:

"Consider haughtiness necessary in dealing with the proud."

Advice of Farid:

Shaikh Farid advised his disciples to develop large-heartedness and honesty in all human relationships. His advice to Shaikh Nizam-ud-din Auliya was twofold: (a) try to placate your enemies and (b) fulfill your obligations. He believed in non-violence as the only method to solve differences in social life.

Through his own behaviour he demonstrated that pacifism and non-violence in the cult of the strong and not the defence of the weak. The *Guru Granth* contains his saying:

"Farid, return thou good for evil,
Bear no revenge in thy heart:
Thus will thy body be free of maladies,
and thy life blest."

At a time when *Qulandars* and *Jawaliqs* made attempts on his life and the *Ulema* criticized him mercilessly, he forgave them with a magnanimity which put even the offenders to shame. It was in his *Jamaat Khana* that Shaikh Nizam-ud-din Auliya, who was known in his earlier days for his superb debating talent and was called *Mehfil-Shikan*, learnt how to discuss conflicting points of view without creating bitterness.

One is constantly reminded of this remark while assessing the impact of Shaikh Farid on our society and culture. His life is one long story of quiet but persistent human endeavour to bring various culture groups and religious communities closer and nearer to each other and to inculcate in them a feeling that all humans should believe in humanism, and restless concern for the weak and the downtrodden in society irrespective of caste, colour or creed, gave to his mystic activity a depth and a dimension which touched the deepest chords of India's soul.

Though seven long centuries have passed since he breathed his last and during this period empires have been set up and pulled down and the country has moved from one phase of life to another; mediaeval institutions have yielded place to socialistic patterns of life, his message still goes on echoing down the corridors treasured with love and respect by Muslims, Sikhs and Hindus alike.

In Punjab his impact was the deepest when Guru Nanak appeared on the scene. Baba Farid's saying which contained the quintessence of the highest moral and spiritual values were current all over. Some of these sayings found place in the *Guru Granth*, while his numerous remarks, incantational phrases, litanies, were absorbed into the complex but attractive pattern of Indian legends.

Baba Farid lived at a time when Persian poetry and culture exercised a dominating influence in the Muslim world. Baba Farid's grandparents spoke Persian at home. Yet, the saint-poet's deepest urge was to carry his message of inward peace to the common people around him, and nothing could be better suited to this purpose than verse in the tongue of the people. He therefore chose to write Punjabi verse and what he wrote has become a beacon of light to the generations that followed. The volume of this verse is meager, but what it lacks in bulk, it makes up in the intensity of sublime emotions that it succeeds in creating.

Theme of Farid's Punjabi Poetry

Some of the themes of Baba Farid's Punjabi poetry are: the verity of youth, physical beauty and worldly wealth; regret over the time wasted in pursuing aims less than the most worthy; the loneliness felt on the departure of one's companions; the tragic failure of even the most painful ascetic exercise; the aches and restrictions of old age; the universality of pain; and finally, the destruction of man himself brought on by the inevitable onslaught of Death that results in void and nothingness. True, he hints at a life beyond the grave, but compared to the overweening force which he brings to describe the reality of Death, it looks rather formal. Among these different themes, the one about the inexorable march of time and the inevitability of death seems the basis of Farid's world view.

Here are some examples of these themes in Baba's verse with their translations.

(It is a common place to say that translation of poetry can never be adequate; we shall, therefore, offer no apology for the poor quality of the translations here presented).

On the paramount significance of death Farid says,

"Man comes into the world with bundles of hopes. When the Angel of Death comes smashing through all closed doors your own dear ones tie you up in the shroud for him. Look, there goes the man, carried on the shoulders of four pall-bearers."

"I was afraid that touch of dust has soiled my turban. Foolish heart indeed! It does not realize that one day this very dust will eat up even my head."

The turban, of course, is a symbol of dignity and honour in the Punjab. Some of the readers may remember the commotion caused in the Punjab by one short line- *Pugri Sambhal Oay Jatta* at the beginning of this century.

How even the most delicate beauty becomes coarse refuse upon death, fit only for the scavenger birds to peck at, is expressed thus by Farid:

"Eyes that once captivated the world; eyes that would not bear a too heavy line of collyrium, I saw them pecked at by birds upon death."

Baba Farid is renowned for the long years he spent in the most intense ascetic exercises. Withal he was a man of high intelligence, deep feelings and creative ability. He, therefore, should be the best qualified judge to pronounce on the usefulness of abnormal ascetic practices. But we find that like *Gautama* the Buddha, he finally gave them up for they failed in their object of revealing God to man.

"Doing penances the body has dried up, become a mere skeleton, crows begun pecking at the body (thinking it dead), yet God has not revealed Himself to his devotee. Look that is the destiny of man!"

And now here is a beautiful piece on the trials and tribulations of one who would tread the path of love, come what may:

"The beloved's home is far; it rains and the path is muddy. If I walk forth my cloak gets wet, if I stay back I break my covenant. Then let it rain ever so much, I will go to meet the beloved and not let the covenant break."

These Punjabi verses make use of many symbols. The meaning of some of which should be obvious to all, but some may not be so obvious. The muddy path and the far distance quite obviously stand for the difficulties of the way of love. But *kambli* or the woolen cloak which the venerable Shaikh is wearing represents the exterior of sanctity. If he does anything to cause a stain on it, there is going to be a rain a (symbol of *malamat* or reproach) against him from the orthodox adversaries. But he shall tread the chosen path of love nevertheless.

With all his preoccupation with the tragedy of pain and death, Farid is not oblivious of morals, he has a code, that of turning the other cheek, which he preached to those who came to him.

"If they smite you, do not smite them back (in revenge). Instead, kiss their feet and go along on your way."

Finally, a verse about the universality of pain, a man thinks that his tribulations are peculiar to him alone, but actually all men have them, only one has to get outside one's narrow self to realize that:

"I thought pain was my peculiar share, (but actually) the whole world is caught in pain. When I viewed the world from a height every home revealed this fire."

This then is Baba Farid, the first Punjabi poet in historical times. The style of his speech is direct, without any poetic embellishments or literary illusions which became popular with the latter poets. He did not tie up his verses with any *ragas* like the latter-day Sufi poets of Punjabi and Sindhi. He uses no symbols from the area of *Trinjans* (spinning circles of women), Such as the spinning wheel, cotton and cotton thread etc., nor does he make use of the female persona to represent him in his verse: he is always himself. But when he does employ the female gender, it is for some actual woman whose plight he wants to show, as in the well known line—*Aj Na Sutti Kant Sainyon*..... "I did not sleep with my husband today."

In all these aspects he is distinctly different from the latter poets. The rare intensity of his verse is owing to the authenticity of his mystic vision and the complete sincerity of its expression. His experiences are varied which give richness to his diction that has the ruggedness of the home spun about it. The significant context of his poetry is that the suffering of man is due to his being cut off from God and his salvation lies in accepting his will- *Raza*. This is his teaching and message.

Baba Farid laid stress on love of man as a means of attaining love of God and service of humanity was part of mystic discipline for him;

"Don't say a harsh word; God dwells in all men.

Don't break a heart, every Jewel is priceless."

He believed, "All is in God." He preached,

"Rise oh! Farid! Do your ablutions

And say the morning prayers.

Behead the head that does not bow before the lord."

To sum up Baba Farid-ud-din Masud Gunj-i-Shakar is one of the greatest saints and mystics and a *Sufi* poet of rare creative ability.

It is said that Farid underwent severe penance and asceticism under Khwaja Qutb-ud-din's stewardship. He hung himself upside down in a well for forty days. He neither ate nor drank but remained attuned to the Almighty. There are a number of references to this experience;

Says Farid:

"My bread is made of wood,
And hunger is my sauce;
Will suffer severe agonies."

Once Sultan Nasir-ud-din is said to have visited Shaikh Farid on his way to Uch on pilgrimage. With him was Balban who later ascended the throne of Delhi. Balban wished to donate a village to Shaikh Farid, but the saint who believed in simple living declined the offer. He would not have more than one blanket for himself. During the day he sat on it, in the night the blanket was used as a cover sheet and if he had to go out, he wrapped himself in it.

It was a lucky coincidence that Guru Nanak met Shaikh Ibrahim, a follower of Baba Farid in the sixteenth century and recorded Baba Farid's poetry which was later on preserved in the *Holy Granth*. Farid wrote a large number of couplets (*Shlokas*) which are very popular with

Punjabi- speaking people. They are noted for their musicality and sweet cadence of diction;

Says Baba Farid,

"I have seen the eyes that lured the world.

A trace of kohl they would not bear.

And birds, to day, have made their nests in them."

Says Farid,

"Why do you roam the jungles with thorns pricking your feet; your Lord dwells in your heart. And you wander about in search of Him."

There is very little difference between God and the angel of Death in Shaikh Farid's imagery. In another couplet he says;

"Had I known the sesame seeds were so small in quantity?

I should have been liberal in filling my fist.

Had I known my lord was not yet an adult,

I would have prided less in myself."

In yet another verse, he says again:

"Had I known the end would slip,

Tighter matters to me as much as you,

Though I have traversed the whole world."

This world indeed appears to Shaikh Farid to be an obstacle in the way of man's union with God.

He says:

"The lanes are muddy, and far is the house

of the one I love so much.

If I walk to him I wet my rug and

Remaining behind, I fail in my love!"

Life in this world is a period of separation from God, which is full of sorrow and pain:

"Sorrow is the bedstead,

Pain the fiber, with which it is woven,

And separation is the quilt

See this is the life we lead, O Lord."

Baba Farid was also a prose writer who wrote in Persian, Urdu and Punjabi. To sum up Baba Farid is one of the greatest saints and mystics and a Sufi poet of rare creative ability.

Popularity:

The main basis of his popularity was his effort to seek oneness with the people he met and his sermons which he preached in the language of the masses. He did not preach any high philosophy, but simple truths affecting the life of the locality. He described his spiritual experiences in Punjabi, which was his own spoken language. His teachings, based as these were on his own experiences as an average householder, had a great significance for both Muslims and non-Muslim and served as a fountain of knowledge not only for the general public, but also for scholars hankering after the higher truths. Shaikh Farid believed that the mind is intelligence per se and it embodies right reason while it is free from selfishness.

Again, according to him, intuitive knowledge is the key to understand the nature of the world, it is not limited to men, but, in a wider sense, it extends to all animate beings. The spirit pervades the universe. Man imprisoned in his physical body, is sometimes separated from it. His intuitive knowledge, nevertheless, is the controlling power of man's life. The extension of intuitive knowledge is the meaning by which men can unite with Heaven, earth and all things. The extension of intuitive knowledge is the extension what comes with action. It is only by acting in obedience to the commands of intuitive knowledge that knowledge can be completed. Knowledge and action, according to the Shaikh, are an indivisible whole; knowledge is the meaning by which men can unite; with knowledge is the beginning of action and action is the completion of knowledge.

As regards the question of life and death, the Shaikh said that if we can understand day and night, that shows that we have come to knowledge of the secret of life and death. The Shaikh declared that truth is like a torch, shining everywhere and the highest and the noblest function of every religion in the world is to show that knowledge is for the establishment and realization of truth. Self-discipline, self-knowledge and self-control are the pre-requisites for the realization of truth. Religion, whatsoever it may be, is really a binding unit; however it may vary between man and man. But in the midst of diversity, unity emerges and it is that unity which helps to bring knowledge and peace and understanding among the warring elements in human society, so that humanity at large may believe that all religions are one and that like rivers, starting from different places careering through different courses, reaches the ocean ultimately, and lead the faithful to the knowledge of that One and the Supreme Lord of the universe, by whatever name He may be called.

The Shaikh, with such teachings as the above, appeared to the people who met him as a big ocean on whose shores infants can play and in whose depths giant souls can swim. In other words, the Shaikh with his spiritual knowledge was a mirror reflecting clearly untarnished ideas from every point of view. The universality of the Shaikh's appeal was well-known. The materialist found in it a code of daily life and conduct; to the men of affairs, the path of action was laid here; while to the devotionally inclined there was the clear path of adoration, till he merged himself into the Supreme. The Shaikh, on the basis of his experience, had a clear insight into the functions of the human mind, which is so just, profound and true to human experience.

All creatures in this world hold life and happiness dear and dislike death and misery. Since all like to live and love life dearly, "live and let live" should be the basic ideal of everyone's life. This ideal can be achieved only if all human beings do good by others, irrespective of their having belonged to any caste or creed, for the heavenly bodies, like the sun and the moon, benefit the whole world and do not differentiate between the pious and the sinners in this world. There is a magic in "forgiveness"; its home is the heart. Existence must cease ere its power departs. Since forgiveness calms one's passions and sorrows, the Shaikh wanted his audience to remember the note: "Forgive and forget" and act upon it so that the world may see its tensions eased.

The other main teachings of the Shaikh, to sum up, centered around the following doctrines which were ten in number: isolation of unification, the understanding of audition, noble fellowship, the preference of preferring, the yielding up of personal choice, swiftness of ecstasy, the revelation of thoughts, abundant journeying, the yielding up of earning and the refusal to hoard. By isolation of unification is meant the non-corruption of the purity of the belief in one Lord by any thought of polytheism or atheism. The understanding of audition enjoined on one listening in the light of mystical experience and not merely in the light of learning. By noble fellowship is meant the society of the highly enlightened souls so that communion with the Almighty may be possible; the preference of professing means that one should prefer what another should prefer, so that one may have the merit of professing. The yielding of personal choice is the surrendering of one's ego and thus leaving oneself open to the will of Lord. Swiftness of ecstasy is realized when the consciousness is free from anything that disturbs one's ecstasy.

The revelation of thoughts means that one should examine every thought that comes into his conscious and follow that which is of God but leave that alone, which is not of God. In order to cut the bonds of materialism and to train the soul, abundant journeying must be undertaken for the purpose of beholding the warnings that are to be found in heaven and earth. The yielding up of earning is with a view to demanding of the soul that it should put its trust in God. The refusal to hoard is only meant to apply to the condition of mystical experience and not to the prescriptions of theology.

Death:

Shaikh Farid left his transitory world on the 5th of Moharram. A.H. 668, corresponding to Monday, the 5th September, 1269 A.D at Pak Pattan. He is buried in Pak Pattan (formerly known as Ajodhan in olden days), where hundreds of thousands of his devotees visit his shrine daily, particularly on the anniversary of his death. And thus approached a glorious end; it was at Ajodhan that the famous *Sufi* saint Nizam-ud-din Auliya, had gone to be the disciple of the Shaikh, when he was only 20 years of age and had, ultimately, succeeded in obtaining the key of the treasury of inward illumination.

Shaikh Farid or Braham:

The Shaikh presented a collection of *Shalokas* and hymns believed to be composed by Baba Farid in the local dialect. The Guru must have gone through these *Shalokas* very carefully and cautiously. The consolation of the aggrieved heart, fear of the consequences of evil actions, love of God and humanity, transitoriness of worldly riches, grandeur and honour, importance of Death as a deterring factor from oppression, tyranny, sin and pride and cultivation of higher moral values is the theme of these *Shalokas*. This message of Baba Farid is really a universal message above sect, creed, community, colour and race. It has a great moral force which ennobles a man and prepares him for the vision of God. Guru Nanak who was a seeker of truth must have been attracted with this message and that is why he included these *Shalokas* in the *Adi Granth** which later on were incorporated in *Guru Granth*.

Before we start writing the literary contribution of Shaikh Farid we must decide that the *Shalokas* and Hymns we found in the *Adi-Granth* are written by Shaikh Farid or by Shaikh Braham? This question has raised the controversy and confusion in the minds of critics and literary figures. Macauliffe in his book *The Sikh Religion* writes, "it is certain that it was Shaikh Braham who composed the Shlokas and Hymns bearing the name of Farid in the *Granth Sahib*. Though he used the name of the founder of his spiritual line as his "Poetical nom de Plume"[11] Dr.Lajwanti Rama Krishna, the author of *Punjabi Sufi Poets* also believes that available *Shalokas* in the *Adi-Granth* in the name of Shaikh Farid actually belong to Shaikh Braham, the follower of Shaikh Farid.

Bawa Budh Singh writes most controversial views. He is not sure to decide that the *Slokas* which we find on the name of Shaikh Farid were written by Shaikh Farid or Shaikh Braham. He says, "I have been told that the *Slokas* named after Farid were written by Braham. Since I have not got the definite proof to give the decisive version on this, still I feel these *Slokas* might have been written by Shaikh Farid."

Actually Dr. Lajwanti could not understand the inner depth of these lines. Persian book, *Syrial Aulia*, is an evident proof that the *Slokas* were written by Shaikh Farid Shakarganj. Author of this book, Hazrat Kirmani, gives the reference of Farid's hymns and *Slokas* in his book. He quotes the *Slokas* of Shaikh Farid also. Hazrat Kirmani wrote the book at least 150 years before the birth of Shaikh Braham. Now the question does not arise that the *Slokas* which are recorded in *Guru Granth Sahib* be named after Shaikh Braham. I think that Macauliffe and

Dr. Lajwanti have not understood the depth in the literature of Shaikh Farid. The beauty of the language and the very refined expression raise the doubt in the minds of these critics and they without understanding the personalities of Shaikh Farid and Shaikh Braham make such judgements. Shaikh Braham does not bear that personality who could compose the *Slokas* and hymns of such a lofty and high literature. The man, who has studied the literature of Shaikh Farid, knows that the *Slokas* reflect the personality of Shaikh Farid Shakarganj and not of Shaikh Braham.

Conception of God:

Baba Farid had a unique personality; unique in the sense that he was a profound scholar and last but not least, a man of great mystic vision and gnosis *(Ma'rifat)*. Therefore, his conception of God was not merely a scholarly presentation of an outcome of logical reasoning but it was the expression of his deep religious meditation and intuition. God, for him, was a living Reality, having an all-embracing Personality present in his intellectual, ethical and mystic experience. It was not the God of deism who after creation became aloof from the universe and left the universe to go on mechanically, nor was it the God of Pantheism who manifested himself in the universe and became immanent in it, but it was the God of Theism who was both transcendent and immanent.

Baba Farid felt as though God was always in his presence. While offering prayers, it seemed that he was communicating with Him. Baba Farid's brother, Shaikh Najib-ud-din Mutawakkil asked him one day, "People say when you pray, you hear God saying, 'I am present, my *Abd* (Creature). Is it so? "It would have been pedantic to say 'yes' to this query", replied Baba Farid. Baba Farid did not want to be oblivious of Him even for a single moment.

God, for Baba Farid, was omnipotent. It was his firm belief that He was the only bestower. Recommending the case of a certain person to Sultan Ghiyas-ud-din Balban he wrote, "I put his case first before God and then before you. If you award him something, you will be thanked for it because you are the agent for this award, but God, in the real sense, is the only bestower; if you refuse it, then you are helpless in this matter, because God is the only refuser." He, in the *Khilafat-Namah* which he gave to Nizam-ud-din Auliya, says, "God alone deserves all praise. He is the first and the last, the Manifest and the Hidden. He elevates, none can bring him down and whomsoever he throws down, none can elevate him. None can bring to light what he has concealed and none can conceal whatever he has revealed."

All the above statements of Baba Farid clearly show that God, for him, was a living reality having an objective existence. He was in personal contact with Him and he had a firm conviction that God was always present to him.

Love of God:

The summum bonum of life, in the opinion of Baba Farid, is the attainment or the realization of God, as expressed in the verse:

"In both the worlds thou alone art the object that I cherish."

For the attainment of this cherished end he prescribed the path of love. He attached so much value to love of God that he used to greet his visitors with these words, "My God give you pain *(dard)* of love. A true devotee in the opinion of Baba Farid, is one who is a lover of God. He says, "Those alone are true devotees whose heart is sincere in love with God. The one whose heart is belied by their tongue are false, inconstant. The true devotees soaked in God attach unto Himself, blessed is their birth; truly fruitful their life, Lord, I seek shelter in Thee, Thou alone the bestower of forgiveness, Grant to Shaikh Farid the charity of the devotion." The above Bani of Baba Farid incorporated in *Adi Granth*,(page 588) truly depicts the attitude of Baba Farid towards God and the importance of love of God.

"Farid, love of God and greed go not together;

With greed love is rendered impure"

Such love is frail as leaking straw roof against rain. Love of God begets union with God and for the union with God- purification of the heart from the evil desires, control of the emotions and passions and the performance of noble deeds are but indispensable. Baba Farid says:

"Listen man, shouldst thou ennoble thyself, then may'st thou have union with the creator and have true bliss; whoever is for God, the world will be for him." Baba Farid also emphasized God's grace. He is but categorical in his statement that it is only through grace of God that union (with God) is possible.

"To one separated from her Lord, what comfort? Through his grace alone may she find union?"

He further says:

"God in his grace my join me to holy company. As I look around, God alone I find my succourer."

Baba Farid as a Humanist:

Baba Farid was a great humanist. The entire mission of his life was to remove the pain and misery of suffering humanity and to provide man with that vigour and energy with which he may face the ordeals of practical life and lead a life of peace, progress and solace in this world and the world beyond. Baba Farid categorically asserts that the resources of human mind, scientific reason, are limited in nature. The scientific reason has no access in spiritual realm. The problems of spiritual realm can only be grasped by inspiration *(Kashf)* and gnosis *(Ma'rifat)*, i.e. by intuition.

Baba Farid's mission was the peace and progress of humanity at large. To attain this cherished goal he prescribed three paths: (i) the path of knowledge, (ii) the path of self-discipline and (iii) the path of love. Baba Farid was a great lover of knowledge and scholarship. It was his firm conviction that without knowledge it was very difficult to discipline the self and to traverse the path of love. Knowledge, says Baba Farid, is a divine gift for the individual. A man should make an endeavour to attain it. The mere desire to attain it does not make a man learned. Had it been so, no one in the world would have been illiterate. Therefore a man should make an earnest effort for the attainment of knowledge. Religion, in the opinion of Baba Farid, can be protected through knowledge. The Prophet (SAW) used to say, blessed is the man whose knowledge of his own faults and defects prevents him from disclosing the faults of others.

Baba Farid assigned a respectable position to a learned man in society. He said, "The *Ulema* (learned man) are nobler than the common people and the *Faqirs* (*Dervishes*) are the noblest of all." While appointing Shaikh Nizam-ud-din as his successor, he remarked, God has bestowed upon you knowledge, reason and love and one who possesses these three qualities can discharge the duties of the *Khilafat* of the *Shaikhs* well."

Baba Farid vehemently condemned ignorance. He goes to the extreme extent and declares, "Do not regard the ignorant as alive." He further says. "Give a wide berth to an ignorant man who poses as a learned one."

After knowledge we come to the discipline of the soul. Baba Farid laid importance on the purification of the soul because for the good of humanity it is but indispensable that every member of the society must possess a noble and exemplary character. And Baba Farid devoted his long life of ninety years in ennobling the character of the corrupted humanity. He gave the highest position in a society to a *Faqir* and defines a *Faqir*, "A *Faqir* purifies everything, but nothing can make him dirty." Thus self-purification is the first and foremost ideal which he wants to inculcate in his followers. For self-purification he prescribes a number of disciplines.

Baba Farid checks his followers from acquisition of material things of the world. A man in his opinion, who buries himself exclusively with feeding and clothing himself, is the meanest of all people. He further says that misery is the by product of mundane aspirations. Therefore one should not pay undue attention to the demands of the physical self; the more one satisfies it, the more it demands.

He forbids his disciples to harbour pride and arrogance. Pride, according to him, turns the whole world into an enemy. Hence, a man should not take pride in committing sin because it makes the heart of a man which is sheet of love and truth, a play thing of the devil.

Baba Farid always tried to impress by his precept and example the importance of consolation and comfort of the human heart, good work, nobility of character, justice, self dignity, character, generosity, showing gratitude, and contentment. These are the positive qualities which the Shaikh (Baba Farid) wanted to implant in humanity at large.

The virtue of charity was ingrained in the nature of Baba Farid. Whatever unasked gifts *(futuh)* came to his monastery, he at once distributed among his visitors. The same spirit of charity he wanted to inculcate in his disciples.

After self-discipline, lastly, we come to path of love. Love is the basic teaching of Sufism. This love includes both the love of God and the love of creation.

Sufis are unanimous that God cannot be loved without loving the creation of God. Through love a Sufi wants to create harmony in the discordant elements of love and goodwill so that a healthy social order free from dissension, conflicts, discrimination, hatred and jealousy might come up. To achieve this goal he organized and himself supervised the *Jamaat Khana*. The *Jamaat Khana* of the Shaikh was a large room where his disciples and visitors used to sleep, pray and study on the floor. It was run by the inmates themselves. Every one of them had to do something for the management of the household. There was no discrimination there on any ground, not even on the ground of piety and penitence. Hindu and Muslims, seniors and juniors, old and new, rich and poor, Sultan and beggar, pious and sinner, every one of them was treated on an equal basis.

Baba Farid himself used to preside over the *Jamaat Khana*. He was a tower of strength for the low born, the down-trodden, and the humble and despised people. In India of the 13th century where the difference between conqueror and the conquered, rich and poor, high caste and low cast, privileged and down trodden was at its height, this *Jammat Khana* of Baba Farid served as an oasis in a desert. This was the holy place where personalities like Shaikh Nizam-ud-din Auliya, Maulana Badr-ud-din Ishaq, Shaikh Jamal-d-din Taunswi and others were being shaped. The higher Sufi ideas were actually translated into actions by the followers of the Shaikh.

The spiritually starved people flocked to it from far and near and men of different temperaments and attitudes rubbed their shoulders and learnt to live together. This humanism of Baba Farid brought about a tremendous change in the land of the Punjab and its neighborhood in particular and in the Indian Subcontinent in general. Today Muslims, Hindus and Sikhs alike have feelings of great reverence for Baba Farid.

Baba Farid led a life of piety and penitence. He was proud of his poverty *(Fakr)* and observed continuous fast. At *Uch* he performed the *Chilla Makus* by hanging head downwards in a well, suspended from the bough of a tree. It is the agreed opinion of the Indian Shaikhs that no saint has excelled Baba Farid in his devotion and penitence. According to Shaikh Nizam-ud-din Auliya it was a moving and thrilling scene to see Baba Farid in his prayer. When alone in his room he would lay his head on the ground for hours and recite, ("I die for thee and I love for thee").

Baba Farid was a living embodiment of love. His excellence was the excellence of his character. There was a complete unanimity in his thoughts, words and deeds. He had a lovable and affectionate nature—truthfulness, honesty, sincerity, love and devotion were the hall-marks of his personality. His private life was a perfect mirror of his public life. There was a complete absence of hypocrisy. He had a very sympathetic and tender heart. He always tried to console the heart of the aggrieved people. He spent his long life in lifting the humanity from the quagmires of sin and superstition. Baba Farid's monastery (*Khanqah*) was open to all, irrespective of caste and creed. Rich and poor, officials and non officials, old and young, Hindus and Muslims, were received in the same way. A stream of visitors flowed to the monastery every day, but Baba Farid never got tired of it. He attended to the problem of every visitor individually and tried his best to remedy his grievance. He furnished the society of his day with infinite moral force which removed the social, ideological and linguistic barriers between the various cultural groups of India. He, for the first time, sowed the seed of emotional, cultural and linguistic integration which later on flourished and in its final shape we have the Hindustani culture and Hindustani or Urdu language.

Delhi, at the time of Baba Farid, was a great centre of Muslim culture. Many refugees from Central Asia had settled there. They generally aspired for mundane honours and positions. Allurements of court life had drawn them to Delhi. Baba Farid too, breathed in that atmosphere for a short time. His fame and popularity spread in Delhi like wild fire. But Baba Farid was not hankering after worldly grandeur and honour. He was in search of truth and solace for the suffering humanity. Therefore, he left Delhi and migrated to Hansi. He used to deliver sermons at Hansi. And very soon he attained popularity there. Then he shifted to Kothewal and from Kothewal he came to Ajodhan where he settled down permanently. Very soon, at Ajodhan, the period of self – discipline came to an end and the seclusion *(Uzlat)* was changed into association *(Suhbat)*. The door of the *Khanqah* was opened and everyone was allowed to visit him without any discrimination. Shaikh Farid-ud-din devoted his long life there to enhance the moral and spiritual culture of the people. His humanity, sublimity of character and spiritual caliber helped in spreading the fame of the *Chishti* order to distant places.

Baba Farid possessed all those qualities which are needed for the expansion of any *Silsilah*. He made Sufism a mass movement. Sufism took root in the life of the people and became more and more Indianized in its character and expression. There was a vital difference of approach between the orthodox theologians and the Sufis. There was no place in the heart of a theologian *(Alim-i-Kabir)* for a sinner or the misery-stricken people. A theologian was just like a lawyer or a judge who was talking in terms of virtues and vices, punishment and reward, Muslims and infidels. But the Sufis, on the contrary, took Islam to the masses. In doing so they (the *Sufis*) exclusively emphasized the moral training and building of conduct and character. They dealt with the problems of suffering humanity at the personal level. Whenever any aggrieved person or sinner came to Baba Farid, he welcomed him with affection and warmth of emotion. He consoled his tormented heart and tried his best to pacify him. As a new born baby gets consolation in the lap of his mother, so the visitor whether suffering from worldly or spiritual troubles or conflicts, used to get solace and peace of mind in the company of Baba Farid. Baba Farid trained a number of disciples and *Khalifas* who spread the *Chishti Silsilah* in different parts of the country. And it can be rightly said that though *Chishti Silsilah* was founded in India by Shaikh Muin-ud-din Chishti, it was popularized in Delhi by Shaikh Qutb-ud-din Bakhtiyar Kaki, but the credit goes to Baba Farid who made it a mass movement and with his effort and with the effort of his illustrious *Khalifah* and successor, Shaikh Nizam-ud-din Auliya, it spread in every nook and corner of India and Pakistan.

The Visitors and their Problems:

The *Khanqah* of Baba Farid remained open till midnight. People of all classes paid visits to it with different objectives. The Shaikh attended to the individual problem of every visitor, without showing any discrimination. In short, Baba Farid spent his long life in the service of humanity and helping those whom he found in distress. He consoled them and inspired in them faith in God.

With his life of poverty, Baba Farid shared the grief of others and suffered for their cause. His sympathetic and kind words provided them solace and in the words of Barani, "he has taken the inhabitants of this region under his wings," a real estimate of the Shaikh by a contemporary scholar.

Baba Farid's Relation with the Non-Muslims:

Khanqahs were the only places where people of different shades of opinion, professing different religions and speaking different languages met. These *Khanqahs* became veritable centers of cultural synthesis where ideas were freely exchanged and a common medium for this exchange was evolved." Baba Farid had contacts with the Hindu religious thinkers and he carried on religious discussions with them. References are available that Hindu *Jogis* very frequently paid visits to his *Khanqah* and the inmates had discussions with them. Shaikh Nizam-ud-din Auliya, while staying in the *Jama'at Khana* of the Shaikh, twice met Hindu *Jogis* and was very much impressed by the method with which the *Jogis* explained to him the Hindu ideas on the subject--- the spiritual and the animal elements.

New Linguistic Synthesis:

The difference in the medium of expression stood as a great barrier. In creating understanding between two major cultural groups-the Hindus and the Muslims--the need of the time was to create a new instrument of self-expression. As such, "a new linguistic synthesis take place: the Muslim gives up his Turkish and Persian and adopts the speech of the Hindu. He thus evolves a new literary medium-Urdu." The Muslim mystics were the first Muslims who came into contact with the lower or working-class groups of Indian society. Among whom they were to propagate the teachings of Islam. As such Baba Farid carried on all these conversations in the language which was spoken and understood by the common people and the gentry. We have evidence of the Shaikh speaking in *Hindavi*, the earliest form of Urdu, which was in later days used by Hazrat Amir Khusrau for his poetic expression. This paved the way for establishing a more close contact between the Hindus and the Muslims and falicitated them in appreciating each others' religious views.

Sufi Dervesh Baba Farid and the *Bhagati* Movement:
Bhagati Movement of this Period

Bhagati Movement is the out-spring of Mahatma Buddha who had taught his Middle Path and expressed his denunciation of *Brahmanism* and priesthood through the language of the people, by traveling himself and by sending out special missionaries and disciples. The new cult adopted both the devices. In early *Buddhism* and *Vaishnavism* both, we have the same spirit of independent inquiry, fearless assertion, ceaseless activity for conversion and unflinching and unsparing loyalty of the disciples to the Master. The teachings of the Buddha were collected in the shape of real and imaginary, psychological dialogues.

These teachings collected by disciples became very popular in the medieval period. Bhagat Kabir, Saint Ravi Dass, Saint Namdev and so many other saints and mystics preached the same teaching in different formation. Bhagat Kabir is considered the exponent of this *Bhagati* movement in Punjabi literature. Kabir was born in the family of weavers. He was the first writer who wrote against social evils, dogmas, superstitions, misconceptions and caste-fanaticism. Analyzing the language of Bhagat Kabir, it can be definitely stated that his language of mixture of *Hindwi, Punjabi, Sadh-Bhasha* and *Brij*. Bhagat Kabir cannot be named as one of the initiators of *Bhagati* movement. Kabir belongs to the group of the mystics like Namdev, Jaidev and Saint Ravi Dass.

Critics can analyze the language of Bhagat Kabir and the conclusion they will get is definitely like this that Bhagat Kabir's language is closely related to the old Punjabi language. Bhagat Kabir eradicated the social evils, meaningless customs and baseless superstitions. Kabir was the forerunner of *Bhagati* Movement which was followed by Guru Nanak, Chaitanya, Ravidas, Namdev and so many other saints of this period. These mystics opened the doors for the study of the soul and the Sublime. In spiritual enlightenment the stage comes when soul intermingles with the sublime-formation of God. So Kabir was an institution in himself, his teachings were preached by the *Sikh Gurus* in the modified form.

A.C. Bannerji says in this connection:

"He was the first leader of the medieval reformation to make a conscious effort for Hindu-Muslim unity in the sphere of religion."

Bhagat Kabir was not the spiritual guide of the Muslim community only but his verse is above this worldly class system. In the world of Macauliffe:

"His *dohs* can be accepted by all types of persons and, if perused without bigotry, are advantageous for the salvation of all persons whether belonging to the Hindu or Muslim faith."

Saint Ravi Dass believed that man is the sublime creation of God. Only in the birth of man spiritual attainment is possible. The cycle of deaths and births goes on and after a long time human birth comes. So it should not be wasted in useless pursuits. Involvement of the worldly temptations should be channelised.

This movement has enriched Punjabi literature and the poets of this movement developed the study of the soul in the Punjabi literature at that time.

Purpose of the Movement

The Saints of this age belonged to the common folk. They led a very simple life. Their opinion was that freedom of spirit comes from concentration on the Supreme Self in solitude, alone, self-controlled, free from desires, free from longing for passion.

Freedom is not in the shouts of armies and the clamour of crowds; freedom is in the life of the spirit. It is a life which may mean poverty and pain. But this poverty enriches, this pain becomes a power of service. All the saints believe that the motion of God's love is a living fountain, and where the channel is free, it flows in and through our individual lives. Unchecked it pours. It irrigates the life within, and the wilderness, the solitary place, is made glad and the desert rejoices as blossoms as the rose, for it fertilizes the soil, and the loveliness of the Kingdom reveals whenever these waters stream and blesses the city of the soul, which becomes the city of God.

G.R. Bhai giving the philosophy of *Bhagti* movement in his book "Glimpses of Meditation and Thoughts" writes, "When a desire comes in one's mind it stimulates thoughts which in turn initiate action that makes one's destiny. Fulfillment of the worldly desire is generally pursued in the belief that it would lead to happiness. However it does not as was preached by Lord Budha." So the Saints from time to time preached the above theory which was followed by the millions. Dr. Gokal Chand Narang is right when he says "The spring of religion had been choked up by weeds of unmeaning ceremonials, debasing superstitions, the selfishness of the priest, and the indifference of the people. Form had supplanted the reality and the highly spiritual character of *Hinduism* had been buried under the ostentatious paraphernalia of sects." (Dr. Gokal Chand Narang)

Farid and *Bhagati* Movement:

As a matter of fact, the extraordinary popularity of the *Chishti* Order in India was, to a large extent due to similarity with Hindu Internalism and mysticism represented by *Jnan Marg* and *Bhagati Marg*. It was Shaikh Farid, "the second Adam of *Chishti* Order" in India, who gave a new turn to the *Chishti* attitude, which culminated in the strictly religious, moral and disciplinarian attitude of the *Chishti Sufis* of the 16th century. But what is even more remarkable is the impact of this religious tilt given to mysticism by Shaikh Farid, on the *Bhagati* movement which was the chief standard bearer of Hindu internalism or mysticism at the popular level. During the two centuries between the death of Shaikh Farid (1265) and the birth of Guru Nank (1469), popular Hindu mysticism or the *Bhagati* movement had undergone a deep change.

The *Bhagati* Saints of the 15th and the 16th centuries, Kabir (b.1440), Guru Nanak (b.1469) and Chaitanya (b. 1485), were all moralists and men of religion. They preached not only individual morality but also wanted to reform their society on moral lines.

It is needless to say that Guru Nanak was the most important of all the *Bhagati* saints of the period. He was the one to point out in most clear and emphatic terms the pitfalls of amoral *Bhagati gnan* and inner perception. He discarded idol worship which had attracted many *Bhagati* Saints and denied the very concept of *Avatar*. For him no one could at any stage transcend the limits of right and wrong. To trace pantheism or the internalist concept of the unity of Existence in Guru Nanak's *Bani* is in my opinion, in no way less difficult than to trace it in the Quran or in the *Bani* of Shaikh Farid.

It was this similarity of attitude that urged Guru Nanak to establish relations with Shaikh Ibrahim, his contemporary successor of Shaikh Farid. It was again due to this very reason that Shaikh Farid's *Bani* was included in *Guru Granth Saheb*.

Guru Nanak had tried to bridge the gulf between externalism and internalism, or between formation and devotionalism. He was burning with the love of God, and yet this love of God did not burn his sense of discrimination between right and wrong, between virtue and vice, between God and the Devil.

Looking around him, Nanak found that among the Muslim saints the closest to him in all these respects was Shaikh Farid. Shaikh Farid too had been a great lover and devotee of God, who hated religious formalism or externalism as much as Guru Nanak. He accepted many unorthodox ways of keeping the fire of God's love burning in his heart, and yet Farid was deeply-rooted in religious morality, he never flouted any explicit command of God, and never stooped to do any thing clearly forbidden by the Prophet. He, too, like Guru Nanak did not pay much attention to pantheism because it tended to blur the moral sense of man. Before becoming the disciple *(Murid)* of Khwaja Qutub-ud-din Bakhtiyar Kaki, he had fully equipped himself with formal religious education, and never ignored these religious teachings throughout his long life of ninety years, meticulously abiding by all the injunctions of the *Shariat*. His moralist bent of mind is manifest in his sayings, a few of which, culled from *Siyar-ul-Aulia* are given below:-

"Invent excuses for doing good

Acquire vision through your faults

Do not consider anything a substitute for faith"

He has described his path, in the following *Sloka* included in the *Guru Granth Saheb*:

"Our path through life is cheerless — sharper than the sword, narrow in extreme, over such a path doth my way lie." (*Adi Granth* Page 794)

This was the straight path of religion and morality. Being a mystic as well as an orthodox scholar both in theory and practice, Farid acted as the most important bridge between the two extremes of internalism and externalism. Two hundred years later, this bridge was consolidated by Guru Nanak.

Baba Farid may be regarded as one of the earliest Sufi poets, who played a dominant role in shaping the *Nirguna Bhagati* tradition in Punjab. Although some Sufi saints had come to India during the 8th century too, the proper propagation of Sufism started with the arrival of the distinguished *Sufi ALIHUJVERI* at Lahore in the 12th century. Baba Farid was also another famous *Sufi* saint of the 12th and 13th centuries. Initially, the advent and the development of Sufism took place within the framework of Islam to begin with; the Sufis had faith in the Islamic Law, but as time passed, the *Sufi* became increasingly independent in their thinking. There was a school comprising Sufis like Juned and Al-Ghazali who aimed at the reconciliation of the two sections. Farid also belonged to this set of *Ba- Shara Sufis*.

Baba Farid was not a narrow-minded, bigoted Muslim of the old stamp; his spiritual discipline was basically, 'Love- oriented, like that of *Sufis*. He received his religious instructions from a learned *Sufi* of his time, Khawaja Qutb-ud-din Bakhtiyar Kaki, who strengthened his belief.

Unlike Al-Ghazali, Baba Farid was not, in the proper sense of the word, philosophical. He was more of mystic and in his mystical experience he appears to have been greatly influenced by the Indian spiritual discipline, particularly the *Bhagati*. In fact, his poetry comes to us as a natural fusion of Islam, *Sufism* and *Bhagati*. He was primarily a, love-oriented *Sufi*, but we find in his poetical compositions almost all the main elements of *Bhagati*. In his Punjabi verse he did not even make a mention of the 'Quran' the 'Prophet' and the *Kalima* which any staunch Muslim would have done.

Love towards God, as the Sufis conceive it, may have two forms:

1. Love with God and the Beloved and the devotee as the lover.
2. Love with God as the Lover and the devotee as the beloved (woman).

The Punjabi Sufi poets have generally represented God as the lover and the devotee as the beloved; whereas in the Hindi Sufi poets God is conceived as the beautiful beloved, while the devotee is his female lover. Baba Farid was the first Sufi poet of the Punjabi language. He has portrayed God as husband-lover and himself as his beloved. All the Punjabi Sufi poets who came after him followed the same pattern. For the Sufis earthly love of men and woman paves the way for the higher relationship between man and God. Consequently, sometimes their descriptions take a sensuous form. Even a Hindi Sufi poet of eminence, *Jayasi*, portrays the consummation of the love between *Padmavati* and *Ratansain*, who represent, respectively, the deity and the devotee in utterly physical terms, employing gross sensual imagery, which clearly shows that even at the stage of such an experience of ecstasy and mystical union with the Divine, the poet has not risen above his physical nature and hence has fallen short of the sublime experience. In Farid's we find a complete absence of such a sensuous tendency. In fact, Farid's mystical experience is completely detached from the physical and worldly allurements. The emphasis that Farid has laid on the illusory and transitory character of human body and the vanity, mutability and the evanescent nature of the earthly world also endorses the theory that the ascetic element in Baba Farid had become sufficiently pronounced. Describing the ultimate vanity and the fall of all the worldly beauty, Baba Farid has said:

"Farid jin loin jagu mohiya se loin mai dithu

Kajal rekh ne sehdiya se pankhi sui bahithu"(19)

(Look the skull that held the eyes that were so delicate that they could not bear the weight of collyrium in them, has been turned into a nest for the birds to hatch their eggs in.)

According to Baba Farid all physical charm and beauty is useless if through it the love of the Lord is not cherished. The ultimate end of all human beings is death. According to Farid the day of death for all is pre-determined. He believes the day a man is born; the day of his death is inscribed on his forehead. This writing cannot be effaced. The marriage with the God of death must come on the appointed day; entreaties are of no avail. The path by which the soul has to pass is subtler than the thinness of a hair.

Shaikh Farid's popularity was not less in weight and volume than the popularity enjoyed by the apostles of the *Bhagati* movement—Chaitanya; Kabir and Guru Nanak. Every one of these was leader of that socio-religious revolution of medieval India, of which one of the torch-bearers had been Baba Farid. Farid is reflected in the speeches of Chaitanya and Kabir, in the tradition of Guru Nanak the wording of Baba Farid's *Shlokas* is bodily incorporated. Guru Nanak received the genuine Farid *pothi* through Shaikh Ibrahim, the 12th Successor of Shaikh Farid. The *pothi* containing 112 Shlokas of Baba Farid became part of the *Granth Sahib* under Guru Arjun.

Why Guru Nanak appreciated and felt inspired by Farid's *pothi* – his *Shlokas* and hymns is a problem which few scholars have cared to study. Perhaps the Sikhs alone approach those *Shlokas* and hymns with deep emotion and respect. On hearing those *Shlokas* and hymns, at least some of them, sung in the early hours of the morning, with spiritual music turn a devotee's mind and he is elevated and transported. 'Those who do not get up in the early hours of morning may be considered as living corpses, says Baba Farid in one of his *Shlokas*. The other *Shlokas* inspire love of God in the devotees' mind and make it visualize death which is a certainty and which must never be forgotten. He impresses on the believer that God is love, and he invokes him in sweet Punjabi as *Kant, Sain Sahib, Pir* and *Shah*.

Keeping in view Farid's description of the horrors of death and hell some critics maintain that Farid was a pessimist. But this conclusion does not seem to be correct. The pessimist gives way to despair and frustration and consequently, turns away from action. He may think even of suicide as a means of escape from his predicament. But Farid's reaction was quite different. He persistently counsels good and noble deeds and he himself practiced what he preached. His is an ascetic approach and not pessimism, continuous pondering over the sinlessness and truthfulness; austerity and contentment; simplicity and renunciation. The gospel of ascetism and renunciation is complementary to the passion of *Bhagati*. According to the Sufis also,

"Love of world and love of God cannot dwell together at one place. Whosoever states the contrary is a liar."

The goal of the Sufi mystic is to attain complete union (oneness) with the deity. This stage of mystical experience is missing in Farid. Of course, he has the urge stage of *Wisal* but the stages of *Hal, Fana* and *Baqa* are absent in his poetry. He does not also have that stage of *Analhaq* which was attained by the famous Sufi Hussain Bin Mansur.

Baba Farid's passion for the Divine lover has steadfastness, purity and strength. Displaying his love for God Farid says,

"The Love for the lover should brook no obstruction; what matters if you have only one garment and the path that lead to him be muddy and even if it be raining heavily. Decide to go to meet the beloved preceptor, never allow any gift to be caused between you and him on any account whatsoever."

He glorifies silent suffering. The pangs of separation and a restless yearning for meeting the lover are also there, but his love lacks the vehemence, wildness, frenzy and ferocity of the other *Sufi* mystics of his class. Farid's love is extraordinarily calm, serene and gentle, which is very close to the love in *Bhagati* tradition. Farid narrates the agony of his love:

"Make thy mind the bed and agony of separation the bed-sheet. Thus should you live the painful life of agony; suffering for the Beloved, telling your tale of woe to him alone. Everybody has praised the agony of love, which is the greatest king who rules the lover."

And then talking of the suffering in separation Farid Says;

"In pining in the separation for the Lord, all the blood in my body has dried up, not a drop can be discovered now. This is ever the condition of the lovers of God. Very lean and thin in body they are."

These sentiments are in perfect conformity with the Indian *Bhagati* tradition. The importance of the recitation of the 'Name of the Lord' (*Nam Samaran*) is accepted equally among the Sufis and the Hindu *Shastras*. The Sufi says;

"If ye seek the lord, seek the company of the Name i.e. repeat it constantly and be sure union will be thy lot, for there is not the least difference between the lord and his Name."

In *Srimad Bhagvata* too we have it, "When in helpless condition the Name even if once repeated or even heard redeems man from all his sins." (Xiii—12-46). Bhaktas like Kabir, Guru Nanak and Tulsi all laid emphasis on efficacy of the 'Name of the Lord.'

Humility and meekness are the two cardinal tenets of *Bhagati*. In Farid we find not only humility and meekness but also the other elements of *Bhagati* such as faith, reliance, self-reproach and surrender of the self. Farid commends the service of his master, the God, in the following words:

Farid Sahb di kar Chakri

Dil di lahi bharand

(Do the service of the master and shed of all your doubts.)

Both in *Sufi* mysticism and the *Bhagati* complete surrender to God is the *sine qua non*. The famous Sufi, Jami, states it beautifully:

"The goal of my body and soul art thou alone, O Lord!   I live and die only for thy service, O Lord! Wherever I go I seek thee."

In this very vein Farid writes, "Get up and offer thy prayers to the Lord; if thy head does not bow to Him, burn it in place of fuel."

Therefore, it will be appropriate to say that most of the elements of *Bhagati* are present in Farid's poetry. Along with the love for God, Farid seems to have imbibed the essence of asceticism and knowledge (*gyan*) inherent in *Bhagati*. As in *Bhagati* tradition, he stressed the need for eradication of the ego, of covetousness, of rapacity of greed, of anger etc, and of acquiring truthfulness, contentment, spirit of service, benevolence, humility and forgiveness. According to Farid it is only after acquiring these qualities and practising well that one can achieve 'perfection of humanity' (*Insan-ul Kamil* or *Purnamanav*) which has been given equal importance both by the Sufis and the Indian *Bhaktas*.

Baba Farid saw the relevance and use of religion in daily life and actions of man and taught us the true and practical meaning of *Dharma* and gave us an understanding of sublime living. Rising above all narrow and intolerant communal feelings, he commended and advocated the oneness of humanity and the need of well-doing. Thus by ennobling the human sentiments and awakening our spiritual consciousness, he made distinct contribution to the progress of human thought.

One more important feature of Farid's poetry is his assimilation of the Indian environment. Probably he is the first foreign Muslim poet who has not only embodied the Indian customs and costumes in his poetry, but has also derived his images and symbols from the Indian environment. This trend became more pronounced in the Hindi and Punjabi Sufi poets who came after him.

A disciple of the great Moin-ud-din Chisti, Baba Farid, left a disciple no less great in Nizam-ud-din Auliya whose tomb at Delhi still draws crowds of Muslims as many as of Hindus. These three great names, Moin-ud-din Chisti, Baba Farid and Nizam-ud-din Auliya are the three great pillars of the *Chishtya* order of *Sufi* mysticism in Indo-Pak subcontinent—a great gift to the composite culture of this land, to the Hindu *Bhagati* movement, to Kabir and Guru Nanak and the like, and the characteristic humanistic ideology that India nurtured as a protest against the traditional priestly and scholastic Hinduism and Islam of the medieval centuries.

To conclude, I can say that the poetry of the Sufi poet Farid is also the poetry of an ascetic and a *Nirguna Bhakta*. It is sweet and satisfying like ripe dates and honey. It contains the nectar of Divine love and it is fragrant with love for mankind at large.

Notes:

1. Probably due to Ghuzz invasion.
2. Frishta writes "His father came to Multan from Kabul during the reign of Sultan Shihah-ud-din Ghuri (*Tarikh-e-Frishta*, Vol. II p.383) Captain Wade places their arrival earlier. He says: the ancestors of Shaikh Farid-ud-din first came to Multan in the train of Behram Shah of the Ghaznavi family." (*Journal of the Asiatic Society of Bengal*, March 1837, p. 192, 193).
3. According to the *Siyar-ul-Arifin* Baba remained in Multan and completed his education as his master had instructed him. Jamali further states that the Shaikh went to Qandhar for higher studies and stayed there for five years. *Siyar-ul-Arifin* by Jamali p.36. According to Muhammad Ghauthi he went to Seistan also; *Gulzar-i-Abrar*.
4. The spirit of Islam by Ameer Ali's Syed, Page 460.
5. A.M.A. Shushtery, "Outlines of Islamic Culture" Page 354
6. A.S. Tritton, "Islam-Belief and Practices"' Page. 108.
7. A.S. Tritton, "Islam-Belief and Practices"' Page. 94.
8. Yusuf Ali, Koran, Page. 175.
9. Contribution to Analytical Psychology, Page 243.
10. Dr. Padma Agrawal, Symbolism in Art (Introduction), Page 9.
11. Macualiffe," *The Sikh Religion*", Vol. VI, page 357.

Harbans Mukhia

Bhakti and Sufi Movements— Significance of the Day

The subject of Bhakti and Sufism is extremely attractive for a number of reasons. One is historical dimension or historiographical dimension or rather not even historiographical, but in terms of a perspective of historical explanation. The second aspect, which I will touch upon, is something which is relevant to the very constitution of the theme of contemporary relevance. I will touch upon the contemporary relevance.

To understand Bhakti and Sufi movement is a mode of understanding history. It is a mode of explaining history. It is a mode of historical explanation, one among many modes of historical explanation. Ever since history which is supposed to be the oldest discipline around, a very paradoxical, mode of explaining history has evolved, it has evolved through innumerable forms. It has evolved in terms of clash of civilization, a clash of civilizations evolved as far back as Herodotus and Gibbon and Berdnov and Samuel of Huntington is propounding. The theory clash of religions is another way in which historical explanation has been offered. The rise of religion is a third way or whatever way in which historical explanation has been offered. Christianity arises a worldview, a perspective on history developed with the rise of Christianity that Christianity is the ultimate truth God has revealed through his son Jesus and therefore ultimately the truth will prevail over the whole of humanity and the whole of humanity will turn Christian one day. That is one perspective.

Within that perspective of Christianity, another very fundamental development occurred with St. Augustine who was the first great religious thinker who had profound influence on the development of understanding of history on historical perspective, namely, history as one single whole. History is not the sum of past, history is not a sort of fashion, history is a kind of unfolding of a pattern; history is unfolding Divine will. It is God's will which keeps unfolding itself and therefore, since it is God's will which unfolds through historical events, in God's will; everything past, present and future is integrated into one single whole. There is nothing which is desperate, there is nothing which is haphazard; there is nothing which is random, everything is fundamentally integrated within that and therefore, we have history unfolding itself as one single pattern.

This is the first sort of perspective on history. St. Augustine's which saw history as an integrated pattern and single whole. 1 am emphasizing this because fascinatingly in my own ways, this perspective of history as one single whole unfolding itself independently of human will, cannot interfere with God's will and therefore independently of human will, God's will is unfolding itself in human history. This perspective of history as one integrated whole has survived amid the perspectives which are the very anti-thesis of religiosity, religion, and theology. It has survived in post-enlightenment rationality which sees history unfolding itself in terms of the advancement of science, technology and rationality, independently of human will. It has survived in Hegelian conception of the world spirit which unfolds itself in history independently of human will; it has survived in Marxian concept of class struggle as almost historical inevitability embedded in the concept of class struggle which unfolds independently of human will. Therefore, St. Augustine's perspective is a perspective which cultivates a great durability which has survived even in the perspectives developed in its adversarial perspectives like: Marxism, Hegehanism, post- Hegelianism, etc. So that many sort of modus of explaining history have evolved. It has evolved in terms of dominance and rebellion against dominance. It has evolved in terms of imperialism and national liberation movements; it has evolved itself in the latest being class struggle; all histories are histories of class struggle; say Karl Marx and Freddy Engel. Therefore, there are many perspectives of history which have evolved with the discipline. There are many ways of understanding history, explaining history, which have evolved with the development of history. All of these perspectives or explanations have been positive as binary opposites, a kind of conflict, perpetual conflict between one religion and another religion, between one civilization and another civilization, between one class and another class, etc.

The fundamental constituents of all of these perspectives had been binary opposite and the further implications of these binary opposites is that each opposite is a composite whole. As each opposite is a complete whole and therefore there is no common space, between the one and the other between classes. Let me focus on class struggle. There is nothing common between capitalist and workers, between feudal lords and peasants, between slave-owners and slaves. There is no shared space between them. Each class or each nation or each religion or whatever is a composite whole complete in itself, undaunted as it were by the other, with no common shared space between them. Each one is a complete whole in itself and these complete wholes are perpetually in mutual conflict with each other.

Historical change then occurs through this struggle between these two composite wholes. In class struggle, for example, historical change, is a very essence of history. How to understand change? Change then occurs through a perpetual struggle between one and the other between the two classes. Let us say just as an example, it could be any other, so that one class which is dominated through perpetual struggle overthrows another class, which was dominating it and establishes its hegemony in turn and therefore a new class formation and a new class struggle begins until this class would be overthrown by next class, etc. That is the essence of the notion of revolution; revolutionary struggle and revolutionary stages of development: feudal revolution, bourgeois revolution, and socialist revolution. By revolution, obviously, is meant revolutionary change, overthrowing of an existing dominant class and hegemony of another class. Revolution is the very heart of change and revolution occurs in a very evocative phrase as coined by Anderson, who has called it catastrophic collision between two antagonistic classes. That is how revolution occurs through catastrophic collision between them and these revolutionary stages even came to be classified in Marxism in particular, slavery to feudalism, primitive communism to slavery feudalism and capitalism etc. It goes on till communism. Thus we have fundamental two antagonistic unities constantly in struggle and in conflict with each other and historical change occurring through this conflict.

Now one characteristic feature of this mode of historical explanation was the contracting space for visualizing any internal cleavages within these unities. If it is national movement against Imperialism, nation is one nation; nationalism is one single whole. There are no internal cleavages within nation. If it is religious struggle between one religion and another, there are no internal cleavages between any religion, which is in conflict with another religion. There are no internal cleavages; there are no internal tensions within any of the units and therefore the completeness of each unit is the fundamental premise of this notion of class struggle or any other struggle between the unities and therefore, it is through this sort of complete units that great revolutions occurred, French Revolution, Chinese Revolution; Russian Revolution, etc. Hence the triumph of national movement or any national liberation struggle in any part of the world, colonized world triumph against colonialism or through the rise of one religion, which overthrows the dominations of a pre-existing religion, etc. Now it is interesting that all of these revolutionary changes, French- Revolution, Russian Revolution or even the birth of Christianity, birth of Islam, etc., all of these are very precisely dated to the day. French Revolution occurred on 14th July 1789; it did not occur on the 13th July or 15th July. It occurred on the 14th July, Russian Revolution occurred on the 7th November 1917. It did not occur on the 6th November or to be very precise, Islam was born on a particular day in a particular year; Christianity was born on a particular day, etc. The very precise dating of these revolutionary changes, which were perceived by their protagonists as revolutionary changes pinpoint the dramatic nature of change. Change is always perceived in dramatic terms.

I use the word 'revolution' again and again because the revolution captures that dramatic nature of change like no other word does. Therefore, Revolution is the mode of change that has been at the Centre of historical explanation throughout the centuries. Therefore, one is completeness of each unity and the other is the adversarial relation between the other unities, whether it is religion or nation versus empire or class vs. class, etc., each is in antagonistic relationship with the other. Now there are also other ways of explaining history and

I think Sufi movement and Bhakti movement are very illuminating illustrations of the other way of explaining history according to which history also evolve through silent corrosion from within constituting an adversarial relationship with something outside, that it is from within and without any dramatic events like French Revolution or Russian Revolution or birth of religion or whatever without any revolutionary sort of dramatic incidents taking place, change still occurs within each unity whether it is based upon religion, nation, class or whatever. Sufi and Bhakti movement, as I said, are the most impressive, most illuminating illustrations of this mode of historical explanation, namely, corrosion of change from within a unity and changes brought about from within that unity. The Sufi movement was solidly grounded within Islam. It was not adversarial to Islam. It was not outside of Islam or adversarial to Islam. It is very much grounded within the structure of Islam. The Bhakti movement was not hostile to Hinduism, either.

The Sufi movement even as it enveloped and enforced or reinforced an Islamic vision of the world, its vision substantially differed from the rulers and the *Ulemas'* vision of Islam, where it brought about change. Sufi Movement or Sufis and ulema are to be considered as unities. I am aware that they are not unities, there are a lot of cleavages, differences, tensions, diversity of opinion and diversity of perspectives, etc. within the movement of Sufis and among the *Ulemas*, there are a lot of shades of opinion. It is not one shade represented by the Sufis and the other shade represented by the Ulema.

I am aware of the fact that essentialization really does harm to any kind; it is quite injurious to any kind of useful analysis, but none-the-less one does essenlialize in order to make a point, a paradigmatic point is still made through essentializaion and through rounding of the edges and in that sense, the Sufis and the Ulema, they do represent different perspectives of Islam, though both of them are grounded within Islam. The distinction in the heirs in the very origin of Sufism first in Arabia in the early decades of Islam in a very sort of feeble kind of assertion, but in its fluorescence in Iran and in India in particular, it is there that distinction becomes further more and more clear. The Sufis distance from the State, their celebration of penury, there renunciation of any overt form of power, all of these are forms of protest against the State, against the Muslim State, against Muslim acquisition of riches and Muslim acquisition of power.

All of these are protests from within the discourse of Islam, not outside it. In excluding themselves from the state, the Sufis were also stopping the state from entering the *Khanqah*. In living in penury, they were also pouring ridicule over the life of the rich among some Muslims. In asserting their moral superiority over temporal power, they were also underlining the ephemeral nature of temporal power. Yet, the protest was internal to Islam, not adversarial to it. Their protest against distortion of Islam did not lead them to posit an alternative to Islam in the future, but a return to the past, even vis-a-vis the State there is a great deal of shared space. It is not adversarial relationship in the sense that on how the Sufis distance themselves from the State for sure, but they were also fascinated by some form of the language as it was not verbal language, but language of symbols which is common to State and the Sufis. When Sheikh Nizamuddin Aulia is recognized at the height of his spiritual attainment, it is expressed in terms of his *Sultan-ul-Mushaikh*. He is *Sultan-ul-Arphheen*, the term that comes to designate him is a term borrowed from the State. When we are told that everybody has to sit solemnly in the presence of the Sufi saint, the great Sufi saint. This reverence is borrowed from the imperial court, where in the presence of the King, everybody has to stand in silence, some of them sit while most of them stand in silence, and not a word is even whispered. When we are told that you are in the presence of the Saint Sheikh, your attainments are graded and you occupy a particular space in terms of your spiritual attainments in terms of the grade of your spiritual attainment, one is also reminded of the standing space for each Mansabdar in the court according to the Mansab that was given to him so that there is a lot of space with language, as I said, language of symbols that is shared between the State and the Sufi. There is, therefore, not an adversarial relationship, there is a great difference, there is a protest and yet it is not as if both of them are two different unities, which are constantly in conflict with each other. One of the lasting legacies of the Sufi Movement is evolution of the Ghazal. I think it is one of the greatest contributions of Sufism among other things. The Central movement in the Ghazal is the celebration of failure which again fascinates me. In Ghazal, you never celebrate success, you always celebrate failure. The poet who writes Ghazal, if writes a 'Nazam' would probably celebrate success, but not in Ghazal. Ghazal is the epitome of celebration of failure. And this celebration of failure which comes from the Sufi ambience, this celebration of failure is a kind of protest against the celebration of success of the high and mighty of the powerful against the ideology of conquest and dominance of the powers that be, whether it is temporary dominance or religious dominance. The ideology of universal love becomes the counterforce.

Every foundation that you see is vulnerable to disturbance, to destruction except the foundation of love. There is a counter positioning here that universality of love which comprehends the entire humanity and the dominance of State, dominance of the religion, dominance of the power and dominance of the mighty which differentiate between the dominant and the dominated, therefore, counterposed to one ideology of universality and of failure. It is thus that the history of Islam has evolved, not merely in terms of its conquest of territories and conversion of non-Muslims. All of these are true conquest of territories, its part of the history of Islam and the version of Islam held by non-Muslims is part of the history of Islam. But there are also other aspects to it, other dimensions to it, there is also evolution of Islam in terms of its own internal conflict and mutations not merely vis-a-vis outside forces. If the 'jallats' amongst the Muslims, amongst the Ulema in particular, though again let me emphasis Ulema is a very heterogeneous group with lot of diversity of opinion almost about everything under the sun, but nonetheless one is juristically speaking of Ulema as one homogenous whole.

If the very orthodox jellots amongst the Ulema treated the Kafirs as adversary, one is always reminded of Ziauddin Berne's very famous or infamous recommendation i.e. Collection of *Jazia* from the Hindus is not meant for collection of revenue. He says the State should not collect revenue, *Jazia* to add to its revenue, to add to its coffers. The purpose of collection of *Jazia* is to humiliate the Hindus. Humiliation is the purpose, not adding to the revenue. To that view is counter-posed the view of the Kafir held by the poets. For Persian and Urdu poets Kafir is the greatest term of endearment. Kafir is the beloved, a sweetheart. It is the greatest term of endearment and therefore when a poet says, "You are willing to give up even Islam for the sake of your beloved. You are willing to sacrifice your life, your religion everything-for the sake of Kafir." Kafir becomes the beloved here, the sweetheart for whom one is willing to sacrifice everything. Kafir is not the enemy, the adversary, Kafir is the sweet heart.

Therefore, there are many dimensions, there are many internal cleavages within Islam. It is just not one uniform history. It is this internal mutation in contrast with all that historical explanations that are talked of which are posited as binary opposites of constant struggle with the other in adversarial relationship. It is this internal mutation within a unity, very long term, very durable not dramatic at all, which is very effective. That transformation occurs through the long-term internal movement, internal protest, internal change which is as effective as French Revolution or Russian Revolution or any other Revolution. Therefore, that is another perspective of history, that is to say you look at history not in terms of adversarial conflicts or catastrophic collusion alone, you also look at history in terms of internal movement, silent almost imperceptible and long term but nonetheless very effective. That is what the Bhakti and the Sufi movements tell us in a way as how to look upon history in a different perspective.

Let us come to the second aspect that has fascinated many scholars, the atmosphere of communal harmony and co-existence. There was virtually not a single communal riot in five and half centuries of so-called Muslim rule in India except towards the end of the 16th century. As we go by record, we go by evidence. The first recorded evidence of a communal riot occured in Ahmedabad in 1693 towards the end of the Mughul period. Eventually, it was the end of the Moghul stream; in Aurangzeb's reign virtually towards the end. In Ahmedbad on the day of Holi, a cow was slaughtered and the communal riots broke out. This is the first recorded riot. In the entire 18th century only five such communal riots have been recorded. Just imagine that under the aegis of the secular state, every year there are about 500 communal riots on record, which are noted in Indian Parliament while during entire one hundred years of 18th century only five riots occurred when the Moghul State had virtually been wiped out. What preserved social peace in medieval centuries, when we know that the State at the political level was engaged in the life and death struggle with Marathas on the one hand, Jats on the other hand, Sikhs on a third front, etc. All these struggles were perceived on both sides as religious struggles whether they were or not. They were perceived as religious struggles on both sides and yet at the social level, peace prevailed during all these centuries. What explains this great phenomenon? I would not say paradox but nonetheless it is a great puzzle. What does it explain? 1 think, the only explanation, which occurs to me is the ideology of the Bhakti and the Sufi movement at the social level. It is this ideology of universality of love, universality of feeling, universality of God rather than the sectarian nature of God. It is this ideology of Bhakti and Sufi movement, which preserved social peace even as the State was embroiled in the stuggle of life and death between various adversaries.

This ideology, it seems to me, also restored and preserved social peace in India at the end of the twentieth century and it still did so in the first five years of the 21st century. Let me briefly illustrate what 1 mean by this. On 6th December, 1992 when the Babri Masjid was demolished, a whole world collapsed for many of us. Many of us including myself, who are athiest, who believe in atheistic secularism. I am still an atheist myself and 1 still believe in secularism of my own kind, but 1 also see a great dilemma before us. For those of us who believed in Nehruvian atheistic secularism, a whole world collapsed before us. The entire world that we had been brought on had collapsed when the Babri Masjid was demolished What shall we do now? Is there any future left for us that was the question hanging before us in a challenging way.

Then communal riots erupted between 6th December, 1992 and about 15th or 20th January of 1993, then around the second week of January 1993, very small bits of news began to filter through one small town here, from another small place there. The news that filtered through was that Hindus and Muslims of this locality in this Gwalior city got together and decided to rebuild the mosques and the temples which had been demolished by the rioters in 1992 and 1993. They together also undertook to see that in case if there arises a riotous situation in future, no outsider will protect a *mohalla* or a street against any outsider intervention there, etc. And then peace began to get restored after those horrendous communal riots. Peace began to return to these localities and to these cities and gradually to the whole nation.

Atheistic secularist as we were, then realized immense power of secularism, probably, not as the best world but challenging the, communal onslaught from every quarter. Power within the discourse of religiosity, the power that invest in rebuilding of mosques and temples rather than in doing away with mosques and temples. There is no immense power in that discourse of religiosity and religion per say, but religiosity. 1 am making a distinction here between religiosity and religion. Religiosity is the Bhakti movement, religiosity, which is universal, religion is a sectarian identity, which may be one or the other. Therefore, this discourse of religiosity which accepts difference of religion and yet it also accepts that God is common to all. It is this discourse of religiosity which brought back peace and harmony after the demolition of the Babri Mosque in 1992 and since then there has been only one big horrendous incident of rioting in Gujrat some years ago. Except the riots organized by state there has been peace on this front for last 12 or 13 years.

Therefore, the contemporary relevance of Bhakti and Sufi movement is as a great resource, a great force an immense power latent in this discourse of religiosity which Bhakti and Sufi movement propound. There is a great power in it for keeping, maintaining advancing and of social peace even in the midst of enormous amount of challenges to it. The challenges have come from everywhere. The challenges have come from Bajrang Dal and VHP and others. The challenges have also come from Al-Qaeda, the challenges also come from Samuel Huntington. All of these are serious challenges and yet it is this immense durable power of Sufi and Bhakti movements, which has given us this ability to survive. After all these horrendous events and incidents and experiences, it has given us this immense ability to survive as one group of Indians on the whole.

Iftikhar Arif

Sufism and the World in Crisis

I am tempted, at the outset, and before we discuss the more specific subject of Sufism in South Asia, to consider the crisis our modern civilization under the captaincy of the West faces, to which thinkers like Rene Guenon, Frithjof Schuon, Annemarie Schimmel, Martin Lings, Gai Eaton, and others have referred to with the binary vision that they possess, having been able to surmount the global divide and seen the world in the throes of a war that now knows no frontiers and which, with the typical superficiality that fast foods perhaps engender, has been explained away as the clash of civilizations. Rene Guenon, who has perhaps gone deeper into the question of civilization in its philosophical and cultural aspects, locates the area of crisis within the western parameters where stark individualism, together with unabashed materialism, has chased away the last remnants of tradition and left the society denuded, bereft as it were, of that intrinsic joy that holds people together, sustains human existence and makes life livable without artificial props.

The Renaissance and Reformation which are much celebrated as perhaps the parents of the modern western civilization are the two developments that Rene Guenon holds responsible for bringing about the rupture with the traditional spirit, the former in the domain of arts and sciences and the latter in the sphere of religion itself. From there on material progress becomes the cult, and man, instead of God, becomes the centre of existence. Science comes down to gadgetry, becoming a docile servant of war mongers, and the social fabric is tattered to make way for individualism on the loose. Greed then becomes the motivating force, the engine of social advancement in a soul consuming competitive society. But does that help the individual or the group. We find it does not. There is perpetual strife, dissatisfaction and insecurity at all levels, be it the individual, the family or the state. One word, progress, that has come to mean everything, is being presented as an unending process. But can man be a companion of this fast moving beast?

Already in the last century millions in the West had started questioning the value system of the modern society. Young people in droves were moving to East in search of some sustainable truth. The growing interest in the works of Jalaluddin Rumi, Yoga, transcendental meditation and the rest of it indicates a growing yearning in the West for a return to tradition, but as Rene Guenon and others have pointed out, that elite group, which would lead and bring about change in thinking at the governing levels of society, is yet to emerge as a force. The possibility is real indeed that while such a build up of opinion is in the process of evolution, there may be a violent change in world view and value systems as a result of some catastrophe for which the world, as it is, has the critical potential.

It is my humble opinion that if Sufism is to be studied, whether with regard to its history, content, its personalities, its message or its place in formal religion etc., it should be studied in the context of the problems that face the modern world and it should be our endeavour to find if it has any relevance in the modern world with its fast changing modes of living and whether it will have a role to play in the future of mankind

Islam, because of the importance it attaches to man's life on earth, has a relevance and a stronger role to play in the modern world than perhaps other systems that separate the church from the state. The break from tradition, which the Christian West has suffered on account of the separation of the divine from the mundane, does not occur in the world of Islam which regards worldly life as the door to the Hereafter. Islam wants its followers to fulfill the demands of human nature within the framework of a moral order. In the opening chapter of his *Ihya ul-Ulum*, Imam Ghazali declares that the "ultimate purpose of man's life pertains to this world as well as to the Hereafter. The attainment of the objects of faith is not possible without appropriate handling of worldly matters, for the world is the sowing field of the Hereafter. The person who considers the world the means to the

Hereafter, for him the life on earth is a means of attaining proximity to God."

So the good Muslim can hold property, engage in economic activity to acquire wealth. He is told not to leave his progeny ill provided, is warned against giving his all in charity, and told to do work to keep the wolf from the door, and not sit idle. Then there are social welfare mechanisms like *zakat*, *infaq* and *siham* to establish equity and justice in society. No other religion intervenes in the individual and collective life of the community as does Islam. Then how, in this comprehensive and integrated life plan for individual behaviour and social practice, the need for a system like Sufism arose?

Whether Sufism was born in the bosom of Islam or came from outside is a question that has long been debated but the widely held view that it can be traced to those companions of the Holy Prophet (PBUH) in Medina who under his tutelage practised piety, led a very simple life and devoted themselves to the service of mankind and were called the men of 'suffa' is not in variance with the other opinion that it grew, in the words of Fazlur Rahman, out of 'an initial native tendency' but experienced external influences later in its development such as notions with regard to monism and pantheism. But the origins of Sufism are traced to some of the Prophet's companions, Hazrat Salman Farsi and Uwais Qarni who are regarded as spiritual guides for later practioners of the order, but the first recognizable groups of people who were called Sufis for their distinctive life style and world view were those from Basra and Kufa in the 8th century. Among them belonging to the ascetic order are such important names as Rabia al-Adawiya, Zulnun Al-Misri, Abu Yezid al-Bustami, Junaid Baghdadi and others whom Fariduddin Attar has mentioned in his *Tazkaratul Auliya*. They are those, who, it is understood, reacted against the opulence and tyranny of the rulers and practiced *faqr* and *twakkal* in their lives.

It is also widely held that when at the end of the rule of the righteous Caliphs the Muslim states deteriorated to imperial polities and society became decadent, some of the pious lot separated themselves from political Islam and took it upon themselves to safeguard the purity of the faith through exclusive devotion to God, service to mankind and bringing peace in society through love and tolerance. The greater systems of Sufism began in the *Ummayad* and *Abbasid* periods spreading to other lands that came under Muslim rule.

The advent of Islam in South Asia is around the 8th century of the Hijrah where, in interaction with followers of other faiths, Sufism moulded a very distinct shape for itself, alongside development of movements like the Bhakti way. The Sufi influence, that gained rapid adherence when the teachings of the saints started reaching the people in their own vernaculars and devotional gatherings acquired a popular pulse through the use of music in the singing of mystic songs of the great Sufis like Khwaja Farid Shakarganj, the first great Sufi poet, and Hazrat Amir Khusrau, who expressed his message of love both in Persian and local dialects, is regarded as a landmark in the acceptance and spread of Islam in the sub-continent.

Sufism added a new element to the intensity of faith among the common believers. Beyond the early ascetic pietism, Sufism spread rapidly both because of its popular appeal as also its attraction for those more spiritually inclined who sought in religion the ecstasy of an esoteric experience that formal rituals did not provide.

There was probably something in the soil of the South Asian land that made people God-seeking which in a way explains the great force and following that Sufism acquired in a few centuries after Islam's arrival here. By the 11th century there were as many as twelve orders flourishing in the Subcontinent two of which were declared heretical for their pantheistic teachings. Both Hazrat Data Ganj Bakhsh Ali Hajwairi and Hazrat Imam Ghazali wrote impressive refutations of pantheism. In the next century the *Qadriya* order came to the subcontinent and soon spread to present day Pakistan, flourishing to the end of the 17th century alongside the *Naqshbandiya* order, which laid more emphasis on observance of Shariya.

The second major order of the Sufi system that made a major dent in the following of the orders in the 13th century was the Suhurwardiya which Sheikh Bahauddin Zakariya established and popularized after setting up his astana in Multan. The Chishtia order arriving from Sistan named after Sheikh Moinuddin Chishti and had followers like Qutbuddin Bakhtiarkaki and Fariduddin Ganj Shakkar. The Naqshbandis were the last to take into their fold a great many adherents around 1600. The fount of their teachings under Sheikh

Ahmad Sirhindi was opposition to the philosophy of *Wahdatul Wajud*. Khwaja Mir Dard on whose poetry the German mystic scholar Annemarie Schimmel has written extensively belonged to this order. But other orders like the Shadhilia, Saadeeah, Rifa'iyya, Badawiyya etc., that flourished in the rest of the Muslim world, made no headway in the subcontinent. The saint, Syed Ali Hamdani, brought the Kubrawiyya order to Kashmir.

These saints used poetry to reach the hearts and minds of the masses of the people where alone the true spirit of the faith could be preserved. And this was beyond the reach of the lay preacher who taught the observance of the rituals in the mosques. Poetry's direct impact on the mind was channeled to the heart through the employment of music that in Sufi orders like the Chistia became a regular collective activity in the shape of sama meetings where the qawwals sang the verses of great mystic poets --- Hafiz and Rumi, Baba Farid-ud-Din Ganj Shakar, Amir Khusrau as well as Sufi songs of local saints like Shah Abdul Lateef Bhittai, Baba Bulleh Shah, Shah Hussain, Mian Muhammad Bakhsh and others. The songs emphasize the themes of love, union, separation, other worldliness etc. the sama meetings created an atmosphere of spiritual ecstasy and helped the disciples to enrich their spiritual life and advance them on the path of Union with God which is every Sufi's ultimate objective. To make the nature of spiritual love accessible to the novice these singing saints have often used love stories from the local lore such as Heer Ranjha, Sassi Punno, Umar Marvi and even Laila Majnoon from the Arab tradition. There is no space here to quote from the vast treasure of this poetry but lines such as Bulleh Shah's

calling Ranjha Ranjha I have myself become Ranjha
call me Ranjha now, let nobody call me Heer

رانجھا رانجھا کر دی نی میں آپے رانجھا ہوئی
سدو نی مینوں دھیدو رانجھا، ہیر نہ آکھو کوئی

or the Sufi's disdain of formal observances in the following lines of Baba Farid

the ways of Farid are all topsy turvy
he neither fasts nor says his prayers
his drinking ways of life are notorious

or lines such as these oft quoted from the poetry Bulleh Shah on the uselessness of empty knowledge

let us put a stop to knowledge, O friend
only one alif is required for salvation

علموں بس کریں او یار
اکو الف تیرے درکار

then we have this very popular theme from Hazrat Amir Khusrau that qawwals all over the subcontinent perform in Sama meetings

نمی دانم چہ منزل بود شب جائے کہ من بودم
بہر سو رقصِ بسمل بود شب جائے کہ من بودم
خدا خود میرِ مجلس بود اندر لا مکان خسرو
محمدؐ شمعِ محفل بود شب جائے کہ من بودم

nami danam che manzil bood, shab jae ke man boodam
ba har su raqse bismil bood, shab jae ke man boodam
khuda khud mir-e-majlis bood, andar lamakan Khusrau
Muhammad Shama-e-mehfil bood, shab jae ke man boodam

Another method that the Sufi saints employed to teach the simple folk was through narration of anecdotes and parables that gave neither locale, nor name or time of the occurrence and as such had a timeless quality and deal with subjects like kindness, love, generosity, forgiveness, compassion etc and are generally termed as *mulfuzat* in the Sufi lore. There are tens of thousands such stories extant and related to nearly every saint whose name lives. For instance this story; a group of people came to see Hazrat Junaid and said they were looking for livelihood. Seek it if you know where it is,' rejoined the Sheikh. They then wanted to know if they should seek it from God. ' Remind Him if you think He has forgotten you' came the retort. Should they wait then at home and practice *tawakkul,* they enquired. 'This suggests a state of doubt, they were warned. Then what stratagem they should employ, they asked. Give up all stratagems, was the Sheikh's response. Another good example is the one about a woman whom a kind man took as his wife. But before she could join him she lost an eye to chicken pox. The man learning of this told the woman about pain in his own eyes and soon declared he had become blind. The woman came to his house and lived with him for twenty years and after some illness died. The man then opened his eyes, which were normal. He had pretended to be blind to save his wife from the embarrassment of being one-eyed. Another very famous dialogue that is often quoted and has a long pedigree quoted in *Risala-i Qushairiya* goes like this: Shaqiq Balkhi enquired from Jafar al Sadiq about the meaning of *'futuwat'* i.e., manliness or chivalry. The Imam asked Balkhi to give his view first. Balkhi said it meant that when the Giver gives us something, we offer thanks; if not, we practice *sabr* (patience or fortitude). The Imam remarked, 'the dogs of Medina do the same." This conversation is also related to Hazrat Rabia Basri and Hazrat Junaid Baghdadi, both living in time a hundred years apart. But the purpose of these *malfuzat* is throwing light on issues that the simple folk could not understand.

When talking about the spread of the various Sufi orders or schools it is often asked if such divisions between the seekers of the ultimate truth were necessary or if these orders represent some difference in the nature of beliefs the masters of these systems held. The Sufis themselves hold no such question in their mind. There is considerable unanimity in the thinking that these various orders of the saints are not variants of faith or in anyway having or leading to different goals. The differences between the various orders are mainly differences of selection, by the founders of the orders, from the wide range of practices offered by the Prophet's own example and recommendation. In fact all paths lead back to the Apostle since all Sufis insist that the Prophet indeed was the first Sufi Shaykh. This is affirmed by what Junayd Baghdadi meant when he said that "all the mystic paths are barred except to him who followeth in the footsteps of the Messenger," and further that "this our lore is anointed with the sayings of the Messenger of God". With particular reference to the origin of

Sufism it is also mentioned that the Prophet gave some teachings which were not intended to become common knowledge. This particularity of Sufism in the ambit of Islam does not lessen its universality, and regardless of what many practitioners of Sufism in the West may like to say about the Sufi path being independent of any particular religion, the Sufi seeks Divine bliss through the Messenger's lore. Nevertheless the Sufi discourse is open and as one sees in Sufism's evolution in the subcontinent, and particularly in the Sufi poetry of Punjab and Sindh, the absorption of local lore and imagery, in fact the actual feel of the land, only goes to broaden and accentuate its appeal, since the objective of the Sufi is to seek God's pleasure in the love and service of His creation.

In the languages spoken in Pakistan Sufi poetry enjoys a prominent place. In fact, one can say with some certainty, that in the entire Muslim world, the way mystic thought infuses the verse tradition in Pakistan, it does not do anywhere else and the quantity and quality of this poetry is also unmatched. Starting with Farid Shakarganj, Shah Hussain, Khushal Khan Khattak, Sultan Bahu, Rahman Baba, Shah Abdul Latif Bhitai, Bulhe Shah, Jam Durak, Sachal Sarmast, Mast Tawakkli, Khwaja Ghulam Farid, Mian Muhammad Bakhsh, , Saeen Ahmad Ali --- to a host of important poets of today, whose work is enriched with the Sufic thought, they present a continuing tradition that does not seem to end anywhere, despite the great influx of new sensibilities, themes and a modern idiom in the poetry of the subcontinent. While reading these poets it is not difficult to recognize the deep refrain of the great poetic works in Persian of Abu Saeed Abul Khair, Sanaee, Fariduddin Attar and Jalauddin Rumi.

As a living force running through the cultural life of the people and giving a spiritual dimension to the practice of religion, Sufism made more advances in Muslim India than anywhere else, particularly in the vale of Sindh where its real creative period started in the early years of the second millennium when Syed Ali Hajvairy migrated to Lahore from his ancestral Ghazni. He had been to centres of Islamic learning in Central Asia and the Middle East and had also spent time in the spiritual nurseries of Muslim saints. A contemporary of Imam Ghazali, he shared with him opposition to extremist Sufi expression and emphasized moderation of thought and behaviour. He was not only a poet but entertained positive outlook on arts and was partial to music.

The saints and mystics who came later, particularly those belonging to the Chishtia order, not only worked for tolerance and communal harmony among people of different religions but also enriched and elevated regional cultures by using local languages for the expression of their devotional poetry. Though Syed Hajvairy's verse could not be preserved, we have the valuable and inspiring verse of Fariduddin Ganjshakkar which no other but a saint and sage of 15th century, Baba Guru Nanak, conveyed to the people, proving how the different faiths coexisted in mutual harmony and respect at that period of time. Baba Farid is regarded as Punjabi language's first poet. In the next generation of the Chishtia order we come across Hazrat Amir Khusrau, lending colour and song to both Urdu and Hindi languages. Together the poetry of these saints won the hearts and captured the imagination of millions in northern India.

In the footsteps of these great men of Sufi tradition followed a whole crop of poets and singers whom history has not preserved but who belonged to the Bhagti Movement and served the cause of bridging the chasm between Ram and Rahim, to bring communities together and promoting love and harmony in the land. In the lead of this movement were people belonging to the lower classes among whom were luminaries like Baba Guru Nanak and Bhagat Kabir, respected by Hindus and Muslims alike.

The poetry of Baba Farid has influenced generations of poets in Punjab and Sindh among whom Rajasthan's Mira Bai, central Punjab's Shah Hussain, Sindh's Shah Abdul Latif Bhitai and southern Punjab's Khwaja Ghulam Farid stand out as the integral spiritual glue that binds the Sufi tradition in this part of South Asia and keeps the stream of cultural sensibility informed of its original fount. But the philosophy of the Unity of Being that was given its Islamic form by Sufi intellectuals like Sheikh-e-Akbar Ibne Arabi could not find acceptance among the Suhrawardy order saints. But it was more readily assimilated by the Qadria order Sufis among whom Shah Hussain, Sultan Bahu, Baba Bulhe Shah and Shah Abdul Latif Bhitai have a strong pantheistic strain in their poetical work. In the 17th century it got further impetus from personalities like Hazrat Mian Mir and his disciples, among whom Prince Dara Shikoh and others represent the high liberal and humanistic tradition of that time.

Now before we return to Sufism's relevance in this era of global uniformity of values and the reduction of all and everything to a soulless commercialism, a word about the themes Sufi poetry of the subcontinent concerns itself with. The central refrain is of course a seeking of the Divine intimations, the Ultimate Reality and the origin of Being. The thirst to have cognition of these basic truths keeps his soul in perpetual agitation; he yearns for union with the ultimate, a dissolution of duality and attainment of that unity in which his own identity is annihilated: So the songs of the beloved's separation from her love. Life's fickleness and man's short and uncertain existence is emphasized to discourage the pursuit of worldly gains. Yet Sufi poetry is not didactic or moral in nature. It gives due regard to high morals as long as these are reflection of inner purity and sincerity. What is most vehemently rejected is hypocrisy and false show of piety. In the end, constant vigil and awareness of the Divine reality is the labour man must perform to save himself from the sin of forgetfulness. But in the state of divine love this labour becomes true ecstasy for the Sufi.

Now the question that this brief presentation has attempted to examine, with reference to the crisis which many serious thinkers of our time perceive the modern world to be facing, is about the efficacy of Sufism in attending to the basic malaise which, as earlier mentioned, is the concept of progress the west swears by and wants all others to follow. It is not just about making more money but generally about having more of everything without any reason, about winning, about fighting, competition, about influence, hegemony and control, about the use of power and the means of securing it. These cherished precepts one can challenge only at the cost of being dubbed as a cynic or a recluse unaware of where the world is going. And this view is shared by a considerable section of opinion in the East also. The haze of rhetoric does not allow the paradox to be seen clearly which is most visibly evident in the failure of technology. Its impressive advancement has not relieved mankind of drudgery. In the most advanced countries of the West the time for leisure has shrunk to a weekend hour of hectic indulgence. The luxury of having time to waste is something only the poorest on earth enjoy. This is the result of breaking loose from the cohesive bond of tradition, giving quality's place to quantity and having substance in place of essence. Now change is the god; permanence is rejected as backwardness. But change does not mean new things. It means more of the same. It means repetition. The drudgery of work, in place of the joy of creation. The breaking down of the family structure, first in the west, and now also in the east, has deprived society of the cohesion in which the individual found meaning and identity.

It is no wonder people around the world are looking for meaning in their lives. They are reading the teachings of Buddha, they are reading Rumi, they are doing meditation, taking up courses in Yoga and so on, as I said earlier. But this is happening at the individual level. At the conceptual level of the society, the value system that governs life continues to be the same. Progress requires constant action but man needs rest and contemplation. Extremism and terror politics have widened the gulf between religions. There is distrust all around and insecurity. But what binds all religions, and is at the core of all faiths, is the Sufi view of life. If the world is becoming a global village with all kinds of communication and information gadgetry, it is time to think of bringing it closer more meaningfully by restoring in our lives, across the boundaries of east and west, the tradition of spirituality the Sufi way offers.

Jigar Mohammed

Relevance of Sufi Thought and Practices to the Promotion of Peace and Concept of Living Together

The socio-religious movements have been a continuous process of dialogue between past and present in terms of continuation of the sources of the cultural developments. It is an established fact that the modern world has made tremendous progress in the scientific and economic fields. The man of the contemporary world is more fortunate in terms of educational facilities, transport, communication, food and dress etc. But it is another established fact that the man of the modern world is facing greater political and socio-economic problems. Existence of the problems is not a new phenomenon of the modem world, but the social tensions, evils, territorial aggrandizement, suppression of the rights of the common people, religious persecution and property disputes have been prevailing in the world since the ancient times. However, in every age people invented some methods for the minimization of their tensions and conflicts. It is known that during the ancient period when social tensions and evils emerged in the different parts of the world and importance of the common people and dignity of work was threatened, various types of religions, social organizations and movements emerged to restore the dignity of the human beings. For example the Buddhism, Jainism, Christianity and Islam emerged against the social injustice of the period. The foundation of Islam laid by Prophet Muhammad (peace be upon him) led to the emergence of equality among the Muslims and all types of prejudices, superstitions and exploitations were challenged and a process of the elimination of the social evils started in Arabia.

However, the emergence of the Sufism, an offshoot of Islam, intensified the process of social justice and social services to the mankind. It is an established fact that the Sufism emerged as a social protest against the emergence of the monarchy in the Islamic world. But it did not confine to the Muslim countries. In the last decade of the 12th century, the Sufism entered India as a social movement. The Chishti *Silsila* was the first Sufi order, which arrived in India. At the arrival of this *Silsila* the Muslim population in India was negligible. But the Chishti Sufis did not find any difficulty in performing their activities. Within short period they became very popular in India. The social popularity of the Sufis was not established because of any political or economic grandeur, but their social activities meant for the common people brought great fame for them. A large number of people found the activities of the Sufis as the source of their peace and progress. The Chishti Sufis' main activities were to organize social discussion at their *khanqah* (houses) to provide financial support to the needy, impart education, organize audition party (Sama), keep themselves far from the state, preach the philosophy of the Unity of Being *(Wahndat-ul-Wajood)*, promote vernacular language, establish dignity of labour and adjust oneself according to the local environment. All these activities were meant for the people of each section of the Indian society irrespective of religion and caste. Khawaja Moinuddin Chishti, the founder of the Chishti *silsila* in India declared that helping the poor and needy was the highest form of devotion. Farid-ud-din Ganj-i Shakar, popularly known as Baba Farid introduced *Iangar* (free Kitchen) for the welfare of the poor. Amir Khusro wrote *Ioris* and *pahelis* which are still popular among the common people of India. The Chishti Sufis established the concept that poverty knows no religion. All these activities of the Sufis were very much appreciated by the Indian society. The Sufis' *khanqah* became a place of social gatherings and meeting place of the Islam and Hinduism. The popularity of the Sufis can be estimated from the fact that after their death their shrines became the places of worship, a symbol of Indian Islam.

In the contemporary world each nation, society, community and social group is trying to establish its domination over oneanother. The concept of exclusiveness is the main trend of the contemporary world. People of one community consider the people of other community as their rivals. The processes of establishing domination over others and to adopt the life of exclusiveness are the causes of international conflicts, social tension, economic crisis and law and order problems all over the world, particularly in the Asian continent. It is important to mention that the teachings and practices of the Chishti Sufis discourage exclusiveness and are helpful in eliminating the causes of the people's miseries. During medieval period the Chishti Sufis established that the concept of oneness was the strongest source of peace and happiness. It is known that during the medieval period there were two ways to make people loyal to a particular authority and social group. Firstly, it was theology and secondly the armed power. Common people did not possess these things. But the Chishti Sufis did not take help of any of them in establishing their base in the Indian society. They believed that performance of social service was the most important duty of the human being. They discarded the concepts of otherness and exclusiveness. Their philosophy of the *Wahdat-ul-Wajud* (Unity of Being) determines the places where people of different social background can sit together and contribute to the betterment of society collectively. For the creation of oneness and inclusiveness the Chishti Sufis recommend the rendering of social services and continuous social mingling.

According to the Chishti Sufis' philosophy and practices, no place of the world can be called backward. Every area has potentialities of the progress provided the people work sincerely for that. For example, when Chishti Sufis came to India they established their centres of activities without any consideration of the prominence of the place. Contrary to it they settled at the places, which were inhabited by the common people. It is known that when Khawaja Moinuddin Chishti came to Ajmer and settled there, it was predominantly Hindu populated area and a seat of the power of the Chauhan Rajputs. But Khawaja Moinuddin Chishti decided to make Ajmer as his permanent residence. His disciple Sheikh Hamiduddin settled at Suwal, a village in Nagaur in Rajputana. It is understood that he was the earliest Muslim settled in the village. Khawaja Qutubiddin Bakhtiyar Kaki, another disciple of Khawaja Moinuddin Chishti, settled in Delhi where he had to face the opposition of the *Wema (hieologians)*. But he did not think to shift from there. Consequently, the people of Delhi in a large number became his followers. His large social support may be justified from the fact that Qutubuddin Aibak (1206-10), the Turkish ruler, constructed

Qutub Minar at Mehrauli after the name of the Sufi.[3] This shows that Bakhtiyar Kaki made the people realize that difficulties of an area were to be solved by the people there. His determination to reside at Delhi despite the opposition of the *Ulema* not only enabled him to serve the people of Delhi, but also the area was honored by the ruling class, birth, religion, caste, class and race.[4] Similarly, it is the duty of a person to perform those duties which encourage inclusiveness. Khawaja Moinuddin Chishti used to say that the generosity was the effective source of the people's happiness.[5] He remarked that the trust in God of only those persons is worthwhile who do not cause problems for humanity *(Khalq-i-Khuda)*[6]. He defines three duties of a person as highest form of the devotion to the God:[7]

- To redress the miseries of those in distress *(Faryad Rasee)*
- To help the needy *(Bechargan)* and
- To feed the *hungree (Gursigan)*.[8]

Nizamuddin describes two types of devotion to the God: 1. Intransitive (lazmi) and 2. Transitive *(mutaaddi)*. According to him, "The intransitive devotion is that by which only the devotee gets benefited, and that consists of prayer, *hajj*, fasting, the repetition of *latanie (awrad wa tasbihat)* and similar other things. But the transitive devotion is that which comes forth in the form of being helpful to others out of sheer love for their good and comfort and the reward of this transitive is immense and immeasurable. Intransitive devotion sincerity is first accepted by the Almighty, while the acts of transitive devotion are acceptable (to God) and would be rewarded in whatever form they are performed".[9] Regarding feeding the people Nizamuddin Aulia observed, "A pious man has stated that serving food worth only a *dirham* before friends carries reward of more than a *sadaqah* (charity) of twenty *dirhams*".[10] He advised his disciples to first greet *(salam)* a visitor and, then serve him with food and make conversation with him.[11]

For the welfare of people the Chishti Sufis propagated the offering of charity *(sadaqah)* to the needy. Sheikh Nizamuddin Aulia remarked that charity was to be given with full sincerity and truthfulness. He puts five conditions for the giver of the charity:

1. Legitimate earning,
2. The intention of giving it to a man of good character so that it might not be spent wrongly,

3. Cheerfulness, humility and open heartedness,
4. Complete secrecy in giving it and
5. After giving it the giver should never talk about it or reveal it to any body.[12]

To encourage circulation of wealth among the people the Chishti Sufis discouraged the accumulation and hoarding of wealth. They encouraged the renunciation of wealth. Regarding the renunciation of wealth Sheikh Nizamuddin Aulia observes "This is no renunciation if one strips himself to the skin, ties the *langota* around his waist and retires (to a corner). The true renunciation is that one puts on (proper) clothes and takes one's food as usual, one is contented with whatever one gets, has no inclination to accumulate that and refuses to be attached to anything. This is Renunciation".[13] The concept of the renunciation of wealth explained by the Sufis is very much applicable to the contemporary world. It generally happens that people of certain areas face starvation because of some natural calamity or non-availability of sufficient resources for survival. But if the people of fertile areas, controller of resources and wealthy persons share a small part of their wealth and resources with the needy the problem of food may be minimized to a great extent.

The Chishti Sufis advised the people that social services were not to be performed through speech but they are to be in deed. It is known that Baba Farid introduced *langar*(open kitchen).[14] By organizing the open kitchen Chishti Sufis not only enabled the poor and needy to feel secured in satisfying their hunger, but more importantly they provided opportunity to the downtrodden to participate in food party without any complex. The concept of open kitchen is not simply an act of helping the needy, but it very helpful in bringing people closer to each other and creating the concept of inclusiveness. In the contemporary world a great disparity exists in terms of class, religion and caste. On the basis of these disparities the concept of others is widened between privileged and unprivileged people. Thus the application of Sufis' methodology for providing food to the needy may help in shortening social disparity.

The Chishti Sufis practiced the distribution of wealth among the needy and poor as service to the humanity. It is an established fact that most of the Chishti Sufis accepted unasked donation or charity *(futuh)*.

They hardly spent the donation on their maintenance, but whatever donation they received was spent on the welfare of the common people. They distributed the donation within the same day on which it was collected. Nothing was to be saved for the next day.[15] Sheikh Nizamuddin Aulia advised his disciples to use only onetenth part of the unasked charity for their personal expenditure. He did not accept any *futuh*, which could be instrumental for the publicity of the giver or distributor. He prescribed the following rules for the acceptance of the *futuh*:

1. No guaranteed payment could be accepted,
2. To accept only the unconditional payment,
3. No acceptance of immovable property such as lands, villages and buildings,
4. Nothing was to be saved for tomorrow and
5. To accept *Futuh* according to the need and capacity of distribution.

It seems that the Chishti Sufis formulated the said rules so that wealth collected in form of charity was not used to make the collector as an exploiter. It is important to mention that Chishti Sufis were against all types of burden imposed upon the people. They thought that wealth was meant for whole society not for an individual. According to Sayyid Muhammad bin Kirmani, "Sometimes *futuh* and *Nazrana* came to *khanqah* in large quantity. Nizamuddin Aulia started to weep (because of difficulty to distribute), but when he heard that all *futuh* had been distributed (according to prescribed rules) among the poor he felt great comfort".[16] It is said that once Sheikh Nizamuddin Aulia was walking on side of Jamna river, he saw that an old woman was fetching water from a well. He was very much surprised and asked the woman when Jamna river was so near to her why was she taking so much pain in drawing the water from the well. She replied that the water of Jamna was so sweet and pure that it increased the hunger very much which she was unable to meet with her resources. Nizamuddin Aulia realized the poor condition of the woman and ordered his disciple Iqbal to "go and ask her how much she needed for her daily expenses and sent her expenses every month without fail". He instructed his disciples to provide two times food which was justified. He also told that it had always been a righteous act to feed the people.[17] It is important to mention that the Chishti Sufis extended this help as their duty to society and not to gain any fame. Since during the contemporary world people stress mainly on the collection of wealth and its expenditure on the personal maintenance, there is hardly any sense of satisfaction among the people. On the contrary people are trapped in social tension irrespective of social background. Thus, here lies the relevance of practices of the Chishti Sufis according to which the collection and distribution of the wealth are to go parallel.

The Chishti Sufis stressed on the enjoyment of the fruits of development with limits so that all member of society could enjoy them. More importantly, they themselves used minimum food, cloth and lived in ordinary houses. They preferred to live in poverty. Both Khawaja Moinuddin and Khawaja Bakhtiyar Kaki did not have their own houses. Baba Farid always lived in brickless *(Kutcha)* house. Even this, too, was built during last stage of his life. When a disciple of Baba Farid expressed his desire to build a masonry house for him, he told his disciple, "Masud will not put brick on brick".[18] Sheikh Naqib-Uddin Mutawakkil, brother, of Baba Farid lived in a thatched house *(Chhappar)* along with his wife and children throughout his life.[19] Sheikh Nizamudin Aulia did not have any house in Delhi for many years. Ultimately, he built a thatched house at Ghiyaspur.[20] By living in simple and lowly accomodation the Chishti Sufis exemplified that a house was to be according to the need of the family. Nowadays some people build palatial houses and large number of people live without roof. Such type of distinction is an important cause of the social tension in the modern world. Sufis' life style in terms of houses may not only provide housing to every body, but it may create congenial atmosphere to the people.

The Chishti Sufis always took small quantity of food and its quality was very simple: In no way the quality of the food of the Sufis was better than the food of the downtrodden. Generally, they observed fast throughout their life. When they broke their fast they took very simple things. Baba Farid broke his fast with *Sharbat,* which was brought to him in a bowl with some rice in it. He distributed half or about two-third of it among the people present in the *Majlis* by mixing it with water in drinking vessels. The remaining of one-third of the *Sharbat* he took and even out of it he gave someone to whosoever he wished. Between *Iftar* and *namaz* he was given two loaves of bread. He broke one of the two loaves to pieces and distributed them among the people around. The other loaf he himself ate and even out of that he offered some to whosoever he wished and thereafter he did not eat till the time of *Iftar* next evening? It may be mentioned that in modern times large expenditure and varieties of food are considered as a symbol of higher status. But the persons of such thinking do not understand that their extravagancy are at the cost of a large section of society. They should understand that the Chishti Sufis lived long because of their moderate habit of taking food and to be concerned about the food of the others.

The medieval period was an age of despotism and persons of armed background were considered the most dominant section of society. But during the same period the Sufis successfully promoted the concept of nonviolence and created large followers. They preached people to promote social harmony and discard the means of animosity. Nizamuddin Aulia observed, "there are two things: lower self *(nafs)* and heart *(qalb)*. The former has acrimony, violence and discord in it while the latter, besides other virtues, has peace, acquiescence, benignity and kindness. If one behaves under the spell of the *nafs,* the other's response should be from the side of the *qalb*. This would rest the *nafs* being overpowered. But if anybody confronts *nafs* with *nafs,* there will be no end to animosity and discord. He further observes, "If a man places thorns (in your way) and you do the same, there will be thorns everywhere".[21] In the contemporary world when arms race is considered as the solution of all the problems the philosophy non-violence by the Sufis may be a guide to happiness and peace.

On the basis of the above cited activities the Sufis emerged as the men of the masses. They not only remained popular in society during their lifetime, but also more importantly, after their death their shrine became the centre of religious activities.

Nowadays a large section of Indian society goes to shrine of the Chishti Sufis to get their blessing for mental peace and prosperity. Thus for the contemporary world it is a lesson that only those persons are glowing part of history and deserve respect who work for the welfare of the humanity. It is important to mention that no body goes to the tombs of the rulers of the medieval period who were symbol of authority. Thus in the contemporary world the Sufis' concept and practice of inclusiveness is more relevant.

Notes:

1. K.A. Nizami, *Some Aspects of Religion and Politics in India during the Thirteenth Century*, Delhi, 1974, p. 186.
2. Amir Plasan Sijzi, *Fawaid-ul-Fuad*, Eng.Tr. by Zia-ul-Hasan Faruqui, Delhi, 1994, p.386
3. Ibid, p. 285
4. Richard Maxwell Baton, *Sufis of Bijapur, 1300-1700*, New Jersey, 1978, p. 79.
5. Sayyid Muhammad bin Kirmani, *Siyar-ul-Aulia*, Urdu Tr. by Abdul Latif, Delhi, 1994,p.56
6. Ibid, p.56
7. Qutubuddin Bakhtiyar Kaki, *Dalil-ul-Arfin*, Urdu Tr. by Arshad-ul-Qadiri, in Hasht Bahisht, published by Maktaba Jam-i-Nur, Delhi, n.d. p.2.
8. K.A Nizami, *Religion and Politics*, p. 185
9. Fawaid-ul-Fuad, p. 88.
10. Ibid., 124
11. Ibid., 185
12. Ibid., p. 122
13. Ibid.,p.122
14. K.A, Nizami, *Religion and Politics*, pp. 205-206, fn.7.
15. K.A, Nizami, *Life and Times of Nizamuddin Aulia*, Delhi, p.63.
16. *Siyar-ul-Aulia*, p. 141
17. *Fawaid-ul-Fuad*, p.94
18. K.A Nizami - *Religion and Politics*, p. 102
19. Ibid, p.199
20. Wahid Mirza, *The Life and Works of Amir Khusro*, Delhi, 1974, p. 114
21. *Fawaid-ul-Fuad*, p.148
22. Ibid, p. 259.

Karan Singh, M.P.

Sufism and Bhakti Movements as Part of Great Indian Culture with Special Reference to Kashmir

In Kashmir, there have been many great religious movements. In medieval times, the interaction between Shaiva Movement of which Yogini Laleshweari, perhaps, was the most glowing figure and Sufi movement at the hands of Sheikh Nurruddin Noorani, whose Mazar is at Chrar-e-Sharif and others was the most extraordinary story of the era. Such interactions and a point where Islam and Hinduism can react in a positive fashion have always fascinated us. There has also been much though, a lot of negative interactions down the ages. The destruction of Martand Temple at the hands of Sikandar Butshikan is an example of such negative reaction. On the other hand, we have traditions in Kashmir of Hindus worshipping at the great Sufi shrines at Chrar-e-Shari, Makhdoom Sahib, Hazrat-Bal Dargah and so on. This is a part of our composite culture.

There has been so much violence and conflict down the ages in the name of religion that it is felt that religion has been one of the major sources of conflict in human history. Religion has a two-edged history. On one hand, much that is great and noble in human civilization such as art and architecture, literature, language, music, dance, moral codes and spiritual classics can be traced back to one or the other great religions of the world. On the other, perhaps, more people have been killed, tortured, massacred and persecuted in the name of religion than in any other name. So the question now in this global society is that what sort of religion are we going to encourage? There has been unfortunately a flow back to fundamentalism in many religions, not only in Islam, which has become the most dramatic example, but also in Christianity and Hinduism. There have been fundamentalist backlashes in Sikhism, earlier, as there was a very bad period we went through. Thus, wherever there is growth of fundamentalism, it has led to death and disaster.

If we start arguing on theology, then there are many differences. There are insurmountable theological differences between religions; some may believe in re-birth, others may not; some may believe in single prophet or a book, others may not; some believe in Unity of Godhood, while others in pluralism of Godhood. Therefore, theologically, we can never get an agreement, but as far as the experimental elements of religion are concerned, a golden thread links together all the great religions of the world. This spiritual realization therefore is really the crux.

The Sufis and the Bhakts had really fallen in love with the Divine and this love binds the two socio-religious movements. In Hinduism, we have four main paths to the Divine. *Jnan Yoga,* the intellectual approach, is the way of the mind. Ibnal-Arabi and Shankaracharya perhaps are those great theologians of this path. *Karma Yoga* is the way of action or the way of good deeds. *Raj Yoga* is the way of *Pranayam* and inner spiritual practices. *Bhakti Yoga* into the way of love, where the heart overflows in love for the Divine. Maulana Jalaluddin Rumi's work deals with the aspect where there is reflection of ecstatic statements of 'love for the Divine'. That love could be for human or for Divine, for in love there is no difference.

Ultimately, it is the transcendental power and sovereign vibration of love that really brings about the meeting of hearts, which Rumi calls "the wine of Divine intoxication". The greatest moments in human history were the meetings of Maulana Jalaluddin Rumi and Shams Tabriz, Ramakrishna and Vivekananda, Plato and Socrates, and Hazrat Amir Khusro and Khawaja Nizamuddin Aulia. These are great moments of human civilization. The tomb of Humayun and the *dargah sharif* of Hazrat Nizamuddin are situated within one kilometer. But none goes to pray at the Humayun's tomb but thousands throng to Dargah Sharif for peace and dance. Dargah sharif of Ajmer is said to be the largest place of Muslim-pilgrimage after Makkah and Medina. A large number of Hindus also visit the shrine.

We have also great traditions of Bhakts singing in devotion to Krishna or Shiva. The *Dervishes* dance also is akin to our devotional dance. In this, the whole thing revolves around love for the Divine. The Sheikh sits in the middle and young devotees sit around him. Then, they get up and start dancing whirling and whirling about; they go round and round and it is really one - which moves the heart and the spirit. It is really astounding and this is still in practice. Raslila could also be almost similar to this.

Thus, whether it is 'Chaitanya Bhakts' who do their ecstatic *kirtans* or the whirling *Dervishes,* all of them are symbolic of the essential golden thread that links together all the great religions of the world. The Christian mystics also practice identical things. Francis Thomson, in one of his poems, says;

> Not where the veiling systems darken,
> And are benumbed conceiving soars,
> The drift of pinions would be hardened
> Beats at our own clay shuttered doors,
> The angels keep their ancient places,
> Turn what a stone and start swing,
> It is he; it is your strange vision
> That miss many splintered things.

This is what is said to be - many splintered light of the Atman, what the Bible calls a light that lighteth over man that cometh into the world; what the Sufis call the *Noor-e-Elahi*, what the Sikhs call the "Ek-Onkar", what the seers of the Upanishads say.

I have seen that light shining like a thousand Suns beyond the darkness. It is that Inner Light which represents the core of the human personality and it is that Inner Light which expresses itself through both the Sufis and Bhakts. Both of them were reactions to very strong and rigid ideologies and wavered reactions of the common people. They were not elitist reactions, and were not confined to the scholars or princes. They were indeed the methodology for the masses to express their innermost sentiments and to participate actively in the process of 'love of loving the Divine'. Every religion looks upon the Divine as merciful. As a worshipper of Shiva, we recite:

"karpoor gaurang karuna aytaram".

Thus, we call Him embodiment of compassion. Muslims similarly begin in the name of God by reciting *'Bismillah-i Rahman-i Rahim'*. *Rahman* means full of compassion and love. And yet in the name of Divinity – so much hatred, so much killing, so much fanaticism, so much terrorism, so much violence, so much cruelty is unleashed. This two dichotom cannot co-exist together. It is like the existence of darkness and light together. Fundamentalist creeds and the fragrance of Sufism and Bhakti movement cannot co-exist because they are opposites of each other. In this global society, when science and technology has united the globe, a small machine makes us talk to anybody on the earth. This is a great miracle where your voice gets bounced off a satellite that is circumambulating the globe, thousands of kilometers away in the air and comes down to the earth. All these technologies are there, but religion still represents an area of conflict. In fact, even today, there are many areas in which religious conflicts are in progress and where in the name of religion, the most terrible atrocities are being committed. Therefore anything that helps to bring about a better realization of the importance of Sufism and the Bhakti Movement is to be welcomed.

Islam is a great and noble religion that has made major contributions to human civilization. Today Islam has been reduced to the 'Jehadis' and fundamentalists. Something has to be done to redeem the image and the soul of Islam, as it were, from a very small minority, which in effect has held it as hostage. After the destruction of World Trade Towers, Muslims are seen with suspicion in many parts of the world. Bajrangdalis are doing the same to Hinduism, what Jehadis have done to Islam. They have defamed us in the entire world.

Therefore, the need of the hour is that, Sufism, its literature and consciousness should be developed. Bhakti movement started from here in the same manner. Bhakti movement is a reaction and it developed in this country, cutting cross religious barriers. Several Muslim saints, like Raskhan and Malik Mohammed Jayasi and so on, were major Bhakts. When you are in love with the Divine, these theological differences make little difference.

In Kashmir, we have had until recently the tradition of everybody going to the shrines for worshipping. In fact, there is a temple in Srinagar where on the upper portion there is a mosque and Dargah and in the lower portion, there is a temple of Kali. There is a *shahandan* in the same building where 700 people came from Iran and practiced Sufism.

Our traditions need to be kept intact and promoted. Our intellectuals should shoulder the responsibility of projecting our rich traditions with sincerity. Indian intellectual elite has been guilty of a serious dereliction of duty vis-a-vis religion, because for them, it has been for many decades unfashionable to talk about religion. They construe that religion means orthodoxy. Instead they embark, upon discussions encompassing "so-called modern theories and thoughts" for instance, progressive and socialist society. As the socialist society also collapsed, now, the intellectual class has discarded the religion of USSR. The discussion of religion was practically left to backward people. They became fanatical and fundamentalists. I have been emphasizing this aspect for the last three decades when I started studying *Gita* and *Upanishad*. When I was in the Cabinet of Indira Gandhi, some had reservations about my observations. It has always been my endeavor however to highlight the deeper thoughts and virtues of Hinduism and Islam. I also greatly admire Sikhism. The land of India has been the land of great saints encompassing all the three religions. The saying of Baba Farid, Nizamuddin Auliya and Amir Khurso are part of our traditions. How wonderfully Bulleh Shah says:

> You may demolish the temple,
> You may demolish the mosque
> And demolish whatever he says
> But don't break the heart
> Where God resides.

The intellectuals need to actively look into our religious ethos and traditions and inculcate them in the youngsters. People tend to call you reactionary if you talk about religion. One need not worry about such comments. There is nothing wrong in presenting our views in our own manner and style. Allama Iqbal talks about, his own self in these words:

> "This *Bulandi of Khudi*" in other words is *Yogn*. *Bulandi* means to make ones consciousness and inner self so powerful that it has direct communion with God. *Yoga* also contains the same thing. *Yoga*

means union i.e. *'Joining the Atman and the Brahman.'*

It is this pursuit, which made us form "Rumi Foundation" in the name of Jalaluddin Rumi. Maulana Jalaluddin Rumi is one of the supreme Sufis. The endeavor is to project a liberal image of religion. Fundamentalism is emerging everywhere, practically among every religious group. I call upon the intellectuals to ponder over these aspects and project a liberal image of our religious ethos and composite culture.

Our composite culture is unique. It reminds me of my childhood, when I observed while going to Shankaracharya temple at Hari Parvat, chaddar was offered first to all the mazars along with it. I also observed that the Muslims maintain the cave of Amar Nath. That was Kashmir, which I know of, where there was no discrimination and in fact, there existed a great deal of mutual respect and admiration for each other. Today there is communal disharmony and identity crisis. Kashmir, which I knew and the Laleshwari which is permeated in me and whose sweet songs we used to listen from our mothers before going to bed, is still deep in my heart. Kashmir is a state of Sufi or Bhakti tradition. Apart from beautiful designs, paintings, 'amri' work and many others, the art and culture of Kashmir is full of Sufi and Bhakti traditions. 'Kanni' weaving was an integral part of Sufism. The number of times that fabric was woven and the songs and the rovers, which were attached to it, were in the same style of Sufi devotion. The fabric which used to mingle with the civilization, which we know by the name of religion, was woven in that fabric, the concept of which we these days teach in the universities, for example, gender issues.

When we ask this question, whether the movements and traditions of Bhakts and Sufis have any relation with the modern and the contemporary world, and if there is any relation what is that, then we might ask ourselves what was Ganga Yamuna culture? Sometimes we call it by some other name. In simple term these were multi-identities. Sufism and Bhakti also have showed this. Whether it was Baba Farid, Bulleh Shah, Nuruddin, Kabir or Nanak, they all were part of great devotional ethos. They were up against the existing power structure striving for a better society. These were movements of dissent of great power which were waged in order to demolish autocratic power.

Today, we know them as movements for civil liberty. Sufi and Bhakti movements were not different from these present-day movements. Bhakti poets in Tamil Nadu who were cobblers or blacksmith said 'we shall demolish the temple' and in the same manner Bulleh Shah said ... If you wish to demolish temples and mosques go ahead, but don't demolish the heart of anybody". Their message like the message of today's freedom movements or movements for civil liberty, was for humanity.

Whether it is poetry of the Sufis or Bhakts - Rumi, Kabir or Sur Uas, their underlining ethos is the same. Rumi says, "I am a goblet and make me a goblet; I am the wind, make me wind".

We cannot bring about global or national harmony through coercive power. No harmon has ever been brought through the power of Powers; no harmon has ever been connected by the assertion of proprietary rights. We have experimented with that model of appropriation of propriety rights, which has already failed. We should now try out the other model represented by the Sufi thought. If we can learn one lesson that the might of the powerless has great value politically and socially, in order to change the political systems, which happen to be that of our voices and by our own actions, we can indeed, transcend this the very great *Rakshas*' of individual and collective ego. We can call it by any name, uni-polar world hegemon, but we know that it is there. The power of the powerless language is the great power of expression. But then, cant these be solved? Most of all can go back to Kashmir, not because Kashmir happens to be mine and I happen to be the receiver of my childhood in Kashmir, but because Kashmir is a model of the confluences of civilizations and cultures. The tensions in which we only talk of Kashmir show that we do not realize the kind of intervention and the blatant violence that we have done to a model of civilization.

Today, we also talk about Afghanistan, Tibet, China and Kashmir. However, it was in Kashmir from where Shavism started. The memorable work of Dara Shikoh took place in Anantnag near Srinagar in Avantipur and where Sufis and Bhakts had left deep imprints. Mir Sahib came from Afghanistan to reach Tibet and he reached Nagarjun or Anantnag. Anantnag is an ideal place for a heritage site. The concept of Charar-e-Sharif started from here. Therefore, it is befitting to have a heritage site here. We have to reconstruct at the national level. From Dal and Nageen to Anantnag. and Kauser Nag and Amar Nath and whereelse at Kolai and Manasbai, at every nook and corner, Kashmiriat, which is talked about or the multiplicity of languages and the cultures, I see it crushed and devastated. If we start a movement of having Anantnag as a heritage site, which would be the central place to spread the message of peace and harmony, which would bring history contemporary and political, and international dialogue together: it will be a great new achievement.

Kazi Javed

Sufism, and the Tradition of Tolerance and Enlightenment in South Asia

There are two types of Sufism: One is based on the metaphysics, of *Wahdat-ul-Wajood* while the other is derived from the philosophy of *Wahdat-ul-Shahood*. These two types are diametrically opposed to each other so far as their socio-political and cultural implications are concerned.

The first type, which is usually referred to as *wajoodi* Sufism teaches tolerance, moderation, peaceful co-existence and humanistic values. This is because its metaphysics implies that there is a unity and oneness in all that exists. The differences, disagreements and divisions among human beings, ideas and all that exists are illusory. They come into being only when we look at things and matters in a limited and biased perspective and fail to see their true reality.

If all differences are not real, then it clearly means that mutual differences of human beings, creeds and cultures are also superficial. They are absurd in the ultimate sense. We should sympathize with those who take these differences seriously and not detest them.

The metaphysics of *Wahdat-ul-Shahood*, on the other hand insists on differences and accords primary to them. This metaphysics developed as a reaction to the socio-political, cultural and intellectual trends that flowered out as consequence of mass popularity of *Wahdat-ul-Wajood* in the 16th century India, Sheikh Ahmad Sirhindi who first presented it as a thought system was a contemporary of the emperor Jahangir.

The philosophy of *Wahdat-ul-Wajood* is Indian in its essence and its origin can be traced to Vedanta. This philosophy was adopted in the early stages of Islamic mysticism. It is commonly believed that Sufism could never have flourished without having accepted this philosophy as its ideological foundation.

History has preserved the name of a Sindhi scholar, Abu Ali Sindhi, who is considered to be the first one who introduced the Sufi intellectuals of the central Muslim world to *wajoodi* doctrine. Bayazid Bastami of the 9th century was the first great Sufi who took lessons from him in it. Jami quotes him as saying in his *Nafahat/-Uns,* "I learnt the science of annihilation and unitarianism from Abu Ali of Sindh."

Majority of the Indian Sufis adopted this philosophy during the middle ages. But we must keep in mind that Sufis were attracted to this philosophy mostly because it was in line with their own ideas and attitudes. The first eminent Indian Sufi Syed Ali Hajveri, for example, belonged to a period when the features of *wajoodi* philosophy had not become popular and prominent. He settled in Lahore in the early years of the eleventh century. His book *Kashf-ul-Mahjoob* still survives and is considered one of the most important books on Sufism. The teachings carried therein are notably humanistic and tolerant. Syed Ali Hajveri preferred a direct and personal relationship between man and God over religion's ritualistic and abstract forms. This preference provided the metaphysical basis of accepting dissent and treating others with tolerance. Here, for example, we can quote Hajveri's opinion about *Hall.* In his, book, *Kashf-ul-Mahjoob,* he supports the idea: "I am surprised at the one who looks for the house of God in the world, but does not experience and witness it in his own heart."

He also had a liking for music and poetry, and did not agree with the religious scholars who believed that Islam had no patience for them. His point of view in this regard is very clear: "the one who says that he does not relish a beautiful voice or music and melody is either a liar or a hypocrite or does not have slightest aesthetic sense."

Lack of taste makes such a person even worse than animals and cattle."

Syed Ali Hajveri laid the foundation of Muslim tolerance in the medieval India through his flexible system of thought. The Sufis and saints promoted these values in the subsequent centuries. Some of the rulers also adopted this policy of tolerance and tried to create harmony among diverse religious communities in India. In this way, they managed to counter the oppression of what we now term as fundamentalism. They not only provided the people with an opportunity to live in a peaceful and congenial environment, but also contributed towards their genuine spiritual and moral grooming. This state of affairs made Thomas Arnold to observe: "During the Muslim rule, on the whole, the level of tolerance exhibited towards non-Muslims was missing in Europe till modern times." The ideology and values that were promoted by the medieval Sufis can be termed as moderate enlightenment. I have borrowed this term from Gerneral Pervaiz Musharraf but I am not going to discuss it here. Anyways this ideology was bitterly opposed by religious scholars who declared themselves custodian of the religious law. Many of these custodians of religious law and orthodoxy did not like Sufism and viewed Sufis with a deep sense of distrust and cynicism. We can imagine the magnitude of opposition between the Sufis and mullahs by the fact that almost one fourth of the traditional Persian, Urdu and Punjabi poetry refers to the conflict between them. The efforts of the religious scholars remained largely confined to highlighting the Hindu-Muslim conflict on the one hand and intensifying differences within the Muslims on the other. Many of them wanted the non-Muslims living under Muslim rule to be treated as sub-humans. They wanted the same treatment to be meted out to those Muslim sects which did not agree with their school of thought. However, the ideas, attitudes, teachings and influence of Sufis hindered the growth of fundamentalism during the middle ages.

It was the Sufis of the *Chishtia Silsila*, or school of thought, who appeared on the Indian scene after Syed Ali Hajveri. This *silsila* was introduced in our region by Khawaja Moeen-ud-Din who came here from his native town of Seistan during the rule of Prithvi Raj. The Sufis of this *silsila* further promoted religious liberalism, tolerance, interaction and humanistic values that were upheld by Syed Ali Hajveri. Khawaja Mooen-ud-Din used to say: "God has created the humans and the universe for the sake of love, and loving God implies loving human beings regardless of their religion, class, color or race. The ultimate goal of religion is selfless love for human beings and their service. The observance of religious law and rituals is not essential as the service of fellow humans". Khawaja Moeen-ud-Din died in 1235 in Ajmer. It was the time when the town of Nagore was emerging as an important centre of Sufi humanism and the culture nourished by the Chishtia intellectuals. This transformation took place because of Hameed-ud-Din Nagori who was a disciple of Khawaja Moeen-ud-Din. He was a poet and a spiritual leader. He made invaluable contribution of combining the finest elements of Hindu and Muslim civilizations to introduce a harmonized culture based on humanism. He also adopted many principles of Hindu mysticism.

The process of adoption was carried on by Baba Farid-ud-Din Ganj Shakar who became the chief of the *Chishtia silsila* after the death of Qutb-ud-Din Bahaktiar Kaki in the fourth decade of the 13th century. He was bitterly criticized by conservative religious scholars for adopting non-Muslim practices. We can take him as the finest personification of tolerant culture created by the Sufis who was to greatly influence the great founder of Sikh religion, Baba Nanak. He presented his teaching in the form of mellow and captivating Punjabi language poetry the major portion of which has been preserved forever by Baba Nanak in *Guru Granth*. The ideas, values and culture promoted by the Sufis of the pre-Mughal period greatly contributed to the development of Bhakti movement despite the narrow-minded and harsh polices of many Muslim rulers and aristocracy. I have discussed the circumstances and factors that gave birth to this movement in some of my books. Many historians now claim that it was a purely Hindu movement, which had nothing to do with Sufis and their teachings. Shushmita Pande, for example, would simply dismiss all links that are established between the two.

The origin, nature and aims of the Bhakti movement have been made very controversial. Anyway, in my humble opnion, we can accept the view that Shankar Achariya and Ramananj of the 10th and 11th centuries revived the ancient Bhakti sensibility in South India. It was a pure Hindu affair but the need to revive Bhakti and its general popularity in North India of the 14th and 15th centuries was a direct result of the cultural and intellectual influence of Sufis. Political influence of Islam also played a role. This is the view that was supported by scholars like Dr. Tara Chand and Professor Humayun Kabir.

In northern parts of India, Bhakti movement produced a number of such Bhagats who had, not only unconsciously but consciously also, absorbed the Muslim influence. Their concept of Bhakti envisaged uniform love for all humans without discrimination on the basis of colour, caste or creed. They sang of love and unity and wanted to bridge between various groups of Indian population.

Many such persons surfaced during the 15th and 16th centuries and their collective efforts are named the Bhakti Movement. The people associated with the movement emphasized the need for a direct relationship between man and God, instead of mere rituals and worship. When the stress is on personal relationship, the religious divisions become irrelevant. Therefore, the hallmark of the Bhakti movements is that it preached religious tolerance, universal love, equality and humanism.

Ramananda was the man who initiated the form of Bhakti we are interested in and which strived for the Hindu-Muslim unity. The liberal elements of his system of thought later embodied themselves in the form of Bhagat Kabir who was born in 1440. Tulsi Das, Bhagat Kabir and Baba Nanak are by many accounts the most refined personalities created by the Indian civilization of the middle ages. They all are representatives of the Bhakti movement. Kabir can be termed as the personification of the most sophisticated Bhakti sentiments and its grandest ideals. Religious tolerance and harmony that he preached took him to such a height that it is not possible to fit him in any traditional religious category; he can qualify both as a Hindu and a Muslim.

The same is true about Baba Nanak. You can hardly find any Muslim in Punjab who will not declare him to be a *pukka* Muslim. Baba Nanak was beacon of tolerance and humanism. He had incorporated the finer elements of both Hinduism and Islam in a refined manner. Now there are scholars who entertain many doubts regarding the Islamic or Sufi influence on Baba Nanak. But it is not possible to deny this influence simply because it is clearly manifest in every aspect of his poetry, thought and personality. In comparison, there is only a scanty influence of his ancestral Hinduism. Baba Nanak gave a great message of tolerance and humanism to the people of this part of the world, but the subsequent political circumstances gave his movement entirely different colour.

It may sound strange but it is a fact of history that the founder of Mughal dynasty, Zaheer-ud-Din Babar, too had absorbed many teachings of the Sufis and Bhakts that were in the air at the time he laid the foundations of Mughal rule in 1526. He did not get a chance to rule for a long time, but during his rule he rejected the narrow-mindedness and intolerance of the Lodhis and adopted policy of religious harmony. A will is attributed to him, which he is supposed to have made for his son and successor Humayun. It is a significant example of religious tolerance and foresight. Babar advises Humayun:

> My dear son! India is inhibited by people belonging to diverse religions. It is a great blessing of God to have made you the emperor of this land. As a ruler, you should accord special consideration to these points: (1) Never let religious bias take root in your heart and, respecting people's religious sentiments and customs, administer justice to all and sundry without special concessions to any; (2) Take special care to avoid cow —slaughter, so that you could win the hearts of your subjects. In this way, " they will become obedient to you out of gratefulness and gratitude; (3) You should not demolish any religion's place of worship and always do justice to all, so that the king and his subjects enjoy friendly relations and there is peace in the land; (4) The preaching of Islam would be better ensured though kindness and love instead of cruelty and oppression; (5) Always ignore the Shia - Sunni differences because they would weaken Islam; and (6) Take diverse traits of your subjects as the various seasons of the year, so that your rule remains free form ills and weaknesses."

The kind of moderate enlightenment emphasized by Babar became the basis of his grandson Akbar's policies. If now we remember him as Akbar the Great, it is mostly because of his policy of religious tolerance and his respect for all religions. I have no intention here to go into details of his policies or his *Din-e-Elahi*. However, I would only say that his policies and *Din-e-Elahi* would never have come into being without the teachings of Sufis and Bhakts. In fact, it were their teachings that created a new culture and circumstances that were reflected in the policies and ideas of the great Mughal.

The polices of Akbar were unacceptable not only to the orthodox religious scholars but also many other sections of the Muslim society. They were offensive to them from the religious point of view. They also feared that the distinction of Muslim and non-Muslim would disappear as a result of these policies, and the Muslim dominance in India would be endangered. The lords and upper class particularly opposed Akbar. They rightly feared that his policies will ultimately deprive them of their supremacy in society. A large number of those lords and other members of the privileged classes had come from the central Asian region. Their vital interests were at variance with those of the Indian people. So winds of change started to blow.

The most aggressive reaction came from Sheikh Ahmad Sirhindi who belonged to the then newly introduced Sufi school of *Naqshbandia*. Sheikh Sirhindi can be labeled as the ideologue that laid the foundation of Muslim fundamentalism in the sub-continent. Allama Muhammad Iqbal believed him to be the 'greatest reformist of Islamic mysticism.' It is interesting to note that many of the orthodox clerics of his day did not like many of his ideas and they came down heavily on him. As has been explained earlier, the foundations of Muslim enlightenment in India rested on the philosophy of *Wahdat-ul-Wajood*. Therefore, it was imperative to strike hard at this philosophy in order to provide a sound intellectual basis for fundamentalism. Sheikh Sharf-ud Din Yahya Moneri who lived away from the central areas of Muslim rule, struck the first blow in the 13th century. He rejected the philosophy of *Wahdat-ul-Wajood*, declaring it unacceptable from the Islamic point of view and demanded to exclude all the un-lslamic ideas and practices from Sufism. His ideas have reached us through a book *Maqtoobat-i-Sadi*, which is a collection of his letters written to his disciple, Qazi Shams-ud-Din who lived in Bhagalpur. These letters carry rudimentary form of the concepts, which were later developed by Sheikh Ahmad Sirhindi.

The basic claim of Sheikh Ahmad Sirindi was that the highest spiritual experience is that of *wahdat-ul-shahood* and not that of *wahdat-ul-wajood*. One experiences *wahdat-ul-shahood* at the level of consciousness and its highest form is revelation. Therefore, the mystical experience and its, proclamation must be within the limits of religious law. This principle enabled the Sheikh to defeat the forces of harmony, tolerance and liberalism on three fronts: first the philosophy of *wahdat-ul-wajood*, on which the foundation of Muslim tolerance and enlightenment in India rested, was declared imperfect; second, no room was left for the fraternal Sufism and third, Ijtehad, which was defined by Allama Iqbal as the principle of movement in Islam, was rendered impracticable. In this way, the future course of the socio-cultural and political life of the Muslims of this region was determined. It ultimately led to the events that took place in our corner of the globe in 1947.

Khawaja Masud

Role of Sufism in Pakistan

The ultimate purpose of Sufism is a lived experience of an internal, unifying encounter between a human being and God i.e., the sense of the infinite and the absolute linked to the divine as taught by Islam, and indeed, by all religions. Mystical contemplation is an individual exercise. It is lived as a gratuitous gift of God, which is reciprocated by the loving gift of the Sufi. Islam encourages communication with God without the mediation of the priests.

When the great Sufi, Mansur al-Hallaj, who was tortured and executed in 922, uttered the phrase, "Ana al Haq" (I am the Truth), the narrow-minded and the close-hearted orthodox elements of the society could not comprehend him and condemned him as a heretic, accusing him of "hulul" (incarnation). Louis Massignon, arguably the greatest authority on al-Hallaj, wrote: "Hallaj tried to reconcile dogma and Greek philosophy with the rules of mystical experimentation."

Louis Massignon's assessment of al-Hallaj underscores the originality and richness of Sufistic thought from the 7th to the 9th centuries in a society where several cultural traditions and currents of thought originating in ethno-cultural groups (mawali) converged. Philosophy was capable of unraveling a mystical experience, just *as* Sufism interchanges of ideas could occur in cosmopolitan cities such as Baghdad, Basra, Makkah (during pilgrimage) and Cairo.

Sufis of the formative period succeeded in remaining solidly rooted in the intellectual terrain of their time, all the time edging toward an existential monoism (wahdat ul wajood) in the words of the great mystic Ibn al Arabi (d.1240). They described their experience with an analytical profundity that elicited admiration even from Allama Iqbal.

Bistami (d. 874) and Junaid (d.910) are two great Sufis among several others.

As Iqbal puts it: "Iman (faith) is not merely a passive belief in one or more propositions of a certain kind; it is a living assurance born of a rare experience."

"In the history of religious experience in Islam", he goes on to say, "which according to the Prophet (peace be upon him), consists in the creation of divine attributes in man', this experience has found expression in such praises—'I am the truth' (Hallaj); 'I am the speaking Quran (Ali);' 'Glory to me' (Bayazid Bistami). 'In the higher Sufism of Islam' says Iqbal, 'unitive experience is not the finite ego effacing its own identity by some sort of absorption into the Infinite Ego; it is rather the Infinite passing into the loving embrace of the finite."

Historically, Pakistan has been one of the greatest confluences of cultural strands, a laboratory of racial inter-mixing of cross-fertilization of religious ideas, of co-existence of languages and dialects. Our country represents fascinating coalescence of cultures: vibrant, regenerative, adaptive and innovative. It is a vivid and dynamic example of unity in diversity. Its survival and continuity of more than 3000 years of recorded history (possible 2000 years of pre-history) makes it one of the oldest and the most plural society of the world. Its characteristics are: continuity (notwithstanding change), assimilation (not precluding conflicts) and synthesis (not overlooking thes's and anti-thes's). Continuity is the result of the triumph of assimilation and synthes's. Assimilation and synthesis in turn have been the two dominant processes of Pakistani society. A peculiar combination of geographical factors interacting with historical forces have marked out Pakistan as a distinct socio-political entity.

In the dim twilight of history, the migration of primordial hordes of ethnic groups from western, central and south central parts of Asia that descended wave upon wave into the Indus-valley provided the first pattern of inter-ethnic mixture in the generous Indus valley that became one of the biggest crucible of races and cultures in human history.

It is not surprising that the composite culture in Pakistan originated in an environment of reconciliation rather than refutation, cooperation rather than confrontation, co-existence rather than mutual annihilation.

The Sufi saints of the Indus valley played a glorious role in the evolution of the composite culture of Pakistan with love as the axial principle of life—love of God and love of mankind as the means of the mystic vision and the unitive state. The central concepts of Islam—brotherhood of man, justice as the governing principle of social ethics, charity towards the have-nots, rejection of priest-hood, monotheism, emphasis on Rehman (the Beneficent) and Rahim (the Mericful) as attributes of God, with implications of mercy and beneficence towards human beings in fulfillment of haquq-al-ibad (obligations to humanity) — form the bed-rocks of the teachings of the Sufi saints. These Sufi saints became popular heroes as charismatic focus of charity, fraternization of different communities, upholders of the rights of the downtrodden and dissenters against the tyranny of the feudal aristocracy and dogmatic intolerant priests. Their khanqahs (monasteries) provided refuge to the wretched of the earth and the disinherited.

Baba Fariduddin Gunj Shakar (1175-1265) firmly advised his followers not to make friends with the rulers and the aristocrats, despite the great reverence in which Sultan Balban (d.1287) held him. His *khanqah* (monastery) became the rendezvous of scholars hailing from different religions. So deep was his influence on Guru Nanak, the founder of the Sikh religion, that the verses of Baba Farid were incorporated in the holy book of the Sikhs, *Guru Garanth Saheb* and have been sung in the Sikh temples for the last five hundred years.

Baba Farid is the first Punjabi poet of Sufism. The rural masses of Sindh, the Punjab and the Frontier province know and sing the verses of the great Sufi saints and poets Shah Abdul Latif, Bulleh Shah, Shah Hussain and Rehman Baba. Their verses steeped in love, compassion and tolerance are the warp and woof of the world view of the people of Pakistan. Fundamentalism, as interpreted in the west, is synonymous with fanaticism, violence and terrorism, because they never appeal to the masses of Pakistan, because they are profoundly influenced by the Sufi saints and poets. Their main thrust was to bring ancient wisdom to the common folk, through the message of love, amity and tolerance in the language spoken by them. The Sufi saints lived for what they preached. Nothing more repugnant to them than hypocrisy and false religiosity. Never was their message was more relevant than today.

Juanid said: "Sufism is another name for correct thinking." Ibn ul Samak said: "Sufism is to adopt sincerity." Maarul Karzi said: "Sufism is to embrace truth."

All the Sufis agree that Sufism is the essence of the Qur'an and the Sunnat (conduct of the Prophet).

As the Qur'an puts it: Create in your self the attributes of God. That is what Sufism stands for, and that **is** the need of the hour. Sufism opens, at one end, to the infinite greatness of the Divine and, at the other end, to the infinite variety of mankind, with love as binding force between the two ends.

Islam regards man as the highest form of divine manifestation. As the Qur'an puts it: We did indeed offer the trust to the heavens and the earth, and the mountains, but they refused to undertake it, being afraid thereof but man undertook it (Quran:xxxiii,72)

Ibn al Arabi compared man with the bezel in the seal of a ring. "He is a sign, a mark engraved on the seal with which God's treasury is guarded", he said. Thus the Sufis developed the concept of al-insan el kamil (the perfect man), with the above-mentioned Quranic verse as the starting point. The Sufis' al-insan al-kamil is outlined not in comparing his merits with those of other co-religionists but by correlation with the Absolute, since the criterion of the ideal as conjectured beyond, or, at least, much above normative standards is not of (his world of ours but heedful of the transcendental while restricted to the bounds of the human ego.

It is when preponderance is given to man's divine essence instead of his biological nature that the choice of such criterion becomes possible. Within the boundaries of Islamic culture, the ideal of the perfect man opposed to the normative one (that is fashioned in exact conformity to dogmatic rules) is al-insan al-kamil of the Sufis, according to whom man's predestination is to be the receptacle of the Divine. The Sufis believe that the Qur'anic verse quoted above affirms their concept of the perfect man.

To justify this supreme divine foreordinetion man must strive to attain perfection. His heart is like a mirror in which God's reflection is to appear. Hence, it must be polished so that reflection should correspond to what is reflected. The *raison d'etre* of man's existence consists in performing the supreme duty of constantly serving to attain self-perfection.

It is not enough to obey merely the prescribed rules and norms of social behaviour. Laws and regulations help one to find one's bearing only in the phenomenal world. Those who enter the Sufi's path should be cognizant of the immeasurable distance between man and the Absolute. Self-perfection, is a long journey of many stages. These stages have been variously described by the Sufis.

Fariuddin Attar, in his *Mantiq at-Tayar* depicts seven "Valleys". The first is the Valley of Search (*talab*) where man is purified from worldly desires and passions, exposing himself to the Divine light. The second is the Valley of Love (ishq) where the mystic life begins. The third is the Valley of Comprehension (ma'rifat) where the mystic is immersed in meditation. The fourth is the Valley of Detachment (istigna) where the soul is enveloped by love for God. The fifth is the Valley of Unification (tauhid) where the mystic, devoid of any images, attains vision of God and unity with Him. The sixth is the Valley of Bewilderment (hayrat) where all vision disappears and the soul is dazzled by the Divine light. The seventh and the last is the Valley of Annihilation (fana) where the human self is completely merged in God.

In Sufism the attainment of perfection comes with adhering to universal human values and practicing them in one's daily life. Then comes ascetic self-discipline and renunciation of temptations which lead to a life illuminated with the quality of *istigna* and deep look into one's self—knowing oneself means knowing the truth. As the *hadith* says: "He who knows himself knows God." Ibn al-Farid wrote in his poem: "After self mortification I saw that he who brought me to behold and led me to my real self was I: I was my own example. My standing before myself; my turning (towards Ka'aba) was towards myself. Even so my prayer was to myself and my Ka'aba.

The Sufi's path to perfection is unending, including expansion of all latent human faculties. His behaviour expresses dissatisfaction with the existing world order and it is a challenge to the social mores which uphold the status quo.

The mystical asceticism manifests the highest degree of altruism in rejecting mundane goods and pleasures. It exalts self-sacrifice. Contrary to the common notion that Sufism rejects life, constant striving for self-perfection and truth testify to real affirmation of life which is in a process of constant change. In search for truth Sufism rejects dogmatism, intolerance and fanaticism. Sufism opens one's heart and mind to kaleidoscopically changing reality. It seeks unity in diversity. Humanism and pluralism are the hallmark of a true Sufi who believes in letting all flowers blossom.

Now, at the end of the second millennium when nationalism and pragmatism rule the world, when the achievements of science and technology have extended man's rule to the boundaries of the cosmos, suddenly there has arisen a heightened interest in the mysticism. What especially attracts people to Sufism is rooted in its vision of man's inseparable connection with the universe. The Sufis believe that to attain perfection man must forsake his self-conceit, disclaim his pretension of arbitrary meddling with the harmony of the universe, realize the value and worth of his own self but of all other human beings, counteract the selfishness of egocentric individualism with the altruistic spirituality of enlightened personality.

Individual self-perfection is an indispensable ingredient in the process of social transformation. Society cannot be perfected without the perfection of individuals, at the same time personal perfection cannot be separated from the perfection of the society as a whole. A true Sufi true to account as fully as possible all the spiritual wealth acquired in the course of history. Hence a dialectical approach is needed that rids human thought of stereotypes and enables it to comprehend and utilize various traditions in their complexity.

A true Sufi striving for perfection bears the cross for the entire suffering humanity. A Sufi rightly claimed and the world acknowledges it that Mansur al Hallaj is the epitome of the concept of al-insan al-kamil, as he gave his life not only in uttering the truth, but upholding it to the end.

M.D. Thomas[1]

Kabir: A Pioneer of Social Harmony and Upliftment

The special presence of the Creator in the human society has always been proved by the emergence of saints and sages, especially from among the common folk. Their life and message, have contributed greatly to the on-going reformation of the human society towards social harmony. One of the most significant of such great men was Kabir,

who is known for pioneering the unique 'saint tradition'. He was not merely a traditional icon of holiness but was a living legend of spiritual achievement and social renaissanceion. The perennial contribution of Kabir to the re-construction of social life was immense and that makes him a stalwart of social harmony.

Kabir was a product of 15th century who supported himself and his family by hard work, and hence wasn't a traditional monk living at the mercy of others. Though he lived in Kashi, he had gone to Meghar towards the end of his life, in order to challenge the traditional belief i.e; to die in Kashi would merit entry to heaven and to die in Meghar, would lead to hell.

Kabir was not scientifically educated, but had enlightened insights, and was a revolutionary. His thinking was practical as well as radical. He was a saint, a poet, a mystic, a great thinker, a social reformer, and the like - all in one. He was so genuine with his experiences and so bold with his expressions, as well. He was a man of the people as he spoke the dialect of the common man, moved with them, thought with them and lived like them.

The Popular Poetic Saint

Saints of the medieval period are known as popular saints. Kabir has been the most significant of all of them. Like others, he belonged to the people, in a special sense. He hailed from the so-called lower strata of the caste-ridden society of his time. He belonged to the discriminated lot of the general public, voiced the cries and sentiments of the 'voiceless', represented the tastes, needs and aspirations of the masses, shared the problems, struggles and life-situations of the ordinary people and was liked by the common folk for his genuineness and admitted for relentless search for divinity which was appealing to people.

Kabir spoke in the dialect of the general public. In his discourses, he adjusted the language to the audience before him. His utterances were spontaneous, poetical and musical, simple, straightforward, and colloquial. To attempt the popular dialect for communication, when Sanskrit monopolized all knowledge and media of official communication, it was the revolution that Kabir pioneered. Through such an approach, he whispered volumes of spiritual messages to the hearts of the general public. No wonder his lines are often found ready at the tips of tongues of people.

The poetic character of Kabir emerged from his inner experience. It had an appeal of spontaneity. The categories Kabir used were taken from the day-to-day life. The images were taken from the nature. The idioms and examples were fully in line with the ordinary experiences of human life. Kabir did not struggle in any way to compose poetry. Poetry was a natural medium for him in the process of his thought and expression. Poetry became an effective tool for Kabir in communicating his mystical experiences. Thus Kabir became a living icon of spiritual poetry and poetical spirituality at the same time. The poetical dimension has added quality to the saintly quality of Kabir and his spiritual experience.

Kabir was deeply involved in the Indian society - its traditions, values, struggles, problems, needs, ambitions and aspirations. His heart and mind were fully alive to the spiritual, cultural, ideological and behavioral patterns of Indian life. He was deeply committed to the diverse dimensions of the genius of Indian worldview, such as spiritual outlook, individual freedom, plurality, integration, philosophical concept, experimental approach, aesthetic attitude and poetic expression.

This Indian character had a universal appeal. While being firmly rooted in the Indian soil, his life and message had ample implications for the whole humanity. Even though his poetical lines were mostly addressed to himself. They communicate many values for the welfare of the entire human family. Their perennial value travels across the boundaries of caste, creed, profession, community and nationality.

Kabir has a powerful message for the humanity, which was firmly grounded in his mystic experience. He never relied on others' utterances or on pieces of hearsay, he counted on his own personal experience.

Kabir could not close his eyes against the rampant forms of enslavement the human society of his time was afflicted with. There were bondages of understanding, the ritualism, fundamentalism, fanaticism, communalism etc. Forms of slavery like prejudice, hatred, and ill feeling were strongly prevailing. Discrimination based on caste, class, sect, office, social status, profession, language, region, etc., was the most commonly found social malady. Kabir attempted a campaign of reformation, with a view to freeing the humans from the clutches of diverse bondages. Only the one who is liberated can facilitate another to get liberated. Personal life of Kabir had a considerable inbuilt spiritual capacity for awakening reformation in societal life as well as spiritual transformation in personal lives. His message of liberation was processed in his own social context, and it was in the light of the personal experience of the divine he was brimming with.

On Social Harmony

Religion is a doubled-sided phenomenon. On the one hand, it is a system of faith, which takes care of the spiritual factor in life. It is supposed to be an agent of all-pervasive liberation. But, on the other hand, the followers get enslaved to a certain perspective, an interpretation, a code and a ritual expression. It is a certain type of conditioning. It is intended to unite human beings. But nothing else has divided the human society so appallingly as religion. The worst of the wars and tensions in the world have taken place in the name of religion. The pages of the world history go thus. No doubt, it has facilitated the humans in the search for the Divine. But the institutionalized and sophisticated details of the religious systems have made the spiritual journey of the followers not only bothersome but also next to impossible, in many respects. There are large numbers of self-styled leaders, who claim to have been 'appointed to rule over the people'. They have no scruple in manipulating the religious fabric in order to suit their personal interests. Pseudo-orthodoxy and discriminatory attitudes based on caste, class, language, ideology, profession, sect, etc. gain undue power. No wonder, the general public feels pushed aside. It is obvious that the religious system failed to maintain the social equilibrium.

This is more or less the story of religion Kabir found himself encircled by. He had his roots in the discriminated section of the society, but he emerged as an extra-ordinary sage. He had deep personal experience of the Divine and was capable of a spiritual leadership intended to awaken social outcome.

Simplicity of Religion

Kabir understood religion in a very simple manner. His spiritual insights were natural. They were accessible to all. They were appealing to the downtrodden and alienated ones. The texture of religion suggested him included such simple threads, like remembering the Higher Power, entertaining sentiments of faith in that Power, singing *bhajan* or praises to that Power, engaging in *satsang* (good company) or in acquaintances which are conducive to a divine atmosphere, being of service to the other, etc. These attempts at self-realization were coupled with values of social behavior, too. The practice of religion was made simple for the common folk. Spiritual experience was brought within the easy reach of the general public. This form of religion, which was lived and highlighted by Kabir, goes beyond the barriers of caste, creed, traditions, community, ideology and sect. This is an approach of religion, which incorporates all faith positions and perspectives of life, in some fashion or other. It is like a world religion for the humanity, which could easily be accepted, this understanding of religion, which is universal as well as simple, capable of liberating the humans from the clutches of the prevailing system of religion complicated as well as degenerated. This message of Kabir was for the re-construction of spiritual experience for social harmony.

Personal Experience

Experience is personal by its very nature. 'Personal' pertains to the core of one's being. When processed by one's own personal involvement, experience becomes genuine and reliable. That is precisely what Kabir means when he says *anbhai saancha,*[3] i.e., experience is true, and true experience is personal. He does not rely on *lektaa lekee, i.e.,* what is written or narrated by others, but on *annkhin dekhee, (Too kehtaa kaagad kee dekhee,main kehtaa aankhin kee dekhee)*[4] what he has seen with his own eyes. He exhorts, 'you think for yourself (i.e., experience); then you will become wise' *(Aap bichaarei so gyanee hoi)*[5] According to him, 'seeing, hearing and touching the reality oneself, thinking and feeling it oneself, experiencing and knowing it oneself, gives one a joy, that is special'.[6] He continues, 'the story of love is indescribable; hardly anything can be said about it; it is like a dump person who has taken jiggery and is not able to express what he or she feels about it, but just smiles'.[7] That would amount to say experience defies expression. God is a matter of personal experience, as love is; one has to know him for oneself. *Kabir* proceeds to a-mystical experience and tells the Lord: 'pondering you again and again I became you; now there is nothing left in me'.[8] His experience of the divine reaches an exquisite culmination when he says: 'I am so full of your presence; wherever I look you are seen'.[9]

The deeper the experience, the richer it is. Pearls are not found at the shore but at deep sea. The personal experience of the mystic saints like Kabir goes to the point of ecstatic communion and is often expressed in striking' analogy between 'drop and seal, 'wife and husband', 'fish and water', 'bird and air', 'peacock and mountain', 'chakor and moonbeams, 'waves and sea', etc. This characteristic of personal experience highlighted by him could be compared to Meera bhai, Ravidaas and Raman Maharshi, Ibn-e-Arabi, Al Mansur al-Hallaj and Rumi and Jesus, Thomas and Paul. This concept is akin to the concept of 'Safa' in Sufism which means purity of heart, mind and body. Without personal experience of the Ultimate Reality religious practices wouldn't produce the intended result for the societal life.

Purity of Heart

Purity of heart makes one eligible for attempting an experience of God- since the Divine is pure, only a pure state of mind can assure an encounter with him. Purity of heart would mean simplicity. That is why Kabir says, 'One is capable of meeting the Ultimate Reality only when the mind clears its crookedness off.'[10] Kabir stresses transparency which is synonymous to purity of heart. Purity of heart is holiness and is the starting point of spirituality. This aspect of the inner religion certainly facilitates a social behavior, which is acceptable to one another in the day-to-day life.

In Dwelling of God

The presence of the Creator in the creation is a fact too obvious to be negated. This common belief underlines the constant awareness of his abiding presence in all the beings. Kabir highlights the intimate and close union with the divine by way of declaring the human heart as the special abode of the divine. He even considers the whole universe as the home of God. He has many categorical sayings to establish the fact: 'as the whole subsists in the part',[11] 'as musk resides in the deer',[12] so dwells God in every being; 'mind (man) is Mathura, heart (dil) is Dwaarika and body (kaayaa) is Kaashee'.[13] The in dwelling of God is materialized in an experience of self- realization, which is a personalized form of the universal presence of God. It makes the existence of the Divine real and meaningful. It permeates in to the diverse dimensions of life, making it effective to the details. Kabir advocated the basic principle of equality in life pausing arguments like 'the image of God is in all'[14] and 'the divine power is present in all'.[15] The spiritual consciousness of Kabir that the human heart is the temple of the divine has far-reaching implications for a harmonious social life.

Kabir found himself amidst staring contradictions of social life as well. Social behavior was in stark incompatibility with the prevailing theories and policies. The general public was being crushed by the clutches of the hierarchical structure of caste and class. The ways of discrimination and exploitation were beyond any logic. Brahmins and high classes monopolized the religious, social and educational arenas. The low-placed people in the realms of caste and class found themselves dominated over. They were deprived of their rights, which were assured even by basic justice. The spiritual insight of Kabir was the product of his own social situation. It enabled him to recognize the seriousness of his awkward social predicament and its tragic implications. He was charged with a great sense of social consciousness. He felt, his being challenged by the social evils. He experienced a passionate urge to respond to it positively and creatively. No matter how unjust and trying his situation was, he decided to prove his spiritual mettle. Like lotus, which remains in dirty conditions but produces immaculate flowers, Kabir, rose to such spiritual height in life that his very life became a living symbol of social resurrection.

Kabir campaigned against evil forces like selfishness, hypocrisy, discrimination, exploitation, manipulation, suppression and fatalism. He was genuinely committed to reforming the society, he emphasized personal values like genuineness, honesty, sincerity, love, service and respect. His saintly way was 'living this alternative value system which he himself proposed. He propagated his message in a subtle poetic language. The values were applied to the respective life setting of the people he addressed. He placed a clarion call to the practice of social values as the religion in practice. He was avowed to making the society a better place to live in. This reformative character of his message is like an ever-flowing fountain, which contributes immensely to better quality of life in the society.

Co-ordination between Theory and Practice

The most reliable test of one's social fitness is the co-ordination between theory and practice. It is the proof of one's genuineness in life. It reveals the level of maturity a person has achieved. The individual fruitfulness and social relevance of one's life is hidden in this hard reality. The life of Kabir, like other saints, has always stood the test of the theory he upheld. His behavioral integrity was not only beyond doubt but was highly inspiring for others. The poetical utterances of Kabir shed light on the details of the problem of disagreement between theory and practice that prevailed in his society. Kabir asks, 'what is the use of that speech which does not correspond to action?'[15] According to him, 'theory is empty, practice is the essence of life'.[17] To give advice to others is easy, but to translate the same into action is very difficult. 'Many are those who say things but few are those who do accordingly'.[18] He appropriates a satirical approach to those who preach without practicing; 'you haven't got water with you; but you pretend to distribute milk to others. Your own mind is not at peace; and you seem to be enthusiastic in consoling others'.[19] This argument has another dimension. When one is not pure in oneself, how could one give advice to others. The basic predicament of spiritual attainment is that doing is difficult and saying is easy. Without living the life oneself, the Divine cannot be attained. This is the double-sided play of the reality of speech and action. Kabir analyses the phenomenon further: 'the speech is sweet like jiggery, action is like poison; but if-you leave speech and do action, then you will attain nectar, in the place of poison'.[20] He observes the sad plight of the learned and categorically suggests an effective treatment to the problem of disharmony between theory and practice: 'the world has (generations have) gone by perusing large volumes of books and no one has ever become learned. The one who learns the single word of love only will really become learned'.[21]

To him, the verbal expression becomes futile if it does not correspond to what it implies. The ideal word is one, which is accompanied by the corresponding behavior. Only this merits the divine approval. One who does not translate the word into practice is like a foolish man who builds his house on shaky ground. Faith without action is dead. What is the use of seeing one's face in the mirror if one does not want to improve his look! Theory is like a treasure that needs to be invested in practice. One's relation to the divine is a theoretical experience, which is not worthwhile without the practical expression of good relations with the human beings and the nature. Loving God is theory and loving one-another is practice. Spirituality has both individual and social dimensions. The social side of one's spirituality - can in no way be underrated.

Kabir advances his argument by his perception that disagreement between theory and practice would mean having a divided heart. One has to be single-minded. Coordination between word and deed and as well as thought and action is the sign of an undivided mind; and that is human integrity. That is why Kabir condemned oral knowledge and appreciated behavioral knowledge. His utterances are as if he was addressing himself! He used to speak out only which was experimented by him in his personal life. That which has come to one's own experience only is worthy of any importance. As the words interpret the action, so the action bears witness to the words. The conflict between theory and practice proves one's state of being disorganized in life, which is to be regretted. Besides, word and deed are complementary to each other. Kabir highlight co-ordination between theory and practice as a radical social message, relevant of the social order of world today.

Equality

The measure adopted by Kabir to re-organize the society, which was scattered by discriminatory behaviors, was the ideal of equality. Different standards were being applied to individuals and communities. Superior inferior attitudes were maintained in the society, too. The approach of Kabir to this mentality of inequality, and discrimination - was basically spiritual. Contemplating the whole reality would help rising beyond the fragmented mind. The internal sphere of the mind is to be concentrated upon rather than the external characteristics of the body. The former unites whereas the latter divides. The quality of the spirit is to be imbibed in order to see the basic oneness. A non-dualistic experience is the basic requirement for equality. It is the divided mind, which discriminates on the basis of caste, color, language, profession, class, creed, faith, conviction, ideology, nationality, and the like. The foundation far human equality is faith in the same divinity. The characteristic of *'rainbow'* inspires one to comprehend the mystery of divine oneness. The rainbow presents seven colours, one different from the other. The diverse colours expressed in the rainbow, are all hidden in the sunlight. It is the same sun and the same sunlight at the root of all these colours. So is the divine spirit—basically *one in experience find different in expressions*. The different colours are different expressions and they are not to be compared with and discriminated against each other. Each has its own singular quality. Together they radiate a beauty. This aesthetic outlook of life is the spiritual motivation for equality. This has been the subtle experience of Kabir.

Kabir presents an awareness of the *common roots,* which elicits a sense of common belonging. By going deeper into the experience of the Divine, one comes to the realization that all beings essentially belong to the same Divine. The supreme truth is that *all beings are of the same God*. All human beings are the creatures of the same God. All are members of the same family of God, the same family of humanity. All have the right to live. Differences are just superficial and often superimposed. The places of worship of the diverse religious traditions represent the same Higher Power that knows neither temple nor *masjid*. The high and low feelings are based on merely external differences. The quality of the human person is more important. The inner quality is the invisible basis of an attitude of equality. To be carried away by the visible world would mean to lead a life on the level of the body, which is not proper life. All beings share the same Creator and the same creation. All share the same water, the same air and the same light. It is indeed foolish for one to make difference between one another. Sorrows and joys, hopes and disappointments, sufferings and struggles, successes and failures, dreams and achievements are a common experience for all. In fact, there is no reasonable ground for discrimination and unsociability. The basic reality of life is just equal for all. The so-called religious and secular leaders of the society erected a system of classification of human beings, where they could satisfy their selfish interests. A divine sanction is attributed to this system, which has no logical basis. This is the sublime realization of Kabir.

Kabir highlights the religion *of good social conduct* as *dharma*. Good behavior towards one another is that which makes a real human society. Kabir challenges the proponents of the caste system, who undervalue others and thus fall short of a social conduct, which is humanly dignifying. He asks in an ironical tone, 'you *Brahmin*, why haven't you taken another way to be born'?[22] He means that if both *Brahmin* and *Sudra* have taken the same way to be born in to the world, what is the difference between them? Both have blood of the same color; both have hunger and thirst as well as needs and problems. One has to learn from Nature lessons of equality and good behavior. The system of caste discrimination is a hindrance to a meaningful social life. What is important is a spirit of equality in the garden of life, which is created and maintained by the same Creator. That is why Kabir categorically affirms the *oneness of religion that is good conduct*.

Kabir suggests a morality of good behavior to one, which is grounded on the perfect equality among the humans, for the establishment of harmony in social life. Unity of the human society is dependent on the behavioral equality in life. Equality takes care of the right approach to life. This attitude does full justice to the human dignity and to the dignity of life. It rules out all narrowness of thinking. It also proves one's genuineness and nobility. Such an open, transparent and realistic disposition assures the right orientation to life.

It liberates the humans from all that is unworthy of the human spirit and promises a healthy tuning to one-another. The welfare of the whole humanity *(Sarovdaya)* is inherent in this elevated state of mind. This is in fact the foundation of social harmony.

Integration of Values

Integration is combining different parts to form a single whole. It is like bricks, stone and the other requisites brought together to erect a wall. It is like different parts fixed together, letters to form a word in the block, or words to make a piece of poem, or harmony of various notes to make music. It is like a body which functions as one unit while having many parts. The many parts exist as one. There is no contradiction or discrimination among them. There is equal importance and dignity shared among the parts. There is mutual understanding and agreement. Integration, thus, is an existence in togetherness and precursor to a holistic vision of life and can rightly be described in the terminology of Indian culture: 'unity in diversity and diversity in unity'. Integration is the positive outcome of the dynamics of human values, which make social life possible. A well-knit social life is dependent on the inter-play between the values the humans live by.

Kabir not only underlined the need of integrating the values of social life but his own life was a lofty example for the same. He was a person of great integrity. He was honest and upright in character. He was simple and straightforward in heart. He was fully committed to the society. The sole mission in his life was an all-out attempt at making the human society a better place to live in. He started this campaign with himself. Kabir suggests a highly imperative single-doze medicine for the disorganized and disintegrated human society: 'the oneness of the human existence". For him, following a particular religious tradition or ideology, belonging to a particular social caste, class or community, holding a particular profession or position, etc., is not important. Becoming a good human being is the most meritorious achievement in life.

Kabir also raised objection about the religious traditions. The human society has accumulated a lot of junk in the name of tradition. Much of it is just a burden, a futile heavy weight, for the human being. There is a dire as well as a continuous need to examine, discern and discard what is out-dated and irrelevant. Kabir gives a categorical exhortation: 'accept the substantial and reject the insubstantial'.[23] The primary things are to be attended first in comparison to the secondary things. The inner element has to get priority in relation to the outer. Quality should gain the first importance. That only can help life progress, and assure a bright future for the human society. Quality takes care of a sense of perfection in life, which is the greatest human motto possible. The motivation for being perfect and the best model of perfection is the 'Higher Power' itself, which never discriminates between the good and the evil. The quench for perfection is life's greatest adventure.[24] This divine characteristic of perfection can be imbibed only by an honest commitment to quality in life.

Integration of values is to be searched for in the quality of concord one maintains with the divine and with the other human beings. The unseen is reflected in the seen. Creatures are the images of the one same Creator. The Divine is to be encountered in the human and in the natural. Commitment to the Creator is to be expressed towards commitment to the creatures. The latter is the measure of the former, too. There is no religion like doing well to the other and there is no paganism like doing harm to the other. Doing well to the other is the right worship of the Divine. Whatever is done to the other human being is done to the divine being itself. To love one's neighbor is to love God. To live in harmony with one's co-creatures, especially the humans, is to achieve harmony with the Creator. This is the Truth of God and the God of Truth as well as the truth of life experienced and communicated by Kabir. Kabir intertwines the visible and the invisible dimension of the Higher Reality in an unparalleled way. Thus he proposes the establishment of social harmony in the human society. This form of integration summarizes all values in life. The consciousness of harmony with the Divine expresses itself in gestures of harmony with one another in the diverse dimensions of societal life.

More than being a holy person, wise and enlightened, a saint is one who is oneself in perfect harmony - spiritually and socially - with the divine as well as human and natural dimensions of life. Kabir was one such great mystic and social reformer who enriched the human society, by his struggle against, various forms of disharmony in the society, i.e. discrimination, slavery, corruption, castes and other abnormalities, he not only expounded the real spirit of religion but also lived it. He was endowed with a special gift of being human as well as spiritual. His life encompassed the diverse dimensions of spiritual and social renaissance and harmony. He highlighted a universal spiritual foundation for human integration, and facilitated a revolution for renewal in view of promoting integrity and quality in social behavior.

Notes:

1. The author holds a doctoral degree in Hindi literature from Banaras Hindu University, Varanasi, on the topic *'The Social Implications of the Understanding of God in Kabir and Christian Thought'* (Hindi). A modified book form of the same was published in 2003 under the title *'Kabir aur Eesaayee Chintan'*. The author was awarded 'Saahityik Kriti Sammaan for 2003-2004 for this book by Hindi Academy, Delhi, in 2005 March. He has also done Pradhma, Madhyama and B.Mus. in Hindustani Classical Music. Since then, he has been involved in comparative research as well as promoting multi-faith relations. Manav Ekta Munch, Ujjain, honoured him in 1998 for his efforts in promoting communal harmony and national integration. The themes of his lectures are *The Saint Tradition of India, Multi-Faith Relations, Cultural Integration, Harmony of Values*, and related topics at various institutes and conferences in the country. He- contributes to books, periodicals and newspapers, both in Hindi and English on diverse themes. He has now over 50 articles and research papers to his credit. His musical compositions on multi-scriptural values are to take the form of an audio-CD cassette very soon. He is doing postdoctoral research, i.e., D. Litt. in the above area. Presently he is committed to the mission of promoting religious and social harmony in the country as the National Director of the Commission for Religious Harmony, CBCI New Delhi.
2. Dr. Rajdev Singh, *Shabd aur arth Sant Sahity Ke Sandarbh Meinf Nand Kishor and Brothers*, Varanasi, 1968, pp. 51-53.
3. Sir David Goodalf Farward R.H. Lesser *Saints and Sages of India*, Intercultural publications of New Delhi 1994f p. xi
4. *Kabir Granthavaleef* Dr Shyam Sunder Daas (Ed), Nagree Prachaarinee Sabhaaf Varanasi, VS 2045, Saakhee 5.4, p. 10.
5. *Too kehtaa kaagad kee dekhee mein kehtaa aankhin kee dekhee'* - Kabir
6. *Aap bichaarei so gyanee hoi*-Kabir Granthaavaleef Padaawaleef 52, p. 79
7. *'Aap hee aap vichaariye tab kaisaa hoi anand re'* -Kabir
8. *'Akath kehanee prem kee, kachu kehee na jai, goonge keree sarkaraa, baithe muskaai'* - Kabir
9. *'Too too kartaa too bhayaaf mujhmein rahee na hoom'* - Kabir
10. *'Jit dekhoom tit toom'* - Kabir
11. *'Jab man cchod kutilaayee, tab aayee milei raam rayee'* - Kabir
12. *'Khaalik khalak khalak mein khaalik'* – Kabir Granthavalee, ibid, Padaavalee, 51, p. 81
13. *'Kastooree kundali basei'* - Kabeer Granthavalee, ibid, Saakhee, 53.1, p. 64
14. *'Man mathuraa dil dwaarikaa, kayaa kaasee jaanee'* - Kabeer Granthawaiee, ibid, Sakhee, 23.10, p. 35
15. *'Jyoon bimbahi pratibimb samaanaa'* - Kabir
16. *'Ghati ghati rahyo samaayee*-Kabir Granthaavaleef ibid. Padaavalee 18.1, p. III

17. *'Kethne Kethee tou kya-bhayaa, je kernee na thahray'* - Kabeer Granthwali, ibid, Sakhee 18.1, p.29
18. *'Kethnee thothee jagat mein, kernee uttam saar'* -Kabir
19. *'Kehtee to bahut milaaf garta milaa na koi'* - Kabir, Sant Sudhaa Saar.
20. *Paanee mile na aapko, auran baksat ccheer; aapan man nichal nahin, auran banthawat dheer,'* - Kabeer, Sant Kavy, Parasuram Chatruvedi (Ed,), p.241
21. *'Kehnee meetha khaand see, kernee vish kee loy; Kethnee taj kernee karei, to vish se amrut hoi,* - Kabir, Sant Baanee Sangrah, Part 1, p 47
22. *'Pothee padi padi jag muvaa pandit bhayaa na koi; ekei ashir peev ka, pade so pandit hoi,* - Kabir Granthavalee, ibid, Sakhee 19, 4, p. 30
23. Je too *banbhan-banbhanee jaayaa, to aan baat hvei kehee na aayaar*-Kabir Granthavalee, ibid, p.79
24. *'Saar Saar ke gahee rehein, thothaa de uday'* - Kabir
25. A French quote

Madhu Trivedi[1]

The Contribution of Sufi and Bhakti Saints in the Evolution of Hindustani Music

Medieval centuries witnessed the evolution of Hindustani music wherein the contribution of Sufi and Bhakti saints is immense. The Sufi saints integrated the west Asian and Indian musical forms and ornamental varieties in a way that it led to the creation of a common musical culture, which was followed by the classes and the masses in north India from about the fourteenth century. It was a long drawn process that began during the time of Mahmud Ghaznavi, who is regarded as the creator of the Muslim culture on the eastern fringe of the Islamic world. It has also been stressed upon by some of his admirers that Muslim religion and civilization passed to the Indian peninsula by his influence.[2] Under his successor sultan Mas'ud, Lauhawar or Lahore emerged as a center of Muslim culture. The isolated culture-groups, which included saints and mystics also, first secured a foothold in Punjab and from there they slowly started moving in the territories of the Hindu *rais,* who had 'always been tolerant of culture-groups without molestation'.[3] And, apparently the Muslim immigrants had considerable freedom to follow their own cultural tradition. One may *quote* here the example of Sheikh Bahauddin Zakaria of Multan (1191-1267), the famous Suhravardi saint whose ancestors settled in Kangra some generations before his birth, that he pursued his education in the Hindu environment and learnt the Quran in all the seven *qirats* (modes of recitation) as well as acquired adequate knowledge of Arabic language.[4] The process of the assimilation of Indian and Perso-Arab music in *sama'* began under him at the *Khanqha* (hospice) of Multan which was also a famous pilgrimage center of the Shaivites as well as the Siddha and the Nath saints who are commonly referred as jogis in medieval literary and folk tradition.

Sama i.e. music which leads to the attainment of the state of mystic ecstasy belonged to the *khanqahs* especially those which belonged to the Suharvardiya and Chishtia *silsilas*. The spiritual congregations were held in them *khanqahs* and people of all castes and creed attended these in large number. The Sufi Sheikh used to hold discourses with wandering Hindu saints such as the Naths and the Siddhas, who made frequent visits to the *jama'at khana* at Multan and at Delhi.[5] The *jogis*. and the Sufis had influenced each other to some extent. The *jogis* who believed in a formless *(nirgun)* God,[6] assimilated some of the Sufi symbols and practices, such as *sahaj samadhi*, which was like mystic ecstasy, while the Sufis adopted their themes, imageries and poetic forms, such as *Chhand*.[7] There were similarities between popular Hindu practices and Sufi practices.[8]

The Sufi *Khanqhas* were thus the most effective venue of cultural assimilation and became instrumental in promoting the composite tradition in art and culture. The impact was felt more markedly in the realm of music which formed an integral part of the socio-religious rituals and festivities, and in this process *sama* began to be influenced by Indian classical music for which the credit goes to Sheikh Bahauddin Zakaria Multani. According to Faqirullah, the Sheikh adopted the folk genre *Chhand* and used it for devotional music and rendered Persian couplets in this form.[9] *Chhand*, it should be noted was one of the verse forms used by the *jogis* in their poetic compositions in lieu of the traditional *prabandh* form. He also adopted the *rag-ragini* system and evolved new *rags*, such as *Million Dhanashri* which are still very popular amongst the *qawwals*.[10] The *Khanqah* of Multan thus initiated the process of Indianisation of *sama* music which culminated in Delhi under the Chishti saints.

During the thirteenth century Delhi began to emerge as a great center of the Chishti *silsila*. According to Simon Digby the preeminence of the Chishti order over other Sufi orders in Delhi was probably established by the 1230s. Sheikh Qutbuddin Bakhtiyar Kaki enjoyed the allegiance of the reigning sultan Altutmish, and of the urban population. The prestige of the Chishti Sheikhs grew in the time of his successor Fariduddin, and perhaps reached its apogee after Sheikh Nizamuddin established an extensive Khanqah at Delhi in the late thirteenth century. The Chishti Sheikhs are much revered by the majority of the Indian Muslims. The most widely attended rituals of pilgrimage took place around their graves (within the capital of Delhi). By the thirteenth century the cult of graves and pilgrimages to local saints, was well established in the Islamic world.[11]

The Chishti saints played an important role in the religious and cultural history of the country, as they adapted well to indigenous traditions and played an important role in promoting friendly relations among followers of all religions. Sheikh Nizamuddin Chishti established his Jama'at Khana in Ghayaspur, a suburb near Delhi in the late thirteenth century.[12] His charismatic personality had created a large following covering all classes of people. A large number of people, irrespective of their religious beliefs came from great distances. Like the Suhravardi saints, the Chishtis also included *sama* as essential part of their *zikr* (*zikr-i jali* or reciting aloud)[13], and Sheikh Nizamu'ddin had many adherents of *sama* in the court circle. Foremost among them were Amir Khusro and Amir Hasan Sanjhari, the author of *Fawa'id al-Fua'd* that he was compared with the celebrated Persian poet of Shiraz, Sa'di (1184-1291), the author *of Gulistan* and *Bostan* of world wide reputation and known as *Sa'di-i Hindustan*[14].

It was, in fact, a unique phenomenon of the early fourteenth century that court culture and popular culture came into close contact through persons who were intimate with both circles and Amir Khusro was the foremost among them. He enjoyed the longest tenure of association with the court. He also had links with the Sufi circle. His musical innovations were instrumental in popularizing exclusive techniques, which had been reserved for the aristocracy and the elite circles. Besides, he also borrowed extensively from folk techniques. Amir Khusro thus tried to link two diverse musical cultures, and this became the foundation stone of Hindustani music.

Amir Khusro not only regularly attended the festive gatherings of the Khilji Sultans 'where chosen ones from the greatest masters of musical arts assembled and performed',[15] he also had strong links with the Sufi circle. He was a devotee of Sheikh Nizamu'ddin Auliya (d.1324) of the Chishti order and was well versed in the practices related to *sama*. Barani referred to him as *sahib-i sama'*, *sahib-i wajd* and *sahib-i hal*.[16] Thus, Amir Khusro had the rare opportunity of acquiring knowledge of exclusive court traditions as well as popular traditions which were taking roots in the *sama* music. At the same time, he was well versed in the Indian musical system. Amir Khusro combined all his knowledge in the forms of *qual, tarana, naqsh, nigar, basit tillana, farsi, fard* and *sohla*.[17] In these musical forms he blended Indian and Persian lyric genres and musical techniques *(saut-u naqsh-i Farsi-u Hindi)*; and in view of its mass appeal the songs were composed in *desi*, the dialect current during that period in Delhi.[18]

Qaul was fashioned in a way that it became similar to *git* in its rhythmic structure.[19] Persian verses were rendered in it along with the rhythmic syllables *yali, yalam, tana, tundrana, tani, tadani*, which were employed in its *sarband*.[20] In its new form *qaul* also began to be rendered in Indian *rag-raginis*. Similarly, *torana* was akin to *git* in its rhythmic structure. Whether in prose or in verse form it included rhythmic syllables, termed as *tana-talli* by Nawab Faqirullah Saif Khan (17th century) in his *Rag Darpan. Tillana*, however, had only *tana-talli* without a song text; *farsi* was a form of *tillana* in which verses from Persian *ghazals* and *qasidas* were rendered along with rhythmic syllables; *fard* had only one verse incorporated in the *tal* oriented song composition. It was also a form of *tillana*,[21] *naqsh* had no *tanatalli* and it was equivalent of *man*, a musical composition of *Prakrit* and *bhakha*, which was known as *pingal*, with a theme of self exaltation.[22] *Nigar* was a counterpart of *suravathi (swar-avartini;* a rhythmic recital comprising a cycle and some patterns moving at even speed); *basit* was like *chhand* and also a kind of *geet*.[23] Amir Khusro's intensive knowledge of Indian and Persian musical systems resulted in the fashioning of many new melodies and tunes in which he combined Indian *rags* and Persian *muqams*, or blended different Indian or Persian airs *(ahang)*.

According to Faqirullah Saif Khan, all these innovations were made at the time of Amir Khusro's competition with Nayak Gopal and popularised through his chosen disciples Samat and Nigar.[24] From now onwards, *qauwal* became a generic term for those who performed *qaul* and allied variants. Mirza Khan mentions in *Tuhfat al-Hind* that those *gandharp* and *gunkars* who excelled in *qaul, tarana* and such other composition are called *qawwals*.[25]

Amir Khusro's appraisal of the *qawwals* provides an idea of the techniques of song and rhythm as developed at Delhi. According to him their musical compositions bewildered the composers *(shakl-sazan)* of Arabia and Persia; they employed handclaps *(zarb-i dast)* for marking the rhythm and hand gestures *(ishara-i dast)* for indicating the *usul-i rast* and *usul-i chap*. They regulated their vocal volume in such a way that a single *bang* (i.e. *tan*) of theirs appeared like a piece of intricate music *(sarud-i pechan)*. Even the most exalted and proud vocalists and instrumentalists were taken aback by their art.[26]

During this period, devotional traditions of the early medieval period, such as *hari-katha*, the Vaishnavite, Nath and Siddha cults as well as the bardic traditions were integrated in the form of the *Bhakti* cult, which also assimilated some of the Sufi practices. The Bhakti poet saints renounced the traditional prabandh form and adopted *chnand, pad* and *doha*. It is in this scenario that most of the musical forms like *karakka, shabad, dhrupad,* and *Vishnu pad* eventually arose. A good part of medieval music, thus, evolved in a religious setting, but one which assimilated strands from both Hindu and Islamic forms and traditions. It did not remain specific to any single ethnic group, caste or creed. All musical forms were learnt by Hindus and Muslims alike who used similar *rags* and imageries for devotional music.

Braj region emerged as a center of poetry and music during the sixteenth century under the patronage of the Mughal emperor Akbar who aimed at creating an atmosphere of trust and co-operation among diverse communities. The Braj-Bhasha treatises *chaurasi vnishinvon ki varta* and *do sau chhappan vaishnavon ki varta* as well as Persian land grant documents of the period reveal the fact very well that Akbar generously granted land to the existing and the new temples in the vicinity of Mathura arid Brindavan.[27] His generosity and tolerant attitude towards other religions attracted a large number of *Vaishnava* poet saints belonging to the Chaitanya and Ballabhacharya sects from diverse places of the sub-continent to settle in the Braj region, which gradually became renowned as a great center of Krishna *bhakti* cult. Vaishnavism gained enormous popularity here because it was interpreted to the people through their own language and through the medium of music, dance and drama, which formed an integral part of the socio-religious rituals and festivities.

A number of new temples were built in the area around Brindavan, which emerge as the town of temples and *ghats* during this period and as Fuhrer mentions there were computed to be within its limit as many as thousand temples.[28] Amongst these the Govind Dev temple, built by Raja Man Singh in 1590, reflects contemporary Mughal style at its best.

Interestingly these temples became the mini replica of the Mughal court and adopted some of the symbols of royalty. The *naubat*[29] was performed here in the same manner as in the courts and a schedule was prescribed for the devotees regarding the *darshan* of the deities Krishna, Balram and Radha who had all the aura of royalty. The temple precincts became the center of various cultural activities attracting a large number of performing artistes and the poet saints, who composed poetry and rendered it as part of devotion. These poet-saints, which included the *asht-chhap* or the eight distinguished poet composers such as Sirdas and Nanddas, had thorough knowledge of poetics and prosody. The proximity of the Braj region to the capital city Agra, which was also the cultural node and the financial hub of the Mughal empire,[30] was an added advantage that facilitated the full fruition of art and poetry in the area. One may add here that the growth of art and literature is intimately connected with patronage and the patronage patterns influence the standard of creativity. Akbar's court was a great confluence of the musical geniuses from different regions of India as well as from all around the Persian cultural sphere. Pandarika Vitthala, the musician and musicologist from south, characterizes his court as '*sangitarnavamandir*.[31] The lavish land grants attracted a large number of *Vaishnava* poet saints belonging to the Chaitanya and Ballabhacharya to the existing as well as new temples in Mathura and its vicinity sects to settle in the Braj region, which emerged as a great center of music and poetry.

Vaishnava poetry is an integral part of the medieval Indian literary culture. The tradition of the recitation of *lila-kavya,* which found manifestation in the poetry of Jay Dev and the devotional songs of Chandidas and Vidyapati, got new impetus in the hands of the *Vaishnava* poets of the 16th and 17th centuries. It also resulted in the stylization of the folk dramatic art, *ras-lila,* as a dance drama, which attained its theatrical vitality as well as ritualistic character during this period. In its new standardized form the *ras-lila,* became an assortment of dance, music and drama. It became part of the ritualistic ceremonies of the *Vaishnava* cult and the temples provided an arena for -its performance. The temple culture contributed to the enrichment of the dramatic content of *ras-lila,* and this presentational form of *ras-lila* owes its origin to Swami Hari Das and Narayan Bhatt. They organized *ras-sthals* and *ras-mandals* for these performances in the Braj area.

Pad, one of the six ingredients of *prabandh,* was a popular lyric genre among the *Vaishnava* saint.[32] Yahiya Kabuli, the author of a renowned Persian musical treatise, *Lahjat-i Sikandarshahi,*[33] written during the reign of the Lodhi Sultan Sikandar Shah (r.1489-1517) defines it as a combination of poetry and the sweet and soft *kalams/kalmat* (phrases) of the instruments rendered in a pleasant voice.[34] Other varieties were *dhrupad* and *bishunpad (Vishnu pad).* The origin of *bishunpad* was attributed by Mirza Khan to Surdas.[35] Another popular verse form was *kavitt* which was a poetic composition set to *tal.* The meaning is interpreted by various gestures, while *laya* (tempo) is marked by feet. When the constituent units of the *tals (alfaz-i usul)* played on the *mrdang* were incorporated, it was known as *taivat* or *tirvat* in the professional music parlance.[36] Nanddas composed such *kavitts* in great number, which were extremely popular among the musicians.

A close study of the poetry of these poet saints brings out interesting details about several facets of musical culture and performance tradition of Northern India during the sixteenth century. The male performing artistes referred in the *pads* and *kavitts* are *kirtaniya, bhagatiyn, bhanvayyn, bahu-rapl,* who may be classified as the medieval theatre artistes.

Most of these poet saints were accomplished musician composers. Of these Swami Haridas, Surdas, Govind Swami and Nanddas were the most renowned. Swami Haridas was an excellent singer also, and traditions have it that Akbar went with Tansen in disguise to listen to the *kirtan* of Swami Haridas, and that he was mesmerized by his divine performance. The court tradition and the *desi* patterns prevalent in the *Brqj-bhumi* and several other regions of the north came in lively contact in the Braj Bhumi. In music the term *desi* appears to be used in a very large perspective during this period. It is not used in terms of a region.

Instead it denotes the recognition, classification and standardization of folk, regional and exotic material in accordance with the current performance traditions.

There is a possibility that the *sama* music also had some bearing on some of these saints. The ecstasy of Chaitanya at the time of the performance of *kirtan* reminds us of *hal*. This is, however, said by way of suggestion. This period witnessed an enormous rise in the popularity of the Chishti *silsila* and the *dargah* cult. The *dargah* of Sheikh Salim Chishti at Fatehpur Sikari, in the close vicinity of Braj Bhumi, was deemed a great centre of pilgrimage and became the most effective venue of cultural assimilation in the area and provided a ground for the mixing of followers of different faith.

The Vaishnavite *kirtans*, rendered in the *dhrupad* and *dhamar* style, have special compositions for the *ras* and the *vasant* (spring festival), which suggest solo, duet and group dance. The dancers are Krishna, Radha and gopis. Krishna is represented as a divine dancer. He is *natwar*, a perfect dancer and the best among dancers. There is a specific *gati* (to and fro movement of the dancer) *Natwari-gati* attributed to him and later on a dance-form, *natwari nritya* was also evolved.

The dance represented in these poetic compositions is a perfect art form depicting various features and techniques of *nritt, nritya* and *natya* as is evident from the varieties of gait and rhythmic pillories of movement and various other dance-motifs and varieties of hand gestures. This attests to the fact that these composers were fully conversant with the current performance traditions as well as classical dance techniques represented in the Sanskrit musical treatises like *Natya Shastra, Abhinaya-Darpnn* and *Sangit-Ratanakar* and so on. *Niratkar* is the term generally used for the dancer in the Vaishnavite literature. In a pad, *'ah main nachyo bahutg gopal'*, Surdas has provided a description of a dancer.

Surdas refers to *swar, tal* and *nritya* while describing the beauty of the flute *(bans)* performance of Krishna. He also indicates the order of movement of various body organs; hands, feet, eyes, neck, and emotional expressions during the course of dance. In conformance to the principles of classical techniques the poets have indicated some gaits *(bhangima)* such as *tribhangi*, and varieties of hand poses, *hastak-bhed*[37], represented by Krishna. There are conventional signs of *tals*, known as *tatkar*. Vaishnava poets generally describe the *ras-nritya* performed by Krishna, Radha and gopis. Interestingly the vocabulary of the *ras* is similar to those codified dance forms, which are described in the Sanskrit and Persian treatises such as *bhramaris*,[38] *parmuḍ*[39] and *mandal*[40] etc. Pundarika Vitthala, the author of *Nartananirnaya*, describes it as a group dance performed by four, eight, sixteen thirty two, or sixty four danseuses *patras*, with four, five or six beats, with *bhramaris* and *charis* executed to the left-and to the right forming geometrical patterns and circles *(mandalibhaya)*, performed without sticks in accompaniment to the *muraj* and other instruments.[41] One also finds mention of various *angs* such as *dhilang, ump, limp, dat, lag* and so on.[42] The frequent occurrence of rhythmic syllables *like ta ta thai thai, and tat thai*, in these *padas* suggest that a large number of these verses were written for use in dance. Hence they display many dance-motifs, specific gestures and movements intended to be sung and interpreted through dance and *abhinaya* (expressive mime) simultaneously. They have the *bols* of *miridang* in abundance, which was gaining currency as a dance accompaniment instead of the *patah* and *huruk*. The poetry of Surdas and Nanddas has many examples of these:

> patur chatur sab ang nirat karat, desi suddh ang gai
> ta ta thai thai ughatat hain harshi man
> urap tirap lag dilt tat- tat- tat thai ta thai thai
> let gati man ta ta thai thai hastak bhed
> --
> gati sudhang nrityati braj nerl
> --
> nirtat mandal madhya Nandlal
> urap tirap lag dat tat- tat- tat thai ta thai thai
> --
> nritya karat udghat sangit pad[43]

The above verses show that the terms *udghat* and *sudhang* appear frequently in the *pads* and *kavitts* of poet-saints of Braj region. *Udghat* is a phonetic degeneration of *udghattana* (striking). In professional parlance the term denotes the recital of rhythmic syllables and patterned sequence or *bol*. Mirza Khan defines *ughat* as meaningless syllables set to *tal*. According to him *ughat* (i.e. *udghnt*), comprised of five syllables-ta, *di, thu, na* and ti/ *tai (thai}*, formed the basis of *nirat (nrtt)*. The *bandh* (rhythmic composition or *bandish*) are formed of these five syllables only such as *tat thai, ta ta thai* and so on.[44] The use of this term in *ras* prompts us to suggest that up to this period the dancers used to recite the rhythmic phrases themselves. This practice was, however, discontinued in the solo dance performances and the rhythmic phrases began to be recited by another artiste, referred as *goyanda* in the Persian sources. This is known as *parhant* in the modern times.

The term *sudhang* (a phonetic degeneration of *shuddha-ang*), which appears so commonly in the *Vaishnava* poetry, is not found in the Sanskrit musicological literature, not even in *Sangit Rataniikar*. The Persian musical treatises of the fourteenth and fifteenth centuries, *Ghuniyat ul Munya* or *lahjat-i Sikandarshahi* also do not mention it. Interestingly there is no reference to *ras* in the sources of the Indo-Persian tradition. One finds casual reference of it in the Sufi *premakhylin, Mirgavatt*.[45] However, we find its description in *Tuhfat al-Hind* as a dance form wherein the units of *tals* are performed accompanied with graceful body movement *(kichol)* and expressive and suggestive postures *(ada u andaz)*. In it a variety of *angs* were performed Mirza Khan has also provided valuable details about some of these *angs*, which according to his description were numerous.[46] Interestingly, this dance-form came to be known as *thai thai naach* during the late eighteenth century among the masses.[47] Later on it was integrated in *Kathak. Natwari Nritya* at Lucknow, the capital of the kingdom of Awadh.

The poetry of the saints also reveals the fact that *mridang*[48] and *bansi* (horizontal flute)[49] were becoming popular as a solo and as an accompanying instrument. Although the *Hast-pats* of the *desi patah*,[50] which are described in detail by Yahiya Kabuli and known as *kotakhar* in the professional music parlance, were also used in the poetry of these *Vaishnava* saints. Other instruments were *mardal, hurakka, chang* and so on.

The poetry reveals the fact very well that even though a good part of the *Vaishnava* poetry and music evolved in a religious setting, it no longer remained specific to any single ethnic group, caste or creed. All musical forms were learned by Hindus and Muslims alike, who used similar *rag-raginis* and imageries for devotional purposes. The poetry of Raskhan is an example in this regard. The author of the Persian travelogue *Muraqqa'-i Delhi* attest to the great popularity of *kabbait (kavitts)* of the *Vaishnava* saints among the musicians of the early eighteenth century in the Mughal capital Delhi, and there was a specific style of their rendition known as the *tarz-i kalawanti*.

This period witnessed an enormous rise in the popularity of the Chishti *silsila* and the development of *dargah* cult. The Sufi dargahs at Agra, Fetehpur Sikri and Ajmer were deemed as great centres of pilgrimage and provided a ground for the mixing of followers of different faith and promoted a liberal and eclectic attitude through various means. There were similarities between popular Hindu practices and the Sufi practices. One of the major reasons of the popularity of the Chishti order was its capacity to adapt itself to the usage and customs of the country.[51]

These Sufi saints believed in the spiritual value of music and patronized professional singers of talent irrespective of their caste and creed. According to Sheikh Fariduddin Bhakkari Nawab Islam Khan Fatehpur Alias Sheikh Alaudam, the son of *Shaikhul Islam* Salim Chishti; maintained *taifas* (bands) of *lulis, huuknis, domnis, kanchanis* and *kamachnnis*, who were the leading classes of highly skilled performing women.[52]

From about the middle of the seventeenth century, artistic and cultural activities shifted from Agra to Shahjahanabad, the new capital city founded by Shah Jahan in 1638, popularly known as Delhi. Delhi always had a two-fold significance: it was the conventional center of Muslim rule in India, the *dar al-mulk* [seat of the empire] of the great Sultans; it also had immense religious significance as it held the *dargahs* of many famous religious leaders which drew pilgrims from all over north India, and it was regarded the center of the circle of Islam (*markaz-i da'ira Islam*).[53] Due to the rise in the popularity of the Chishti *silsila* under Sheikh Kalimmullah (1650-1729) the cult of *curs* became exceedingly popular at Delhi during the period, and many important cultural event became associated with these. During the reign of Muhammad Shah (1719-1748), the *Qila'-i Mubarak* had become the center of cultural activities. A modem scholar remarks: 'The brilliance of Mughal culture, as described in non-political sources of information, stands out sharply against the background of political turmoil and the gloom and the depression caused by it.[54] In this perspective, music played its own role in enlivening the cultural atmosphere. The musical arts received patronage of an exceptional nature not only from the court and the elite circles, but also from a large section of the local populace who, too, evinced unprecedented taste for music. Dance and music became a favourite pastime as well as an integral part of all festivities. No occasion of mirth or festivity was ever wanting in these two arts. *Mehfil-i sama'* were regularly arranged at the tombs and shrines of saints on the occasion of 'urs and on other dates of the month, especially *nauchandi*. Musical sessions *(mehfil)* arranged by nobles, affluent people and eminent musicians attracted large audience.[55] During this period, the classical traditions of the Mughal court were synthesized with the regional musical patterns of the Delhi region. This resulted in the fruition of the skill of the *qawwals*, who integrated *qaul-tarunn* and other allied variants into a composite musical style which came to be known as *qawwali*.[56] The *qawwls* who belonged to the dom and dhadi classes,[57] incorporated the stylistic features like *tan- palai* and *alap* of khayal which was the leading vocal genre of north Indian music during the early eighteenth century. However the time measure *(tal)* applied in it were of Persian origin such as *usul-i fakhta*. This style became extremely popular among the people. According to Dargah Quli Khan, the author of *Muraqqa'-i Delhi*, the foremost *qawwal* of the period was Taj Khan. His voice moved the people to ecstasy and he created pleasing images like the painting of Behzad. He captivated the listeners by the magic of his voice.[58] He was attached to the royal court.[59] Another *qawwal* of eminence was Mu'inuddin. He had tremendous command over the high and low pitches. Burhani and Jatta *qawwal* were also renowned for their talents. Jatta was a prominent figure in the *mehfils* of the Sufis.

The musical culture and tradition of Hindustani music, nurtured in the Sufi Khanqahs and the temple precincts of the Braj-Bhumi provided the background for the development of Hindustani music and dance, which is performed with the same ethos.

Notes:

1. University of Delhi
2. wne, E.G., *A Literary History of Persia*, Vol.11, pp.117-8.
3. Ammad Habib, *Politics and Society during the Early Medieval period*. Vol. 1, p. 68. 3.
4. Ibid.

5. Amir Hasan Sijzi Dehlavi. *Fawa'id al-Fua'd*, ed. Muhammad Latif Malik, Lahore, 1386/1966, pp. 59-60, 404-5,417-18; English Trans., Bruce B. Lawrence, *Morals for the Heart*, New York, 1992, p. 97.
6. Ibid., pp. 178,355.
7. 1 owe this information to Dr Sudhir Shanna, Department of Hindi, University of Delhi. *jogis* adopted *chhund'm* place of *prabandh*
8. Shaikh Nasiuddin Chiragh brought out the importance of yogic breathing exercise. For details see *Khair ul Majalis*, 48th *nwjii.'i.* p. 157
9. Faqirullah Saif Khan, *Rag Darpan* ed. Nurul Hasan Ansari and Shatrughna Shukia, Delhi, 1981, pp. 22, 41: Persian edn and English Trans. by Shahab Sannadee, *Tarjuma-i-Mankutahal* & *Rialla-i-Ragdarpana by Fac/zrvllah (Nawiib SaifKhan)*, IGNCA, Delhi, 1996 pp. 59,117.
10. Ibid., p. 25; Kaumudi, The Mingling of Islamic and Indigenous Traditions in Indian. Music', *Indian Historical Quarterly*, 'XXVI, pp. 130-133.
11. For details see *Tabarrakat* and Succession among the Great Chishti Shaikhs of the Delhi sultanate in *Delhi through the Ages*, pp. 63.64.65.
12. Barani. *Ta'rikh*, pp. 343-44.
13. Tarachand, *The influence of Islam on Indian Culture*, p. 55.
14. Ibid
15. Ibid., p. 287.
16. Barani, *Tarikh-i- Firuz Shahz* (Aligarh edn), vol. II, p. 190.
17. Ibid., pp. 35-6; Persian edn and English Trans. by Shahab Sarmadec, pp.101, 103.
18. Ibid. 101
19. Faqirullah Saif Khan regards it as the equivalent *of git:* see *Rag Darpan*, p. 36; Persian edn and English edn. by Shahab Sarmadee. p.103.
20. Mirza Khan bin-i-Fakhru'ddin Muhammad, *Tuhfat al- Hind*, ed. Nnurul Hasan Ansari, Tehran, 1950, vol.1, pp.353, 359.According to Mirza Khan, *tarana* and *tillana* are similar.
21. *Rag Darpan*, p. 40.
22. Ibid.; Mirza Khan. *Tuhfat al-Hind*, vol. 1, p. 350.
23. *Rag Darpan*, p. 36.
24. Ibid., p. 36.
25. *Tuhfat al-Hind*, Vol. 1, p. 359.
26. Ibid., p. 280.
27. For details of these grants see Tarapada Mukherjee and Irfan Habib, 'Akbar' paper presented at the 48th Session of Indian History Congress, Goa, 1987 (A.M.U., Mimeograph), 65-117.
28. A Fuhrer, *The Monumental Antiquities and Inscriptions in the N W. Provinces and Oudh*, Delhi reprint, 1969, p. 98.
29. The *naubat* is the Imperial orchestra, consisted originally of *tabl* (a pair of drum) and *naqqara* (a large kettle-drum), and it was played at stated times before the gate of a king or prince. It was a west Asian tradition introduced in India by Sultan Iltutmish (r. 1210-36), and was a symbol of political authority and the most effective and visible mean to announce and communicate power, It also heralded the activity of the emperor and traveled with him wherever he went. Otherwise it was located at a prominent point of the entrance of the royal residence, and the place was called *Naubakhana*. Initially the *naubat* was performed five times a day coinciding with the time of Muslim prayer During the Mughal period, however, it came to be performed in accordance with the Indian system of dividinK the day in eight *pahar* (from Sanskrit *prahar*) or *ghari* (watches) and at each *ghari* eight different instruments were performed.

Jahangir particularly mentions about *kuwarga, karana (kara-nay), suma (sur-nay)*, which were wind instruments, and a pair of drums for playing the *mursal* (an overture or some introductory strain) as part of the orchestra *Tuzuk-i Jahangiri*, English Trails., A. Rogers, Delhi, Reprint, 1%8, Vol. II, p. 79.

30. Madhu Trivedi, *Imperial Agra as the Cultural Node: late 16th to early 17th century'*, paper presented in a Seminar on Qazi Nurullah Shustari, held on 18th- 20th January, 2003 at Agra; K. K. Trivedi. The Emergence of Agra as a Capital and a City: A Note on its Spatial and Historical Background *JESHO*, Vol. XXXVII. Leiden, 1994, pp. 147, 161, 165, 166, 167; for details also see *Agra: Economic and Political Pro file of a Mughal Suba*, 1580-1707, Pune, 1998, chapters 2 & 4.

31. *Ragumanjari* (2.78), as in R S. Sathayanarayana ed. *Nartananimaya* (Introduction), Vol. 1, p. 14.

32. The other ingredients *(ang)* were: *sur, virud, pad, tenak. paat* and *tal*. Prabandh were musical compositions of three types, *sudakram, alikram* and *viprakarinn*. These were further divided into various sub-types. *Sudakram* had twenty two sub-types like *ela*: *alikram* had twenty four varieties like *panchtaleshwar* and *Viprakirna* thirty six varieties such as *tripadi* and so on. Only few forms were current in our period of study, which are mentioned by Abu! Fazl in *Ain-i Akbari*, English Trans., H. S. Jarrett, Delhi, Reprint, 1978, vol.111, p. 265.

33. Yahiya Kabuli, *Lahjat-i Sikandarshahi*, undated, Persian, ed. Shahab Sarmadee, Delhi, 1999, pp. 479,488,492-493.

34. Ibid. p. 492

35. Ibid

36. *Tuhfal at-Hind*, vol. 1, p. 351.

37. *Hastak* (handposes) is defined as generating aesthetic appeal in dance. The hands are of supreme importance in *abhinaya*: anything could be symbolized through *hastas*. These hand gestures along with the movements of the eyes and eyeballs are employed in *sumanyabhinaya* (basic representation) and *citrabhinaya* (special or variegated representation). Varieties of *hsata* are three: *asamyuta* (uncombined, gestures shown by single hands), *samyuta* (combined, gestures shown by both hands), and *nritta-hasta* (the dissemination of meaning with both hands in special formation in dance): *Nritta-hastas* are of five kinds: They are known to be movements upward, downward, on the right, on the left and in the front. The author of *Ghuniyat ul Munya*, the musical treatise of the fourteenth century uses the term *hastak* and tells there are sixty four varieties of it *(shust u chahar shaki darad*, p. 64).

38. *Bhramari* is whirling movement in dance and has many varieties such as *bahyabhramari antarbhramari, tiripbhramri ,chhutrbhramari* and *chakrabhramari*.

39. The origin of the term *primlu* is from *pillmiru;* which is derived from *pillauru*. *Pilla* means diminutive in the Deccani language, while *muru* denotes a turning, twisting rotation in dancing. The term, thus, denotes a smaller version *of muru*. It is composed of a variety of *tal-prahandh* (instrumental compositions) especially the *yati-prabandh* and follows the song and *tal* closely, as one may notice in the account of Mirza Khan. These instrumental compositions were integrated in the vocabulary of kathak as *primlu ke bol;* in the opinion of some music scholars the term originates from *parmul*, which is the phonetic distortion of *paramel*. In the professional parlance the term indicates the blending of sounds of various percussion instruments such as *naqqara, pakhawaj, jhanjh, manjira, tasha* etc.

40. *Mandal* is a male instance, in which the two feet are placed on the ground, obliquely, such as both hips and knees are aligned to this line and are still.

41. Pandarika Vitthala, *Nartananimaya*. edited and translated by R S. Sathyanarayana, Delhi, 1994, Vol. ill, p. 45, *Slokas,* 665, 669-71.
42. *Ang* is the component of *tal* used in the context of movement of different organs of body in a dance. *(Tuhfat al-Hind,* Vol. 1, p. 439). According to Mirza Khan *urap* and *tirap* were characteristic of jumping and to and fro movement, while *lag* and *dat* were charecterised by brisk movements *(Ibid).*
43. *Sur Sagar, Khand,* 1, p. 655, as cited by S. Awathi, 'Raslila an Operitic Drama', *Marg,* Vol. Xll, No.4, Bombay, September, 1959, p. 56.
44. *Tuhfat al-Hind.* Vol. I, p. 437-8;
45. For details see Madhu Trivedi, *Art and Culture as Reflected in the Sufi Premakhyans: Chandayan and Mirgavat,* paper presented in a seminar on 'Culture Economy and social Change in Medieval India 12-18 century', held on 5-7 January, Aligarh, 2002.
46. Ibid., Vol. 1. p. 440.
47. Mir Amman *Bagh v. Bahar* (1803), Urdu, Calcutta, Delhi edition. 1995, p. 153.
48. *Mrdanga:* is a barrel shaped membrane phone. The vernacular synonym for *mrdanga* was *pakshavaj* or *pakhavaj,* which is, apparently, used for the first time in NN, (see *mrdanga lakshanam,* sl. 47, pp. Vol. 1, pp. 172-73. Here PV mentions it clearly that *mrdanga* is synonymous with *mardal, muraj* and *pushkara* and that people also describe it as *pakshavaj.*
49. Yahiya Kabuli's description is very exciting regarding flute. He enumerates fifteen varieties of it and describes their distinguishing features as well as illustrates various styles of playing flutes. It was a popular instrument and there were exclusive *vrind* (orchestra) offlute players. These were comprised of a master musician and four supportive artistes (pp.479-483).
50. According to Sarang Dev the popular name for *desi patah* was *addavaj, S.R. 6.824);* Avaj or *avuja* seems to have functioned as a generic name for the class of instruments of the *mrdanga* type. For instance, *hurukka* was called *skandhavaj* by professional percussionists. (Nartananirnaya, Commentary. Vol.1, p.293).
51. Tara Chand, pp. 36, 82.
52. *Zakhirat ul Khawanin,* p.441.
53. Hakim Maharat khan Isfahani, the author of an early eighteenth century geographical work *Bahjat* al- *Alam,* Persian Manuscript Collection, Ethe 729, India Office Library, folio. 34a, as cited by Stephen P. Blake, 'Cityscape of an Imperial Capital: Shahjaahanbd' in *Delhi through the* Ages, 1739, p. 155.
54. Zahiuddin Malik, The Reign *of Muhammad Shah,* 1729-48, Delhi, 1977,p.345.
55. Dargah Ouli Khan, *Muraqqa'-i Delhi,* pp. 81, 85, 86; English Trans., pp. 75, 82, 83.
56. For details see Madhu Trivedi, 'Hindustani Music and Dance: An Examination *of* Some Texts in the Indo-Persian Tradition', in The *Making of Indo-Persian Culture: Indian* and *French Studies,* eds. Muzaffar A lam, Francoise 'Nalini' Delvoye and Marc Gaboriean, New Delhi, 2000, pp. 281-306.
57. Crooke. Ill, p. 496.
58. *Muraqqa'-i Delhi,* p.778.
59. Ibid.. pp.85.

Maqsood Ahmed Rahi

Mysticism in Kashmir

There is no denying the fact that Islam began to prosper in Kashmir in the reign of Shah Mir, who patronized the religious personalities coming to Kashmir from Turkey and Persia. The official patronage facilitated the preaching of Islam in all the states of Kashmir in general and in Ontipura and Maten in particular. Numerous Islamic centers and *Madrassahs* were established where information about Islamic faith was imparted to people and they were persuaded towards the path of welfare and goodness.

In the middle of 14th century A.D. Islam dominated the valley of Kashmir. The *Sufi* religious saints played a vital role in the promotion of Islamic faith. These mystics were the epitome of humanism and they won the people's hearts by absorbing the teachings of all the faiths into one religion.

The vacuum created by the absence of an all-embracing faith in times of political uncertainty and changing social values was fulfilled by the teachings of the *Sufis*. Their teachings and personalities were the manifestation of faith and morality.

Lilah Dedi or La Yashuri was the most prominent among these *Sufis*. Lilah cast deep influences on the lives and thoughts of her contemporary Kashmiris and even today her sayings echo in the hearts of every Kashmiri.

Lilah Dedi or La Yushiri a Perfect Saint:

Lillah Dedi occupies an exalted status in *Rishi* movement. She was a perfect saint. The fame of her spiritual powers is a vivid manifestation of her spiritual greatness. Even the great saint Noor-ud-din Noorani received his spiritual training in her lap. Lillah Aarfah's advent is one of the momentous and fortunate spiritual incidents that occurred in the fourteenth century. Lilah Dedi played a key role in propagating Islamic faith in Kashmir.

She was born in 1335 in Sampura near Srinagar in a *Pandit* family. She was married to a *Pandit* of Padmanpura in a very young age. Her in-laws treated her ruthlessly and even her husband, misguided by her mother-in-law, was bent upon killing Lillah Dedi. Unconcerned by these cruelties of fate which she had to face she was undergoing a spiritual transformation. She was absorbed in the love of God. One day this secret was revealed. Once she entered her house carrying a water pitcher on her head which her husband broke with a stick. The water became still over the saint's head. She filled all the pots of her house with that water and threw the rest in the desert where a pond appeared. The talk of her spiritual feats spread far and wide. Her husband became puzzled by her spiritual powers and sent her out of the house. Lillah was already disillusioned by the world and was always engrossed in God's meditation, so she resigned to her fate. She wandered in jungles and deserts completely unconcerned about herself in a naked state.

During these wanderings, she met Sadhu Srikanth Maharaj and started singing the songs of *Shivism*. She sang hundreds of songs in this state of meditation. These *Vikyas* are important part of Kashmiri language. She also learned *Yoga* from Srikanth. At that time, the unrest was prevalent in Kashmir and her fellow countrymen needed guidance. Lillah came back to her people and produced a revolution in the people's hearts. Her songs gave courage and strength to the people. She gave the lessons of patience and forbearance to the people in the reign of tyranny and cruelty. During her ascetic life, thousands of Hindus and Muslims used to run after her but she used to disappear in the jungles and mountains. She had to face many hardships too. During this time Muslim *Sufi* Saints were busy in spreading Islam in every nook and corner of Kashmir. Lillah Dedi met veteran *Sufi* saint Hazrat Jalul-ud-din Bukhari Makhdoom Jahanian Jahan Gasht and embraced Islam. Then she headed towards the destination of *Saluk*. Lillah undertook long journeys to far-flung areas with him. Hazrat Jalal-ud-din from Bukhara was an important Saint of *Suharwardi Silsalah*. His family later shifted to Bhakkar (West Punjab). He was a learned scholar and disciple of famous Sufi Saint Hazrat Baha-ud-din Zakarya Multani.

Lillah Dedi also remained under the patronage of Mir Syed Hssain Simnani and then she met her cousin Mir Sayed Ali Hamdani.

After meeting him, her way of life was entirely changed. Lillah stopped wandering naked after that. She played a pivotal role in spiritual training and evolution of Hazrat Noor-ud-din Noorani. According to a tradition she designated Hazrat Shaikh Noor-ud-din Rishi as her spiritual heir. On the instructions of Hazrat Meer Sayed Hassan Simnani, her spiritual guide, she went to Sidra Moji who was about to give birth to Noor-ud-din Noorani. She transferred her spiritual powers and knowledge to Hazrat Noor-ud-din Noorani when he was 22. Lillah Dedi died in 1400. She spent her youth in guiding, training and educating Noor-ud-din. Lillah Dedi preached equality. She advised people to keep away from worldly rites and custom; to abolish, caste rituals and religious differences. She was rebellious and antagonistic towards Brahmans as they had made her homeless and had been cruel to her. Lillah plunged deep into her heart, undertook a spiritual journey then expressed the truth before people. Lillah's songs are sung by every Kashmiri child, youth and old folk even now. Lillah established a culture of love; therefore, the followers of every religion respect her. She occupies an important place in mystic poetry. She was a critic of religious festivals and religious fundamentalism. She had strong distaste for social inequality and class system prevalent during her times. She raised her voice against the class system. Her poetry reveals many aspects of life and death. Her poetry is characterized by spirituality, the transitoriness of life, love with the creator, and trust in God. She established the bonds of friendship and love among different religions which was the need of the hour. She can be ranked among *Sufis* like Rumi, Hafiz, Kabir, Khayam, Bulleh Shah and Rabia Basri.

Below is given the English translation of some of her Kashmiri poems.

O! Silly man
You cannot become virtuous
Just by keeping fast and
Performing religious rites
The idol is made of stone
The temple is of stone
Everything which is above and below

Is one and the same
Whom will you worship?
O silly, *Pandit*
First strike a consonance
Between your mind and heart
....

If the world defames me
I harbour no grudge against it
As I am a true admirer of God
Is it possible for ash
To leave a speck on mirror?
When my mind
Became free of impurities and wickedness
It became clean like a mirror
Free from dust and dirt
I recognized myself
When I found Him (God)
Residing inside me
I felt that Being
Embracing all
And felt myself as nothing
....

Lillah Dedi occupies a prominent place among the *Sufi* Saints born in Kashmir. Some remember her as a poet, some as a spiritual leader; some know her as *Sufi Yogi*, and a follower of Shivaji Maharaj. Some consider her as an *Autar*. However, she is an intellectual for the Kashmiris. They read her poetry with great devotion and respect. She enriched Kashmiri language with her poetry. She influenced her cotemporary generations and even today her poetry is a driving force for Kashmiris, though scholars differ about her correct religious beliefs. But a Muslim historian Beerbul Kichro (1919-46) regarded her as Laila Aarfah, Lillah, Lillah Majzooba and even Rabia Basri.

Nandu Rishi Baba Hazrat Noor-ud-Din Noorani:

Shaikh Noor-ud-din Noorani remembered as Nundo Rishi by Kashmir people was the spiritual heir of Lillah Dedi and right hand of Sayed Ali Hamdani. He was born in a village Kemva of Lagam on the day of *Eid-ud-Azha*. His father's name was Shaikh Salar-ud-din and mother's name was Sidra. They were both newly converted Muslims. They both embraced Islam at the hands of Saint Yasmin Rishi and both used to spend their time in his service. They met renowned *Sufi* Saint Lillah Dedi there who presented a fragrant flower bouquet to Sidra, after which she gave birth to Shaikh Noor-ud-din. Shaikh Noor-ud-din did not wish to be fed by her mother but when Lillah Dedi asked him, he allowed Lillah Dedi to feed him. So Shaikh Noor-ud-din was attached with Lillah Dedi from his infancy. Lillah also loved him very much and regarded him as her son and predicted the sainthood (*Wilayat*) for him. Once, Lillah Dedi took Seikh Noor-ud-din to Shah-e-Hamdan, who also blessed him. Shaikh Noor-ud-din had to face cruel sufferings: his step-brothers became his enemies and imposed a false charge of theft on him. He separated from his brothers. He started trade but adulteration, dishonesty and base tactics of trade made him disillusioned with the world. He left his home in search of truth. He wandered from village to village and remained engrossed in meditation. He was always in a state of lamentation and prayers. He became unconcerned with the world. He wandered in jungles, mountains and fields, left eating and fed himself on *Kasni* for twelve years. For next 12 years, he only drank milk then left it, too, considering it as un-conducive for his state of piety and lived on the water of a stream for next two and a half years. So he did not touch grain or bread for 26 years. He therefore was called Rishi Baba. He saw the Prophet (PBUH) in his dream and stepped into practical life. He started preaching Islam far and wide and followed the teachings of Prophet (PBUH). According to another tradition he also met *Sufi* Saint of *Suharwardi Silsalah* Hazrat Shaikh Baha-ud-din Zakariya Multani, and Hazrat Jalal-ud-din Bukhari and Farid-ud-din Ganj-e-Shakar of *Chishti Silsilah* and the *Qalander* of his time Lal Shahbaz Qalander. These saints filled Shaikh Noor-ud-din Rishi's chest with 18 fountains of scientific knowledge. His being was immersed in light after that. He found himself soaked in light. In this way he headed towards his spiritual destination when he was 30. He remained busy in prayer in a cave and led an ascetic life for twelve years. He kept fasts and fed himself on vegetables and water. According to the Rishi tradition, salvation can only be attained by tormenting the body. He opted for this way and practised it for 25 years. But when he came under the influencee of

Hazrat Mir Hussain Hamdani and Hazrat Sayed Ali Hamdani he gave up asceticism. This is mentioned in a letter by Hazrat Mir Hussain written on 15th Rajab in 814 Hijra which is still preserved in *Khanqah-e-Mua'lla* in Srinagar. He made him his special disciple. He acknowledged Noor-ud-din Noorani's spiritual status.

Hazrat Noorani was also influenced by Mir Sayed Hussain who had inspinred his father to embrace Islam. He also had intimate relations with his contemporaries Shaikh Baha-ud-din, Sultan Pakhli and Baba Oham. He became very popular in his life and the people were deeply moved by his simple life and poetry.

Nandu Baba had 99 disciples and a number of caliphs but four of them are renowned: Baba Bam-ud-din Rishi, Baba Zain-ud-din Rishi, Baba Nasir-ud-din Rishi and Baba Latif-ud-din Rishi. His followers included the people of every strata of society like laymen, princes, farmers, people from the lower class and *Brahmans* of high class, Rajputs and atheists. Both the illiterate and the scholars used to come in his company. All these people caused a social movement and waged *Jihad* against injustice and cruelty under his leadership. Baba Daood Mishkati writes in *Israr-ul-Ibrar*.

"Nandu Baba and his followers led a very simple and clean life. They lived on water, dry wild grass and vegetables. They never saved anything for themselves and whatever they got they used to give it away to the poor, fed beggars and travelers. They were harmless people who did not give any harm to even birds and insects."

His mystic poetry (*Ashlok*) is highly inspiring. His poetry which is termed as *Satrokh* in Kashmiri is soaked in oneness of Allah (*Tauheed*) and love of Prophet (PBUH).

The English translation of the selected poetry from his collection of poetry *Rishi Nama* is presented below:-

God is one
But it has hundreds and thousands of names
Even the thin blade of grass
Is absorbed in Allah's remembrance
I avoided everything to attain Him
Days and nights passed
In His search

I plunged deep into myself
And felt Him
Thus, I won the cognizance of myself and Him
I am near Him and
He holds me close

In the era of Shah Hamdan, the Muslims of Kashmir were attached to their old customs and rites in one way or the other which was disliked by Nandu Baba. He wrote *Satrokh* to show his feelings regarding this.

His poetry is widely popular which enthralls the reader; even the writers and critics of modern Kashmiri literature are impressed by his poetry. The main features of his poetry are mysticism, the temporariness of life, attainment of purposeful life, the reality of death, self-control and avoidance of greed.

Only those know
How to read Quran
Who repent by
Day and night
At last they are reduced
To mere skeletons of bones
And become dust with the dust
Pay careful heed
To Quran and Hadith
As one day they will
Lead you to paradise

I attain ecstasy in His Company
To search at other places
Was of no avail
The abode of my beloved
Is in my inner self
Only he will be deemed successful
In both the worlds
Who has an unflinching belief
That the Prophet of Islam
And his four Caliphs lead

To the path of truth
Their deeds are like key
To the solution of sorrows and sufferings

Most of those who
Claim to be saints
Are modern Pharaohs
They indulge in fun and pleasure seeking
But those who hold themselves
Away from all pleasures
And die on the way of Allah
They become like pure Gold
After burning into fire
Oh! *Pandit* how you can avoid fire without good deeds
Your ego has turned your knowledge useless
You forget that you will
Become dust one day
And your wealth and comforts
Will be taken back
They have become
Strangers to themselves loading books
Like donkeys who are loaded by books
Always remember God
And remain near Him
Control your passion, employ reason
Make a necklace of diamonds and think
The fountains of wisdom
Will originate within
Then you will see God everywhere
He is your Master, you are a slave
Always be absorbed in His remembrance
Then you will hear the echo
Of his beautiful names within

He was an epitome of explicit and implicit knowledge; a manifestation of inner and outer light, uniquely blessed in treating ailments. Mir Muhammad Sayed Hamadani gave him the title of *Kutb-al-Afaq*. He was a born saint. He passed away in 843 Hijra/1438.A.D.

He is buried at Charaar Sharif. He is also known as *Alamdar-e Kashmir*, *Shaikh-ul-Alam* and *Surkheel-e-Rishyan* His tomb is the centre of attraction to all and sundry.

Mian Muhammad Bukhsh Qadri (R.A):

Mian Muhammad Bukhsh was a peerless scholar, a unique saint, a teacher inspired by divine light, and a universal poet. He belonged to that *Silsila* (chain) of *Sufis* who enchanted peoples' heart with their poetry and inspired them to replace the hatred, differences, and malice with love, peace and tolerance. Baba Bulleh Shah, Sachal Sarmust, Baba Rehman, Noor-ud-Din Rishi and Shah Abdul Latif Bhitai, all of them were enlightened by the same source of light.

Mian Muhammad Bakhsh was born in Khari Sharif, MirPur, Azad Kashmir in 1865. His father Mian Shams-ud-Din was the *Mutawalli* (incharge) of the *Khanqah* (monastery) of Hazrat Peeray Shah Ghazi Qalandri known as Damri Wali Sarkar. There is difference of opinion about his correct year of birth. Mehboob Ali Faqir Qadri in the preface of his biography *Saif-ul-Malook* has written his date of birth as 1246 Hijra / 1825 A.D. This same date is written in *Shahkar Islamic Encyclopedia*. At some places it is mentioned as 1830 and at other places it is 1843. Mian Muhammad Bukhsh has himself mentioned this in *Saif-ul-Malook* that when he completed the book in 1863 (1279 *Hijri*) he was 33 which means that the correct year of birth is 1830 (1246 *Hijri*). His father Allama Shams-ud-Din Qadri was a prominent and authentic scholar.

His father paid special attention to his education in a religious atmosphere. His piety, mental and spiritual maturity was the result of his father's training. After acquiring the external forms of knowledge, he developed a passion to fathom the secrets of wisdom, spiritual knowledge and purity of self. So his brother Mian Bahawal Bakhsh enrolled him in the *Madrassah* of Hafiz Muhammad Ali in Samwal Sharif. There he learnt Arabic, Persian, grammar, *Surf-o-Nahu*, Holy Quran, *Hadith*, *Fiqah* and *Tafseer*, *Ilm-ul-Kalam*, philosophy and mysticism. The brother of Hafiz Muhammad Ali, Hafiz Nadir, was an ascetic who had given up worldly affairs and lived in the mosque of Samwal Sharif. Mian Muhammad Bakhsh used to read *Yusuf Zulekha* with great interest in melodious voice and Hafiz Nadir used to listen to it with rapt attention. He was only 15 then. When his father got very sick he called all his relatives, pupils and local nobles and declared to transfer all what he had got from Ustad Peeray Shah, Ghazi Damri Wali Sarkar to Mian Muhammad Bakhsh. But Mian Muhammad Bukhsh insisted that his brothers should not be deprived of this blessing. His father became very pleased on this and nominated him as his caliph.

A few days after that Shams-ud-Din died. After the death of his father, he went to the *Khanqah* (monastery) after spending 4 years in his home. He led the life of an ascetic. Though he was nominated caliph by his father but he had a strong feeling that he should make a *Sufi* saint as his mentor. So after completing the formal education he started the search for a perfect saint. He wandered place to place but could not find his destination. So he made *Istikhara* (divine consultation) to get guidance from God Almighty. He was guided by Shah Ghazi Qalander known as Damri Wali Sarkar to have initiation by Saint Ghulam Muhammad. He went to him and told him the purpose of his arrival. He, at first refused to do so. He went to him again and again for many years and during this he passed through various stages of spiritual purification. At last, one day moved by his devotion and respect, he endowed him with initiation and asked him to go to Kashmir to Shaikh Ahmed Wali. He made him aware of some spiritual secrets and made him his caliph. He then stayed in Kashmir for a month enlightening people with his poetry. He raised his voice against cruelty. His heart deeply ached on the helplessness and wretchedness of the Kashmiri people. He also asked the rulers to stop the atrocities against Kashmiris.

Hasphet Rai, the ruler of Kashmir, assured him that the Muslims of Kashmir will be given equal status. After one month he came back to Khari Sharif where he benefited people with his knowledge, wisdom and spirituality. He was nominated the spiritual successor of *Darbar-e-Alia* Khari Sharif in 1298 *Hijri*. He had completed most of his publications till then. He was about 51 or 52 years at that time. He spent all his life in worship and meditation and acted upon the *Shariah*. He used to go to the tomb of Hazrat Peeray Shah Ghazi and swept it daily. He used to be engrossed in *Darood* and *Wazaif* (forms of prayer)

Though he belonged to a rich and prosperous family he was averse to the worldly things, power and pelf. He led a simple life. He ate a frugal repast and in the last part of his life his food was reduced to very little. He always remained engrossed in worship and prayer. Those who visited his company were enriched by the love of God, the respect of God's saints and the wealth of spiritual purity. He had innate devotion and love for *Ahle-Saadat* (The family of Holy Prophet (PBUH)). He never used to disappoint anyone and was generous to every visitor.

He even blessed Partab Singh who harbored a desire to father a child when he was very old. Mian Muhammad Bukhsh prayed for him and also warned Partab Singh not to take the child to any temple. He fathered a male child when he was 60. In the celebrations of the childbirth Partab forgot to fulfill his promise and the queens of Partab's palace took the child to the tomb. A few days after that, the child passed away. Main Muhammad Bukhsh also predicted the fall of Dogra Empire. The last ruler of Dogra Empire Hari Singh, too, did not refrain from tyranny and injustice. He destroyed thousands of Muslim families. So at last, he had to abdicate his throne in 1947, where he was compelled to sign the accession to India which ended the Dogra Raj.

He authored numerous memorable publications which bear witness to his scholastic status, devotion, abundance of spiritual strength and extempore poetic talent. His publications include:

(1)*Tuhfa Rasool* (2) *Gulzar-e-Faqr* (3) *Karamat-e-Ghous-e-Azam* (4) *Tuhfa-e-Meeran* (5) *Hidayat-ul-Muslameen* (6) *Nayrang-e-Ishq* (7) *Tazkarah-e-Muqeemi* (8) *Sakhi Khawas Jan* (9) *Kissa Shaikh Sana'an* (10) *Mirza Saheban* (11) *Shah Mansoor* (12) *Sohni Mahiwal* (13) *Shireen Farhad* and *Saif-ul-Malook*, which became widely popular. He is remembered as *Jami-e-Punjab* and *Rumi-e-Kashmir*.

His interest in *Sufism* had led him to write poetry. At first, he composed a *Qaseedah* for his spiritual mentor. He started writing poetry by composing stories into poetic form. His poetry has a rich store of Arabic and Persian words. He has also written a comprehensive review of *Qaseedah Burda Sharif* by Albuseri. His poetry has been translated into many languages. His book *Saif-ul-Malook* occupies a prominent place in Punjab literature. His poetry is also tinged with *Potohari* tone and style. He played prominent role in the preaching of Islam.

He expressed his views and feelings in simple language and style which is comprehensible to everyone. Though all the *Sufi* poets have conveyed their message in an impressive way, but Mian Muhammad Bukhsh's style was unique and unparalleled. He always remained immersed in the remembrance of God. The depth, sweetness, simplicity, metaphors and similes found in his poetry are unparalleled by other *Sufi* poets. His spiritual services are immeasurable. He contributed a lot in the preaching of Islam. His life was devoted to humanity. His mystic poetry contributed to spread his spiritual message. He always preached love and harmony. There was a unique pathos in his poetry and voice. His poetry penetrated the heart. He didn't become aloof from the world in forests, caves and deserts and made extensive travels to spread the word of love and peace. He strived to free people from the clutches of hatred and ignorance.

This great mystic poet, champion of humanity and love, breathed his last on 7th Zilhaj 1324 Hijri / 1907 A.D. He was buried in Khari Sharif near the tomb of his spiritual mentor, Peer Ghazi Damri Wali Sarkar. Thousands of people visit his tomb even today to pay their respect.

Below are given the English translation of his selected poetry:

"This river (life) can't be crossed without the spiritual mentor
Whosoever steps in it all alone is destined to drown."

"Those who drink the draught of the spiritual wine
Are so intoxicated that they forget the act of speech
and ignore every sort of conversation"

"You are the subject, ruler, chief and the clerk yourself
Who else may be raven or a hunter?
You live alone within yourself
No one is your partaker
You are the worshipper and worship your own self"

"The fragrance of gardens is useless without friends
If I meet my friend, He will free me from thousands of sufferings
I shall thank my lord immeasurably"

"I have made ties with someone higher than me
And entangled myself

None else, but only my friend can comfort me"

"Once arrested by love,
One can never be free
It is a pirate which robs the wayfarers"

"Don't be proud of your startling beauty,
The twigs are not evergreen,
The flowers will not always be fragrant
Neither the lamp will always give light,
Nor the moth will burn,
The hands will not always be colored by henna,
The bangles will not always strike"

"O Lass! Fill your pitcher in the daylight
With water as much as you wish,
At evening, you will fear to go home
Unaccompanied by your lover"

"No one reaped fruit by befriending the base
By guiding the vine on the pricks
I injured every grape"

(Translated into English by Khurram Khiraam)

Notes:

1. *Hikayat-e-Sufiay-e-Kashmir, Maqsood Ahmed Rahi, Five Star Publications, Islamabad, August 2008.*
2. *Mian Muhammad Bukhsh Shakhsiat aur Fun by Hameed Ullah Hashmi, Pakistan Academy of Letters, 2007.*

Mohd. Zaman Azurdah

Elements of Sufism in Nundo Reshi's Poetry

They valley of Kashmir has always been a seat of intellect and a habitat of saints and Sufis. Kalhana's Rajtarangni is a witness to the valley's rich past, the oldest chronicale available in the sub-continent. Later on, a number of histories of Kashmir written by various authors at different period of time which also show that Kashmir has not only been geo-politically, and strategically important but also intellectually, it has been significant enough.

Sense of historicity and intellect has always been in the genes of Kashmir's. Only a few know that the history of Avadh, "Sawaneh Salateeni Avadh" was written by a Kashmiri called Syed Kamal-ud-Din Hyder, who was an employee in observatory at Lucknow. The most remarkable thing about this history is that he not only wrote it but also protected it from British wrath by remaining underground, leaving his house and hiding himself along with the copy of *the MSS* in villages of Avadh.

Besides history writing and Sanskrit literature, Kashmiri's have contributed to Persian, Arabic and urdu literatures as well. Needless to mention, whether it was Abhino Gupt, Mamat, Bilhan, Ghani Kashmiri, Sheikh Yaqoobi Sarfi, Mullah Mohsin Fani, Birbal Kachru, Ratan nath Dhar Sarshar, Brij Narayan Chakbast, Brij Mohan Datatarya Kaifi, Khalifa Abdul Hakeem, Sir Mohd. Iqbal, Saadat Hasan Manto or the literature on the present literary scene. All these are basically Kashmiri's, who have written or are writing in different languages at different places.

As mentioned in the beginning the valley has been a seat of religious scholars, saints and Sufis. The fourth Buddist conference makes it more authentic. Saints of the valley comprised of a large number including Lala Arifa and Sheikh Noor-ud-Din. Sheikh Noor-ud-Din is widely known as "Nunda Reshi" in Kashmir. He belonged to Reshi cult of Kashmir. Reshi's cult of Kashmir performed the same job what Sufis played at the other places of the world. Reshis were Sufis in seclusion and social reformers in public life. They roamed and went from place to place to reform society. This was the reason that Sheikh-ul-Alam is known as "Alamdar-i-Kashmir" i.e. the standard bearer of Kashmir. His spiritual, social and Reshi stature was both in theory and practice. He did what he said and spoke what he performed. His fear of God "Taqwa" and Trust in God "Tawakul" never allowed him to bow before rulers. He had the domain of his own in which he was all in all.

In his love of God he practised and preached total surrender, without any worldly fear or reward. He ironically once said:

Kungh yiyi tehe kun Be Gharzayay
Kas Aasi Dilas Teoth Wusat
Janti Ki Tamha To Douzkhinr Bayay
Daya chhi karan Ibadat

O God people worship thee for the fear of Hell and Temptation of Heaven. Who will march towards you selflessly whose heart can be so vast and deep"

In fact Nundu Reshi wants total and whole-hearted surrender before God Almightly, without any rhyme and reason. In his vision, God is so great and supreme that people should bow towards him out of love and love only. Love of God forms the basis of Sufism. Sheikhul Alam in fact does not believe in rituals. He believes that God is above all rituals. No ritual can move him. He is to be won through selfless love. He says:

"Ami Tasbeehi, Aasi Ta Jando
Ami Phandi Su Athi Yiyee Noa"

You cannot find him through *Tasbeeh*, stick and robe. These tricks do not work with Him. Sheikhul Alam Sheikh Noor-ud-Din believes in *Qana'at*. He neither himself wants to become a glutton nor likes others to behave like that. He says:

ELEMENTS OF SUFISM IN NUNDO RESHI'S POETRY

> "*Tagi ye Bochhi Buzun Dize*
> *Manas Greshizan Kea Chhay zaat*
> *Tsawab Sasi Goan Pravize*
> *Yoad Bayi Nund Karakh Ravi Na Zaat*"

O my brother! you should burn your hunger if you can, look at your heart, do not count your identity. You will earn thousands of credits. If you do virtuous deeds, you will not loose your identity.

He further says:

> "*Manay Khen Anis Aichh Roshan*
> *Maney Khen Chhay Poshan Boyee*
> *Maney Kheni Aasi Shaitan Roshan*
> *Maney Kheni Chhuy Sit Farishtan Khoie*"

Eating in lesser quantity is the eye sight for blind. It is the fragrance of flowers and by eating less the devil goes away. Angels like the person who does not eat more.

Element of Qana'at has been very dear to Sufis. It is not with the eating only but in all spheres-of life except love of God, that Sufis want to be patient, tolerant and keeping themselves from worldly attraction.

Sufis have not been giving any importance to worldly appearances, riches and physical comforts. Their goal has been to restrain self from indulging into worldly affairs. The apparent world they have treated as a field for sowing seeds to harvest after this life. They have been trying to discover the path to reach Almighty Allah, who is the source of their creation. Sheikhul Alam Says:

> "*Rizq Chhuy Bronh Moat Pati Patay Dunyah*
> *Chhuy Shahruk Wata Gath*
> *Sar Tan Khoday Gar Tihinzi Watay Yeti*
> *Mali Rozan Nek-u-bad Kath*"

Your fate "whatever is in your store" is ahead of you and your death follows you. This world is like a traveller's temporary stop. You try to find God and trace his ways. What remains here is the talk of someone's being good or bad.

He further says:

> "*Awal ti Suy Aakhir ti Suy Nada Bal Wasith Mal*
> *Kaaso*

Das Guil Gandith Tais Kun Aaso
Devi Kuni Douzkhaninari Laso"

He is the first and He is the last. Go to the river and remove the dirt of heart. I folded the hands and came to Him and this act of mine may perhaps save me from the fire of hell.

While going through the poetry of Sheikh-ul-Alam, one comes across the elements of Sufism, much often. Late Abdul Abad Azad commenting on Sheikh's preaching and poetry Writes:

> "The essence of Sheikh Noor-ud-Din's preaching (Which of course comes through his poetry) is restraining of self, seclusion, trust in God, contentment, patience and gratitude for what God bestows with and indifference towards the world etc."

Prof. Rahman Rahi writes:

> "While studying and taking stock of Sheikh's poetry, one thing is necessarily to be kept in mind that Sheikh basically is a Reshi (Sage) in whose poetry we occasionally find mystic experiences"

One does not hesitate to agree with Prof. Rahi, that these elements of mysticism are occasionally found in the poetry of Sheikh Noor-ud-Din, but these occasions are too obvious, forceful and strong to be ignored by a reader.

However this is not true of his later poetry, where we find him like a true standard-bearer, coming closer to public and preaching the practicing life like a true human being. His message does not deny his own belief in love for God and act for God but at the same time brings people nearer to the human beings. He shuns seclusion and no more sits in caves but practises the real life. He refutes Mullahs and tells them that they are misguiding commoners with their false images.

Muhammad Ali Siddiqui

Mysticism and Humanism

The Mystics have played an important role in mediaeval times when the concepts of territorial integrity of states, human rights of people and threshold of dissent were easily dispensed with on the whims of invading hordes.

Mysticism has its origin in Vendanic, Greek and Neoplationic thought.

Max Muller, in his Hibbert Lectures, says that Monotheism is a stage next to Fetishism (worship of the inanimate objects and animals) & Monotheism[1] (objects in which man first suspected the presence of the invisible) Monotheism led to Devism (denial of the old Devis) and it is only after this stage that belief in one Being, the Self of all selfs, took its shape. I think that Max Mueller had a brilliant flash according to Lilaram Watanomal Lalwani to conclude that the philosophy of the Self leads us to mysticism, in *Upanishads*, which is very close to Islamic mysticism.

What is Vendata if not the summing up of *Upanishads*? The Keynote point of the *Upanishads* is 'know thy self'. It is to lead one to discover it in the highest, the eternal self, the one without the second, which underlines the whole world. The principle of individuality self embraces the idea that it is the eternal intelligence or consciousness that keeps the body alive, guides our motions and the senses to that respective functions.

The author of *Dabistan-Mazahib*, a Persian work translated by David Shea and Anthony Troyer, says that according to the followers of the

Vendanta, the really existing holy being is *Paramatma* i.e. the most excellent *Barahma*, the supreme and the most excellent spirit.

According to the account of the revealed unity of God, all is he ( ) and yet to show their attainment to the height of philosophy the Vedantians would prefer to say "All is one ( ) which is ( ) in Sanskrit.

This is the extent of similarity between the concept of "self" "All is one" having close resemblance to and in Islamic mysticism.

Looking into the import of the Greek speculative thought about 'self' and its relationship with the creator, the first point to consider is that with the capture of Alexandria in 641 AD the Arab conquest of the Middle East was virtually complete. The Greek thought got due response in Egypt, Syria and Iraq since the time of Alexander the Great. The Chef product of the Greek influence in the Middle East was the sway of Neoplatonism, founded by the Egyptian Plotinus (d, 270AD) and his most famous disciple the Syrian Porphyry of Tyre (d 303 AD).[2]

The earlier version of mysticism in Islam was Ascetism. We notice that from the end of second century & early third century of Hijra[3] the intermingling of Islamic and Non-platinic concept began with the first translation into Arabic of Plotinus[4] great work Enneads into six books of nine chapters. In Arabic it was called Kitab al-Rabubiyah (The Book of Divinity) much of Greek metaphysical ideas were assimilated by the Arab (through Egyptian, Syria, Iraqi & Iranian) and we have a whole body of rationalization of Islamic belief- known as *Ilmul kalam* and the thought of Neoplatonism and Neopythagoreanism being grounded in Al-Razi, Al-Farabi (950), Ibne Sina & the Brethern of Purity taking hold of Muslim mystics in a great measure.

It finally resulted in the sway of Ishraq (Illumination), reconciliation of Neoplatonism & Sufism of Al Suhrawardy & Mulla Sadra (P111-113)[5] until we reach a stage when we reach in Ishraq and Ibne Arabi's brand of mysticism's close resemblance to Vendantic to Platonic thought so much so that al Husain Ibn Mansur al-Hallaj was accused Manichaen influences of Hullol (transmigration) in addition to his utterances (I am God and I am the eternal self).

Buddhistic Influence

According to Buddhism man is essentially a moral being and the primary objective of religion is to build the character and personality of the individual, and through the individual mankind at large.

It was according to the above axiom that Buddha confined his teaching to Ethic, and refused to discuss Neta Physics with which India was already over-saturated according to Imran Nazar Husain (1976). [6] Buddha is silent about the existence or non Existence of God. His parting words to his disciples before he died were:

All component things are subjected to decay. Work out your own salvation with diligence (Imran Nazar Husain, 1976)

However in actual terms the Manayana Buddhism has transformed the religion of no-God into a religion of 'Gods galore'- big and small, strong and weak, male and female. The 'Man-God Buddha, like Dalai Lama, appears on earth in human form from time to time.'

And hence the vogue of Buddhist mysticism took a new shape, acquisition of spiritual power through meditation through opening the door of the transcendental dimension.

As Buddhism had its full sway in Central Asia (including Bactria) and present day Afghanistan the Budhist practices of contemplation, meditation, and self- mortification also attracted attention of some of Muslim mystics originating from these areas.

We have very distinct influences of such influences on some mystics eg. Baba Fareed Ganj Shakar and some other mystics.

It is quite wonderful that all great mystics, whether they belonged to Vendatic, Greek a Islamic schools of mysticism have always been sympathetic to the common masses. They have tried to act like their creators vicegerents and their responses could be taken as the divine solutions to the problems of the laity. The faith which these mystics, enjoyed with the masses could not be possible unless they were accepted as the ultimate models of piety and virtue

When we study the role which mystics have played all over the world we can't keep concluding that they have been, infact, the beconlight of hope to all those who have needed it most when only despair stared them in their faces. Hope is the pre-requisite which keeps on kindling the flame of Love and Compassion and brings the best in the human beings, and it is equally a theological virtue.[5]

Even though some secular institutions have tried to sideline the importance of mysticism. All that the present day humanism & theosophy have done to alleviate the sufferings of humanity couldn't be deemed equal to the task of serving more than one fourth or one third of humanity.[7]

We choose to restrict the field of action still further. Just imagine yourself to the poverty and human suffering in the subcontinent just look askance and see the steadily increasing flash-points of tension in our midst. All of these problems could be adequately addressed if we imbibe the teachings of great mystics. What are they in a nutshell: control thy propensities to mess up others problems and be careful not to allow malice greed and avarice take control of your thought process.

I am sure that the minimum course of action suggested above could render this planet worth living for all of our peoples.

In Islam the oldest type of mysticism, according to Prof. Reynold Nicholasm, was ascetic and devotional rather than speculation and the word 'Sufi' first appears in literature as a name applied to a certain class of ascetics. It was only in the second century of Hijra that the element of world flight and self-abnegation crept in. In almost every religion of the world we came across a tendency to go after the 'essence', the source of divinity, and these are always some individuals who have tried to reach out 'essence' through exercises of self-mortification, which has means to many a bit too hard on the body.

It was with the upsurge of Helenic influences that the Islamic asceticism took the shape of mysticism as it is understood today.

It is strange that some Muslim scholars have objected to the intrusion of Vedantic or neo-Platinic elements the mystical thoughts of some Muslim mystics which it is always within the domain of possibility to be influenced by mystics whose destination is no other than God and metaphysical truths cannot be monoplosed by my religion, specially when religions prior to Islam have a vast treasure of mystical thought.

It is a pity that mysticism has fallen on lean days now a days and the reasons adumbrated for the same are that science and technology have been steadily narrowing the domain of the unknown. The industrial age is said to be the undermining factor[8] and before it is averred that renaissance in the west gave birth to humanism which has not let mysticism remain the sole mainsprings of humanism. The modern humanist, it is said, doesn't need any spiritual yearning to look upon the poor and underprivileged as the center of his attention. The secularizing tendencies of human institutions & movements, like moral rearm, Human Rights Commission and scores of international relief agencies are not letting spiritual instincts to monologize the role of good Samaritan.

Materialism of our times, if is partially correct, is not providing as much space to mysticism as the God-fearing & the religions aura around Mysticism of the yester years did.[9] There was a time when the capacity to expect astonishing miracles from the saints and saint like persons touched utmost proportions.

How could the present day advances in sciences, technology and neglect of spiritual domain in general can obliterate the great humanistic role which the mystics have performed in history. Their role was so important that even today the oppressed & neglected section of humanity look upon them as the great saviors of humanity in general.

The message which is constantly going out of their mausoleums is that the human beings, regardless of their colour, creed, language and region deserve our respect and love as they are the creatures of a creator who doesn't admit of my discrimination between them.

There is another aspect of some important mystics which should accord them important place in our scheme of them. There are quite good examples that some of them have actively fought for the rights of the common men.

For example Mansur Hallaj, being an Iranian in origin, was a discipline of Imam Hambal an Arab, but his sympathetic were for the Shuaibia movement which favored the Non-Arab Muslim struggling for equal rights with the Arabs.

Quite a few mystics' poets of 12th & 13th century AD, offered solace and shelter to this oppressed people fleeing from Halagu & his successors raids.

Take the example of Mian Mir who didn't regard Sikhs as deviants of the correct path as is understood by many Muslims today. He laid the foundation stone of the Golden Temple of the Sikhs in Amritsar. He belonged to this party of Dara Shikah and was a Qadiri himself. He apposed his brother Aurangzeb.

We cannot forget the role of Shah Inayat al Qadri of Sindh who openly sided with the landless peasants of Sindh the mystic poets of Punjab eg. Bulhe Shah, Waris Shah and Shah Hussain have openly chided Afghan invaders. Ahmed Shah Abdali in particular for the look and plundeng of the common masses of Punjab.

Shah Latif in his Sur Sri Rag has been critical of Portuguese & English for their in roads in Sindh as against those agenda or traitors who collaborated with them.

Almost the majority of eminent mystics of the mediaeval times have been interceded on behalf of the common masses and second dismissed of the Governors of their areas on complaints against the misdeeds of the Governors of their areas.

Notes:

1. Lalwani, *The Life, Religion and Poetry of Shah Latif*, Sindhi Kitab Ghar, Karachi, 1985, P23
2. Fakhry Majid, *A Short Introduction to Islamic Philosophy & Mysticism*, One World Publication, Oxford
3. *Tarikh-i-Tasawuf*, Yusuf Salim Chisti, Auqab Board, Lahore
4. Fakhry, Majid, *A Short Introduction to Islamic Philosophy and Mysticism*, One World Publication, Oxford, 1997, Page 6
5. Fakhry, Majid, *A Short Introduction to Islamic Philosophy and Mysticism*, One World Publication, Oxford, 1997, Page 6 Husain, Imam Nazar, *Islam & Budhism in the Modern World*, World Federation of Islamic Mission, Islamic Centre, Block B, Nazimabad, 1976
6. Elton, *Lord Edward King & Our Times*, Geoffrey Bles Ltd, London, 1958
7. *Islam and Buddhism in the Modern World*, World Federation of Islamic Missions, Islamic Centre, Block B, Nazimabad, Karachi, 1976, P9
8. Lings, Martin, *What is Sufism*,
9. Arberry, R.A, *Muslim Mystics*

N.A. Baloch

Shah Abdul Latif, The Great Saint Patron of Music

Muslim saints and sages in the East from South Asia to Indonesia, patronized music in general and devotional music in particular. From the 14th century C.E. onward, saints of the Chishtiya Order in South Asia continued to inspire the masses with devotional music. 'Wali Songo' (Nine Saints) did the same in Indonesia. The Muslim saints Sunan Kahjaga in Yogyakarta (Jawa) had endeared himself to the people by putting their traditional themes (including 'Ram-Sita') to the music.

Amir Khusrau and Shah Abdul Latif

However, Amir Khusrau of Delhi and Shah Abdul Latif of Bhit (Sindh) may be singled out for their unique contribution in the revival of music of their times. Both were great poets, and also well versed in music. A long period of four centuries separated the two: Amir Khusrau flourished in the 14th century and Shah Abdul Latif in the 18th century. Amir Khusrau was a courtier and had his association with rulers, while Shah Abdul Latif belonged to the non-elite social strata and moved freely among the masses: Amir composed in Persian which was the state language and Latif composed in Sindhi which was his mother-tongue and a provincial language. Despite these difference, the consummation of genius in poetry and music and their sufistic devotion equated them in their achievements in the domains of poetry and music. Particularly in having unshered in new eras in the development of music in their own times.

The ancient music of India, continued by tradition from bygone times, was temple based, being part of the Hindu religious worship. Its models and modes of performance were handed down by the early worshipers. Being sacrosanct, it was not to be deviated from what was handed down by sages from the past. It was after the advent of Muslims in the Subcontinent that, for the first time, Amir Khursrau explained that music was part of knowledge to be learnt and cultivated as a science (*ilm*). In this discourse on differentiation in the fundamental and the subsidiary principles of music as well as in his well known Qita' , he has referred to *Ilm-i-Musiqi*, i.e. 'Science of Music'. Amir Khusrau (1255-1350 A.D) was born in Delhi and had educated himself in the music tradition of India as well as of the Middle East/Central Asia. The latter was highly developed by that time under the patronage of Muslim rulers from Cardoba to Bukhara. In his writings on music as well as through his performances, at courts and Sufi gatherings, he had brought about a synthesis between the two in the new secular system of 'Hindustani Music, as distinct form the sacrosanct Hindu Music'.

From the 14th century A.D. onward, 'Hindustani Music' began to develop as a secular art based in exactitude of the goals and the newly defined sargam formulae, and the *ragas* were sung to the accompaniment of the newly devised instruments specially Sitar and Sarangi. With further progress made during more than two centuries, theorists and performers of 'Hindustani Music' achieved the heights of their glory during the Mughal period.

Then came the decline, -- the new generation of musicians ceasing to be creative, even though excelling in executing the music patterns left by their predecessors. Shah Abdul Latif flourished during the reign of Muhammad Shah (1719-48) when sophisticated music models and techniques had eclipsed the creative interpretation and natural music appeal of the early masters. In order to bring about a renaissance. Shah Abdul Latif founded a new music institution at Bhit in 1731 A.D after he had settled down there.

Shah Abdul Latif (1102 H./1690 A.D) was born in a revered Sayyed family of Sufi poets. His father Shah Habibullah (d.1144 H. /1731 C.E) often composed verses a few of which have survived, while his great grandfather Shah Abdul Karim (d.1044 H./1634 C.E) was a great Sufi poet. He had also established devotional Sufi Sima' sessions, which were later continued on by Shah Abdul Latif.

Shah Abdul Latif's stature as a great poet has overshadowed his contribution in the domain of music. In fact, poetry and music became integrated in his compositions. His verses represent music expressed through harmony of works. The late Allama I.I. Kazi, explains the great authority of Shah Abdul Latif, "Latif never thought of his poems as 'works' because they did not entail labour. He created them in ecstatic moods when no work as work was possible". Each one of his *bait* and *waee* poem, is musically composed in order to be sung, and these are being sung to this day even by the village folk.

During his wanderings in Sindh and beyond Sindh in his youth. Shah Abdul Latif had associated himself with the masses, and became familiar with their problems. He gained knowledge of the folk music tradition and also of the professional performers. Flashes of this rich experience are reflected in his verses (*bait* and *waee* composition). These were put to writing and compiled by his disciples and admirers and the compilations became known as *Shah-Jo-Risalo* (Shah's Poetic Compendium). It is a thesaurus of more than three thousand of his *bait* and *waee* compositions. In its importance, it has often been compared to the *Mathnavi* of Maulana Rumi which was a constant companion of Shah Abdul Latif along with 'Discourse' of his great grand father (Bavan-al-Arifin) and the Holy Quran.

The *Risalo* and the music institution of *Surud Latifi* or *SHAH-jo-RAGA* founded by him (see below) are the two main contemporary sources to appreciate Shah Latif's superb poetic thought of universal import once and his contribution in music.

Shah Abdul Latif's perception of Music

In the *Risalo* a number of elemental forms of human voice as also a variety of other echoes with music strain find mention in different verses under different themes. Most of the musical instruments have come under reference. These include *danburo, surando, keenro, rabab, murli, kamach, nadr (nay), duhl, damama, tabal, naqara, bher, chang, murchang*, and also other popular folk music instruments such as *singirryun kani, kanjho, chhinnka, charra/lar, sanbhar/sanbhar. Kharkyun, ghand, ghandirree, tunto, tubirree*. Terms pertaining to performance/style such as *sur, taan, chherr, roop, raag* occur under different themes. Of the professional groups of singers and musicians, references are made to *qawwal, ata'ee, raga'ee, path, jajik, kirtia, managanhar, charan, langha, bhan, rababi, tunbair*. This indicates a wide range of his knowledge of the music tradition,-- historical, social and professional.

His sensitive mind put into bold relief some natural sounds, such as of water of the eroding Indus or of rain and thunder of the monsoon season. Besides, sweet notes of birds have come under reference. Under *Sur Sarang* (the chapter of Monsoon Rains), "the seasons resounds with sweet callings of taro bird". There is a unique mention of the 'song of the white swan' (under 'Sur Karayal') a rare perception of our poet.the heroine Sasee's wailings in desert in search of her love (Punhu) are:

- a cry in desert, as if a flaminge's kirking!
- a cry in desert, as if a parrot's sweet note!
- a cry in desert, as if a Sarangi's strain!

Indeed, Shah Abdul Latif had imbibed an intensive 'music feel', a unique music appeal, which is interpreted in a waee compostition under *Sur Ramkali* of the Risalo. It represents his homage paid to the 'Spirit of Music'. The translation which hardly reveals the original ethos and earnestness in as under:

A mere Singrree for the wishful ones,
It is a Secret of the secrets!
It will cause me to die one day!
It is not like the Nadr played by the Jut folk
Marli it has crushed, and Tunburreeis not its equal
It transcends the Bells which inspired Suhni to swim the Indus
It is sharper than the String which killed Diyyach
Its brilliant notes resounds in hundred and thousands
The like of it is neither in North, nor in Sindh or Hind
Has sour to the inimical, sweet to the loving ones:
Sweeter than the sweetest for those who taste with feeling!
Go for it, follow its echoe, sit not, move on…

SHAH ABDUL LATIF, THE GREAT SAINT PATRON OF MUSIC

Those who listened to it became accomplished ones.
Admired by the Praised one, it needs no praise.
It surpasses thousands of instruments.
Those subdue ferocious animals, this subdue the zamans.
This: says Abdul Latif, brings the dead to life!

Allusion to 'string' in one of the above lines is to the music of the 'gut string',--"the queen string" in the Sindhian 'Surando' instrument. Shah Latif composed one whole Sur (charrer), the 'Sur Sorath', of his *Risalo* to highlight the power music. This is not the string's resonance but a secret of the sounds.

They say it is 'instrument', but in fact these are the musician's hands that play.

Be a falcon, and swoop fast to be able to achieve some things!

In his characteristic manner. Shah Latif does recount the details of any story in his composition but brings under floodlight only the most meaningful aspects of it. He has highlighted the power of music as well as supreme devotion to it by the true lover of music,--viz. the accomplished musician Bijal playing the Surando with zest and the munificent Rau Khanghar of Junagadh being overwhelmed was pleased to reward him with his own head which the musician had asked for. In Latifs words:

Bijal: I have never asked for a handful of corn in my bowl
plenty of horses are available to me.
Neither I play music to have an elephant
I want but the jewel of your own head!

Khanghar: Thanks to you, that you have asked for my head!
Had you asked for something I hand'nt got,
My failure would have been a blot for munificents.

         * * * *

I will give away my head as reward for you.
But it will not be enough or of any worth to you!
         * * * *

Had I thousands of heads on my shoulders,

I would have severed them one by one.
Any yet your music would not be compensated.

Foundation of a New Music Institution

By about 1142 H/1729, when Shah Abdul Latif was forty years old, he chose his abode, which he had frequently visited, on a high sandy elevation (bhit) with sand dunes all around creating a lovely scene particularly in monsoon rains. It was then that his disciples would often sit at night and sing his bait and waee compositions, and the bhit resounded with sweet echoes. This pleased Shah Latif and he permanently settled down there. His biographer Mir Sangi has stated that it was because of the music that he had settled down there. For the next ten years he remained busy building his houses and the mosque and developing the village and settling his disciples there. Those with music talents were trained to a proper vocalization and singing of his *bait* and *waee* compositions. The *baits*, being serious in thought content, were to be recited line by line by each singer in order to facilitate understanding by all while the *waee* compositions, lyrical in nature, were to be sung in chorus.

It is reported that most of the Latif's disciples were struck with fever. Being ill and adversely attracted, they related their predicament on revered Site. He than instructed them that they should make it a pant to hold "Surud Latif" sittings and sing his compositions every week on the 'Friday night' (between Thursday and Friday). They acted accordingly and recorded fully. They would commence singing sessions after the passage of 14th of night and continue until the early morning. But after some days, when they ceased to be regular, they were again afflicted with fever. Therefore, they became strictly regular. Since then the Friday night performance continues on to this day (1881)"[(2)].

Both chorus singing and solo recitation became the two important features of this new performance. The *bait* compositions with their higher thought content were to be recited by each singer line by line, following their leader, while the *waee* compositions, more lyrical in nature, were to be sung by the group together in chorus.

The *saregaies* (musicians) who were 'established to perform regularly at Bhit' were recognized as *Addi-ja-Faqir* (The Established Group). Of them, the one more well versed in the text of *bait* and *waee* compositions as well as in rendering them in the specified Music modes (*ragas*) was designated as *Agwan*, the 'Leader' to conduct the *rago* session. Together, they were to sing to the accompaniment of a new instrument, *Danburo* (Tanboor) which Shah Abdul Latif himself devised and got constructed at Thatta. The original one is still preserved at his mausoleum at Bhit.

A New Music Instrument

The conventional *tamboor* was "chao-tara", a four stringed instrument, to which one more string was added. Our present study of it indicates that of the five strings, the outer one (to the right), was tuned at pancham note of the *Taar Saptak* (the Higher Octave): It was called 'Tand' (the 'String') or *Zuban* (the tongue) which was to spell out the raga. The next one called *Ghore* is tuned on the 'SA' of Lower Saptak. The next two, *Jariyoon*' or Twins, are tuned at the 'SA' of the Madh Saptak (Medium Octave); the last one called *Teep* is tuned to the 'SA' of the *Taar Saptak*. The chamber of Danburo (newly made bigger in size) was also to serve the purpose of *daff* or *Dholak* for the accompanying rhythm (taal).

Under his institution, Shah Latif simplified the taal procedure and employed only two *taals*, the *dedhi* (1-1/2 times) and the *dutali* (the double time). However, he preferred free execution by the artist without being subjected to the limitations of *taal*. As such, he created a kind of 'soft free touch of strings' of *Danburo* called *chherr*, and specified the *waee* compositions which were to be sung accordingly, so that the *alaps* (voice modulations of the singer) were not be constrained by any external *taal* (rhythm) but where to harmonize with the ecstasy and feelings of the singer. This brings us to the vocal music organization under *Sarud Latif/Shah-jo-Raga*.

The Vocal Music Organization

Long before Shah Abdul Latif, music in Sindh had developed as a function of her own ethnology and culture. With the advent of Islam it further developed with assimilation from the Arab-Persian musicology and its modes and melodies such as Yaman, Husaini and Zangola were integrated into Sindhian Music and gained wider popularity to become eventually a part of Hindustani Music.

The Risalo is the repository of that development as both Yaman and Husaini, in their original nomenclature are the headings of the Surs (chapters) of *The Risalo* which were also sung in their original *maqams*. 'Husaini' as one of the twelve *maqams* or *ragas* in the Arab-Persian system, and 'Yaman' also belongs to the system. Both these melodies, in whole or in part, were also used by Amir Khusrau in combination with other Indian melodies to creative new ragas. Thus, *Aiman* and *Aiman Kaly* were derived from 'Yaman', while 'Husaini' was crossed within other local melodies. By using Amir Khusrau's created notes of Husaini, the later master invented such melodies as *Husaini Kanra* and *Husaini Todi*. But Shah Abdul Latif was the first to adopt the original 'Yaman' and Husaini in the scheme of his music institution.

Secondly, professional minstrels in Sindh during the dynastic rule of the Soomara (1050-1350) and the Samma (1350-1520) had excelled in their artistic narration of the Epic of Dodo-Chanesar and some other romantic stories. Each story was artistically narrated and sung in a specific music mode or "Sur" which was roled in the lore of a particular geo-historical setting. With the integration of "music theme" and "music mode" developed the 'Tremetic Sur Music' within the domain of Sindhian music. It became more clearly defined under the institution of *SURUD LATIF/ "SHAH-JO-RAGA"*

This development took place gradually during the course of nearly a quarter of a century, beginning from the foundational stage (1144-1155 H) and then through the culminative stage (1155-1165 H) when Shah Latif's *bait* and *waee* compositions of different themes had substantially increased in number requiring them to be sung in different *ragas*. The earliest available compilations of these compositions (Risalo form) indicate that the theme of the Romance of 'Sasuee and Punhu' was then more popular and, therefore, Shah Abdul Latif composed it in five different modes each to be sung in a specific *raga*. As are noted in the earliest manuscripts, and also sung to this day, these were *Abiri* (aabiree), *Ma'azoor, Kohiyari, Desi* and *Husaini*. No such *ragas* existed in Hindustani Music. Shah Latif chose Husaini from the Arab-Persian system and the four others from the music tradition of Sindh and Balochistan regions (to which belonged the 'Romance of Sasee and Punhu'). Desi was, most probably, a local raga of southern Sindh (where Bhanbhor is located) and was different from Desi of Hindustani Music; *Ma'zoor* was the melody of western *Kohistan-Las Bela* region

SHAH ABDUL LATIF, THE GREAT SAINT PATRON OF MUSIC

where it has survived to this day; and *Kohiyari* (i.e. of Kohiyar was a melody of the *Khuzdar* region. 'Kohiyar' being the Sindhian name for Khuzdar. The origin of Abiri cannot be traced satisfactorily. What is important to note is that by selecting these locally popular melodies Shah Latif wanted to raise the peoples' own music to the level of high art under his institution.

In so far as these *ragas* belonged to a specific theme (story of Sasee), they were part of the thematic music. Similarly the following ten melodies were chosen from the area of thematic music of Sindh:

1. Rano, the melody in which the people were singing the Romance of Moomal and Rano.
2. Lilan, melody of the Lilan – Chanesar Romance.
3. Suhni, melody of the Suhni-Mehar Romance.
4. Noori or Kamod, melody of the Jam Tamachi-Noori Romance.
5. Marui, melody of the story of Umar and Marui.
6. Sorath, melody of the story of Sorath and Rai Diyach.
7. Khahorri, melody of the 'Utmost Toiling Ones'.
8. Ghatu, melody of the 'Daring Fishermen Huting in High Seas'.
9. Kapa'itee, melody of the 'Weaver Maid'.
10. Pirbhati, melody of the early morning homage paid by the professional minstrels to their munificent chiefs.

Beside these specifically thematic melodies which were raised to the level of high art as *Ragas*. Shah Latif also composed on other topics which were to be sung as newly created *Ragas*:

11. Rip, melody of love's heavy burden.
12. Karayal, melody of the Swan song.

Beside Yaman and Husaini taken from the Arab-Persian system, ten *ragas* were chosen from the domain of classical tradition of Hindustani Music, either in their original form or as modified and Sindhized under Sindhian Music. These were *Kalya, Sri-Raga, Bilawal, Asa, Ramkuli, Purbi, Dhanasri, Khumbhat, Baruva* Sindhi and Sarang. The actual performance of these ragas as continued on under the Institution of Shah's Raga to this day, indicates that *Kalyan, Bilawal* and *Khumbat* were retained in their original (*shudh*) forms.

In all, Shah Latif's own compositions were sung in 29 *ragas* under the new Surud Latif institution. These Ragas, also called *Surs*, are the headings of 29 chapters of the Risalo. It is only in these chapters that Shah Latif's own authentic compositions are listed. In his own times, or after him, some other compositions were also sung by the performing Faqirs. These are listed under other chapters with their Ragas headlined as *Kedaro, Seenh Kedaro, Beraag Hindi, Dhol-Maru, Hir* and *Basant*.

Inclusion of large number of melodies from the area of folk music in the scheme of *Ragas* in the new shah-jo-raga institution shows that Shah Abdul Latif had thought of raising the status of popular melodies to the high art of Ragas; he explored the inexhaustible and ever-fresh reservoir of folk music to revitalize the music tradition which had lost its appear for the generality of the population due to the dominance of technique and formalism.

It is to be concluded that in order to bring about a renaissance, Shah Abdul Latif founded the new institution Surud Latifi or *SHAH-JO-RAGA* at Bhit. He trained musicians from amongst his disciples to sing in the new style, created the new instrument of *Danburo*, detailed the bulk of his compositions under different themes which were called *Surs*, and each Sur was specified by the *Raga* in which it was to be sung. The night preceding Friday was fixed for regular weekly performances of *Shah-Jo-Raga* had a great impact on revival of music in Sindh. Founded long back in 1144/1731, this institution has a place of honour in the history of world music for its originality, antiquity and continuity for more than two and a half centuries. It needs to be studied, developed and preserved as an institution of national and world heritage.

Paul Jackson, S.J.

Maneri's Inward Journey and its Impact

The whole thrust of this paper is on movement. Sharafuddin Maneri, a person who died in Bihar Sharif in 1381, and yet is still very much alive in the hearts and minds of millions of people, has certainly made an impact. This whole process can rightly be called a movement as it involves a personal transformation for the better. This, in turn, has had an impact on society in general. No movement can prolong unless it has some structural element to focus and guide its energy. This aspect also has to be noted.

Arguing back from the fact of Maneri's widespread impact during 627 years after his death leads us to the man himself. He was a man physically on the move for the first half of his life, and continually on the move as far as the geography of his inner life was concerned. This twofold journey has to be explored in order to understand the way in which this extraordinary man acted as a catalyst in transforming other people's lives. In addition to the structures and the people associated with him we possess a considerable corpus of writings, either by Maneri himself, or recording what he had said. Let us begin with a survey of Maneri's tangible legacy.

The Present-Day Scene

A visitor to Maner, about twenty-five kilometers west of Patna, will be struck by an imposing mausoleum. If the visitor has some knowledge of Indian architecture it will be immediately apparent that this structure is from the Mughal period of Indian history, not from the late fourteenth century. It actually contains the tomb of Shah Daulat, one of Maneri's Sufi descendants, and dates from the early seventeenth century. It is the finest example of Mughal architecture in the whole of the eastern region of India. To the east of a very large, century's old-tank, a flight of steep steps leads the visitor up to the simple tomb of Yahya Maneri, the deeply religious father of Sharafuddin Maneri. If the visitor proceeds to the residential complex, the *khanqah*, he or she can ask to see a wooden bed which is reputed to have been used by Bibi Razia, Maneri's pious mother, at the time of her confinement. It certainly looks old enough to be what it is claimed to be.

The next port of call could be *Rajgir*. Here a visitor will head for Makhdum Kund, a site composed of several buildings at the base of one of the hills. The spring of water used by Maneri still flows, but there is now an enclosed pool there. The cave where Maneri lived is well supervised and maintained, and the tiny mosque on the hillside is still used for prayer.

The main attraction for a pilgrim, however, is Maneri's tomb and the buildings that surround it on the southern outskirts of Bihar Sharif. It is an impressive sight. and a visitor will rarely find himself or herself as the only visitor to the shrine. It will be noticed that Maneri lies buried beside his mother, whose tomb he had been in the habit of visiting while he was still alive. There is a steady stream of visitors during the year and, on the occasion of Maneri's feast-day, the crowd can be so great that movement becomes difficult. For example, in 2002 a photographer could not lift his hands to take a photo because of the rush of people around him. People come to honour the saint; to present some gift to him; to ask him to intercede on their behalf for some serious matter in their lives; or to thank him for having obtained some boon due to his intercession. About half a kilometer away from his tomb is situated the *khanqah* where Maneri's present descendant, commonly known as the Shah Sahib or *Sajjada Nishin,* resides. A *hujra* - prayer cell - is situated nearby and is reputed to have been used by Maneri. A steady stream of visitors comes to consult the Shah Sahib on various matters and also to request him to pray on their behalf.

Another aspect of the present-day scene is the literary activity associated with Maneri's writings. 'Translations have appeared in Urdu and English, and a recently launched Urdu quarterly, *Makhdoum*, has proved to be quite popular. Moreover, the Firdausi *Silsila* (Sufi Order), dating from the person of Manori himself, has adherents in Pakistan,

Bangladesh, England and the United States, in addition to those in Bihar and Kolkata. The people who continue to invoke his blessings at crucial moments in their lives are numbered in millions. What do we know about this remarkable man who has such an impact on the lives of countless Muslims, and on many Hindus as well, down the centuries? The answer to this question lies in the source material.

Source Material

A person who wants to get a feel for Maneri could visit the places mentioned, as well as Sonargaon in Bangladesh and the tomb of Najibuddin Firdausi near the Qutub Minar in Delhi, and think about how Maneri passed his days in these places. The visitor will probably make some inquiries and will be given a certain amount of information. How accurate will this information be? It will vary from place to place and from person to person. Obviously the Shah Sahib, being a learned man, had possessed a lot of knowledge, but can the others be expected to have made a detailed study of the original Persian source material in manuscript form? This is highly unlikely, as a visitor can easily ascertain through personal experience. What can be expected is some accurate knowledge about the particular shrine, together with a number of stories which highlight, in a popular form, the miraculous powers of the man. After all, the vast majority of visitors are devotees who come to pray at these various shrines. Having already formed a high opinion of Maneri's saintliness they easily and uncritically accept stories, which highlight his miraculous powers. For example, he is reputed to have visited the Ka'ba one night, although he never left India, nor even ventured further west than Delhi.

In the same vein, a visitor who reads either the Hindi or Urdu version of a brief outline of Maneri's life, painted inside the impressive gateway to the *dargha* complex, would probably accept what is written there. It says Maneri was born in Maner in 1263; after completing his studies in Sonargaon and then visiting Delhi he spent 30 years in seclusion in the jungle of Bihiya and the cave in Rajgir. This was followed by about 50 years in Bihar Sharif, where he died in 1380.

If the visitor happened to be a historian who was also familiar with hagiographical writings he or she would be immediately struck by the age at which Maneri died - 117 years according to the Gregorian calendar, or 121 according to the Islamic calendar. While this was possible, it was more likely an exaggeration. The question about the chronology of Maneri's life would then arise. It could be settled only through recourse to the manuscript evidence of works written either by him or about him. This evidence would have to be examined in the context of the known history of the period.

This brings us to the manuscript writings. At this point another word of caution is needed. Muhammad Habib and K. A. Nizami, for example, have both warned us about spurious hagiographical literature, especially about the early Chishtis. Thus the manuscript material needs careful scrutiny. Is a particular manuscript clearly and wholly authentic? This question requires an answer based on careful study.

Manaqib- ul-Asfiya (The Glorious Deeds of the Saints), an early fifteenth century biographical work reputedly written by Sheikh Shu'aib, son of Maneri's cousin, Jalaluddin, contains the following: "I have heard that once Oazi Zahid, a learned man and traveler along the Way, who had a firm belief in the Master of the World, said: Master, I have heard that you didn't eat anything for thirty years, and that your natural functions ceased. How could this be explained?' Sharafuddin replied: 1 had not eaten a cooked meal for thirty years. As the need arose, I used to eat something from the jungle. After my natural functions had ceased for some years, I had a nocturnal emission. It was extremely cold weather. I went to the waterside. The thought came to me that 1 would perform my ablutions with sand and then perform my prayers. Afterwards I thought my carnal soul is seeking refuge in the Law! Immediately I rushed into the water and fell unconscious. When the sun rose, I came to my senses. The result was that I missed my morning prayer that day."[1]

In the next section an argument will be advanced to show that the historical evidence militates against an extended period of thirty years in the jungle of Bihiya and the Rajgir cave. This calls into question the whole framework of Qazi Zahid's question. Did he make a mistake about the time involved? Scarcely, for he was a very senior disciple, as the following description, gleaned from the *Wafat Nama* (Death Account), written by Zain Badr Arabi, clearly indicates: "Catching hold of Qazi Zahid's hand, the Master placed it on his blessed breast saying: 'We are the same! We are both mad with love! Then, humbly, he added: 'Rather, we are dust beneath the feet of those maddened by love!'"[2]

Granted that Qazi Zahid knew Maneri very intimately, and granted a sojourn of only a few years not 30 years, the apocryphal nature of the account becomes clear. Maneri himself has this to say: "Nor does a person stay healthy if he fails to eat and drink."[3] In terms of the story itself, Maneri should have drowned. He himself is unsparingly realistic, for he says: "Whoever takes poison, and at the same time trusts in God's mercy, will perish!"[4] On the other hand, certain portions, of the *Manaqib* have been copied from a reliable *malfuz* (a record of what transpired at assemblies presided over by Maneri) entitled *Ma'din ul-Ma'ani*. This is accurate. One final remark about the *Manaqib* is that only 20 of the 152 pages in the printed text are devoted to Maneri. As the title and contents combine to reveal the mindset of the author - whoever it may be - the work clearly has to be utilized with extreme caution. This attitude of caution is not evident in the writings of devotees.

Another possibility also has to be taken into account that of doctoring the text. For example, the printed text quoted on page 132, clearly says of Maneri: *Nikah kard Az a yek pesar shud.* (He got married. From that he had one son) This work was printed in 1895. In a manuscript written by Shah Turab Ali in 1813 and located in the *khanqah* of Sheikhpura, where Sheikh Shu'aib, the reputed author, is buried, we find the following: *Kanizaki dasht. Az an kanizak yek pesar shud.* (He took a slave-girl. By that slave-girl he had one son). The difference cannot be ascribed to scribal error.

We are faced with a choice. Do we uncritically accept the mindset of the author and the picture of Maneri painted in the *Manaqib*, based on a very limited knowledge of history to say nothing of doctored portions of the text? Or do we critically utilize a text like this, in conjunction with other material, to be as accurate a knowledge of Maneri as is humanly possible? A man of his stature deserves such an effort on our part. Fortunately there is a corpus of *maktubat* (letters) and *malfuzat* which are clearly genuine and which provide us with a considerable amount of information about the man. Even here however, one 'must be alert. For example, in five different manuscripts of the second collection of letters, the couplets found in letters 9, 10, 11, and 12, taken as a random sample, and number 94, 71, 26, 61 and 47 verses have clearly been added, but the prose text has been respected.

Life

An examination of Maneri's reminiscences, culled from his *mulfuzat* in conjunction with the known history of the period, yields the following account of his life.[5] He was born to Bibi Razia, daughter of Shihabuddin Jagjot of Jethuli, east of Patna and Yahya Maneri, around 1290. He was the second of four sons, and he had at least one sister. His early schooling was in Maner itself. When he was a teenager a famous scholar, Maulana Abu Tau'ama, passed through Maner from Delhi on his way to Sonargaon. Maneri went along with him to continue his studies under his guidance. This was in 1304, or shortly afterwards. He remained in Sonargaon till 1323. The picture painted by the *Manaqib* is of an ascetic who begrudged the time spent on meals, so he ate by himself. It is quite likely that this is an exaggerated portrayal of a life that was certainly dedicated to serious study. His commitment can be inferred from the fact that he fell ill. The physicians recommended intercourse as a means of overcoming his sickness. The remedy prescribed indicates some form of tension-induced ailment. As we have seen, he took a slave-girl and had one son by her, Zakiuddin. This was probably when he was in his mid-twenties.

A perusal of the reminiscences found in the malfuzat literature, on the other hand, portrays quite a different picture. Maneri notices how his teacher, Abu Tau'ama, has the habit of running his fingers through his long hair when absorbed in seeking a solution to a problem.[6] He joined in a little fun during class. One of his fellow-students was Abu Tau'anna's younger brother, Zainuddin. He knew the Quran by heart. Sometimes his teacher, who was not a *Hafiz* himself, and neither was Maneri would ask for the location of a particular quotation. For the sake of a little fun Zainuddin would pretend he hadn't heard. When pressed, he would give the answer?[ ] The same Zainuddin had a wonderful voice and greatly pleased Maulana Ziauddin, the Sheikh ul-Islam, who sent this message to him through his friends: "I won't let you go! I have a daughter and I want you as my son-in-law." His friends came to him "in high good humour."[8] Obviously Maneri was one of the friends involved, for this vivid account dates from more than twenty-five years after the event. It still carries an element of infectious joy! On the other hand, he was deeply moved by the sudden death of the son of Qazi Husamuddin Shangarfi, the Sadr-i-Jahan.[9]

The material also makes it clear that Maneri had already made his mark as a scholar. The source: material shows him in regular contact with the leading men of the city, and his numerous personal references to Sultan Shamsuddin Firuz Shah (1301-22) of Sonargaon, indicate that he was frequently in attendance at the Sultan's court. While describing a court scene he remarks that "the –Sultan had the habit *('adati bud)* of turning to look at anybody *ru'i bedu qwardi* who had some words of wisdom to offer."[10] The tense 'used to' indicate habitual action which is of significance. When Sultan Shamsuddin died Maneri was present and when his son, Qutlugh Khan, made Maulana Zainuddin his prayer leader.[11] According to Ibn Battuta, Qutlugh Khan was killed by his fratricidal brother, Bahadur Shah.[12] It was probably in 1323, after the assassination of Qutlugh Khan, Maneri left Sonargaon with his small son, Zakiuddin, and returned to his mother in Maner, into whose care he entrusted Zakiuddin. His father had died during his absence. He remained for only a very short time in Maner and then set out for Delhi with his elder brother, Khafiluddin, in search of a spiritual guide.

After Maneri's meeting with Nizamuddin Auliya (d. 3 April 1325), who told him that he was not meant to be his guide, and Bu Qalandar Panipati (d. 3 September 1324), who was so lost in ecstasy as to be unable to act as a guide, Maneri felt discouraged and wanted to return home. It was Khaliluddin who urged him to meet Sheikh Najibuddin Firdausi. He reluctantly did so and the two men experienced an instant rapport. Maneri became his disciple. These events probably occurred early in 1324. While it is true that the reminiscences dating from Maneri's time in Delhi are fewer than those from his period in Sonargaon, they are nevertheless sufficient and detailed enough to establish a somewhat prolonged sojourn there. Maneri's main focus of attention was to tread the Sufi Path under Najibuddin's guidance, but he also attended the lectures of some of the more outstanding scholars, such as Maulana Ziauddin Sunami.[13] One has only to read what Maneri said about the difference between *pir-i tarbiyat* (discipleship by training) and *pir-i suhbat* (discipleship by association)[14] to realize how much he was influenced by the time he had spent with his sheikh. This impression is greatly reinforced by reading letters 5 and 6 in his *Hundred Letters*. "Until the novice falls completely in love with the beauty and saintliness of the sheikh, he will not come under the full influence of his guidance."[15] These words flow from personal experience. When

Najibuddin died on 5 October 1332 there was nothing to keep Maneri in Delhi. He set out on the road back to Maner.

In point of fact, however, he did not reach Maner, for he veered off into the jungle of Bihiya in quest of God by being alone with the Alone. He probably stayed there for about a year before settling into a cave in Rajgir in a spot now known as Makhdum Kund. While Maneri's aim was to be close to various ascetics living in the Rajgir area and give himself over totally to the quest of God, his fame became known and people began to come to him and request him to write applications for various things to the local administrator *(malik)*. This was upsetting for him, but a visiting Sufi, Sheikhzada Chishti, noticed how upset he was to be continually interrupted and said: "Yes, it is a

vexatious business, but do take up the burden of the people!"[16] Maneri realized that God wanted him to help people, to bring comfort to hearts - *rahat bedilan rasanidan* - as he constantly mentions.

Some disciples of the late Nizamuddin Auliya used to come from Bihar town to consult him. Finally, he suggested that he would come to Bihar for the Friday prayer and people could meet him after the prayer. He began doing this and Maulana Nizamuddin had a small hut built for him to stay in. The Sultan, Muhammad bin Tughluq heard that Maneri had emerged from seclusion and ordered the governor, Majd ul-Mulk, to have a hospice built for him and to assign revenues from Rajgir for its upkeep. On the plea that his life would be in danger if Maneri did not allow him to do as the Sultan had ordered, Maneri reluctantly agreed and a hospice was built. This work probably began in 1337, after Maneri had been going regularly to Bihar for some time. He spent the rest of his life there until his death on 2nd January 1381.

The Inward Journey

We have seen Maneri's outward journeys and have tried to situate him in as accurate a chronology as possible. Now it is time to examine the inward journey, which found its manifestation in his life as it has been described. It could be summed up in the traditional saying used to express acceptance of God's will when confronted with the reality of death: *Inna Illahi wa inna ilayhi raji'un* (We all belong to God and unto Him we shall return, Q2:156). While the meaning of these words is clear, the grasp of the reality they convey varies from person to person, as well as from one stage of a person's life to another. We shall trace their growing reality in Maneri's life.

In his early childhood he had the inestimable good fortune of having pious parents. God was the central reality of their lives. This naturally had a beneficial impact on young Ahmad, as Maneri was called by his parents. The same could be said about his other brothers, but they did not attain anything like his stature, so we have to probe further to discern the process of his distinctive growth. We are immediately struck by his keen desire to study. It was he, not his elder brother, for example, who asked his father for permission to accompany Abu Tau'ama to Sonargaon. Was he keen on further studies in order to obtain an official post? Or .did this desire spring principally from the natural desire of an intellectually gifted person to feed on the store of knowledge that was available to him in his day and age? All indications in Maneri's own life point to this latter interpretation. There is no indication of his ever having hankered after any official position. This interpretation tends to be confirmed by his words to Muzaffar Shams Balkhi when he became his disciple and asked for training along the Sufi Path. "This cannot be acquired without knowledge. Whatever knowledge you have acquired was for the sake of rank and position. You didn't obtain a number of its fruits. Return to your studies with sincerity of purpose, doing them for God's sake."[17] This injunction undoubtedly echoes Maneri's own disposition.

The thrust of Maneri's studies could be expressed as his efforts to listen carefully to the word of God in the Quran, and strive to understand what it means through the study of *tafsir,* the word used for a commentary on the Quran. Maneri mentions the *Tafsir-i Kabir* of Fakhruddin Razi (d.1209), but his favourite commentary, to which he constantly refers, was the commentary in Persian known as *Tafsir-i Zahidi.*[18] The very fact of his frequent reference to this commentary in his later years implies that he never got tired of his effort to understand the word of God. Serious scholars devoted much time to the study of the various *Hadith* collections of Traditions about the Prophet in order to enhance their knowledge of how he lived. This was to be able to imitate him in their own daily lives and also guide others to do the same. This study is referred to as *fiqh* or jurisprudence. Reference is made to Maneri's ongoing study of Bukhari's *Al-Jami as-Sahih.*[19] He also possessed an excellent copy of Muslim's work by the same name.[20]

As he enjoyed reading Muzaffar Shams Balkhi's commentary on *Mashariq ul-Anwar* by As-Saghani[21] he was obviously familiar with the original work. The *Hidaya* by Sheikh Burhanuddin Ali (d.1197) finds frequent mention. These and other works cited indicate clearly that Maneri continued to consult such works as long as his eyesight permitted him to do so. He never tired of gaining an ever-increasing mastery over a subject that helped him discern the will of God for himself and others.

This brings us to his journey from Maner to Delhi in search of a spiritual guide. What were the dynamics involved in this move? It was precisely because Maneri had become such a competent scholar that he realized that knowledge could fill the mind but not the heart. His sensitive soul craved for an experience of God, not further knowledge about Him. He wanted someone to guide him in such a way as to enable him to come face to face with God Himself, so to say. The most famous Sufi of the age, Nizamuddin Auliya, said he was not meant to be his guide, and Bu Qalandar Panipati was himself too engrossed in God to be able to act as a guide. This role was fortunately undertaken by Najibuddin Firdaus. Maneri learnt from personal experience that it is only by curbing the unruly demands of his selfish soul, his *nafs*, that he could become fully docile to the multi-faceted influence of his guide. It was like opening a door and allowing the sun's rays to illumine and warm the interior of a dark room. It could be said that he opened his heart and soul to the full influence emanating from the heart and soul of his guide, catching the reflected divine light and warmth, so to say. Maneri was thus able to derive full benefit from the various spiritual exercises Najibuddin guided him through, such as the *chilan,* a forty-day retreat. In a nutshell, he became a transformed person.

When Najibuddin died, Maneri left Delhi and set out for Maner but before arriving there, he left his traveling companions and headed for the jungle of Bihiya. He had learnt a lot about God in Sonargaon. He had been exposed to the beneficial influence emanating from his guide in Delhi. All that was left was to expose himself, as far as humanly possible, to the direct activity of God. With this in mind he headed off to the radical solitude of the jungle. What happened there? "God alone knows what happened between Himself and His devotee during this protracted period," is how the *Manaqib* sums it up.[22] Unfortunately the author did not need the implications of this profoundly insightful statement! It will be good for us to do so. It is obvious, however, that the final stretch of Maneri's inner journey lifted him beyond a desire to be fully open to God as an individual, experiencing much divine light and warmth, but acting like a sponge, so to say, soaking it all up for himself. It became clear to him that he was meant to be as fully open and attentive to the needs of the people as he was to God Himself. In other words, he was meant to be a source of understanding and comfort to others, "bringing comfort to hearts" as he himself frequently put it. This, of course, involved a shift of focus from self to an understanding of himself as related to others, as being a conduct of grace for them.

Maneri's Widening Influence

For a period of about forty years Maneri's influence continued to grow. It emanated from his *khanqah* in Bihar town. It is not possible to number the thousands of people who came to pay their respects to him; to seek his advice; or to request his prayers in some difficult situation. Many people attended the assemblies he conducted. As in each *majlis* (assembly) people could ask him questions; or read out some portion from a book, either connected with Quranic exegesis, jurisprudence or with Sufism, and request an explanation. Maneri was extremely fond of Persian mystical verse and his letters are replete with quotations from his favourite poets. Undoubtedly these poets and their works were discussed during the assemblies. While it is evident that we have no full record of all that transpired during the assemblies. It has to be added immediately of which various records called *malfuzat* are available.[23] These are sufficient to enable us to form a good idea of what occurred during the assemblies.

For our purpose we can pause to take a look at the variety of people mentioned as attending the assemblies. There were scholars, civil and military administrators of varying importance, as well as disciples of famous Sufis, for the *malfuzat* abound with such titles as Qazi, Maulana, Malik, Sheikh, Mufti, Sayyid, Sheikhzada and Khawaja. These titles indicate men of importance in the socio-religious set up of the day. The literature makes it abundantly clear that all these men held Maneri in high esteem. There can be no doubt about his influence on them. He clarified their questions about the meaning of particular passages in the Quran. He advised them on how they should act in accordance with the Law. He gave them an inspiring example. Even as he lay dying, for example, he" insisted on praying. The Master then performed the ablutions by himself. After this, he asked for a comb and combed his beard. Then he called for his prayer mat and performed two rounds of prayer. He ended the prayer with thanksgiving to God and salutations to Muhammad (P.B.U.H) and his descendants.[21] Those present were "amazed at the care and punctiliousness shown in such a condition."

The reins of government lay in the hands of these men. It does not require a spectacular leap of the imagination to appreciate the multiplier effect Maneri exerted for the common welfare by virtue of his influence over them. They could not help but catch something of his concern to be of service to people. Letter 71 in his *Hundred letters* is a beautiful exposition of a type of service, which is inherently an act of divine worship. When the topic of service arose in one of the assemblies he spontaneously had this to say: "Service is a wonderful work. It is one of the doors leading to blessings and mercy. Many promises are associated with service' ... "he spoke with great earnestness saying: 'Service is a wonderful work, a great work"[25] There can be no doubt that Manori's own spirit of service was caught and acted upon by these men, resulting in a movement, not for structural change, but for the betterment of the lives of the common people. This has to be seen as having a social dimension.

Maneri's influence was not restricted to those who came in person to meet him. Muhammad bin Tughluq, in addition to sending him a Bulgarian carpet and ordering a *khanqah* to be built for him and arrangements made to meet the expenses associated with it, also wrote a personal letter to him requesting him to pray for the success of all his ventures as well as write something about Sufism specifically for him. Maneri wrote a very polite letter in reply, but pointedly did not accede to either of the Sultan's requests.[26] Anyone who reads Maneri's letter, and is aware of Muhammad bin Tughluq's character, realizes the esteem in which Maneri must have been held, for nothing happened to him! We have a letter he wrote to Muhammad bin Tughluq's successor, Firuz Shah Tughluq.[27] It is in a completely different tone from the former letter. We are left with the impression that Maneri's request on behalf of Khawaja Abid Zafarabadi would have been acceded to by a letter written to Dawar Malik,[28] son-in-law of Muhammad bin

Tughluq, which is very revealing. Dawar Malik had heaped praises on Maneri in a letter he had sent him. Maneri shows incredible ingenuity in wriggling out from beneath all this praise. The essential point is that Dawar Malik held him in high esteem.

In addition to such exalted personages, Maneri's second collection of letters was addressed to the same variety of people who attended his assemblies and were sent to places such as Delhi, Sonargaon and even Daulatabad in the South. Again it has to be pointed out that his letters touched the hearts and minds of their recipients and effected a change for the good in most of them.

It should be mentioned that Maneri's teaching about following the Sufis path is impregnated with a sense of realism born of his own varied experience it is a far cry from mere bookish knowledge. He obviously knows what he is talking about and this instills a sense of confidence in his disciples and readers. They realize that they are not wandering about in a jungle of words but are being directed along a path sure to lead them to their goal of union with God in this life and the vision of God for all eternity in the life to come.

Conclusion

Maneri's journey to his innermost recesses was also a journey towards the abode of the Lord of his being and of the entire universe. It was because of the depth of the experience garnered along this journey that he was able to be of such immense assistance to others who were making this very same journey but with more faltering steps. The various levels of transformation thus resulted in widespread benefits for many .people. And yet the praise goes to God, for Maneri asserts, as he lay dying, that he is merely "dust-beneath the feet of those maddened by love."[29]

Notes:

1. Shu'aib. Sheikh. *Manaqib ul-Asfiya*, Nur ul-Afaq Press, Calcutta, 1895. p.136
2. Jackson, Paul. *The Way of a Sufi: Sharafuddin Maneri*, Idarah-i Adabiyat-i Delhi, Delhi. 1987, p.243.
3. Jackson, Paul, *Sharafuddin Maneri: The Hundred Letters*, Paulist Press, New York. 1980 p 74

5. Ibd.,p.74
5. For a detailed account of Maneri's life, with quotations from the *malfuzat* concerning him, see *The Way of a Sufi*, pp.1-82. It is possible that more fine-tuning of the chronology may occur, but any major change is unlikely.
6. Jackson, Paul, (translator), *Khwan-i Pur Ni'mat: A Table Laden with Good Things*, Idarah-i Adabiyat-i Delli, Delhi, 1986, p.l9.
7. Quoted from *Ma'din ul Ma- 'ani*, in *The Way of a Sufi.*: 47. 8. Ibd.,p.48.
9. Ibd., p.50.
10. *Malfuz us-Safar*, 15 Jamadi II.
11. *Mukh ul-Ma'ni*, quoted in *The Life of a Sufi*, p.43.
12. Quoted from *Tlie Rehla of Ibn Battuta* in *The Way of a Sufi*, p.45.
13. *Ma'din ul-Ma'ani*, quoted in *The Way of a Sufi*, p 57.
14. *Khwan*, pp.148-9.
15. *The Hundred letters*, p.32.
16. *Khwan.* p.57.
17. *The Way of a Sufi*, p.89.
18. This work was completed in Bukhara on 9th Shawwal 519 A H (1125 A D.) by Abu Nasr Ahmad bin Hasan bin Ahmad Sulaiman ur-Raruhaki.
19. *The Hundred Letters*, p.236.
20. *The Way of a Sufi*, p.127.
21. Ibd., p.127
22. *Manaqib.* p.133.
23. For an indication of the number of *malfuzat* available cf. *The Way of a Sufi.* pp 251-3
24. *Wafat Nama*, as quoted in *The Way of a Sufi*, p.249
25. *Khwan.* P.146.
26. *The Way of a Sufi.* pp 112-114.
27. Ibd., pp 115-6.
28. Ibd., pp 111-2.
29. Ibd., p. 243.

S.A. Hasan

Jalaluddin Rumi's Mystic Thought— A Message of Love & Human Resurrection

The difficulty of understanding Maulana Jalaluddin Rumi correctly does not lie in his lexicon or his grammar. He does not use rare or difficult words and his phraseology is simple and very clear. However, there is also hardly a poem not posing a problem. Perhaps Maulana also knew that the readers of his poetry may make the matter more complicated.

Philosophy, particularly mystic, was one of the avenues in which modern thought expressed itself in the Christian world. It is also the same way through which European ideas and views were spread over the colonial empire. Maulana Jalaluddin Rumi's *Mathnavi* is a storehouse of traditions, stories, and allegories some of which, like the story of the blind and the elephant which can be traced back to Indian sources and is now commonplace in Sufi literature, have especially attracted the interest of Western scholars.

This story has been brought to light in the West by the first investigator into the history of Sufism in Europe, F.A.D. Tholuck, in his interesting booklet published from Berlin in 1821. Then, for a certain time, the interest in Maulana's ideas diminished in Europe. According to other sources, the first European scholar to draw the attention of philologists and theologians again to these lines of Maulana was the Swedish Orientalist, K.V. Petersen, when he, in collaboration with Nathan Soderblorn, translated a few stories for his personal collections in 1908 (it includes an introduction to Maulana's life and works also). In the meantime, in 1914, R.A. Nicholson, to whom the elucidation of Maulana's work owes so much, had, in his book *Mystics of Islam*, quoted some stories in order to show: "for Jalaluddin man's love is really the effect of God's love". Later on, both Soderblom's and Nicholson's works are quoted by F. Heiler, who in his standard work on prayer has mentioned Maulana's verses as the most beautiful example of the fact that it is well known not only in Christianity but also in Islam, an idea that is repeated again and again by many contemporary scholars. [1]

One look at figures denoting the years in which the Christian message thrived and religious reform became successful will show the source of these views. These were the years when the attacks on the priests were at the highest. The same period also witnessed continuous slackening of restrictions on inmates of monasteries and marriage. Nothing of this kind ever appeared before Europe's contact with the Asian civilization.

With the perpetual contacts made between the Persians and European societies, and then, between their minds and beliefs, a new mentality and a new learning to interpret things and to introduce reforms appeared. The European scholars sometimes propounded theories, which were in agreement with the Persians and sometimes differed with them. But difference does not mean to ignore the original source and does not also obstruct formation of new thought in Islam and Christianity. The Muslims called Ghazalias "Hojjatul-Islam", meaning "the proof of Islam". Dante, on the other hand, named Saint Thomasas "The Glimpse of the Heavenly Light". But the question remains that these two had different line of their perceptibility both in letter and spirit.

All these potential developments of the idea of love and divinity had taken place and shape and entered Persian poetry long before Maulana. This is, of course, an Iranian element. We, find their traces in one of the earliest Persian poetry in which the poet confesses having chosen four things of the world: ruby lips, the sound of the harp, purple-colored wine, and the religion of Zoroaster (*Zabihullah Safa, Tarikh-e-Adabiyyat dar Iran*, Tehran 1965, Vol.1, 409). Professor Nicholson in his book *Legacy of Islam* referred to the similarities between the theories of Muslim mystics and the European Christian mystics like the German Eckhart and the English Edward Carpenter who lived later. Nicholson has dealt nicely with the subject of the relation between Christian and Islamic mysticism. If such a relation is improved it should cause no surprise. It has the testimony of history and logic. But it should be surprising if the same is denied by the people knowing that Maulana is the key factor towards a better understanding of divinity in the Western society. Similarly, it is surprising if the relation between the Christian and Muslim mystics were denied by the people who knew that not a single sign of European renaissance was possible before the contact of the East with the West. With the weakening of intellectual and Gnostic elements in Christianity (if we understand by gnosis that illuminative knowledge which Sufism calls '*irfan*' and which is the very heart of Sufism as a every authentic and complete spiritual tradition), the rational faculty of Western man became gradually estranged from the twin sources of all immutability, estability and permanence: namely, revelation and intellectual intuition. The result was that on the one hand the nominalist trend, which destroyed philosophical certainty, and on the other, the reduction of man to his narrowly human aspects, cut off from any transcendental elements; such is the man of Renaissance. This way of conceiving man itself implied his total involvement in sheer change and becoming. This effect can be seen even outwardly during that period in the rapid transformation of Western society which have given the Renaissance its transitional character. [2]

The Iranian mysticism rubbed shoulders with the ancient Indian and Platonic mysticism. Maulana did borrow certain theories and ideas; but while doing so he contributed many of his own in the same way. The elements of Islamic mysticism found in verses of the Holy Quran contains all the principles found in Buddhist and Platonic mysticism.

"Nothing is like Him; and He is the Hearing, the Seeing, so flee to Allah. Surely I am a plain Warner to you from Him", is akin to the Buddhist mystic theory which says that worldly life pollutes the happiness of soul and that the salvation lies in renouncing the world and devotion to God alone.

Understanding comes only through love and not by training or by means of organizational methods. Maulana stresses: that the form in which ordinary emotional religion is understood by organized bodies is incorrect. The veil of light, which is the barrier brought about by self-righteousness, is more dangerous than the veil of darkness produced in the mind by vice.

Maulana is against submitting dogma to study and argument. The real religion is something else and not what the people think it is; why then should dogma be examined? He says "In this world there is no equivalent to the things which are called the (the Throne), (the Book), (the Angels), (the Day of Reckoning). Similes are used and they are of necessity merely a rough idea of something else."

To Maulana, Dante's phrase regarding Homer might be applied: 'He flies above other poets like an eagle.' He was a mystic first and a poet afterwards, that is, he valued his poetic gift as a means of spreading his theosophical ideas and his spiritual experiences, and he did not, like Hafiz, use Sufi phrases as a mere poetic ornament." [3] Truly speaking, the real basis of the poetry is a loftily inculcated ethical system, which recognizes in purity of heart, charity, self-renunciation and bridling of the passions as the necessary conditions of eternal happiness. Attached to it we find a pantheistic theory of the emanation of all things from God, and their ultimate re-union with Him. Frequently the thought flashes out, that all religion and revelations are only the rays of a single eternal Sun; that all prophets have only delivered and proclaimed in different tongues the same principle of eternal goodness and eternal truth which flows from the divine Soul of the world.

He was Puritanical in the sternness with which he inculcated the necessity of mortifying the flesh in order to reach the final goal. He differs from many Pantheistic teachers in emphasizing the reality of the free-will and responsibility of man. In common with the other Persian mystics "he regards outward Rites as insignificant in comparison with the spiritual truths which they embody," [4]

Maulana declares that the world has not read properly into the message of love as given by the Holy Quran and the religious fanatics have stigmatized it by their evil behavior and wrong interpretation. He inspires all religious minded people to turn towards introspect rather than to search outward for the realization and it is therefore he declares openly:

> "I have taken out marrow from the Quran and cast bones to dogs,"

It is the spirit which tackles the intricate problems of life to its full solution, through the heart, and not through the brain, which concerns itself with things physical and mundane and not the metaphysical. A person so equipped transcends all discriminations of caste, creed and color.

> "The soul is concerned with wisdom and knowledge; it has nothing to do with an Arab or a Turk,"

Therefore such advanced souls do not belong to one country or nationality and they deliver their message not for any one group of people or community, but they are a common heritage for the entire humanity and their message is universal. To Maulana love is the message of all religions and panacea for all the ills of the world, when he says:

> "Be happy of my love of nice intoxication,
> physician of all ailments,
> The religion of love is separate from all the religions,
> For lovers God is their religion."

To him the true Kabah is not the square shrine, which the Muslim pilgrims perambulate at Makkah but the human heart. "You may circle round the Kabah a thousand times", he explains, "God cares not for it if you hurt a heart," With regard to (ablutions) he says, 'Yes your hand can wash your body but what hand can wash your heart?" Dr. Johnson writes about Maulana as follows:

> "He makes plain to the Pilgrim the secrets of the
> way to unity and unveils the mysteries of the path.
> to Eternal Truth."

The great message of Maulana Rumi, as of all mystic poets, is centered in love. He has always sung of love and announces that it is love which is dominant in every being or thing which originated from God who created the world for the manifestation of His love.

He says:

His love is manifest and the Beloved is hidden, the Friend is outside and His splendor is in the world.

Which is the object is not the form, whether it be love of this world or that world. Real, Beauty in mankind is like gilding. For that beauty is the lasting; its lips give the drink of life. 'Love whether it be earthly, narrow or selfish, will develop to pure, selfless and divine love and ultimately proceed to that stage, where there will remain no difference between the Lover and the Beloved: "He loves them" is complete in itself where there remains "they love Him". [5]

The Philosophy of Maulana Rumi, like the philosophy of all the Sufis, starts from the conception that not only Being, but Beauty and Goodness belong exclusively to God. Though they are manifested in thousand mirrors in the phenomenal world. God was and there nothing was beside Him, and it is now even as it was then. God, in short, is pure Being and what is "other than God" only exists so far as His Being is infused into it, or mirrored in it. He is also pure God and Absolute Beauty; Real Beloved, and Eternal Darling. His doctrine of unity is, God alone really exists, there is nothing but God, not merely that (there is no God but God).

He says:

"Who are we? In this tangled world what (think
other than He indeed) hath He (who is ONE) like
the letter Alif? Nothing, nothing."

He also says:

"The Beloved (God) is all in all, and the lover only a veil, the Beloved is the Living One, and the lover a dead thing."

Love according to Rumi is the greatest force in human life. It is indescribable in any language and any attempt to describe it merely makes it more baffling. Love presents a paradox in as much as in it by diving we take, and by dying we live. With the help of this unadulterated love the soul transcends through all the discriminations and barring and sees, the One Reality, coming out in bold relief from every created object." [6]

Of Jalal as of Shelley it might be said: "He learnt in suffering what he taught in song," His great *Mathnavi*, a collection of apologues and moral reflections, in twenty-six thousand couplets, opens with the .plaintive notes of the reed-flute longing to return to its osier-bed, ever as the soul longs to return to God." [7]

> "Hear how you read, in sadly pleasing tales,
> Departed bliss and present woe bewails!
> With me from native banks untimely torn
> Love warbling youths and soft-eyed virgins mourn;
> O, let the heart by fatal absence rent,
> Feel what I sing and bleed what I lament;
> Who roams in exile from his parent bower;
> Pants to return, and chides each lingering hour."

The *Mathnavi* is esteemed by the Persians, for its poetic, literary and mystical content that it is called the Quran in the Pahlavi language. Professor Cowell in the *Oxford Essays* (1855) says: "The stories themselves are generally easy, and told in a delightful style; but the disquisitions which interrupt them are often darker than the darkest clouds, and unintelligible to the Persians themselves without a copious commentary. When he is clear no Persian poet can surpass his depth of thought and beauty of Imagery. The flow of fine things runs on unceasingly as from a river-god's urn." [8]

The richness of ideas in *Mathnavi* makes it as it were a very seed-bed, where there is oft times more meaning in a single sentence than in learned tomes; comprehensive as well as rich, the truth of Islam supplemented by the truths of all other religions. Not only does it furnish a centre for the multitudinous sects of Islam, but it presents a platform on which theistic Hindus and Muslim, meet.

The *Mathnavi*, says Nicholson, "is a grand story book. Following, or, rather adapting to his own needs a method long established in Sufi poetry, Jalaluddin sets a matter of his discourse within a framework of tales, which introduce and exemplify the various topics, and are frequently interwoven with explanation of their inner meaning." [9]

It has all the "pantheistic beauty of the Psalms, the music of the hills, the color and scent of roses, the swaying of forests; but it has considerably more than that. These things of scent, form and color are the Mirror of the Beloved, these earthly loves take the journey down the valley into the Rose-garden where the roses never fade, and where Love is immortal." [10]

While comparing his two books, the *Diwan* and the *Mathnavi*, Prof. Nicholson says, "We have seen that the Sufi theosophy is the fountain head of Jalal's inspiration. From this the *Mathnavi* and the *Diwan* descend by separate channels. The one is a majestic river calm and deep, meandering through many a rich and varied landscape to the immeasurable ocean. The other is a foaming torrent that leaps and plunges in the ethereal solitude." [11]

But tributes paid to Maulana by Western scholars pale into insignificance before the tribute paid to Maulana by the world-renowned poet Allama Muhammad Iqbal Addressing to himself, he writes:

> "Your half-opened eyes even now do not see things in their proper perspective, your existence is still a secret to you. The string of the harp of your Self is broken because you are not aware of Rumi's melody." [12]

Jalaluddin Rumi made more public the preliminary aspects of the Sufi philosophy which Attar pursued. He is now no more, but his influence is considerable in the West as well as on poets who came after him. The sublimity of Rumi's thoughts can be best appreciated in the realm of mystic poetry. He points to the ways in which (Seeker) can find fulfillment, but fulfillment through the Sufi understanding. The keynote of Maulana's teaching is Love. He does not belong to one particular group or religion.

With Maulana Jalaluddin Rumi's *Mathnavi* which provides a picture gallery of mystic ideas and images, the Iranian mystic tradition touches its highest watermark. No mystic water before or after him had succeeded in portraying soul movement and its subtle inexpressible experiences with such perception and intellectual vigor. He believed in the creative urge of the self and visualized a long and unending process of its evolution and growth. The earliest reference of *Mathnavi* is found in the *khairul-Majlis* conversations of Chishti, saint; Sheikh Nasiru'd-Din, Chiragh-e-Delhi. There is, thereafter, hardly any mystic writer, who does not quote him. "It is significant that Rumi has selected many stories of Indian origin in his *Mathnavi* and there are many words in it which are common to Persian and Hindi and Arabic and Hindi. During the regime of Shah Jahan, the Mughal emperor, Abdul Latif Abbasi who had also prepared a commentary on *Hadiqa*, has compiled a glossary of *Mathnavi*, entitled *Lataiful-Lughat* in which he identified those words in the *Mathnavi* which are common to Persian and Hindi and also those which are common to Arabic and Hindi." [13]

Maulana prepared Sufi mind in India to receive Ibn-e- Arabi's pantheistic ideas. He had a philosophy of life, a vision of moral and spiritual needs of man and society, a fine spiritual sensibility and powerful imagination, which made his delineation of delicate spiritual experiences a magical performance. In India the mystics were so enamored of the *Mathnavi* that they taught it to their disciples, heard it in their audition parties, and expounded mystic ideas to their audience in the light of the anecdotes given in *Mathnavi*. They drew inspiration from Rumi's moral and ethical ideas and admired the cult of *Ishq* but "an integrated approach to his work on which could be based integration of individual personality and regeneration of human society is still far off. It was left to Iqbal to turn to Rumi for inspiration and guidance for this purpose." Iqbal's philosophy, his concept of (Ego), his ideal of human excellence, his spiritual goals were all determined by Rumi.

"Iqbal gave new interpretation to Maulana's *Mathnavi* and found in him a real guide in the arduous task of resurrecting the individual and the community. Iqbal saw Maulana in his imaginary excursion to the other world addressing him as Zinda-rud (Living Stream)" [14]

Conclusion:

No nation is required to originate a culture of its own entirely different from all other cultures. Similarly, there could be no objection to a nation's attempt to acquire learning when it becomes possible for her to do so. What is objectionable is that a nation may prove itself unworthy of keeping the flame of human culture burning after it has been passed on to her, generation after generation from the beginning of the human history. It is highly praiseworthy on the part of the Iranian poets and philosophers that they have been very particular in quoting the name of each author for their theories. They were full of praise whenever they came across a theory, which appealed to them.

But the same could not be said about the Westerners. They ignored mentioning and giving the credit for the learning they acquired from other sources. Moreover, the study of philosophy was not restricted to the philosophers only in the Persian world; all learned and semi-learned people had easy access to it. *Maa az paye Sanai-o-Attar amadeem* is known to even the blind followers of Maulana. This gave rise to the assemblies attended by the later composers too. The Quranic verse "He is the First and the Last and the Manifest and the Hidden, and He knows all things and everything will, perish but He", covers the entire field leaving nothing of the mystic theory that God is eternal and immortal. God has no attributes of time and space and His knowledge covers universality and particles. And it is for the same reason that Maulana comes out openly in these words:

"What is to be done, O my friends, for I do not know my own identity: I am neither a Christian, nor Jew, neither Zoroastrian nor Muslim.

I hail neither from the East nor the West, neither from land nor from sea; neither from the mine of nature nor from the revolving spheres.

Neither from dust nor from water; neither from air nor from fire; neither from the throne of God nor the earth; neither from existence nor entity.

Neither from India nor China; neither from Bulgaria nor Scythia; neither from the land of two Iraqs. Nor from the province of Khurasan.

Neither from this world nor the next; neither from heaven nor hell; neither from Adam nor Eve; neither from paradise nor the garden of Eden.

The placeless is my place; the traceless is my trace; I have neither body nor soul for I belong to the soul of beloved. " [15]

Notes:

1. Des Gebet-1923, Stuttgart- 1961.
2. S. H. Nesr, *The Encounter of Man and Nature, the Spiritual Crisis of Modern Man*, London, 1968, p.63
3. *Persian Poetry*, Claude Field, Herbert and Daniel, London.pp 175
4. *Persian Poetry*, Claude Field, Herbert and Daniel, London.pp 176
5. *Quran* 5, 57
6. *Indo-Iranica*, vol.vii, Bkl.pp.30
7. *Persian Poetry*. Claude Field, Herbert and Daniel, London.pp 175
8. *The Persian Mystics*, Rumi, pp.41-42
9. Rumi-A Genius, Indo-Iranica, vol.3,pp31
10. *The Persian Mystics, Rumi*, H. Devis,pp.43
11. *Rumi—A Genius Indo-Iranica*,vol.3,pp.31
12. *Zarbe-Kalim, Kulliate-Iqbal*, Eiteqad Publishing House, Delhi, 1941, pp.12
13. *Mystic Ideas of Iran and Their Impact on Sufi Thought*, Prof. Khalique Ahmad, Indo-Iranica. vol.34, pp. 1 07.
14. *Mystic Ideas of Iran and their Impact on Sufi Thought*, Prof. Khalique Ahmad, Indo-Iranica. vol.34, pp.108.
15. *A Golden Treasury of Persian Poetry*, Prof. Hadi Hasan, pp.154-156

Saleem Raz

Sufism in Pashto Poetry

Faiz Ahmad Faiz had once said in an interview:

"Our mental relation exists with the Sufis. There is a conflict between the men of the external and internal values, in our poetry. The mystics taught the humanity, love and peace while opposed the worldly ostentation, bigotry, hate and imperialism."

It is the true tradition of Sufism that Sufis are usually the interpreters of the cultural and spiritual context of their contemporary age and as such they stand as the true preachers of revolutionary thoughts. The Sufi poets of every age, land and nation achieved the same purpose with their poetry.

Sufism is something very different from the religious insanity, sectarianism and bigotry. It teaches us moderation and it believes in love and unity amongst the human beings. That is why one of pioneers of the progressive writers, Ali Sardar Jaffery, has called it a reaction against the social injustice. According to renowned social scientist Sibte Hassan, the behavior of the men of mysticism (Sufis), is a conduct, beyond religious sectarianism.

History shows that the Sufis have always led the people to fight against the discrimination of the ruling class and establishment. They have always taught them to cultivate liberty of thought. On the contrary, the men of knowledge and broad mind have always been called pagans by the Mullas, who have always supported the ruling classes. It is true that the Sufis have always been the supporters of democracy and the censured Sufis have always opposed the feudal and discriminating classes in the light of the rules of class struggle. They have encouraged the people for getting their rights by awakening class consciousness among them. Thus they have paved the way for democracy by eradicating tyranny, constraints and discrimination.

The tradition of Sufism has inherited the same heritage from history, which is playing an important role in leading the people towards their mental evolution.

The Sufi poets of Pashto have also been of such conduct and have always led the people to get their rights and become conscious of liberty. They made them realize their responsibilities. They dared to unveil the social evils, injustices and corruption. They raised slogans against the discrimination, tyranny and sectarianism and as such they led the people to be honest and truthful. In this manner they promoted the conception of making. The social life better and prosperous.

Roshanette movement was the first organized movement of Sufism and mental liberty in Pashto literature and history, which had been founded and led by Bayazeed Ansari, known as Pir Rokhan, Bayazeed was accused as Pir Tareek by the narrow minded religious elements and agents of the discriminating rulers of those times. Pir Rokhan (931H---380H) was a great scholar, Sufi and revolutionary thinker. He was the author of a number of books and a linguist of Pashto, Hindi, Persian and Arabic. He was not only a writer but he practically struggled and resisted against the Mughal imperialism, feudal classes and narrow-minded religious elements. During his struggle, he was martyred but he left behind an organized movement of high virtue, which was later on continued by his sons, grandsons and followers, who met with their responsibilities for leading the common people through ideological and political movement against the discriminating ruling classes of their age.

Pir Rokhan appeared as a preacher and interpreter of reality and truthfulness. He opposed the retrogressive, royalist, extremist and discriminating element, who also assembled against him and launched a campaign to eliminate the movement of Pir Rokhan. Pir Rokhan was strongly supported and backed by the lower classes, particularly the peasantry in that long struggle for getting their rights. The movement was some times led by the women of Pir Rokhan's family. It is to be remembered that 500 years ago, Pir Rokhan had not only made efforts for the rights of the women but he had given their rights to them equal to the men. He had also provided them the opportunity to worship in the assembly of men. In response to these revolutionary thoughts and practical steps. The rulers of those time gave the verdict of paganism against him through their hired Mullas.

Some of the most important Pashto poets had been the members of Pir Rokhan's movement, who

laid strong foundations of Sufism in Pashto poetry. Mulla Arzani Khaweshki (1523 A.D - 1601 A.D) is the first Pashto poet, who introduced Sufism in Pashto poetry in a regular and organized manner. According to the latest research, Mulla Arzani is not only the first Pashto Poet having a collection of his poetry but he also introduced poems on different subjects in the Pashto poetry. he was a great scholar and had knowledge of four different languages. He was the first to descuss the different stages

of the Sufism in Pashto poetry. Some of his verses are:

دَ دۀ زړۀ دَ حق بُلبُل دے

دَ بُلبُل شُغل له باغه

(His heart is a nightingale of truth and hobby of such nightingale is to sing in a garden)

دا بُلبُل طالب دَ ګل دے

دے خبر دے له سُراغه

(This nightingale is a lover of a flower and be knows the clue of that flower)

Mirza Khan Ansari (988H---1040H), Daulat Lowani (died after 1058H), Wasal Rokhani and Ali Muhammad Mukhlis (1019H---1077H) were the other prominent poets of the Roshanette movement, who strengthened the tradition of Sufism in Pashto poetry in to early period of its history.

چې مې یار په نظر کښې نه وت
له جهانه مې زړه ستون شۀ

(My heart returned back from the worldly people and others, whenever I saw my beloved)

(Mirza Khan Ansari)

زه فقیر دولت مُرید دَ میاں روښان یم
له فتراکه به یې نۀ کاږم آسان لاس

(I, humble Daulat, disciple to Mian Rokhan and I am not ready to leave him so easily)

(Daulat Lowani)

کۀ عاشق راپسې وَمړی غم یې څه دے
دَ حیات نسیم یې زۀ یم پرې لګېږم

(The lover should not take any care of his death because I am the breeze of life him)

(Wasal Rokhani)

اے مُخلصه! دَ توحید تمثیل څر گند دے
دا مولیٰ مانند سیاهی، خلق حروف

(The belief in one, can be easily understood because God is the ink and the People are words)

(Ali Muhammad Mukhlis)

Sufism in Pashto poetry appeared in a very mature and fascinating from in the period of Khushal Khan Khattak and Rahman Baba, which is known as the second period of Roshanette poets in the history of

Pashto literature. It begins from the versatile literary personality of great Khushal Khan Khattak (1022H---1100H), who depicted the Sufism in a very organized and popular form in his poetry. it is pertinent to mention here that the poetry of the Roshanette poets had been usually limited to Sufism while Khushal Khan Khattak showed more versatility of subjects in his poetry and as such he bravely mingled Sufism with other subjects, relating to contemporary life.

Khushal Khan Khattak was not only a poet of beauty and dignity, rather he spent his life in battles with Mughal Rulers. He was simultaneously a poet, a scholar, a thinker, a politician and a brave commander, besides which he was also a poet of Sufi thoughts. The great literary figure of 20th century and Sufi personality, Ameer Hamza Khan Shinwari, has written a complete book on the below cited verse of Khushal Khan Khattak:

په هر څه کښې ننداره دَ هغه مخ کړم

چې له ډیرې پیدایۍ نه ناپدید شو

(I see the face, which has faded from the sight due to its superfluous emergence, in every place and thing)

Here we have Sufi ideology of Khushal Khan Khattak in these few verses:

کۀ مسجد غواړې ، کۀ دیر

واړه یو دی نشته غیر

(The Mosque and the Temple are the same for worship)

یو ئې دین دې سره دوه اویامذهبه

خُدایه!څۀ بنی آدم فریق فریق شو

(There are 72 different religious classes in one religion. O' God! The man has divided into so many groups)

SUFISM IN PASHTO POETRY

هغه کارچي په نرمۍ ترسره کیږي
څه حاجت چه رسوهٔ شي تر جنګونه

(The matter resolved with mild behavior, does not need to be resolved with force and battle)

In the 17th century, Rahman Baba is a poet of outstanding features and characteristics, not only of the period of Khushal Khan Khattak, but a Pashto poet of high status in the entire history of Pashto literature. Though he was a representative of the contemporary poetry of his peiod but due to his tendency towards Sufism, he is reckoned as the greatest Sufi poet in the history of Pashto literature. The main characteristic of the poety of Rahman Baba is that he popularized Pashto poetry among the common people and enabled them to absorb the philosophical teachings through this medium. As such Sufism was also popularized by Rahman Baba and the common people understood and found the secrets of Sufism. Some of his verses are:

دغه ګل دے، دغه خار
دا منصور دے، دغه دار

(This is the flower and this is the thorn. This is Mansoor and this is the gibbet)

دا رقیب دے، دا حبیب دے
دغه ګنج دے، دغه مار

(This is the rival and this is the beloved. This is the treasure and this is the snake)

Rahman Baba introduced humanism and peace in a very understandable language in the from of poetry. He taught moderation and tolerance to the human beings and reiterated the moral virtues for a perfect member of the society as:

هغه زړه به له طوفانه په امان وي

چي کښتۍ غوندي دَ حلقو بار بردار شي

(Those hearts are safe and secure from the storm, who share the burdens with other people)

ادم زاد په معنىٰ واړه يو صُورت دي

هر چي بل ازاروي خپله ازار شي

(All the human beings are same and similar. One who harasses other, is harassed with his own acts)

په سبب دَ ظالمانو ، حاکمانو !!

ګور اؤ اُوراؤ پيښور دري واړه يو دي

(The grave, the fire and Peshawar are equal and same for me, due to the tyranny of cruel rulers)

دا هُنرنۀ دے چي خاؤري څوک سرهٔ زر کا

چي زر خاؤري کا رحمانه ! هُنر دا دے

(The conversion of soil into gold is not a skill. O' Rahman! The real skill is to convert the gold into the soil)

Abdul Hameed Baba, Kazim Khan Shaida, Abdul Qadir Khattak, Maazullah Khan Mohmand, Misri Khan Gigyani, Abdul Azeem Baba, Kamgar Khattak, Pir Muhammad Kakar, Muhammadi Sahib Zada, Hafiz Alpuri, etc. are other eminent poets of the age of Rahman Baba, whose attractive poetry depicted the subject of Sufism in a very admirable manner.

Ameer Hamza Khan Shinwari (1907 AD---1994 AD), father of Pashto Ghazal, being a modern poet, is a recent interpreter of Sufism in Pashto poetry. He presented great values of Sufism in his poetry and as such continued the journey of Sufism to the present era and onwards. In other words we can safely say that Ameer Hamza Khan Shinwari modernized Sufism in Pashto poetry, in this regard some of his verses are given here;

کله کله چې اسره مې پاتې نۀ شی

هسې وایم چې جوړ تۀ راسره مل شوې

(I feel your company, whenever I found none with me)

حمزه! ډیر مُسلمانان شته، هُم کافر شته په دُنیا کښې

زۀ اَشنا دَ هغه کس یم چې روش یې دَ انسان وی

(O' Hamza there are so many Muslims and pagans but I support the humanity)

Consequently we find that Sufi poetry in Pashto has a strong tradition and the entire Pashto Sufi poetry leads us towards humanism, realism, optimism and secularism. It teaches us the love, humanity, peace and other moral virtues and values which elevate Pashto poetry to a universal level. The subject of Sufism is also presently appearing in some of the modern Pashto poets. Continuation of the values of Sufism in Pashto poetry is very essential and necessary to enable people of our time to eliminate and eradicate sectarianism and terrorism from the society.

It is very necessary to develop the spirit of love, peace and unity amongst the people through the splendid verses of the Sufi poets to promote a liberal, secular, democratic and broad-minded culture free from religious, regional, linguistic, cultural, sectarian bigotry. It is the duty of every member of the present society to discourage the Klashankov culture, a harmful fruit of the dictatorship and to make efforts to their best for the establishment of peace. Sufism can be helpful in bringing together civilization and countries in friendship and peace for the ultimate prosperity of the people of the entire world.

Translated by Mustafa Kamal

Saral Jhingran

Sufi Experience of 'Fana' as Basis for Religio-Ethical Life Today

An unbiased study of world religions would show that—though there are different religions, there are also as many differences within each religious tradition as between one tradition and another. Secondly, corollary of it would also reflect that, these different strands of one religion find an affinity in similar strands in other religions. The Sufi mystic would find a greater concordance with Indian saints of Bhakti tradition than perhaps with their own orthodox one. Thirdly, in spite of all the differences of race, culture and religion, there is a basic affinity between humankind's innate responses to the Divine Reality as the source and ground of all creation. Fourthly, this affinity could be found best at the level of religious experience, rather than any other aspect of religion, which may mean that religious experience is more basic or central to religion than is usually recognized.[1] All religions must involve some transition from the empirical, the egoist, the petty concerns of every day life, to a profounder and more spiritual level of experience and action. That commutes true religion starts only when it has become a matter of inner experience, an ultimate- concern of one's life.

The claim of religious experience, as basic or central to religion is contested both by theologians and philosophers of Semitic religions. While the theologians contend that the claim on the part of individual to have direct experience of God undermines the authority of 'revelation'; philosophers just cannot appreciate inner experience, and argue the unreliability of individual experience.

However, every aspect of religion, e.g. belief, prayer, ritual and values (though not the details or peripheral matters) get their meaning in and through experience. The intensity and profoundness or lack of it may vary from individual to individual, but some experience must be there in order to give meaning to religion. In spite of all intellectual arguments against religious experience, we 'know' and 'commune' with God in and through it only. Ramakrishna Paramhansa used to speak of his experience of God in indubitable terms:

> "I do see the Supreme Being as the veritable Reality with my own eyes. Why then should 1 reason? 1 do see that it is the Absolute which has become all things around us. One must have an awakening of the spirit within to see the Reality".[2]

Basic religious experience, it essentially consists of an overwhelming consciousness of God which envelops and devours, as it were, the individual's ego-consciousness, so that the devout individual forgets himself and is conscious of God alone both within and without. The Sufi concept of *fana* comes closest to what is probably the profoundest core religious experience common to all religions. *Fana* is self-negating or transcending the ego in order to come closer to the Divine Being. Abu al-Qasim Junaid (9th century) thus opined:

> "As long as a person preserves his individuality, he cannot attain the full state of Tauhid, as the continued existence of his personality means that something other than God is still persisting".[3]

The argument of the Sufis here is ingenious. To think of one self as other than God", they say, "amounts to polytheism."[4] To them, 'there is one God or Absolute; if someone postulates any other reality, e.g. the world or the soul, even if to preserve the transcendence and glory of God, he is challenging the absoluteness of God. Those who are familiar with *Vedanta* would be surprised to find how close such an assertion comes to Shankara's *Advaita Vedanan*.

A later Sufi, Sharaf'ud-Din Muneri says that his God told him, "Clinging to self means 'you'—you cannot reach. To come to Me, you must forsake yourself."[5] Kabir testifies to this experience when he says that, "When I was there, Hari (God) was not; and when Hari is there, 1 am not."⁶ It implies there is place only for one at the center of human consciousness, so that there can be either the ego or God there. God can become the centre of consciousness only when the ego is displaced from its central place.

However, the Sufis, nurtured as they were in the Islamic tradition, did not probably mean any ontological identity between the creature and the Creator. They were simply talking about an existential experience in which the human lover is so much lost in the 'Divine Beloved' that he is conscious of nothing else—neither the world, nor his own individual self. This is the other side or corollary of the 'consciousness of God being all-in-all'. The mystic on tune with this realizes, "I am not, but God alone is." Probably in this state of minds Mansoor-al-Hallaj pronounced 'Ana al-Haq or 'I am the Truth' which led to fierce controversy and his execution. Similarly Abu Yazid, when called by some acquaintance, retorted, "Go away, there is none here except God." He used to repeatedly assert that 'he is not there, only God exists'.⁷

Neither Mansoor, nor Abu Yazid was declaring that they were God; rather, what they meant was, 'I am not. God alone exists, both outside and within me'. This is *fana* or dying to oneself. Countless Sufis have testified to their experience of *fana*. *Fana is* not an assertion of identity with God, for Sufism is the religion of love of God, and love implies the 'duality of the lover and the beloved.' This is the core to the concept of *fana* which I have deliberated upon elsewhere.

According to Sufi philosophy, *fana* or self-naughting is followed by *baqa* or residing in God, that is, being conscious of God and God alone, alongwith a feeling of a profound affinity with Him. Fariduddin Attar gives expression to this experience thus:

> "There is naught but Thee in the whole world Everywhere in the universe, it is Thy face that we see. In whatever direction I turn my eyes there art Thou. Without Thee there is nothing that there is".⁹

It does not mean merely that God is everywhere in the outside universe; above all. He is within our hearts or souls. The best place to search for God is the heart. To quote Attar again:

"Seek for the Reality within thy own heart, for Reality in truth is hidden within thee. The heart is the dwelling place of that which is the essence of the universe. Within the heart the soul *is* the very essence of God".[10]

This is at once an assertion of the Sufi vision and philosophy of God being the only Reality, the all-in-all (*Tawhid,* as understood by most Sufis), and an expression of the existential experience of God's presence within implying a basic affinity between the two. Such utterances may not mean an ontological identity, as they do in *Vedanta* and some Bhakti traditions. It may be only an expression of some profound mystical experience.

In India, there was a razing controversy regarding the metaphysical doctrines of *Wahdat al Wujud* (Unity of Being), vs *Wahdat ul Shuhud* (Unity of Witnessing). Without going into details, suffice it to say that the supporters of the first doctrine asserted the Unity or 'all- in-all' of God in such a way that every thing - every being becomes a manifestation of God. Masud Bak a contemporary Sufi of Gesudraz, who had contested the 'wahm' of the later on comparison of 'wali' and 'prophet' had expressed this Unity thus:

> "Oh God! Thou pervadeth the soul of every human being
> The blackness of Kufr doth emaneth from Thee;
> And Thou art the light of every faith.
> Idol worship, prayer, Kaaba, fire worship in temple,
> To me art identical for the essence of each faith art
> Thou.
> How long should I say 'I am Thou:
> For only Thou existeth, and not Masud
> In reality it is not I who reciteth these verses,
> Thou reciteth them"[11]

This is a very beautiful expression of the experience of *Fana* because it highlights both aspects there of the perception of every thing, every being as a manifestation of God, and self-negation or self-transcendence. Sufis and other mystics of the world, in virtue of their self-transcendence or dying to the self *(fana)* live in through God *(baqa-)* and are best instruments of God's will. Explaining a *Hadith,* 'Whosoever know himself knows God,' Abu Said contended that

'Whosoever knows himself as non-being *(abd)* knows God as real Being (Wujud)'.[12] Thus, Sufi experience of *fana* is integrally related to that of residing in God. In plain terms it means devout experience of transcending one's ego.[13]

The overwhelming consciousness of God which makes one forgets oneself is ever rare now man's consciousness is either 'ego-centric' or 'outward-oriented. In religion we find either an externalist religiosity, or fanaticism, a distorted version of religious faith. If so, how can the experience *fana* be a paradigm to be emulated for modern day man and woman?

Let us ask why a man is led to a path of evil, dishonesty, selfishness and even violence. Unequivocal the answer would be—man is immoral and violent, because all his thinking is self-centered, and all his actions are motivated by self interest. Often a person is ready to do anything, indulge in any dishonest or violent act if it seems to serve his own interest. If man is not conscious or at least obsessed with his ego or his self interest, he would not be driven towards immoral or unrighteous acts.

Though it is difficult to inspire in others the profound and intense religious consciousness of *fana* or total self-forgetfulness, the understanding as to how an experience of *fana,* or at least something approaching it, could make a better human being out of each of us. Today's western culture embodies a conception of the individual as the focus of both rights and duties, an emphasis on maximum realization of one's potentialities, and even striving hard through cut throat competition to achieve one's aspiration. Try to conceive a situation wherein not the ego, but the family, community or neighbors are a matter of greater concern for the moral agent than self-aggrandizement. This was not an impossible scenario, say a century ago, at least in the sub-continent wherein the extended family and neighborhood or *mohalla* were great concern for the individual; and sacrificing one's personal interests and aspiration for the sake of duty or love for others came natural for individuals. This approach may not make you progress as fast, but it is catalyst to inner peace and satisfaction. Emotional deprivation, depression etc. were, and are, much less in those societies in which others, and not the individual's ego, are the chief objects of concern. By acknowledging others as the chief concern of one's life and consciousness, the self or subject gains manifold in terms of peace and tranquility within. Recent studies by anthropologists, sociologists and psychologists have confirmed that people in the East (including Middle-East) are generally happier even in adverse circumstances than those in the West. In caring for others more than ourselves we transcend our egos which are the source of both immoral conduct as well as inner discontent and unhappiness.

If some one were to interject here that it is not what the Sufi concept of *fana* means, one would be both right and wrong. The profoundest dimension of religion probably consists in transcending or losing one's ego into some transcendent Divine Reality. So, it seems that without reference to this Divine Reality religion is not possible. At the same time. Buddhism does not believe either in a transcendent Divine Being, or even in a soul or self. However, not only the religious spirit is present in Buddhism, it gives a firm foundation to a life of morality and altruism. Its arguments is unique, if there is no self or soul *(atma)*, then there is no reason why the moral agent should prefer his/her selfish interests than those of others. The denial of the individual ego thus becomes the basis of Buddhist message of universal compassion *(Karuna)*.[14] Interestingly, however, not believing in a transcendent Divine Being, Buddhists still take refuge in Gautama, the Buddha, an ideal human being. Can it mean that the essence of religious spirit lies in giving up our petty ego to some thing much higher, much more comprehensive and spiritual? Often dedication to art, especially music, takes us beyond our petty selves. Similarly, for some of us service of the people, transports them from the world of egoistic worries to a spiritual plane of inner peace and happiness.

The concept and experience of *fana* implies a transcendent Divine Reality. Though most of us are religious, our religion is often confined to adherence to outward rituals, or in the case of popular Sufi practices and most Hindu ones, approaching the supernatural powers for personal gains. Sufism tells us that religion is not either of these. Sufism connotes loving God for His own sake, and while loving Him forgetting our own petty selves. Rabi'a al-Basari thus prayed:

> "I pray for Thy sake' and prayed God to send her to
> Hell, if he was praying to save herself from Hell and

exclude her from Heaven, if he was praying for sake Heaven.

Not all Sufis believed in *fana,* and asserted the existence of the ego, implying the duality of the creature and the Creator.[15] And yet, they all loved God with an intensity which can but result in 'self-forgetfulness'; the degree and intensity may vary, but it was core to basic thought of Sufism. Baba Farid or Sheikh Faridud'din a leading Chishti Saint asserted that his only desire in life was to love God for His own sake.[16] The Sufi kind of love, makes us understand that real religion consists not in mere outward conformity to the creed and rituals of one's religious tradition, but in love of God. This tells us how transcending the ego is the key to all higher things in life inner happiness to greatest achievements in culture and science, as well as to a true more sincere religious faith.

The Sufi way mainly consisted of two steps — *taubah* (repentance) and *tawakkul* (complete trust in God). *Tawakkul,* for the Sufis, meant an absolute and unconditional dependence on God for sustenance. But they taught their lay disciples to earn livelihood to sustain their families in a righteous way and depend upon God for the success of their efforts. This is exactly the message of the *Bhagavadgita*. Most Sufi and Bhakti saints were householders, which means that neither the Sufi conception of *fana,* nor that of *tawakkul,* demand one to renounce the world. Sheikh Nasiru'd-Din told a disciple that if a person is reciting the *Quran,* or is repeating the name of God while doing his worldly duties, he is practicing *tawakkul.*[17] the message therefore is not to give up one's duties, but only to give up our egos (which is what the sentiment of *tawakkul* implies). In the end, it is transcending or restraining our egos that count most, both for one inner religion and righteousness in our worldly dealings.

The experience of *fana,* thus, is fulfilled in the experience of God being the all-in-all, so that the mystic (Sufi) can see nothing else but God: As expressed by Baba Kuhi of Shiraj:

> "In the market, in the cloister only God 1 saw.
> In the valley, on the mountain only God 1 saw.
> I opened my eyes and by the Light of His Pace around me,
> In all the eye discovered only God 1 saw[18]

In the Bhakti tradition Kabir has given the most wonderful and clear expression to this vision of Unity as absolute equality of all human beings and its practical implications. To quote just a verse from him:

"Numskull! You have missed the point.
From one drop a universe.
Who is a *brahmin*? Who is *shudra*?..
Kabir says plunge into Ram!
There is no Hindu! no Turk"[19]

This vision of the unity of all life can be truly derived only from a mystical experience of the Unity or all-in-all of one Divine Reality. Though it involves a difficult process but it is easily understandable that if God is one (Unity or *Tawhid*), then all His creation being derived from one's source, would be essentially one. And thus differences on the grounds of religion, cast, creed, sex, class, status or position are meaningless. They do not refer to the essence of humankind which is derived from the same Divine source, or in the words of Kabir '*Nur* (Glory)'.[20]

This vision has two practical implications— First, if all human beings have their source in and are sustained by, the one 'Divine', all man-made distinctions become superficial; and there is left no basis for enmity and ill-will between man and man. Secondly, the Unity of Divine Reality implies that the same 'Divine' is also the source of all religions. If all human beings are essentially the same, this realization naturally leads to a religion or morality of intense compassion for all. Thus, the love of man is derived naturally from the vision of God being present everywhere; in every living being.

Sheikh Muinu'd-Din Chishti and Sheikh Nizamuddin Auliya were embodiments of love and compassion. According to Sheikh Muinu'd-Din the greatest act of obedience to God is, "To answer the call of those in distress, to fulfill the needs of the helpless and to feed the hungry." He added that all those possessing the three virtues of generosity like the ocean, benevolence like the sunshine, and hospitality (or humility) like the earth were friends of God."[20] Sheikh Nizamuddin used to say that there are many paths to God, but the greatest consists in giving solace to a grieving heart. He advised, 'As far as you can, bring comfort to hearts, for the heart of a believer is the seat of the mysteries of Providence.[21] Not only was his free kitchen open to all the needy and hungry, he used to take extra care to look after the welfare of those in the neighborhood. Above all, he listened to their tales of woes, and gave comfort to their hearts. At the end of his daily fast, he found it difficult to eat as the thought of so many hungry people around him made it difficult for him to swallow his food.[22]

The vision of one eternal Divine Self *(Atman-Brahman)* in all beings is the basic vision of Hinduism, and is well-recognized by all Bhakti saints. They declare the absolute equality of all human beings; and almost all the Bhakti saints hail from the so-called lower castes while some of them were Muslims. However, the second natural implication of their vision, that is, universal compassion, is not so preeminent in them, except Kabir and Nanak. Other Bhakti saints equally sing prayers of kindness and compassion, but generally they are absorbed in their religio-spiritual experience; and the practical expression of the milk of human kindness that we find in Khawaja Muinu'd-Din and Nizamu'd-Din Auliya is not to be found anywhere else. Thus, the Sufi vision of one Divine Being as the source and ground of all human beings can give the soundest basis for a morality of absolute equality of all, and an attitude of kindness and compassion for the needy and the deprived.

Another message from the Sufi vision of God's Unity and His being the all-in-all is, as we have seen, that the same 'Divine' is the source and object of all religions; so that there remains no justification whatsoever for feelings of ill-will or intolerance towards each other's religion. Kabir gives a clear expression to this idea:

> "Brother, where did your two gods came from
> Tell me who made you mad?
> Ram. Allah, Keshav, Karim, Hari, Hazrat
> So many names.
> So many ornaments, all one gold.
> It has no double nature
> For conversation we make two.[23]

Actually, it is a logical conclusion from the Islamic doctrine of Unity of God, and His omnipotence, that He alone can be the source all world religions.[24] If so, differences of religion can never be the basis of mutual enmity and violence. Religious toleration is innate to Hinduism and the saints of Bhakti tradition. However in Semitic religions Sufi saints were the first to advocate religious tolerance. Khawaja Nizamu'd-Din was once witnessing Hindus celebrating their religious festival; and he observed that "every community has its own path and faith, and its own way of worship.[25]

Sufis, though, practiced namaz., roza etc. rigorously, they were far from being orthodox and even dashed with the *'Ulema'*, the orthodox elements in Islam. Chishtis were broad minded. They were liberal, tolerant and even receptive towards other religious faiths.[26] The saintliness and compassionate behavior of early Chishtis made local populace in large numbers, become their followers.

Sufi *Khanqahs* or *Jama' t khanas* were not only centers of religious training but were also the meeting ground of different streams of religious thoughts and practices. Baba Farid's Khanqah at Ajodhan was such a meeting ground where not only Sufis of different orders (silsilas) but jogis (wandering yogis), other seekers of truth, as well as travelers found refuge, and interacted with each other. The learning was not a one way traffic for the Baba, which he proved, by learning yoga from Nath Yogis' and practicing it rigorously.

As observed by M. Mujeeb, the sincerity and intensity of religious fervor of early Sufis gradually declined. The most prominent change came in their life style. The earlier ecstatic abandon gave place to more conservative version of the mystic life. On the other hand, fifteenth century onwards was also a period of greater interaction between the Hindus and Muslims in all fields of life— political, cultural and religious. Many Sufis, especially in the countryside, were very much at home with Hindu beliefs and mythology. Muzaffar Alam presents a strong case of how these Sufi saints of 16th and 17th centuries interacted with Hindu *sadhus* and *jogis*, and were respected among them as the true *bhakts* of Rama and Krishana, without for a moment undermining their own faith. Especially, there is a definite evidence of close contact between Hindu Nath jogis and later Sufis. Alam gives the story of a simple Sufi saint, Abdur Razzaq Bansawi of Awadh (17th -18th centuries). He kept a close contact with Hindu jogis and Bairagis. Neither the Sufis' nor Bairagis' respective religions came in the way of their mutually understanding and respecting each other's faith, and more than that, a sense of mutual affinity.[27] Those Sufis, with a few exceptions, were not only tolerant of others' beliefs, they like the

Hindu jogis and Bhakti saints, believed that the one God can be reached through many ways. To quote Mujeeb:

> "The outlook of the Sufis was broad enough for them to recognize without inhibitions and reservations the possibility of many paths to God. God has a different secret, a different mystery, different relationship with each person.[28]

Some of the Sufis translated Hindu religious texts. Sheikh Abdur Rahman translated the *Bhagvadgita*, presenting it as an ideal exposition of the Sufi doctrine of *Hama Ust* (all is He). There was a constant effort by some of the later Sufis to understand Hinduism and search for commonalities. As Muzaffar Alam observes:

> "The emphasis in religious circles was on an open and non combative interaction, and in order to avoid conflict, on integration and assimilation within limits.[29]

Thus, mutual harmony, not uniformity, was the goal of Sufi saints; and that is the greatest need of contemporary world. That again makes *fana* immensely relevant, as it attempts to free man from 'self-consciousness' or 'ego centrism' and provides space for realization of God by the process of 'self arbitration' or probably for some, by sacrifice of self for the welfare or others — the needy, the desolate and the poor.

Notes:

1. See Writer, *The Roots of World Religions*, New Delhi: Books & Books, 1982, Chapters 1 and 5, especially pp.10 ff.
2. *Sayings of Sri Ramakrishna*, Madras: Ramakrishna Math, 1975, pp.316-317
3. Quoted in Saiyid Athar A. Rizvi, *A History of Sufism in India*, Delhi: Munshiram Manoharlal, 1978, Vol. 1, p. 55.
4. Paraphrase of the mystical verse of Ibnu'l-Farid's *Tai 'yyatu- 'l-Kubra*, tr. by- R.A. Nicholson, *Studies in Islamic Mysticism*, New York: Cambridge University Press, 1989, p. 220.
5. Quoted in Paul Jackson, The *Way of a Sufi: Sharafu'd-Din Maneri*, Delhi: Idrah-i-abadiyat-i-Delhi, 1987, p-225.
6. *"Jab main tha tab Hari nahin, ab Hari hain main nahi."* From Kabir Grantbavali, ed. by Shyam Sundar *Das,* Varanasi, Nagri Pracharani Sabha, 6th ed.; writer's transl.

7. "I am not I, because I am He, I am He, I am He." Abu Yazid, quoted in A.J. Arberry, *Revelation and Reason in Islam*, London: George Alien & Union, 1965, p. 98; Abu Yazid also quoted in Arberry, *Sufism: An Account of the Mystics of Islam*, New York: Dover Publications, 2002, pp. 54-55.
8. See Writer, op. cit., chapter 5, especially pp. 154 ff.
9. Farid '1-Din Attar, *Jawalvir 'I Dhat*, quoted in Margaret Smith, *Persian Mystics: Altar*, London: *The Wisdom of the East* Series, 1932, p. 99.
   "Thou art the breath of life in body and soul. In every form Thou dost manifest Thyself- according to Thy will... Thou the Creator art seen in the creatures. Spirit shining through given matter....... Thou art the Divine Essence dwelling in the midst of each one of us. Thou art the Sought and the seeker." *ibid*, p.99 cf "To Allah belong the East and West. Wherever ye turn, there is the Face of Allah."The *Holy Quran* II. 115 *(The Meaning of the Glorious Koran*, tr. By Marmaduke Pickthall, Delhi: World Islamic Publication, 1979)
10. Attar, quoted in Margaret Smith, op. cit., p. 94 cf "O servant, where dost thou seek Me?
    Lo! I am beside thee
    I am neither in temple, nor in mosque...
    Kabir says, 'O Sadhu! God is the breath of breath."
    Tagore, *One Hundred Poems of Kabir*, Delhi: Macmillan India Ltd., 1972, p. 21.
11. Quoted in *Rizvi, op.eft.*, Voll, p. 243.
12. Quoted in Nicholson, op. *cit.*, p.50
13. "Does Khuda live in a mosque?
    Thou who lives every where?..
    Every man and woman born,
    They are all your forms, says Kabir.
    The *Bijak of Kabir*, p. 74.
    There is a difference here between the Hindu and Muslim religious traditions. While for Muslims the realization of Unity mainly leads to love and compassion for all human beings, for Hindu Bhakti saints, believing in the continuity of all life, the same vision leads to compassion for all living beings. Significantly, Kabir gives the most emphatic expression to this view point. He passionately opposes both animal sacrifices and even meat eating. See *The Bijak of Kabir*, pp. 46, 64, 88,115 etc.
14. See Har Dayal, *The Budhisattva Doctrine in Buddhist Sanskrit Literature*, Delhi: Motilal Banarsidass, pp. 95,178 ff.
15. Both Sheikh Sharafu'd-Din Muneri and a! Husaini Gesu Daraz were ardent Sufis; but they rejected the metaphysical doctrine of *Wahdat al Wajood*, saying that the difference between the two can never be bridged. See Rizvi, *op. cit.*, pp. 229 ff., 251 ff.
16. "I pray to love only for the sake of loving Thee. wish to become dust and dwell eternally under Thy feet. My principal expectation from both worlds is that,I should die and live for Thee."
    Quoted in Rizvi, *op. cit..*, p. 148.
17. See M. Mujeeb, *The Indian Muslims*, Delhi: Munshiram Manoharlal, 1967, pp. 128-129, and following.
18. Quoted in R.A. Nicholson, *The Mystics of Islam*, London: G. Bell and Sons, 1934, p.59.
19. *The Bijak of Kabir, p.67.*
20. Quoted in Rizvi, *op. cit.*, Vol I, p.124; Mujeeb, *op. cit*,p.146.
21. Quoted in Mujjeb, *op. cit.*, p. 144.

22. See Rizvi, op. cit.. Vol. I, p.164., Mujeeb, *op. cit.*, p.144.
23. *The Bijak of Kabir, pp.50-51.*
24. See refer, no. 11 supra.
25. Quoted in Rizvi, Vol. I, pp.. 166-167.
26. Rizvi argues that the two doctrines of *Wahdat al Wujud and Wahdat al Shuhud* influenced the attitude of their supporters. The advocates of the first were much more liberal than those of the second. See Rizvi, *op. cit.*, Vol. II, pp. 460-461.
27. See Mujaffar Alam, "Assimilation from a Distance: Confrontation and Sufi Accommodation in Avadh Society," in R. Champaklakshmi, S. Gopal, eds., *Tradition, Dissent and Ideology: Essays in Honour of Romila Thapar*, Delhi: Oxford University Press; 1996, pp. 174 ff.
28. *Op. cit.*, p. 160.
29. *Op. cit..* p. 175.

Shah Muhammad Mari

Must Taukli- A Great Baluchi Mystic Poet

The era in which Must Taukli was born was an era in which the grip of British rule was very weak on his ancestral tribe as he was very young in the war of 1839 and after that in his entire life there erupted no war. It was 19th century Baluchistan with no major movement, no economic unrest, and apart from the turbulence caused by the famine of almost a half year, there was complete peace. Must Taukli, a lover, a mercurial-tempered person, a Sufi, a philosopher and a poet sowed the seeds of motion in Baluchistan. His philosophy was based on universal truths. The central origin of Must's philosophy is Sammu, his beloved. The theme of her love runs though all his poetry.

Ishq (Love) combined by thousands of elements, making Sammu's beauty the main cause, continued to pinch the flesh of Prometheus junior like a desert raven. Must was a follower of that major Prometheus who had stolen the fire from the heavens and lit it in Must's heart as well. This fire blows out, dissolves and blinds. Must, heaving sky-rocketing sighs passing from desert to desert, was compelled by the immeasurable heat of love.

His travels span the desert of Baluchistan to Arabia and from Dera Ghazi Khan to Delhi and Baluchistan which is the sacred touchstone of his love. One has to revert to it again and again as it is the only place that offers comfort, guidance and peace. This is the choice, Taukli Must of Sherani tribe and Samnu of Kalwani tribe and the most sacred blessing of humanity the revelation of love. Shah Mureed and Taukli Must have been two widely traveled ones in the history of the lovers of Baluchistan. The former's beloved was snatched by the chief of the clan and was hurled into the den of separation and the latter was trapped into the torture cell of a married and unachievable woman. And both of them had to spend their entire life in finding escape, searching shadow and the place of comfort. Shah Mureed mixed among the *Jogis* of Shah Lateef and ultimately reached the holy city of Mekkah. Whereas the travels of Must are greater in numbers and longer in duration than any other *Sufi* saint. The peace of the body is a product of the peace of the soul. The restlessness of the soul is the essence of love. The purer and the truer the love is the more intense anxiety, sleeplessness, and restlessness becomes. In the kingdom of love restlessness is a blessing and peace is a bane.

As Must Says:
My soul is a vagabond
And heart obsessed by Sammu

This is not a momentary condition of soul. It is a limitless madness formed by many small fits.

Like a writhing snake the fits turn me over
And my soul and body are assailed
By these waves a thousand times

All his life he remained like a nomad, wanderer lost in deserts, and mountains.

This year we had to leave the Kohlu
Had to roam in Sindh
Had to hang our rifle on Guz Tree
Our destination, the vast plains of Sindh

Love and restlessness are close companions. The intense ecstasy and deep sorrow are interwoven in Must. Ecstasy leaps like a flame and sorrow burns like a burning ember. Must has lost himself, wandering in Sindh or India, crying. During his absence someone gave away his lands to farmers. Some have built communes in Paris and someone is known as Abu Zer Ghaffari (May God be pleased with him). The mundane has no meaning in this world. The thing which is considered sin in mundane life is a virtue among these people.

This is not a deformity in love
if your eyes flow out weeping

(Khushhal Khan)

The restlessness results into wanderings and Must was the Baluchi saint with most wanderings. Must was also suffering from this disease. His eyes, heart and soul wept. But if he would not have suffered this anxiety of love and Sammu's grief, he had been a person without insight. He would have been a common shepherd chasing sheep and at last died a purposeless death. He would have been facing death, disease, and war like the other Baluch. The submission to love made Must great, filled him with kindness and pain. And he to fan these wounds in his heart, ran from one place to another and to comfort his heart he sought the replica of Sammu (Who knows whom he was searching for)

This restlessness of love serves as an impetus for lovers' search and training. There is no greater knowledge and observation than in the wanderings. But how Must did acquire this destructive blessing. This must be explained by a line:

"To be kind to me God made Samnu an agent"

My heart often yearns to wander
Once, when this yearning increased
I saw in the foots of mountains,
The same day in the rhythmic drizzling
Torrential rain
I sat for a while in Sammu's tent
She is charming like lemon fruit
The memories of the damsel like a pearl
Singed and held me
My heart is a lunatic, insists on insanity
And hankers for the Zamer Tree of arduous Rock
Like a pampered child it yearns
For the beans of that tree (locks)
It over-powered all implorations
Oh, my beloved, come! I am helpless
Before this desire
I writhe like a snake
Rush to the mountains
Her delicate lips aflame
Have set me on fire

Her beady teeth
Burnt me like saltpeter
Her attractive peeping eyes
Made be roam in the mountains
I flew beyond Sindh like a raven
Then Must ran in search of remedy
South, North, East and West

Sammu your memories are evergreen
Smoldering like the Kaheer's wood
The flames of love have singed me
I am burnt from head to toe
Like a stick
Helpless, humble like the sinful
I shall dispossess your memories
In the sandy plains of Sindh
I have come beyond the sandy plains of Sindh
My feet, hardened by continuous walking
Like that of a camel
The blood frozen in the eyes
From the vigils

I love you as Mureed loved Hani
Like Gullan searching for stars in the deserts
....

The waves rise in our heart
Like the rains in rainy season
Like in the seas, fast flowing flood
Rivers and deluge

When one's heart is the victim of such floods the condition can be guessed. It's like living in death. One has to face many lashing waves simultaneously and helplessly. How can one free oneself from the piercing memories of the beloved. The vulnerable heart is the victim of these poisonous waves.

Must runs towards the heights of Tadri rock to escape.

These efforts to escape are made to avoid an omnipresent enemy. No place is free from the beloved's memories, no nook, no gap, no valley can stop them.

I departed from the slopes of Baghan the day before yesterday.
I crossed the Manjhra brook with my shoes on.
The pilgrims go for the pilgrimage
And I, to see Sammu
I am sad for your eyes like a lunatic
Would that, one day I were coming with the season.
Remembering God for help
Putting expensive arms and remembering Hazrat Ali.
I may spend a whole year in lush green Sindh
The birds may return from Sindh the next season.
The song of the bird is not
A remedy to my heart
My cure is Sammu's sweet laughter.
Birds are returning I should also leave
I'll also mix with the group of birds
I'll also fall in the line of birds
Birds fly for migration and I for Sammu.
Birds are flying, I am on foot
The Birds went to Khurasan from Sindh
The birds will fly ahead, I shall stay in Sibbi
My heart yearns to meet Sammu
The South wind blows in the evening
The noise of ships rises from the East
High rocks are bridled by gods
We adorn the hand-flag with flowers
Nora forbade me and warned
Must, if you slipped
Sea animals and turtles
Will devour you
But I shall not be strayed
I am guided by the lovers
Durrak, Wikramu and Shah Mureed
Granted me the powers
Pir Suhri and Shah Baz Qalander

Granted me sainthood
All the saints of Multan
Are guiding me with Bhawal
My lord Shams Tabraiz will come to help me.

My thoughtful heart makes many intentions
My heart goads me to dig a tunnel
Into rock like the lovers of past
So that I might control the burning memories of Sammu
Wretched, I have been walking
In my beloved's love from Keech to Makran
Believe me I have been running
To far flung lands
Due to this wandering the blood is frozen in my eyes
The chiefs of famous regions come for me

All the preparation of journey starts with your thought
I reach in the valleys of Pub at midnight
I have no meals and live on the fruits of wild trees
Injeer and Patreek are my food
Your lover eats only this
Simil's friends also eat this
The angels bore my message
On their speedy shining wings
I received the messages of Simil's soul yesterday
My soul is mad and urges me to write poetry
I admire my beloved from the depth of
My humble and oppressed heart
I admire my beloved and the bounties of my lord, the prophet
His four friends and angels
The Mausoleum of the Prophet
I keep fast and perform my religious obligation
I recite the pronouncement of faith and Surah Yasin.

What is love? To understand the beloved and to carry out his/her will is love. The expulsion of all except the beloved from the heart is love. Love is a light which illuminates the heart and the soul. It reaches those destinations of perception where mundane means and causes become meaningless. A lover can hear the heartbeats of the beloved from miles through love. It hears the rhythm of breaths. At this point words and expressions become meaningless. To comprehend the beloved there is a heart to heart and soul to soul communion.

But how hard it becomes if the beloved is in someone else's shelter but even if one has control over one's heart and soul, one cannot control the body and material resources.

When Must went to Delhi, he was humiliated there and then he badly missed his Baluch brethren.

This is Delhi, a city of merriments and joys
The black and tanned people of Sindh are gathered here.
The threats and admonitions of Yazids
The cowards are pushing me hard
What a pity, my siblings from Mari tribe are not here
Mehrullah Khan and Shehdad Shirani
The forefront fighter Wadera Lakha is not here
Neither Meer Hassan nor Yar Muhammad Nautani
And Shehbaz Khan, neither respected Raheja of Dera Bugti
Nor Soharb Khan Dombki of Kichi
Neither Kohli chief, nor Mewa Nautani
Neither Hewtan of Masuri nor Baseel Khan
And nor Kadir Khan Mazarani of Barkhan.

While attending the courts of Sufis and after listening to their successors and intellectuals like *Malangs* and to the words of wisdom and philosophy, listening to the poetry with the musicians and understanding the craft of music, he used to become a part of this culture. He used to observe these stalwarts of mysticism and comprehend their philosophy. He remained close to them, appreciated their way of living and held the love of wealth and pomp in low esteem. He used to carry their peace-loving nature, humanism and universality in his heart. He propagated these teachings till the next refresher course. Must faced the local authority. The authority was Nawab Jamal Kahan Leghari. Must got the service of humanity from the rest of the chiefs through friendship. Must reacted against the *Mullahs* (Muslim clergy). He prayed for the welfare of the people, rains, and prosperity, wrote poetry and prayed.

He also made the observation on the high mountains of Baluchistan, experienced the mysterious silence in the mountains, and collected the data regarding the insects and plants and included it in the teachings of the shrines.

I shall keep biannual fasts
Staying in the mountain
Though eating and drinking is also useful
But the charity is the blessing for hereafter.
I remember my God through day and night
Repentance is good
It absolves one from the sins

Though his views apparently seem to be commonplace but if viewed carefully one discovers their philosophical dimensions.

Save poppy for the rainy day
As it is rare in the mountains

Unfortunately Must's mysticism was viewed and perceived in the context of his lunacy in an illiterate, uninhabited and unorganized tribal life. There were neither the facilities nor the objective conditions to understand his philosophy. If he had been in the area with the facilities of the Press we would have greatly benefited from his Utopian socialism. Our fate is unchanged even after two centuries. How many of us have tried to fathom the philosophy of this philosopher? How many champions of Utopian communism have read this Guru of welfare carefully? Let us carefully read his poetry.

I received the commands of my Lord there
I was to go to vast Kichi
To a canal beside the Said Kaheri gardens
In the vicinity of Kucho Bazar
I saw a well-to- do family of gypsies
And had meals there for a year
Then the water of two streams mingled
We were saved by *Shah* (Ali) from this flood.
I remained stainless
I stepped on stairs
Held golden jewelry in my hands
One should have a perfect guarantee

One should buy those thing which
Nobody has seen
Red like the fruits of olive
brought from the colorful palaces
Of the paradise
Refreshing like the beauty of morning breeze
Those riders are very handsome
Who are sweetened by the union
The eternal riders
Conversant with *Hyderi* speech
Their cups are full of red gold
Brought by the celestial angels
They pin their hopes on Khawaja
Run to the deserts and those
Who are made to run
Carrying carts on their shoulders are the ignorant
The carts are carried by fast-paced servants
This is the order for the servants
The night is always luminous for the chosen ones
The believers are always in meditation
No woman should wash the turban with soap
Come and rely or our mysticism
My Almighty lord, appear in the moon
Grant freedom to the prisoners
Like you freed Meeral from the grip of pagans
From the unjust and merciless prison
He returned to his home safely
He was lucky to see the court
Of the chief of his tribe
My beloved will wash me
With her tender fingers
The pilgrims go for pilgrimage
I shall be under the sway of my friends

Must sang spiritual symphonies, songs of monotheism, and kindled the fire of wisdom and knowledge throughout his life. He planted such flowers of mysticism and intuitive knowledge whose fragrance is still fresh. Must introduced the delicate themes of mysticism on a constant basis. He left an immortal mark on the Baluchi language and literature.

The one and only God is great
He is the Monarch, His name is sacred
If he is displeased, none can stay before His might
If pleased, he is merciful and benevolent
Oh the Almighty
We need your bright view
Which we shall have on the Day of Judgment
I am a lunatic like *Majnun*
And the aspirant of God's blessings
A seeker who seeks you
I am a sinful person
The bridge of *Siraat*
Care for me inspite of all its thinness
All the prophets have passed through
Our era spans both the worlds
Many will be at His right hand.

We find the pearls of wisdom, philosophy and intuitive knowledge everywhere in his poetry. Mysticism in general and eastern mysticism in particular is centrally characterized by the existence of God as Sufi enjoys intimate relationship with God. He prays, complains and argues with Him.

The God, Prophet (PBUH), the four Caliphs, Ali and his siblings and the saints of subcontinent are inseparably attached with one another in Must's philosophy of mysticism.

Every one is mortal except God,
He is everlasting, No need to count others
I am under the luminous sheet of my Friend
Cast a look of love at me
The matter started with Adam
I am thankful o God
For the day, when he granted
Ascension to the Prophet
Two kinds of angels escorted him
And handed him over to His Lover
The young cows carried him
And strong camels carried him
Contented and sympathetic camels

At the other side there are brisk boats
Which rush to other countries lifting the burden
They are also in the Heaven's gardens
And brought fruits of forgiveness
And laid on the mausoleum on Lal's Patan
Must is intoxicated by feelings
He experiences them in waves
These are heavenly, major bounties
I saw an old man there
Long live the city of beauties
You are holy, the absolver of sins
Fond of creation, a prolific creator
You are the sustainer, care for the helpless
We are at war with the Murderers of Hussain
I am at Hussain's side
With the innocents of Shah
With the instruments and shining sword of Shah
Bright face and beard
I shall shadow the fragrant turban on his holy head
Made up of Zamer and flowers
I shall shield him from Yazid's dagger
I shall accompany my friend
I seek your will
I am averse to the worldly greed and avarice
To the wives and children in this short life
Bravo! For the virtuous, the truthful
Who admire God's bounties
And obey His orders
Thank for His blessings
Of sweet and ripe fruit
Our prophet (PBUH) was
The prophet of mercy
Victory and Bravery originates from Ali
He is joyous and ever living
Like shining silver and full moon
A great warrior who is never defeated
The word of the Brave is always shining
Hazrat Ali is protector

Who always frees us from sufferings
He won the victory full of signs
From Delhi to Kharasan
There are two *Qalanders*
Both are Ali's friends
Must lives in Koh Suleman
He nurtures Ali's love and thoughts
Friends part from each other
By showing glow in eyes
Give me by virtue of your generosity
One whom I Love
Every sort of garden and fields are decorated
The Bride is to meet her groom
Hazrat Ali is famous for his bravery
The master of *Ummah* has said this
"The country is not mine it's blessed by God"
Taukli raises a lover's call
Lucifer indulges in war
The crown belongs to Muhammad (PBUH)
....

I fear God's wrath
I am his humble servant from eternity
I hope for his blessings
My beloved hides in a veil
The eye knocks at the door of love
I seek wine of God's mercy
Which is filled in two-colored glass
Shah's sons used to drink that
I am desirous of drinking from
Delicate lips
....

    Must builds the nest of his wisdom and consciousness by the straws of his predecessors' wisdom i.e. the veterans of mysticism, literature and philosophy and Baluchi language and literature. The wisdom, found wherever, was taken by Must to his province.

He always mentioned Jam whenever he composed poetry as the fire was fanned by Jam. He mentions Jam in his poetry frequently as a teacher and an inspiring mentor.

May Sayed Jalal facilitate the union of hearts
Those were the balls, which Mir Chakar Khan held
Those were the battles, which revengeful Baluch fought
That was the poetry, which Bueragh did
Promises were those which
Umar and Jam fulfilled
That was the charity, which generous Nuz Bundagh did
Love was of Laila and Majnu
I make wonders in my poetry
I love you, as Shah Mureed loved Hani
I seek you as Akhtar did Gulri from desert to desert
I regard Sammu as the fruit of those trees
You are among the Maheris of Guhar
O! Melodious singer, come to the door of the beloved
And fix your musical instruments
Give your moustache a bend
To signify the start of music
Shower like clouds,
Admire me like a groom.
Wretched are those who hinder
The course of lovers
....

One day, our sighs will strike them
I will go to Sindh with Sufis hundred times
I will visit all the seven mausoleums during the pilgrimage
....

Once while traveling in his area he saw a Jogi(ascetic) in a ridge who was mixing something. Must said to him whimsically:

"Oh! The ascetic with the ears similar to the camels
Give me some *Bhang*
So that I may forget
Sammu's memories

The ascetic looked angrily at Must and then towards the sky. Must felt his spiritual powers famished. He realized his mistake as love is only intensity pain, pray and sincerity, sacrifice and humility.

Then he addressed the ascetic in a humble way.

"Oh! Generous ascetic
Give me some *Bhang*
So that I may forget
Sammu's memories"

A lover acknowledged the strength of another lover. *Ishq* embraced *Ishq*.

Must got his powers again with a lesson that in the way of love there are lovers at every step. One should not feel proud. The ascetic after drinking *Bhang* gave the remaining to Must. When he demanded more he was answered that as he was already filled with the *Ma'rfat* (spiritual knowledge) so he did not need more. Must had completed his education without going to any Pagoda, Bukhara and Sikandriya:

These are the prerequisites of Must's spiritual education:

(1) awareness—vigilance
(2) heart
(3) Intensity
(4) Intoxication

After drinking a cup of sharp *Bhang*
I cover the heights of *Ma'arfat*
As it shakes my soul

Must Taukli's entire poetry is replete with love, and a desire for union. But inspite of suffering from painful pangs of separation there is no tinge of disappointment in it. There is great inner lyricism and music in Must's poetry. He used to frequently visit the spiritual institution *(Dargahs)* of the Sufis of Sindh and Punjab, where Sufi poetry was composed in various musical *ragas* which trained his lyricism. He was a humanist and a secular intellectual. He had no religious prejudice. He had catholicity of vision; he expressed life and its manifestation in the language of human passions. His poetry is a product of civilization and wisdom. He was an intellectual who emphasizes the nobility of conduct, self-respect, humanism, fraternity, search for truth, love of beauty, aversion to worldly pomp, and patriotism. We also find deep love of nature in his poetry. He loved Baluchistan. His style, art and tone are unique and distinct. He was great master of similes and images which he picked from his times. He enlivened Baluchi language. His poetry is in the hearts of every Baluchi. His poetry is quoted in the daily interaction of Baluchi people; he had become immortal in Baluchi language.

After the death of his beloved Samnu, he passed away in 1896 when he was 65. Must Taukli's tomb is known as *Must'e Maidan Gari* which is frequently visited by all and sundry.

(Translated into English by Khurram Khiraam)

Notes:

1. Mazari,Sherbaz, *A Journey to Disillusionment* ,Oxford University Press, 1999
2. Lashari, Mazhar Ali Khan, *Baluch Tareekh Kay Ainay Mein, Ilm-o- Irfan* Publishers, Lahore,2001
3. Timple, Aresi/Mian Abdur Rasheed, *Hikayat-e-Punjab* (Part-111),Majlis-e-Taraq-i-Adab,1992
4. Shah Muhammad Mari, Musteen Taukli, Sangat Academy of Sciences, Fatima Jinnah Road,Quetta.

Shehzad Qaiser

Khawaja Ghulam Farid's Doctrine of Oneness of Being (*wahdat al wujud*) and its Universal Realization

From the dawn of civilization to the era of the present day postmodernism, the questions of epistemology (knowledge) and ontology (being) have remained living issues in one form or the other. There have been many a thinkers in all cultures and times, who have understood the problems of knowledge and being at varying levels. The world has mainly witnessed two main streaks of thought. The first streak comprises the prophets, metaphysicians, mystics and theists who demonstrate the possibility of knowledge of the metaphysical world i.e. a world that exists beyond the sensible one. It not only embraces the empirical world in simultaneity but also embraces the inner self of Man by virtue of which one experiences the ultimate Reality or God. This world demonstrates the metaphysical identity of knowledge and being and constitutes all the great traditions and religions of the world including Confucianism, Taoism, Hinduism, Buddhism, Jainism, Judaism, Christianity and Islam. The second streak comprises the atheists and the agnostics who not only deny the existence of the metaphysical world but also deny any faculty of knowledge in Man laying claim to any such knowledge and thus create an unbridgeable gulf between knowledge and being, which has led to the crisis of the modern world.

Kant, a German Philosopher, in his *Critique of Pure Reason* made a distinction between Phenomena and Noumena i.e. Appearance and Reality. He built his epistemology (knowledge) on the assumption that one could have knowledge only of the phenomena and the knowledge of the Noumena or Reality was not possible. He laid claim to the impossibility of metaphysics on the ground that metaphysics as a science was not possible and this claim in different forms is the dominant trend of the modern times. This constricted epistemology constricts the ensuing ontology too. The separation of knowledge and being has alienated Man both from his inner and outer world. The modern Man, thus perpetually commits, what I call, the Fallacy of Delimitation by delimiting the realms of both epistemology (knowledge) and ontology (being). He delimits knowledge and thereby delimits being. This is a foremost challenge faced by different spiritual revivalist movements in the world on the spectrum of time. Resurgence of Sufism as a universal movement for peace and development, for instance, faces this challenge and tends to defeat it on intellectual grounds.

The presence of the mystics in all countries and ages belie the epistemological and ontological assumptions that sense –experience is the only source of knowledge and knowledge of noumena or the ultimate nature of things is impossible. There is no ground in assuming that anything not traceable to sense perception is beyond knowledge. In addition, there is no basis to assume that the ultimate Reality or God is beyond the province of knowledge. Such an arbitrary denial of higher forms of knowledge leading to a denial of higher levels of reality is fraught with serious consequences for humanity. There is no denying the fact that Science is a legitimate discipline but when scientists overstep their boundaries by denying other forms of knowledge that are beyond the province of science, then science is metamorphosed into scientism. Man locked in human finitude has no way to achieve true transcendence. It is pertinent to note that metaphysics or higher religion does not come in conflict with any sphere of knowledge, which legitimately remains within its own individual domain. The conflict arises only when the individual sphere of knowledge attempts to usurp the universal by turning the true relative into a false absolute.

The essential problem of the modern Man is that he is strands on the spectrum of horizontality without any inkling of the vital dimension of verticality. The metaphysical concept of Universal in the modern world has undergone displacement by the horizontal concept of Globalization, which fails to offer space for larger life. Globalization is not going to solve the problems of the modern Man. It is a simply fixed finite energy, which is flattening out. Only the metaphysical or universal principles can unify knowledge and being and thereby provide a metaphysical basis for universal peace and development. There can be no real and lasting peace without a transcendent principle, which is immanent in each human being, created with a cosmic purpose in this universe. Unless the Divine purpose shines forth in human purpose, there cannot be true, genuine and authentic freedom, equality and solidarity in the human society. Iqbal rightly says "Humanity needs three things today—a spiritual interpretation of the universe, spiritual emancipation of the individual and basic principles of a universal importance directing the evolution of human society on a spiritual basis'. Notwithstanding, the great strides in technology, the modern Man has become spiritually impoverished. How can spiritual impoverish-ment lead to universal peace and development?

Religious phenomenon in our times is succumbing to the onslaught of modernism and false compromises like false promises are in the process of making with the so-called forces of progress. Intellectuality is giving way to rationalism and religion is turning into a bad philosophy. Religion is also becoming apologetic and defensive in the face of modern science that is transgressing its legitimate bounds. Spiritual virtues suffer displacement by social values. The outer form of religion is stifling the very essence of religion. The stages of religious life have become static and the highest stage of discovery has fallen in oblivion. Ritualism and militancy have emerged as a reaction to the loss of spirituality in our times. It is no coincidence that the religious militant movements in the world of Islam have taken a negative stance towards the spiritual dimension of religion. They negate the Sufi phenomena and have more or less aversion to spirituality. The negation of the spiritual element in the constitution of religion is the very death of religious life. The spiritual people belonging to different ages and countries have always considered spirituality as the essence of religion. The Sufis, for example, are folks of intellectuality and spirituality. They have reiterated the creative possibility of having a direct contact with living God. Finding God essentially is finding one's own Self.

The great religious traditions of the world, more or less, have the inherent strength to live in conformity with the universal principles and they have the vitality to meet the genuine needs of its votaries in different periods. However, they have to purify themselves from within i.e., in the light of their own ideals envisioned by their founders, and not through modern seduction or any external inducement or threat. This factor of purification has been a continual phenomenon in different traditions and at different times. The contemporary times have made it exceedingly imperative that the process of purification quickens and heightens in order to provide a spiritually real world to the contemporary Man, who is on the threshold of severing his last link with the Heavens. It is incumbent upon all traditions of the world to strive for spiritual space, which alone can accommodate the anguishing humanity. The modern Man needs courage to be spiritual. Nevertheless, one has to remain aware of that form of mysticism, which stands for life denying attitude.

Resurgence of Sufism as a universal movement for peace and development is a marked phenomena in the present times. The resurgence has taken one of the most vital forms in the revival of the doctrine of Oneness of Being (*wahdat al wujud*) in the hands of Khawaja Ghulam Farid (1845-1901), a Saraiki Sufi poet par excellence, belonging to this part of the world. The universal aspect of his thought is that unlike the religious metaphysician who delimits his approach by starting from the Divinity or differentiated Reality, he as a traditional metaphysician starts from the Essence or undifferentiated Reality. His starting point is the Supreme Principle. He calls it '*Haqq*'. It is formless unlike the divine form that equates with God or the Ultimate Ego. He goes beyond the individualized conception of God, Man and Universe and does not consider Man-God polarity as final as envisaged by Iqbal's religious metaphysics but experiences it as merely provisional that transcends ultimately. He lays a traditional metaphysical edifice for universal peace and development by following the doctrinal teachings of Ibn Arabi, Mansur Hallaj, Bayazid Bistami and his spiritual master Khawaja Fakhr i Jehan. He is the precursor of the metaphysical thought of the contemporary times evident in a number of original thinkers including Rene Guenon, Frithjof Schuon, Titus Burckhardt, Ananda Coomarswamy and Martin Lings.

Khawaja Ghulam Farid does not delimit knowledge but extends its boundaries. From the perspective of metaphysical knowledge, he considers ordinary knowledge as veiled for it is tied to the subject and object structure of reality. There is no real connectivity of knowledge and being.

He says:

علم فریدے ہے حاجب بے شک بے عرفان

Farid! Knowledge is veiled. It is undoubtedly bereft of gnosis.[1]

Ordinary perception considers the sensible world or phenomena as real and ends up in the 'materialization' and 'solidification' of the world whereas the phenomenal reality is devoid of Being (*wujud*). Men are in a state of sleep, the Prophet is reported to have said, and they will wake up when they die. The world is an illusion. It is bereft of real existence. It is an imagination (*khayal*) It is neither independent reality nor autonomous from the Absolute. It is the shadow of Reality. "The whole world of existence is imagination within imagination." However, it does not mean that the world is vain, groundless and false. The metaphysical truth is that the world is not the Reality itself but it "reflects the latter on the level of imagination" in a 'vague' and an indistinctive way. It is "symbolic reflection of something truly real". It is a dream meaning thereby that it is symbolic and we have to interpret it as we interpret our dreams to go beyond dream symbolism. Man does not see the Reality itself in a dream but sees it in a form of a symbol of the Reality, which we have to understand in reference to its origin. It is going beyond sense experience and reason that one sees "the metaphysical transparency of natural forms and objects." Thus, reality is not a subjective illusion, whim or something imaginary. It is "objective illusion." It "is an unreality standing on a firm ontological basis." Thus, the world is an illusion (*wahm*) for it is not the Reality itself. It is an imagination (*khayal*) for it is not independent or autonomous from the Absolute and it is a dream (*khawab*) for its symbols point towards the Reality beyond the dream symbols. Khawaja Ghulam Farid says:

جگ وہم خیال تے خواب ے
سب صورت نقش بر آب ے

جے پچھدیں حال حقیقت
سن سمجھ اُتے رکھ عبرت

جیویں بحر محیط ہے وحدت
کل کثرت شکل حباب ے

نہیں اصلوں اصل دوئی دا
خود جان ہے نسل دوئی دا

گیا پُھوکا نکل دوئی دا
ول اوہی آب دا آب ے

"The world is illusion, imagination and dream. All forms are marks on water. If you ask about the state of reality, then listen, understand and take a note of the fact that the sea encompasses unity. All the multiplicity is bubble-faced. Duality has no essential reality. Know yourself that duality is not everlasting. The airy duality vanishes. The water essentially remains the same water." 2

The traditional cosmologies have outlined cosmological principles to understand the reality of the cosmos and its linkages with the Absolute. A failure to understand the metaphysical meaning enshrined in cosmology brings in an unwarranted criticism against the cosmologists. Khawaja Ghulam Farid has developed a cosmology in consonance with the traditional cosmological principles. It is exceedingly imperative to understand these principles of cosmology in order to understand his metaphysical concept of Nature. The unity encompasses like sea wherein all the multiplicity is bubbled faced. Duality has no essential reality. The airy duality vanishes while the water remains essentially the same.

He considers knowledge as innate. All knowledge inheres in the luminous substance of the Intellect. Heart is the repository of metaphysical knowledge. He says:

نہ کافی نہ جان کفایہ نہ ہادی سمجھ ہدایہ
کر پرزے جلد وقایہ ایہا دل قرآن کتابے
ہے پرم گیان وی دلڑی ہے بید پُران وی دلڑی
ہے جان جہان وی دلڑی دل بطن بطون دا بابے
وچ صورت دے ناسوتی وچ معنے دی ملکوتی
جبروت اتے لاہوتی دل اندر سب اسبابے

"Do not consider 'Kifaya' (a book of jurisprudence) as sufficient. Do not consider 'Hidaya' (a book of jurisprudence) as the guide. Just tear to bits the pages of 'Wiqaya' (a book of jurisprudence). Our heart is the immanent Qur'an (corroborated by the earthly Qur'an). Heart is love and gnosis. Heart is the essence of life as portrayed in Hindu Scriptures: Vedas and Puranas. Heart is the artery of the universe. Heart opens to infinite depths of interiority. It is terrestrial in form. It is celestial in meaning. It is omnipotent and beyond space and time. All possibilities of knowledge inhere in the heart." [3]

Real knowledge is the knowledge of the permanent essences of things and it is attainable by virtue of 'ishq' or intuition. Khawaja Ghulam Farid says:

عشق ہے ہادی پرم نگر دا عشق ہے رہبر راہ فقر دا
عشقوں حاصل ہے عرفان

"Love is the guide to the city of affection. Love steers the way to ontological nothingness. Love leads to the realisation of gnosis." [4]

Looking within posits the possibility of experiencing God in the infinite depths of one's own being or consciousness. He says:

فاش فریدا اے وعظ سناتوں   عالم جاہل شاہ گدا کوں
جے کوئی چاہے فقر فنا کوں   اپنے آپ کوں گولے

"Farid! Openly narrate this spiritual discourse to the knowledgeable, ignorant, king and beggar that any one who wishes to attain the consciousness of his ontological nothingness and annihilation should search within himself." 5

اپرم بید بتاؤں   میں اگیانی کو گیان سناؤں
سرت سرندھ ہاتھموں لے کر   پریم کی تار بجاؤں
پانچ سکھی مل رام دوارے   ست گر کی جس گاؤں
کونج گلی میں شام سندر سنگ   ہوری دھوم مچاؤں
میت چیت پچکاری ماروں   پریت گلال اڑاؤں
کہاں اجودھیا سنبل متھرا   کہاں گوردھن جاؤں
چھمن رام کنیا کلگی   اپنے آپ موں پاؤں
دیسوں کہاں بدیس کو دوڑوں   جوگ براگ کماؤں
سورج چاند کو سنمکھ راکھوں   سن سمادھ لگاؤں
پیپل تلسی کاہے کو پوجوں   کاہے کو تیرتھ ناؤں
اور سے کام فرید نہ میرو   آتم دیو مناؤں

"I am disclosing the supreme Veda. I am imparting knowledge to the ignorant. I take the violin of knowledge in my hands and play the tune of love. I laud the Divinity by integrating five intimates (senses) in the temple of God. I celebrate 'Holi' in the beautiful streets with

"'Krishan' (my beloved). I squirt the love laden and make the colour of love soar. Why should I wander at Ajodhia, Sanbal, Mathra and Gurdhan (Hindu pilgrimage centres)? (When) Lachman, Ram, Kanaya and Kalgi (deity incarnate) are within me. Why should I leave my native abode, run to unfamiliar places and undergo hard spiritual exercises or become an ascetic? Why should I keep the sun and moon opposite my face for concentrating on the focal point (ritual)? Why should I worship (peepal) a tree and (tulsi) a shrub? And why should I go for a bath to the sacred place? Farid! I have no business with otherness. I am realising the Spirit within myself." [6]

ره توحیدی ریت فریدی   اپنے آپ دا دھیانے

The way of unity and the Faridi tradition is watchfulness of one's inner self. [7]

He understands the metaphysical reality of Man by dint of Intellect or Spirit (Ruh) that is in Man but is not his. It is the presence of this universal element in Man and not ego, self, soul or 'nafs' that make him transcend the narrow circuits of his individuality. He does not equate Spirit (ruh) with soul (nafs) and thus, goes beyond the problem of pantheism that has no cause of origin in his traditional metaphysics. He wants Man to understand his Origin and Centre. He says:

کس دھرتی سے آئے ہو تم   کس نگری کے باسی رے
پرم نگر ہے دیس تمہارا   پھرتے کہاں اداسی رے
تم ہو ساگی تم ہو ساگی   واگی ذرہ نہ واگی رے
اپنی ذات صفات کو سمجھو   اپنی کرو شناسی رے

"Which is the place of your origin? Where are your dwellings oh? Your habitation is in the city of love. Why are you wandering forlorn, oh? You are the real and you are the truth. You are neither fake nor there is an iota of a counterfeit in you, oh. Do understand the reality of your essence and attributes. Realise yourself from within, oh." [8]

This universal realization embraces both the inward and the outward. It takes spiritual nourishment from the inner world to bring a real change in the outer one. Thus, when he talks of peace, harmony, concord and tranquillity, he does not lose sight of the freedom from oppression, which is the absolute guarantor of peace. He does not advocate a passive attitude towards life but wants Man to struggle against the forces of oppression in order to find himself and thereby emancipate humanity. Khawaja Ghulam Farid integrates contemplation and action in his advice to Suba Sadiq Khan in these beautiful verses:

سبھوں پھلوں سبجھ سہاتوں بخت تے تخت کوں جوڑ چھکاتوں
اپنے ملک کوں آپ وساتوں پٹ انگریزی تھانے

"You readily choose to grace your seat and with fortune establish yourself in full power. You make your dominion prosper with your own hands and uproot the seats of colonial oppression." [9]

However, this struggle against oppression is not born out of any negative considerations. It does not exhibit even an iota of hate or transgression from the universal law of things. Rather, it is realization of universal love in this distinct mode that authenticates such an act. Love of humanity warrants a genuine struggle against the forces of exploitation. Failure to put such a struggle is a betrayal of love.

Khawaja Ghulam Farid has assigned a vital role to love in his scheme of things. His metaphysical thought, in a certain sense, becomes the metaphysics of love. He considers 'ishq' or love itself as inspiring the Reality or God to create the universe. He says:

کنتُ کنزاً عشق گواہی پہلوں حب خود ذات کوں آہی
جیں سانگے تھیا جمل جہان

"'Hidden Treasure' testifies love itself. Originally, the Essence inspired itself with love. It caused the entire universe." [10]

He brings out the various dimensions of love in these beautiful verses:

عشق ہے ڈکھڑے دلدی شادی عشق ہے رہبر مرشد ہادی
عشق ہے ساڈا پیر جیں کل راز سنجھایا

"Love is the delight of the suffering heart. Love is the mentor, spiritual master and guide. Love is our spiritual teacher, who has made us realise the whole secret." [11]

بندرا بَن میں کھیلے ہوری   شام دوارے میرو لال
اِدھر مدھر مون بنسی باجے   چوراسی لکھ ساج آواجے
بھلی کایہ مایہ موڑی   سن کے گیان انوکھے خیال
ترکھٹ جمنا ترپھٹ ناؤں   درمت دویت پاپ مٹاؤں
پی کے پے سنگ پریم کٹوری   ناچت گاوت رنگرس تال
انہد گھور گگن موں گاجے   چنگ مردنگ لکھو لکھ باجے
لاگی جوری سبد ٹھکورے   برست گر پرتیت گلال
برج موں دھوم پری دھن لاگے   ابھماں ٹوٹے کبدھیا بھاگے
بانہہ مروڑے بنگری توڑے   کنور کنّھی چنچل چال
داس فرید آکاس ہمارا   دیس ایہو ابناس ہمارا
آتم سوں کی لاگے جوری   ہوں میں سنسار ہت پتال

"My beloved plays Holi in the temple of Krishan in Bindraban. The flute is harping on enchanting songs. There are eighty-four lacs musical tunes forming songs. I have absolutely forgotten wealth and myself after listening to the mystical and Gnostic thoughts. I bathe in the river Jamna (of triangular characteristics) to my heart's fill. I wash myself of the sins of alienation and duality. I drink the cup of love in the company of my beloved, while dancing and singing on the tune of love. The divine flute is harping clamorous tunes in the heavens. It seems as if thousands of harps and long tom-toms are sounding. The beat of words is striking the pair of drums. The love of the spiritual master is bestowing colourful blessings (likened to '*gulal*' that is red powder thrown on one another during the festival of Holi). There is dawn of merriment in the world. Haughtiness, pride and ignorance have fled away. The charming beloved has made a playful move by twisting my arms and breaking my bangles. Farid! Heavens is our original abode. The world (terrestrial) is ephemeral. Do heartedly realise your Spirit. Otherwise, you will be condemned to the infernal world.[12]

کیا ریت پریت سکھائی ہے   سب ڈسدا حُسن خدائی ہے
ڈسدی یار مٹھل دی صورت   گل تصویر اتے گل مورت
ہر ویلھے ہے شگن مہورت   غیر دی خبر نہ کائی ہے

"What a tradition love has made me realise. The Divine beauty is manifest everywhere. I see the sweet form of my friend in its complete picture and full face. It is a good omen to see the form of my friend every time. There is no trace of otherness (or non divine)."[13]

Love has a great might and it moves with an irresistible force. He says:

حسن فرید کئی گھر لوٹے   رلدیاں پھردیاں جنگل بوٹے
سے سسیاں لکھ ہیراں   ڈیکھو عشق دی شدت کو

"Farid! Beauty has ransacked many a home. There are numerous Sassis and countless Heers, who are wandering, wretchedly in forests and marshes. Do hereby witness the intensity of love."[14]

The alchemy of suffering in love transmutes the base metal into gold that helps in attaining individual and universal realization. He says:

درد فرید ہمیشہ ہووے   سارے پاپ دوئی دے دھووے
رہندی تانگھ تے تاں   پہونچاں پریم نگر وچ

"Farid! I am having constant pain. It wipes out all the sins of duality. I have insatiable longing to reach the City of Love." [15]

Khawaja Ghulam Farid's doctrine of Oneness of Being (*wahdat al wujud*) understands the Reality or God as the Absolute, the Infinite, the Metaphysical Whole and the Universal Possibility. It broadens the metaphysical concept of the Universal to contain both the vertical and horizontal dimensions 'existent and operative everywhere under all conditions without any limit or exception'. It embraces not only the global but the cosmic as well. It talks about the inward and the outward. It realizes Man's ontological nothingness in Face of the Absolute or God. It ascribes all reality to Being itself and considers the whole universe including Man as its manifestation. The phenomena or manifestation has no self-subsistent reality. In other words, it has no reality in itself but derives it from the Supreme Reality. It is nonbeing in reference to the Being, which is sheer reality. Such a metaphysical view caters for the perspectives of both transcendence and Immanence. It is not merely a theoretical doctrine but has the corresponding possibility of realization as well.

Khawaja Ghulam Farid says:

ہمہ اوست نہ بھید نیارے   جانن وحدت تے ونجارے
ہر ہر شے وچ کرن نظارے   اصل تجلی طوری نوں

"The mysteries of Oneness of Being are remarkable. They are known by the dealers of Unity. They behold the real Sinai theophany in each and every existent." [16]

The doctrine of Oneness of Being (*wahdat al wujud*) considers 'the Indivisible One and Only' as the 'One and All'. He says:

ہر صورت وچ یار کوں جانیں   غیر نہیں موجود
سبھ اعداد کوں سمجھیں واحد   کثرت ہے مفقود
وصل فرید کوں حاصل ہویا   جب ہو گیا نابود

"Discern your Friend in each form. There is no otherness (self-subsistent reality except the Reality). Understand the essential unity of

KHAWAJA GHULAM FARID'S DOCTRINE OF ONENESS OF... 397

all numbers. Plurality is impossibility. Farid attained union (identity) by ceasing to be." 17

سوہنے یار پُنل دا ہر جا عین ظہور
اول، آخر، ظاہر، باطن اس دا جان حضور
آپ بنے سلطان جہاں دا آپ بنے مزدور

"My lovely friend Punnal is openly manifest. Witness his presence in the first, the last, the outward and the inward (in all dimensions). He himself assumes the form of the sovereign of the world and He himself assumes the form of a labourer." 18

رکھ تصدیق نہ تھی آوارہ کعبہ، قبلہ، دیر، دوارہ
مسجد، مندر، بکرو نور

"Do verify and do not remain on the periphery. The House of God, the direction of prayer, the idol-temple, and the Sikh place of worship, the mosque and the temple manifest the same (essential) Light." 19

یار فرید نہیں مستورے ہر جا اس دا عین ظہورے
ظلمت بھی سب نور حضورے اسم فقط بیا آیا ہے

"Farid! My friend is not hidden. He is openly manifest at each and every place (Omnipresent). Darkness too is the pervasive presence of Light. It has just been named differently." 20

اِک جا روپ سنگار دکھاوے اِک جا عاشق بن بن آوے
ہر مظہر وچ آپ سماوے اپناں آپ کرے دیدار

"He exhibits ornamental beauty at times and at times recurs as lover. He dwells in each manifestation. He contemplates Himself." 21

Khawaja Ghulam Farid's doctrine of Oneness of Being (*wahdat al wujud*) remains committed with harmonious development, which is the development of all the aspects of life. It does not subscribe to lop sided growth, which is malignant in nature but integrates both inner and outer development of Man and Society. And in this process of developing it does not become oblivious of the metaphysical concepts of the Absolute, the Infinite, the Reality, the Truth, the Freedom, the Beauty, the Good, the Light and Love, rather it is in the universal realization of these metaphysical truths that that there can be peace and development. He invites humanity to concentrate on the Reality, which is manifest in all forms and is 'Non Delimited Being' itself. The phenomena of falsehood, evil, ugliness and hatred, for instance, arise in the process of manifestation of the Reality, which is necessitated by the Infinite that is All-Possibility. All of them can only be produced in a world of contrasts. They are privations for they have no being in themselves. In other words, they are devoid of being. However, they have a positive function of highlighting their negative counterparts. The remoteness of each from its source is not absolute and thus each is brought back by virtue of cosmic cycles to its original source to become purified of their negative characteristics. Since, falsehood, evil, ugliness and hatred are not absolutes therefore we must not treat them as such but keep ourselves integrated with the Source, which is the Truth, the Good, the Beautiful and the Love. It is such a metaphysical understanding that can usher in an era of universal peace and development.

Khawaja Ghulam Farid says:

حسن قبح سب مظہر ذاتی   ہر رنگ میں بے رنگ پیارا

Beauty and ugliness are the manifestations of the Essence. The lovely colourless is in each colour. [22]

ہکدے سانگے ہکدی سوں ہے   خیر بھلی شر وِسریا

I swear by the8 One that for the sake of the One, I have become oblivious of both good and evil. [23]

غافل شاغل ناسی ذاکر   صالح طالح مومن کافر
سب ہے نور قدیم دا شان

All is the Splendour of the Primordial Light (manifest) in the unmindful and the devotee, the neglectful and the attentive, the virtuous and the vicious and the faithful and the infidel. 24

حق باطل سبھ حق ہے حق ہے   پر اے راز بہوں مغلق ہے
یار ہے یار ہے یار ہے یار   سوہنا کوجھا نیک اتے بد

"Truth and falsehood is essentially truth itself but it is a much profound secret. The beautiful, ugly, virtuous, and vicious are our friends, companions, comrades and intimates." 25

Khawaja Ghulam Farid's doctrine of Oneness of Being (*wahdat al wujud*) is the metaphysical ground of understanding the principle of unity in diversity. It presents a universal perspective of witnessing opposing things and events. It brings home the message that light, essentially remains light in case of both reflection and deflection. It demonstrates the possibility of conflict even among different shades of rightness and the mode of resolving it. It tends to eradicate negativity about negative things by the tremendous force of love. Love has the capacity and strength to transcend all that is ephemeral in life. It makes Man live beyond the polarity of truth and falsehood; good and evil; beautiful and ugly; love and hatred by absolutely concentrating on the Truth itself, Good itself, Beauty itself and Love itself respectively. It is the metaphysical perspectives of Oneness of Being (wahdat al wujud) that can help usher in an era of universal peace and development.

(Paper presented in the International Conference on "Resurgence of Sufism as a Universal Movement for Peace and Development held from 18-20 July 2008 at Hafiz Hayat Campus, University of Gujrat, Pakistan)

Notes:

1. Diwan-e-Farid, Kafi 139(the rendering into English prose is my own)
2. Ibid. Kafi 200 (the rendering into English prose is my own)
3. Ibid. Kafi 200 (the rendering into English prose is my own)
4. Ibid, Kafi 134 (the rendering into English prose is my own)
5. Ibid, Kafi 181 (the rendering into English prose is my own)
6. Ibid, Kafi 85 (the rendering into English prose is my own).
7. Ibid, Kafi, 247 (the rendering into English prose is my own)
8. Ibid, Kafi 248 (the rendering into English prose is my own).
9. Ibid, Kafi 240 (the rendering into English prose is my own)
10. Ibid, Kafi 134 (the rendering into English prose is my own).
11. Ibid, Kafi 8 (the rendering into English prose is my own)
12. Ibid, Kafi 70 (the rendering into English prose is my own)
13. Ibid, Kafi 254 (the rendering into English prose is my own)
14. Ibid, Kafi 150 (the rendering into English prose is my own).
15. Ibid, Kafi-28 (the rendering into English prose is my own)
16. Ibid, Kafi 119 (the rendering into English prose is my own)
17. Ibid, Kafi 32 (the rendering into English prose is my own).
18. Ibid, Kafi 52 (the rendering into English prose is my own)
19. Ibid, Kafi 50 (the rendering into English prose is my own).
20. Ibid, Kafi 218 (the rendering into English prose is my own)
21. Ibid, Kafi 60 (the rendering into English prose is my own).
22. Ibid, Kafi 7 (the rendering into English prose is my own).
23. Ibid, Kafi 13 (the rendering into English prose is my own).
24. Ibid, Kafi 134 (the rendering into English prose is my own).
25. Ibid, Kafi 30 (the rendering into English prose is my own).

W.H. Siddiqui

Baba Farid, Great Humanist of All Times

Professor Khaliq Ahmad Nizami, the distinguished scholar of Medieval Indian history was the pioneer historian who highlighted the contributions of Chishti saints of India and painfully expressed forty eight years ago: "But now a stage has been reached in our historical studies when we should turn to the humble dwellings of those saints and sages who, unspoilt by wealth and power and uncorrupted by court life dedicated their pious lives in the spiritual uplift of man. At a time when race for political power was the prevailing madness, they reminded men of their moral and spiritual obligation and in a world torn by strife and conflicts they strove to bring about harmony of a perfect orchestra." [1]

It is painful that most of the medievalists continued to follow the British treatment of historical literature for reconstructing the imperial history of political, upheavals, struggle for supremacy of different dynasties and biographies of kings and noblemen. No serious attempts were made to study the socio-economic and technological developments of Indian society in the middle ages. The people at large, their aspirations, moods, tensions of the common man, their yearnings, their financial distress general frustration because of autocratic monarchial rules did not receive the due attention of scholars. In fact the medieval society also suffered from age-known bias of casteism and unsociability for centuries and the religious fanaticism was another serious obstacle in the development of liberalism or dispensation of equal justice to every class of Indian society. It was really impossible to think of equality before the law in those days. Inhuman punishments were the known system of meeting the end of justice since ancient times. With the establishment of the Sultanate of Delhi a sort of a new order was introduced by the Muslim Turks who had but little experience of Islamic concept of state which did not allow injustice and cruel punishments besides making any difference between one class of people with other as commanded in Quran and Hadith. However with the advent of Muslims and establishment of their rules the rigid caste system received a setback. According to Professor Mohammad Habib, the low caste artisans and workers who used to live in separate dingy localities outside the fortified areas started living in the precincts of the cities. The craftsmen and weavers found opportunities to live in the towns and cities for serving the changed requirements of the new settlers. [2] Thus new arts, crafts and manufactured goods became popular both in India, Iran and Central Asia. This boosted Indian and foreign trades and precious commodities earned substantial amount of foreign exchange.

Construction of new roads led to the growth of new towns and cities. Though India remained predominantly an agricultural country yet the establishment of new urban centers and the growing need of foreign goods and implements attracted hoards of foreign architects, craftsmen, calligraphers, scholars, poets teachers physicians and Sufi saints who contributed a lot to the development of Indo-Muslim art and culture. The interaction of Vedantic philosophy and Islamic Sufism developed a new social consciousness and exchange of views of Yogis and Sufi saints led to the unique combination of socio-spiritual system in India. In this socio-religious context the life and works of Sheikh Faridud-Din Ganj-i-Shakar (1175-1265 A.D.) are extremely relevant in the present scenario. Baba Farid is one of the must revered and distinguished Sufi saints of Medieval India. For more than fifty years his *Khanqah at Ajodhan*, the modern Pak-Patan (now in Pakistan) was a place of pilgrimage for millions of people of all communities belonging to different faith, castes and walks of life. Millions flocked to his *khanqah* and found spiritual solace in his company. In fact the life and works of Baba Farid are the significant aspect of the spiritual history of medieval India during its most crucial socio-political upheavals, which led to the deep unrest among the masses both Hindus and Muslims. The monarchical autocracy, conflicting ideologies of orthodox Mullahs and rigid interpretation of Brahmmanical outfits the poverty - stricken poor suffered from moral and spiritual unrest. At such a crucial phase of time the entire country was resounding with the din and clatter of the arms of the Sultans of Delhi followed by repeated onslaughts of the blood-thirsty hoards of Mongols. Baba Farid sat cool and collected in his tumbling hut in a far-off town of Punjab, propagating lessons of infinite humanism, affection and of love, which was the essence of Muslim mysticism at large. It aimed at creating harmony in the discordant elements of society. "True to these ideals Baba Farid strove day and night to create that atmosphere of goodwill and love - a healthy social order free from dissension, intrigue, hatred and jealousy among different classes of people. The imperial rule of the Sultanate injured the hearts of the people of all caste and creed. In such a pathetic and unjust phase of lime Baba Farid boldly told "Do not give me scissors" to a visitor who had presented him a pair of scissors, "give me a needle to sew" since I do not cut (injure) said he. [3]

Baba Farid's more than ninety years long life was devoted to the service of humanity by helping poor destitute and people in distress. Hundreds of people came with their worries and problems to him every day and he gave his sympathetic consideration and prayed for them in such a manner which created unshakable faith in God, respect for moral values, self-restrain and forbearance so that one could face ordeals of life peacefully and patiently.

"What Professor Mohammad Habib has written about Sheikh Nizamuddin Auliya may with striking aptness be said with regard to his teacher Baba Farid "He was not a miracle - monger of ordinary sort. He never flew in the air or walked on water with dry and motionless feet. His greatness was the greatness of a loving heart; his miracles conquer the miracles of a deeply sympathetic soul. He could read a man's inner heart by a glance of his face and spoke the words that brought consolation to a tortured heart." [4]

If ever the overcrowding of visitors prevented him from paying individual attention to everyone he would cry out "come to me one by one so that I may attend to your problems individually." [5]

Tales of human sufferings racked his heart and scared his soul. He suffered for others and shared their grief. His kind words of sympathy and advice were the balm to the afflicted ones that came to him. How correct is Baranis estimate of the Sheikh when he says, "He has taken the inhabitants of this region under his wings" [6] Baba Farid used to pray: "May God give you *dard*", and as Sheikh Nizamuddin Aulia has explained, by *dard* the saint meant an eye full of tears, and a heart full of compassions. One day when his loving disciple, Muhammed Shah, came to him excited, "why do you look so unhappy" enquired the Sheikh "My brother is ill, replied Muhammad Shah, "He may have died since I left him." "Muhammad Shah said Sheikh Farid, "As you are in this moment, I have been like that all my life, but I have never expressed it to any one." [7]

The biographers of Baba Farid were highly impressed by his excellence as a man truthful, honest, sincere, affectionate and considerate—he was a living embodiment of all the moral virtues he preached to his disciples and visitors. Itis extremely warm loving nature sweet words and disposition responded to the most ordinary person and destitute to share his sufferings. In fact Sheikh Farids miracles were unique in as much as these were of a deeply sympathetic soul and his greatness was the greatness of a morally perfect man. Humanity and modesty was deeply ingrained in his spiritual experiences. He concealed his identity and created the impression as if he was referring to some other saint. Thus with his pleasing and forgiving nature Baba Farid had become a loveable figure of his time. His visitors were captured by his charming and sympathetic looks which inspired faith and confidence in their hearts. [8]

He strictly followed the teachings of his revered teacher Hazrat Qutbuddin Bakhtyar Kaki who advised Altutmish : "O ruler of Delhi! It is incumbent on thee to be good to all poor people, mendicants, dervishes and helpless folk. Treat all men kindly and strive for their welfare. Everyone who thus behaves towards his subjects is looked after by the Almighty and all his enemies turn into friends." [9]

Baba Farid was fully conscious of the selfish attitude of the kings and their nobles therefore he advised his disciples and visitors to avoid their company, which would spoil their spiritual attainment and the life hereafter. His thought inspired the imagination of common man to realize the significance of an individual and the society irrespective of caste and creed in the unhospitable monarchical and feudal order of thirteenth century A.D.

He firmly believed in unity of man and God and had irrevocable faith in Almighty who made no difference between man and man. He often recited the Persian verse:

"In both the worlds thou alone art the object that 1 cherish; I die for Thee and I live for Thee."

Baba Sahib tried to remove the blind submission to the authority and unfounded superstitions. He used to advise not to believe in superficial whims and thoughts. One should try to think about the causes of his distress and failures. He should take lesson from such adverse happenings. The belief should be supported and protected by education and knowledge. He did not believe in renunciation and complete isolation from the world. He used to say that bread (i.e. earning) was the sixth article of faith (of Islam).

Baba Farid emphasized that knowledge should be the means of doing good to the people. According to him acquiring knowledge was one of the best mode of worship.

In his Jama'at Khana there was no discrimination on the basis of high and low, officer and subordinate, rich and poor race and color. His religion could be defined as perfect humanism, which he himself practiced and taught his disciples and visitors alike. He had profound knowledge of Islam and other religions. [11] Like Mahatma Gautam Buddh he addressed the people in their own language. Instead of Arabic and Persian he gave his messages in simple 'Slokas' in his own Punjabi language which touched the heart of the masses, though he was a great scholar of religious sciences of his time.

Islamic Sufis believed in traveling to different parts of the world which they rightly considered means of gathering knowledge and experience. This taught them toleration and understanding of different people, their beliefs, customs, languages and traditions.

Baba Farid was widely traveled person, he had visited Baghdad (Iraq), Damascus (Syria), Samarqand Bukhara (Uzbekistan) and Nishapur (Iran) where he studied and exchanged views with the distinguished scholars and saints of the time. In those days there were few colleges of higher studies except in Budayun, Delhi and Muhan etc. In *Jamil 'ul-ulum* of Hazrat Makhdum Jahnin Jahangasht it is recorded that one hundred eighty subjects were taught of religious and secular nature in the Madrasa of Firuz Shah Tughlaq, established in 1352 A.D. [12]

However Jama'at Khanas of the saints were the centre of spiritual knowledge. This included the Jamat Khana of Baba Farid, Arabic and Persian used to be the medium of studies in the medieval India. But Hazrat Baba Farid and his favourite disciple Hazrat Nizamu'ddin Auliya preached in local languages that led to the development of Punjabi, Hindi and Urdu languages. If a scientific research is carried out it will be discovered that Hazrat Sheikh Farid Ganj-i-Shakar had immensely contributed to the awareness of the masses regarding their distinct identity as human being:

> The slavery kills the heart in the body and due to
> serfdom the soul becomes burden to the body.

Although a profound scholar of Arabic and Persian languages Baba Farid deliberately selected his own language Punjabi and expressed his spiritual concepts, experience and thoughts to make them understandable to the common people whose social and political consciousness were revolutionized. Islam which was considered an alien religion in the subcontinent became one of the agreeable faith and its simplicity, sense of humanity, social and religious equality, humanism mercy and compassion which were repeatedly emphasized in Quran and Hadith, attracted both illiterate and literate masses:

> "O Farid! Do not humiliate the earth because nothing is greater than it since during life it is under the feet and after death it covers your body."

Baba Farid adopted very simple and practical similes and metaphors in poetry, which kindled the imagination of the peasants and scholars alike.

> "The crop which is rotten and damaged for want of water; it cannot be made green (revived) even if immeasurable quantity of water is given (i.e. irrigated) similarly if a person led his life against the wishes of God, his deeds would go waste and he would be frustrated forever."

The long river is flowing to erode the banks but the storm cannot harm if the shipman is conscious. It is a philosophical expression about the distressed life of the ordinary people who continuously struggle for existence. Baba Farid's sensitivity can be judged when he advises not to break any body's heart since every body's heart is invaluable pearl that is extremely delicate and once broken cannot be restored. Prophet Muhammad (peace be upon him) had said that hurting human heart is a great sin.

The transistorises of life which has been common theme in poetry of all languages of the east particularly in Persian, Punjabi, Hindi and Urdu, Baba Farids treats this subject in a unique manner when he says,

"O Farid! I was protecting my turban from the dust and dirt but I was not aware of the fact that one day the earth would eat away my head itself."

At another place he expresses with a pathos:

"Those whose heads were covered by royal umbrellas whose presence were announced by drums and *shahnaiyan* (flutes), the panegyrists used to recite eulogies in their glory, they are sleeping in the graveyard and mixed up with the distillates."

There are hundreds of miracles associated with Hazrat Baba Farid's spiritual attainments besides his title Ganj-i-Shakar. In Sufi literature particularly in *Mulfuzat* and genealogies the saint's miracles and extraordinary spiritual performances are recorded. Therefore, the life of Baba Farid is no exception in this respect.

But his association with the historic city of Farid Kot is remarkable in as much as that the people of Farid Kot consider him their great spiritual guide and his miraculous event of serving as a forced labourer is not only mentioned in Sikh records but frequently painted in the religious manuscripts and walls of the Gurdwaras. M.A. McAuliffe, the historian of the Sikh religion has respectfully recorded his miracle associated with Farid Kot in his notable work. Mokal the local chieftain who had forced him to work as a labourer was extremely astonished to know that the basket full of mortar (mud) was hanging on the head of Baba Farid while he was walking towards the site of construction. He begged pardon and became the disciple of Baba Farid and named his fort and city as Farid Kot. [20]

The humanism and profound emotional attachment of Baba Farid with the sufferings of the helpless people inspired him to compose verses in Persian and Punjabi languages. Moreover, by preferring Punjabi as the medium of expression and vehicle of his saintly poetical thought. Sheikh Farid raised it to the level of a literary language and set an example to be followed by later mystics, poets and thinkers of medieval India.

The extreme popularity and reverence of Baba Farid's compositions may be judged from the fact that Guru Nak Dev collected his hymns and verses and preserved them for posterity and Guru Arjun Dev incorporated them in the *Adi Granth*, which immortalized Baba Farid's unparalleled thoughts and expression and his *Vani* became part of the Sikh scripture.

Notes:

1. Nizami, K.A., *The Life and Times of Sheikh Farid-ud-Din Ganj-i-Shankar*, Aligarh, 195, p.ix.
2. Mohammad Habib, *Eliot and Dowson's, History of India as Told by Its Own Historians*, Vol.11 (Aligarh), p.59.
3. Nizami, op.cit., p.2.
4. Mohammad Habib, *Hazrat Amir Khusro of Delhi*, p.34.
5. Nizami, op.cit., p.2.
6. Barani, Ziyau'd-Din, *Tarikh-i-Firuz Shahi Aligarh*, (1957), p.131.
7. *Fawaid'ul-Fuwad*, op.cit, p.121, Muhammad Ghauthi bin Hasan bin Musa Shattari scribed by Abul-Makarm in A.M. 1093 (1682 A.I.) MSS in Rampur Raza Library, folios 56-63. Nirmant, op.cit, p.3.
8. *Hazrat Amir Khusro of Delhi*, p.34; Nizami, op.cit, p.2.
9. *Risalah-Hal-i-Khanwadah-i-Chisht*, MSS, f.17B,; Nizami, op.cit, p.20.
10. Nizami, Khaliq Ahmad, *The Life and Times of Sheikh Farid-ud-Din Ganj-i-Shakar*, op cit, p.2.
    Tarikh-i-Mashaikh-i-Chisht(Nadwat'ul Musannifin Delhi, 1955).
11. *Life and Times of Sheikh Farid Ganj-i Shankar*, op.cit., pp.50-51.
12. Makhdum Jahaniyan Jahangasht, Mulfuzat., *Jami'ul Ulum MSS*, Written in A.H. 782 (A.D. 1380), folio 4-5 now in possession of the author.
13. Muhammad Masu'd Khalid, *Baba Farid*, Urdu (Fiction House, Lahore, 1996), p.48.
14. Ibid., p.15, 96.
15. Ibid., p.18, 97.
16. Ibid., p.150.
17. Ibid., p.151.
18. Ibid., p.152.
19. Ibid., p.154.
20. *Baba Sheikh Farid Life and Teachings*. Edited by Professor Gurbachan Singh Talib (New Delhi, 1973), p.13.